# SEPARATE
## AND
# UNEQUAL

# SEPARATE
# AND
# UNEQUAL

## HOMER PLESSY AND THE
## SUPREME COURT DECISION
## THAT LEGALIZED RACISM

HARVEY FIRESIDE

Introduction by MARC H. MORIAL,
former Mayor of New Orleans,
President of the National Urban League

CARROLL & GRAF PUBLISHERS
NEW YORK

**To Edward T. "Ned" Chase for his advice and encouragement**

SEPARATE AND UNEQUAL
*HOMER PLESSY AND THE SUPREME COURT DECISION THAT LEGALIZED RACISM*

Carroll & Graf Publishers
An Imprint of Avalon Publishing Group Inc.
245 West 17th Street
11th Floor
New York, NY 10011

Copyright © 2004 by Harvey Fireside
Introduction copyright © 2004 by Marc H. Morial

First Carroll & Graf edition 2004

Library of Congress Cataloging-in-Publication Data is available.

ISBN: 0-7867-1293-7

Designed by Paul Paddock
Printed in the United States of America
Distributed by Publishers Group West

# CONTENTS

# INTRODUCTION

## EMERGING FROM PLESSY'S SHADOW
### BY MARC H. MORIAL,
#### PRESIDENT AND CHIEF EXECUTIVE, NATIONAL URBAN LEAGUE;
#### FORMER MAYOR OF NEW ORLEANS

*Marooned in a vast sea of cruelty.*

Those are the words a colleague of mine at the National Urban League uses to describe the predicament African Americans found themselves in at the effective end of the brief post–Civil War period of Reconstruction. The Hayes-Tilden Compromise that decided the presidential election of 1876 ended any hope that the white North would extend to African Americans the *inalienable rights* the Constitution of the United States had pledged to all Americans. Instead, it made plain that the majority of white Americans had decided quickly after Appomattox that adhering to those self-evident truths about the essential equality of all human beings announced in the Constitution would be too costly for them to bear.

For one thing, it was too costly psychologically. It was not just a matter of the white South demanding that the price of a familial reconciliation with the white North be the re-subjugation of African Americans. The white northern majority itself gave vent to its own racist attitudes: destroying slavery and preserving the Union was one thing, but accepting the civil and political equality of African Americans was something else entirely. And the decision to abandon African Americans was made all the easier because the flood of white ethnic immigrants beginning to wash over the country was combining with the revolutionary processes of industrial capitalism in the workplace to produce a period of unprecedented political, social, and economic turmoil.

Black Americans were indeed an island marooned in a vast sea of cruelty: subjected to a pervasive reign of terror by the Ku Klux Klan and its many sympathizers, denied the protection of the forces of law and order, and systematically stripped of their political and civil rights by white state legislatures and the white judiciary.

The turning away of the white majority from their fellow Americans, from the American Ideal—and from human decency—would culminate symbolically and practically in 1896 in the momentous U.S. Supreme Court decision in *Plessy v. Ferguson*.

The road to and from *Plessy* is the American tragedy Professor Harvey Fireside explores with such intelligence and empathy and implication and comprehensiveness. His exploration of the political and military necessities that produced the Emancipation Proclamation; of the political maneuvering and the practical and ideological forces behind the brief triumph of the Radical Republicans in implementing a Reconstruction designed to give the newly emancipated and free-born African Americans a chance to become citizens; and his portrayal of the destruction of that possibility, are magisterial—and indicate how much of this crucial story of American history continues to be obscured in the popular discourse about the Civil War and its aftermath.

Fundamentally, *Plessy* declared that the decision of the Supreme Court led by Chief Justice Roger Taney in the *Dred Scott* case of 1857 was correct: African Americans had no rights that white people—from the lowest in status to the highest—needed to respect. And it sought to prove Abraham Lincoln wrong. Lincoln had famously said that America could not exist half-slave and half-free. *Plessy* asserted that America could indeed live with half of its population "free," and the other half penned up in something very close to slavery: a regime of legalized segregation in the South, maintained by extralegal violence, and a custom of racism in the North which by and large had the force of law.

In effect, *Plessy* disclaimed the ideal of equality among different peoples within America that the U.S. Constitution had held out in promise, if not in fact. Instead, Plessy affirmed that the fundamental premise of the Confederacy should be America's guiding principle as far as the "Negro Question" was concerned. That principle was enshrined in the five so-called "Negro Slavery" clauses of the Confederate Constitution of 1861; and it was spelled out even more clearly by Alexander H. Stephens, the former U.S. Senator from Georgia who became Vice-President of the Confederacy.

"The prevailing ideas . . . of the leading statesmen at the time of [the U.S. Constitution]," Stephens said in a speech given at Savannah, Georgia, on March 25, 1861, "were that the enslavement of the African was in violation of the laws of nature; that it was wrong in *principle*, socially, morally, and politically. . . . Those ideas were fundamentally wrong. They rested upon an assumption of the equality of the races. This was an error. . . . Our new government is founded upon exactly the opposite idea; its foundations are laid, its cornerstone rests upon the great truth, that the negro [sic] is not equal to the white man; that slavery-subordination to the superior race is his natural and normal condition. This, our new government, is the first in the history of the world, based upon this great physical, philosophical, and moral truth. . . ."

In fact, the extraordinary advances African Americans had made from the end of the Civil War to the 1890s showed how equal to the task of citizenship African Americans were.

Of course, in the twisted logic of anti-black bigotry, that made it even more imperative that the suppression of African Americans be supported by law. As Leon Litwack, the noted historian, has put it, "What had [angered] the White South during Reconstruction was not evidence of black failure, but evidence of black success, evidence of black assertion, evidence of black independence, and evidence that black men were learning the uses of political power."

Thus, what Grace Hale, another historian of this era, noted about the Jim Crow laws in general could be applied to the *Plessy* decision itself: They, and it, were "intended to accomplish what it was clear the [racist customs] were not going to—which was to make African Americans act inferior. . . . [I]f white people couldn't make black people be inferior, then they could make them act inferior."

So the North had been victorious in the four-year military phase of the Civil War, but the South won the political war that lasted for the next three decades. That the immoral principles of the *Plessy* decision—the great legal scholar Charles L. Black, Jr., said the decision was one in which "the curves of callousness and stupidity intersect at their respective maxima"—would dominate the discourse and behavior of white America for the first six decades of the twentieth century was a tragedy of the highest order for America as a whole. Its true cost has still yet to be calculated.

And yet, something else must be said about the story of the road to and from the *Plessy* decision: that the story is also inspiring. Professor Fireside knows this well; his narrative is laced with this quality of inspiration from the beginning—because part of the story of the road to and from *Plessy* is about the refusal of African Americans, and their white allies, to submit to a great evil. African Americans living in the 1870s, 1880s, and 1890s could not help but know that the battle they were waging was going to be lost; the evidence was all around them. And yet they carried on, as best they could—be they the black Creoles of Louisiana, of whom Plessy was one; or the young, brilliant W. E. B. Du Bois, envisioning that education could lift up the mass of black Americans and rational discourse could defeat racism; or the young Ida B.

Wells, determined to forge a political activism that would bring black Americans their rights; or hundreds and hundreds of others. This part of the story is about the humanity and resourcefulness and indomitable will of African Americans and their white allies to hold up the ideal of the American prospect and live as human beings against overwhelming odds.

Homer Adolph Plessy did not "just happen" to be in that first-class car. He did not "just happen" to decide, without any fore-thought, at that moment that he would not move—any more than six decades later Rosa Parks's actions on a public bus in Mont-gomery, Alabama would be just a matter of happenstance. Homer Plessy had been *prepared*, as Rosa Parks would be prepared. From 1619 to 1896, there had always been African Americans and some whites who were prepared to challenge America's racist hege-mony. One purpose of the *Plessy* decision was to put a stop to that, to crush the spirit of resistance to White Supremacy.

Despite the devastating effect it had both immediately and for decades to come, which Professor Fireside discusses in detail, in that regard, *Plessy* would fail miserably. It did not crush the spirit of resistance. In immediate ways and over the long term, it fomented it. Three crucial pieces of evidence for that point of view occurred in the decade or so after the decision was handed down. One is that black and white "radicals" increased their agitation over the race question, leading to the great meeting of the Niagara Movement at Niagara Falls, Ontario in 1905, and in 1909 the formation of the National Association for the Advancement of Colored People. A second was the establishment a year later of the organization I now head, the National Urban League. But the truly surpassing reac-tion to the gauntlet White Supremacy had thrown down in the form of the Plessy decision was the one which inspired the cre-ation of these two organizations: the Black Migrations.

That was the beginning of that great flood tide of humanity out of the rural South to the urban North. In the *Plessy* decision, White Racist America had demanded through its spokesmen, the U.S. Supreme Court, that African Americans *stay in their place*. Instead, in literally millions of ways African Americans declared over and over again: I will be free. That was the greatest consequence of the *Plessy* decision itself, and, let it be said, the great legacy of Homer Adolph Plessy and the black Creoles of Louisiana.

Marc H. Morial
October 31, 2003
New York City

# Chronology of Major Events in the History of Civil Rights in America

1791   The first ten amendments to the Constitution, known as the Bill of Rights, are ratified.

1857   The *Dred Scott* decision by the Supreme Court denies United States citizenship to Negroes even if they have been freed under state laws.

1861   The Civil War begins.

1863   President Lincoln's Emancipation Proclamation frees all slaves in any state in rebellion against the United States. It does not apply to border states or to territories controlled by the Union Army.

1865   The Civil War ends.
       The Ku Klux Klan is organized to resist perceived threats by Union occupation troops and Negroes.
       The Thirteenth Amendment is ratified, abolishing slavery.
       Southern states begin to pass Black Codes that, in effect, reimpose the caste division of the slave system.

1867   Reconstruction Acts divide the South into military zones and make readmission of former Confederate states to the Union contingent on their ratification of the Fourteenth Amendment.

1868   The Fourteenth Amendment is ratified, granting, to anyone born or naturalized in the United States, citizenship, the privilege of due process of law, and equal protection under the law.

1870   The Fifteenth Amendment is ratified, affirming that neither the federal government nor states can deny the right of citizens to vote on account of their race, color, or previous condition of servitude.

1876   Rutherford B. Hayes is elected president, having told his southern supporters that, if elected, he would not enforce the Fifteenth

Amendment. He is inaugurated in 1877 after a commission narrowly settles election disputes in his favor.

1877    Reconstruction ends, and "Redeemer" (white elite) governments come to power in ten former Confederate states.

1890    The Jim Crow car on trains becomes the law in Louisiana when the legislature passes Act No.111, the Separate Car Law.

1891    The Citizens Committee is founded in New Orleans to challenge the state's Jim Crow car law and other racist laws.

1892    Homer Plessy defies Act No.111 by refusing to leave a railroad car reserved for whites. He is arrested.
        The state supreme court of Louisiana upholds Judge John Ferguson's decision that Act No. 111 is constitutional.

1896    *Plessy v. Ferguson* is heard by the Supreme Court, which upholds Louisiana's segregated railroad cars as being "separate but equal," therefore constitutional.

1905    The "Niagara Movement" is founded, led by W. E. B. Du Bois, to create a new political force in the black community.

1909    The National Association for the Advancement of Colored People (NAACP) grows out of the Niagara Movement, with Du Bois serving as its only black officer.

1932    In a landmark decision, the Supreme Court finds that the inadequate criminal defense of the "Scottsboro Boys," young blacks tried for rape in Alabama, violated their right to due process.

1950    The Supreme Court acknowledges, in decisions on two cases challenging segregation in higher education (*McLaurin* and *Sweatt*), that segregated educational institutions deny "equal protection of the laws" to black students.

1951    *Brown v. Board of Education of Topeka* is heard in a federal court that upholds public school segregation in Kansas as providing "separate but equal" education .

1954    Rosa Parks refuses to yield her seat on a bus in Montgomery, Alabama, to a white passenger, inspiring a strategy that would be used six years later to end segregation in all forms of interstate transportation in the South.

1954    In *Brown v. Board of Education* and four similar school segregation cases, the Supreme Court rules that segregated schools are unconstitutional and violate the Fifth and Fourteenth Amendment guarantees of "equal protection."

1955    *Brown II*, the enforcement of the school desegregation ruling in *Brown v. Board of Education*, is ordered by the Supreme Court "with all deliberate speed."

1957    The Southern Christian Leadership Conference is founded, headed by Dr. Martin Luther King Jr. until his assassination in 1968.

1960    The first lunch counter sit-in takes place in a Woolworth's in Greensboro, North Carolina, inspiring a wave of protests throughout the South.

1961    The first affirmative action order is issued by President John F. Kennedy, directing businesses having contracts with the U.S. government to treat employees without regard to race, ethnic origin, religion, or gender.

1962    The U.S. Department of Justice issues injunctions to end all forms of segregated interstate transportation, following two years of "freedom rides" organized by CORE, the Congress of Racial Equality.

1964    The Civil Rights Act is passed by Congress, guaranteeing federal enforcement of voting rights, school integration, equal employment opportunity, and desegregation of public accommodations.
        Three civil rights workers are murdered in Neshoba County, Mississippi. Indictments against nineteen suspects are dismissed in federal court.

1965    President Lyndon B. Johnson pushes through the Voting Rights Act, barring "tests and devices" used by state officials to prevent

African Americans from voting, and empowering federal observers to ensure its enforcement.

1967   A federal jury in Mississippi convicts seven men for the 1964 murders of three civil rights workers, for the first time convicting whites for murdering blacks or civil rights activists.

1974   The Supreme Court overturns school busing in Detroit.
Allan Paul Bakke, a white, files suit against the medical school of the University of California at Davis, claiming he was twice rejected for admission due to preferential treatment for minority applicants.

1977   The Supreme Court orders Allan Bakke admitted to the University of California at Davis medical school in a mixed decision on the validity and course of affirmative action.

1989   The Supreme Court rules that state and local programs requiring preference based on race are unconstitutional unless preference is designed to compensate for specific instances of past discrimination.

2003   The Supreme Court rules that the University of Michigan's point program for minority applicants is an unconstitutional quota, but finds the admissions program of the University of Michigan Law School legitimate in its "indeterminate weighing of race as one of many factors ensuring diversity."

# PREFACE

The genesis of this book is buried deep in my childhood history. In 1940, as a boy of ten, I managed to leave Vienna, Austria, with my parents. On board the *Roma*, one of the fabled last boats to shepherd refugees from Hitler's Reich, we made our way from Trieste circuitously to New York, then on to relatives in Danville, Illinois. The only racism I had become aware of up to that point was the Aryan variety, which denied supposedly lower forms of life like us the right to exist.

Then, in the United States, I was shocked to see people treated as inferiors merely because of the darker shade of their skin. I couldn't fathom why Berenice, my aunt's kindly maid, was not allowed to share her sandwich with us at the kitchen table, nor why Cecil, the handyman at my uncle's clothing store, was the first person laid off when business turned bad.

In 1945 we moved to New Brunswick, New Jersey, a town divided into ethnic enclaves: Germans, Hungarians, Poles, Italians, Negroes, and "real" Americans. For a social studies project, I interviewed a woman at the Urban League on the extent of the Negro ghetto. I was amazed to see that not only Jews were kept out of certain neighborhoods by racists. Perhaps naively, I later persuaded Oscar, a football hero who was my friend, to join me in picketing the "Y" where blacks and whites could not go swimming together. I didn't understand why he was so concerned that he might anger his parents and jeopardize his future in dental school by holding up a protest sign, but we did prevail. In 1948, the local "Y", was integrated.

Later, as a scholarship student at Harvard, I appreciated that a decades-long small Jewish quota under President Abbott L. Lowell had finally been lifted. But I was also aware that out of a class of some twelve hundred, there were only three Negroes.

When I enlisted in the army in 1955, I encountered southern racism. At Camp Rucker, Alabama, after advanced infantry training, I applied for a day pass to nearby Dothan. "You two aren't thinking of going together?" asked the sergeant, indicating my black friend Chuck. "Why not?" I wondered. "Because if you did go out together," he answered, "you wouldn't come back in one piece." So much for the protection of a U.S. Army uniform.

In those youthful days, I joined marches for Martin Luther King in New York. Later, as a professor at Ithaca College, I worked on a committee trying to recruit minority students. Eventually, three young black women lived in our house in exchange for babysitting, and my wife, Bryna, made them part of our extended family. We later helped secure scholarships and housing for a dozen Muslim students from Bosnia whose education had been interrupted by the war. Neighbors warned of possible problems, but we welcomed the newcomers. It has been rewarding for all of us to reach out across racial and ethnic barriers. Yet, after writing several books for "young adults" on civil rights, I am also aware how deep-seated our social barriers are.

Forty years ago, as we sought to bring down those barriers, many people—black and white—made a real difference: the students and other activists who transformed the South by enrolling black voters; freedom riders who risked their lives to end Jim Crow; youngsters who "sat in," marched, picketed, and turned a new page in American history. Universities look different today. The Indian student who helped carry my bags at my fiftieth class reunion boasted that Harvard had become the most diversified campus among its peers. A new group of black leaders has appeared—in congress, cabinet posts, and the courts—as well as in the business and professional worlds.

Now, a national debate rages about so-called affirmative action programs. Admissions policies at University of Michigan were rejected by the Supreme Court as amounting to quotas. Yet the admissions system at the University of Michigan Law School, one that encourages racial diversity without setting specific numbers or percentages for minority applicants, was approved by the Court in a 5–4 decision. But even if a few additional black students continue to be admitted into elite schools, it will only marginally affect their communities. Disproportionate numbers of black children grow up in poverty, their lives eroded by crime and poor health. Many will not attain their potential, because their schools lack the funds, the facilities, and the vision to teach them. For complex reasons, the richest society in history refuses to improve this situation and, thereby, surely benefit us all.

Six years ago, I began researching the *Plessy* case, which had legalized injustice in America until 1954. As I peeled off layer after layer of data, I saw that this story could serve to reveal the multiple distortions that my generation was taught in school. We had simply swallowed the myth of the "tragic era" of Reconstruction after the Civil War, which had been concocted by southern historians and their Ivy League disciples. It rested on the stereotype of diabolical northern "carpetbaggers" and their pliable Negro tools—a dominant academic view for about eighty years. The purveyors of this "truth" had denied the betrayal of Negro rights after their supposed "emancipation" in 1862.

Only rarely in courses on constitutional law were students told that the Fourteenth Amendment was hijacked for the benefit of corporations, instead of securing the citizenship of former slaves. I have yet to find a survey of American history that mentions the vibrant culture of the "free people of color" who flourished in New Orleans until they were scattered and submerged by segregation laws affirmed by the Supreme Court in 1896.

I could not have explored this story with a critical eye without the guidance of the scholars who lighted the way. The groundbreaking was done by W. E. B. Du Bois, with his essays and book on "Black Reconstruction," a work that lay fallow too long before it was rediscovered. Du Bois was the seminal force that led to the many studies cited throughout the following text. I am greatly indebted to the histories of John Hope Franklin, C. Vann Woodward, Kenneth M. Stampp, and Eric Foner; the biographies of Otto H. Olson and Richard N. Current; the legal analyses of Judge Loren Miller, Richard Kluger, Don E. Fehrenbacher, and Linda Przybyszewski; as well as the special studies of New Orleans by Mary Gehman and John W. Blassingame.

I am also grateful to the American Political Science Association for a research grant that allowed me to consult primary sources; to the Historic New Orleans Collection and the Southern Institute for Education and Research at Tulane University for granting access to their archives; to the Chautauqua County Historical Society in Westfield, New York, for its collection of the Albion W. Tourgée papers; to the Cornell University Law School for permission to use its library; and to my daughter, Leela Ruth Fireside, for her legal expertise.

A special thanks is due to my agent, Liz Trupini Pulli, as well as my excellent editors, Phil Turner, Phil Gaskill, Keith Wallman, and Doris Cross, who supplied the chronology.

# Chapter 1

# AN INTERRUPTED JOURNEY

The story, based on century-old documents, appears deceptively simple.

On June 7, 1892, a young man in his late twenties waited at the Press Street depot in New Orleans for the train that would leave at 4:15 p.m. for Covington, a town on the other side of Lake Pontchartrain, near the Mississippi border. The local train was supposed to take about two hours to make the journey thirty miles to the north. The man had just purchased a ticket for a seat in the first-class carriage. He showed no outward signs of nervousness, although, according to the laws of the state of Louisiana, he was about to commit a crime.

Homer Adolph Plessy appeared no different from the other passengers when he climbed aboard the carriage. He was dressed in a suit and wore a hat, the proper attire of gentlemen traveling first class. After he had taken his seat, Plessy handed his ticket to J. J. Dowling, a conductor of the East Louisiana Railroad Company. Then he spoke the words he had carefully rehearsed: "I have to tell you that, according to Louisiana law, I am a colored man."

The conductor looked in evident surprise at Plessy, whose features were as white as those of the other passengers. Yet by admitting to some obviously remote Negro ancestry, Plessy was, by definition of state law, not a white man. Dowling told him that according to Louisiana law, he had to move to the "colored car." That was a vehicle known in common parlance as the Jim Crow car, named for a comical character in a blackface minstrel show. Such cars were generally hitched right behind the locomotive, reeking of soot and smoke. Plessy repeated what he had prepared to say: that he had properly bought a first-class ticket and was therefore entitled to stay right where he was. He politely but firmly refused the conductor's repeated order to move from his cushioned seat to the wooden benches of the Jim Crow car, which were set aside for Negroes, drunks, and derelicts.

Dowling seemed nonplussed. What was he supposed to do with this well-dressed and well-spoken gentleman who kept insisting that despite his white skin he was a Negro, yet refused to get up from a seat legally barred to any person with a drop of "colored blood" in his lineage? The other passengers were stirring, becoming impatient at the train's delayed departure. Dowling called out for police assistance. Officer Chris C. Cain, who appeared in short order, identified himself as a private detective, although he seemed to hold deputized police rank. After he was briefed by Dowling on the situation, Officer Cain asked Plessy to come with him.

Without further argument, Plessy accompanied Cain to the Fifth Precinct police station on Elysian Fields Avenue, one of the streets evoking the French past of New Orleans. There, Plessy was booked for violating the 1890 state law that segregated railroad cars by race, then taken by a police officer to the jail of Orleans Parish (in Louisiana the equivalent of a county), to spend a night in confinement. In the morning, the police escorted Plessy to the recorder's court of the City of New Orleans, where criminal cases were heard. Here he faced his official charges, being arraigned for "remaining in a compartment of a coach [to which] by race . . . he did not belong, to wit, a compartment in said coach assigned to passengers of the white race . . . all against the peace and dignity of the State."

When the preliminaries were over, Plessy told the judge that he waived his right to a hearing at this time. Instead of being taken back to the parish jail, Plessy found a bail bondsman. This man, who had evidently been awaiting him, guaranteed the defendant's appearance at a later criminal trial. The bondsman offered his own house as security, equivalent to posting a bail of five hundred dollars, a considerable sum at that time. Plessy was then released, able to return home to his wife, Louise, at 244 1/2 North Claiborne Avenue, and resume his trade, a respectable one of making leather shoes and boots to order. The Plessys lived in the part of town known as the Faubourg Trême, an integrated middle-class district of New Orleans.

Plessy's trial was scheduled for nearly five months later, on October 28, before Judge John H. Ferguson of the state criminal district court. The parties submitted their written briefs to the judge two weeks before the trial. For the State of Louisiana, assistant district attorney Lionel Adams had filed a formal complaint known as an "information." Here he spelled out the provisions of the law, segregating railroad cars by race, that had been passed by the state legislature two years before, on July 10, 1890. Adams also cited police testimony showing that Plessy had deliberately broken the law. Adams claimed that the segregated railway law, far from discriminating against blacks, made it just as illegal for white passengers to take seats in the "colored car" as for blacks to enter cars set aside for whites.

The law had called for "equal but separate" accommodations for both races on the state's railways, with the same exact penalties for either whites or blacks who took seats to which they had not been assigned. (Of course, there was no earthly reason for a white traveler to want to be seated in the Jim Crow car, nor was there any case on record of such an event ever having happened.) The state's motive, said Adams, was merely to avoid racial friction by placing white and black passengers in separate cars. Louisiana enjoyed the right to enact such a law by virtue of the Tenth Amendment, which "reserves powers not delegated [to the federal government by the Constitution] . . . to the States respectively, or to the people."

James C. Walker, a local attorney, presented the case in Plessy's defense. In the brief he filed on October 14, Walker outlined his major argument: that the Louisiana law clashed with the United States Constitution, specifically the Thirteenth and Fourteenth Amendments that had been ratified at the end of the Civil War. In short, Walker said, the state had undermined Plessy's rights as an American citizen. Although slavery had been abolished in 1865 by the Thirteenth Amendment, Louisiana had attached to Plessy a "badge of slavery" by confining him to a segregated "colored car." Louisiana's official excuse—that its action was "promoting the comfort of passengers"—was not a good enough reason for enforcing a law that treated Plessy as a second-class citizen, thereby flying in the face of the Fourteenth Amendment's prohibition (as of 1868) against any state's abridging the "privileges and immunities of citizens of the United States."

Walker summed up his argument to Judge Ferguson that the segregated railway law was unconstitutional because it had established:

> . . . distinction and discrimination between Citizens of the United States based on race which is obnoxious to the fundamental principle of National Citizenship, perpetuates involuntary servitude as regards Citizens of the Colored Race under the merest pretense of promoting the comfort

of passengers on railway trains, and in further respect abridges the privileges and immunities of Citizens of the United States and the rights secured by the XIIIth and XIVth amendments to the Federal Constitution.

In short, Homer Plessy was asserting that, thanks to the amendments to the Constitution ratified in the wake of the Civil War, he should enjoy the full benefits of national citizenship accorded to blacks and whites alike. Forced seating of blacks in the Jim Crow car revealed to one and all that Plessy was being robbed of his right to travel in a carriage reserved for "whites only." A basic constitutional privilege, Walker said, could not be denied by a state law on the spurious rationalization that it made all passengers feel more comfortable to travel without encountering those of a different race.

Lawyers on the two sides—for Plessy and for the State of Louisiana—appeared before Judge Ferguson on October 28, 1892, to present their oral arguments.

District Attorney Adams seemed to have the easier legal sledding of the parties. He was able to cite precedents from other cases heard in federal courts in which judges had found nothing amiss in segregating various means of public transportation. Then he focused on the 1890 Louisiana law that Plessy was challenging. Adams argued that this law was eminently "reasonable" on grounds that were patently racist. He claimed, for example, that white railway passengers had a right to be shielded from the "foul odors" emanating from blacks, and that the state's task was preserving the peace by keeping at a distance whites and blacks who could not stand to be near each other. Yet he supplied no facts to back up such prejudices, such as citing a single instance where fights had broken out because of mixed-race seating on trains.

James Walker, arguing in Plessy's defense, had a difficult legal assignment, because he was essentially trying to get Judge Ferguson to make what would amount to new law instead of following the precedents cited by DA Adams. He wanted Judge Ferguson to concede that he did not have jurisdiction in the case because of fundamental flaws in this Louisiana statute. Walker claimed that the law's violations of Plessy's constitutional rights were so obvious that this trial should not even go forward. Plessy had been unlawfully arrested and imprisoned when all the evidence indicated that he had behaved impeccably. He had not used foul language, was "respectably and cleanly dressed, . . . was not intoxicated or affected by any noxious [i.e., infectious] disease." (If Plessy had been drunk or rowdy, *that*, rather than his self-identification as "a colored man," would have kept him from being allowed to sit in a first-class carriage. Disorderly passengers, regardless of their race, were sent to the Jim Crow cars.)

Plessy sat through this initial hearing without saying a word. No other witnesses were called. Judge Ferguson heard the attorneys out, then said that he would require more time to decide whether or not there would be a trial on the merits of the case.

Three weeks later, on November 18, the parties reassembled in court; the judge was ready to issue his ruling: Plessy's trial could proceed, because the Louisiana law segregating the state's railroads was constitutional. Judge Ferguson first complimented Plessy's attorneys on the briefs they had submitted; he found they showed "great research, learning and ability." But the judge said that he ended up accepting the prosecution's arguments, basically since the precedents they had cited all supported the right of a state to assign seats in railway cars as part of its legitimate function of keeping public order.

Walker, as Plessy's counsel, declared that he was taking exception to Judge Ferguson's decision by filing an appeal to the Louisiana supreme court in Baton Rouge, the state capital. District Attorney Adams announced he would counter this defense move with his own opposing brief. As Judge Ferguson assembled the papers filed in his court for shipment to the next highest level, he must have known the odds were against Homer Plessy. Once Plessy had exhausted his appeals at the state and federal level, the ball would likely be back in Ferguson's court, where the temporarily suspended trial could eventually proceed.

The November judicial hearing was a minor event, which aroused little notice locally, let alone capturing national attention. The New Orleans newspapers, reflecting the white elite's point of view, applauded Judge Ferguson's ruling. The *Times-Democrat* editorialized its praise of the judge, expressing the hope "that what he says will have some effect on the silly negroes who are trying to fight this law." A caustic commentary in the *Picayune* lectured local Negroes that "the sooner they drop their so-called 'crusade' against 'the Jim Crow car,' and stop wasting their money in combating too well-established a principle—the right to separate the races in cars and elsewhere—the better for them."

So much for this chapter of the judicial story, which would conclude in 1896 with a notorious decision, *Plessy v. Ferguson*, second only to *Dred Scott v. Sandford* (1857) as the most likely candidate for the all-time most shameful chapter in U.S. Supreme Court annals. The apparent simplicity of the narrative so far, however, is deceptive. The chief actors in this drama were obviously performing scripted roles, but they were also puppets of complex forces behind the scenes.

Generations of law, history, and political science students have studied the case and attempted to deconstruct its casuistic logic. The more astute students boggle at the string of seeming coincidences: Why did someone identified as an "octoroon," with seven white grandparents and only one black one, protest the law that technically barred him from a seat in the first-class carriage? Why didn't Plessy just keep quiet about his racial origins, since his skin was by all accounts indistinguishable from that of the white passengers around him? Then, how do we explain the immediate appearance of Officer Cain? And the subsequent availability of the bail bondsman who secured Plessy's release from jail? Finally, what was the judicial quadrille in court all about? Why did the prosecutor and defense attorney politely present their learned briefs to Judge Ferguson, who was prepared to forward his decision on the law to the state's highest court en route to the U.S. Supreme Court?

More persistent students may have been able to find professors who revealed another dimension of the *Plessy* case. It has long been an open secret that throughout the South, post-Reconstruction laws such as the Louisiana railway segregation act evoked a good deal of opposition, not only from African Americans, who were consigned to dingier though supposedly essentially "equal" accommodations, but also from railroads, which would have to go to considerable expense to provide a separate car even if only one black passenger boarded a train. What is not generally known, though, is that in Louisiana, one particular group was fighting such segregation because of the unique roots of its members.

Mainly in New Orleans, a highly educated group of Negroes had enjoyed the privileges of freedom for nearly two centuries—since the days of French rule that began in 1718, followed by a brief interlude of Spanish dominion starting in 1767, then the territory's return to France in 1802 until President Thomas Jefferson arranged its purchase from Napoleon in 1803. The Louisiana Purchase allowed the fledgling United States to acquire a huge tract of territory—stretching from the Mississippi River to the

Rocky Mountains and from Canada to the Gulf of Mexico—for future expansion at a bargain price ($15 million). For most of its resident Negroes, however, it spelled a shift from tolerant French rule to a harsher American version of slavery, with no more opportunities for education and social progress. Only in southern Louisiana were the liberated Negroes from French days able to maintain some of their status.

These *gens de couleur libre*, or free people of color, also known as black Creoles, formed a special caste between white masters and their slaves toiling in the fields. Many of them were the offspring of white slave owners and their black mistresses, a not uncommon relationship in the easygoing port city of New Orleans, where there was a perennial shortage of white European women prepared to face the hardships of frontier life. The French administrators had made special provision for light-skinned black women in their Caribbean colonies, and they imported them from West Africa and islands such as Sainte Domingue (later the Haitian half of Santo Domingo island) into New Orleans.

The French—and later the Americans—also rewarded some of their Negro slaves for heroic service in their armies by manumitting them. When General Andrew Jackson fought the British in 1812 along the Gulf Coast, he recruited free black men experienced in battling the Indians and actually putting down the last major slave revolt in the state the previous year. Despite the disapproval of his superiors, Jackson promised them pay equal to that of white troops, plus a gift of 160 acres of land each. More than six hundred of these soldiers played a crucial role in the final stage of the war, from the end of December 1814 to early January 1815, concluding with the decisive battle on January 8 at Chalmette Plantation, south of New Orleans—the only major U.S. victory of the conflict. Although the battle was fought two weeks after a peace treaty had been signed at Ghent, it made Jackson a national hero. The general honored these troops, though they never received the promised acreage, because his military superiors would not approve it. They were allowed to march together with the white veterans in parades on the annual anniversaries of the Battle of New Orleans into the mid-1800s.

By the nineteenth century, one-third of the so-called Negro population in and around the city were black Creole, some of them successful enough to own household or agricultural slaves of their own. (The slaves who toiled in the Louisiana fields were mostly employed by the sugar or cotton plantations.) These people primarily spoke French and became known, depending on their racial legacies and the increasing degrees of lightness of their skin, as mulattoes, quadroons, and octoroons. The term "mulatto" was derived from the Spanish word for a young mule and, therefore, carried a derogatory sense of half-breed; but the other terms were actually marks of social distinction, "quadroon" being used by white men for all light-complexioned women whom they sought out at annual "quadroon balls" held through the 1850s. The term "octoroon" was applied not just to persons with one black great-grandparent but more broadly to those of Negro ancestry who could pass as white.

Black Creole circles included a considerable share of the area's professionals—doctors, lawyers, writers, and businessmen and women—with extensive property holdings. The brightest were sent to France to complete their education. Even the middle-class tradespeople such as Homer Plessy lived in comfortable houses. Some of these black Creole buildings have survived in the French Quarter of New Orleans to this day. When the Civil War broke out, the sympathies of these *gens de couleur libre* were mostly with the Confederacy, but they were ready to abandon it when it became a lost cause later in the war.

The Civil War lasted only a little more than a year for the

people of New Orleans, making their postwar readjustment relatively easy. Admiral David G. Farragut's Union naval force had
been blockading the mouth of the Mississippi. On April 24,
1862, these two dozen ships bombarded Forts Jackson and St.
Philip, which were guarding the delta. Then they bulled their
way past the forts and through the defensive fleet and crashed
through a boom erected between sunken hulks to block the
river. Although the Union ships were not ironclads, the gun-
boat crews had wrapped chain cables around their engines to
protect them.

The following day, the fleet found New Orleans abandoned by
its defenders. It thus became the first major Confederate city to
surrender. Farragut's ships brought Union troops, commanded by
General Benjamin F. Butler, to occupy the city before they sailed
up the Mississippi to capture Baton Rouge and Natchez. Farragut
won later victories, notably at Mobile Bay in 1864, when Congress created the ranks of vice admiral and, in 1866, admiral, especially for him.

General Butler, a man of little distinction as a strategist, had
become known as the first commander to accept slaves fleeing
north as "contrabands of war," meaning that they were property
of military value, subject to confiscation. Able-bodied males
among such fugitives, simply called "contrabands" by northern
newspapers, were taken into the Union army. (Other runaways
who could not be outfitted were returned to their masters.) When
the city's women screamed insults at the Union soldiers to demor-
alize them, Butler, on May 15, 1862, ordered that any such action
would henceforth cause the offender to be treated as "a woman of
the town plying her vocation," in other words, as a prostitute who
could be arrested and jailed. Confederate president Jefferson
Davis denounced Butler as a felon and an outlaw; British critics
spoke against the general in Parliament; and Butler, who had

become known locally as "the cross-eyed beast," was eventually transferred to another post when Lincoln's advisers caved in to the diplomatic pressure.

While still in command at New Orleans, Butler continued to improvise policies, with mixed success. He organized a "compulsory free labor system," assigning former slaves to work on plantations at guaranteed wages, forbidding corporal punishment, and ensuring children access to schools. Though they needed their employer's permission to leave their workplace, these workers at least enjoyed a modicum of freedom and economic security for the time being. Butler also helped to set up a Reconstruction government for the state, in which members of the black Creole elite played leading roles. One of the most prominent, Louis A. Martinet, who had earned both law and medical degrees, was elected one of the New Orleans representatives to the state legislature. There he spearheaded a group of seventeen members who protested the reimposition of racial segregation after the old white elite returned to power in 1877. He also edited the *Crusader*, a New Orleans newspaper, in which he first suggested a boycott of the railroads if the legislature passed a law requiring "equal but separate" railway cars for whites and blacks.

Later, Martinet proposed a different tactic to circumvent the new racism pervading the state. "We'll make a case, a test case," he wrote, "and bring it before the Federal Court on the grounds of invasion of the right of a person to travel through the State unmolested." On September 5, 1891, a year after the law was finally passed, some of the most prominent black Creoles organized a group to plan the legal strategy for a test case and to collect funds to pay the costs. The names of this committee's officers reveal their French roots: Arthur Estèves, president; Firmin Christophe, secretary; and Paul Bonsigneur, treasurer. Money and support were solicited not just from the privileged "free people of color" but also from ordinary freedmen who had tilled the fields and served their masters during the long, bitter years of slavery. With contributions from northern abolitionists, the legal fund grew to thirty thousand dollars.

This coalition represented quite a dramatic change of attitude among black Creole leaders, who had long prided themselves on their superior culture, wealth, and status. Even if belatedly, they now realized that the so-called white Redeemers, though supposedly intent on overturning Reconstruction laws, would nonetheless insist on putting rich and poor African Americans alike into the same grimy Jim Crow cars; the only criterion would be whether or not they had at least one drop of "colored blood" in their veins. (In the curious physiology of racism, such a minuscule legacy would stigmatize the offspring, while more substantial amounts of allegedly superior "white blood" was not deemed to outweigh it.)

The situation of Negroes throughout the South had changed dramatically after the disputed election of 1876, when Samuel J. Tilden, the Democratic governor of New York, appeared to have won the presidential election after taking a majority of votes. However, Rutherford B. Hayes, the Republican governor of Ohio, offered a secret deal to the electors of three southern states—South Carolina, Florida, and Louisiana, the only former Confederate states that were still under control of the Republican party. If these members of the Electoral College would assign their challenged votes to him, Hayes promised that once installed in the White House, he would withdraw all remaining Union troops from the eleven former Confederate states.

After a closed-door meeting of the election review board in Louisiana and other backroom maneuvers, all the disputed electoral votes of the three states were reassigned to Hayes. The board, which was composed of eight Republicans and seven

Democrats, gave him the presidency by a single vote in the Electoral College. Thousands of Tilden ballots had been thrown out in these three states to award Hayes a narrow victory instead of a major defeat. Without northern troops to protect them any longer, the last Reconstruction governments of the southern states collapsed, leaving resident Negroes—no matter how educated or wealthy they might be, or how pale their skin—once more at the mercy of their former white masters. Whoever dared to challenge the reimposition of that antebellum system in its new incarnation found his life threatened by the hooded night riders of the Ku Klux Klan, who had been driving out Republican party governments by violence in state after state. The new Republican president thus enabled the southern Democrats to establish the "Solid South" regimes that would last until 1948.

In this hostile political climate, the New Orleans organizers of the Citizens' Committee to Test the Constitutionality of the Separate Car Law knew there was much more at stake than being forced to sit in dirty, uncomfortable seats on railroad trains. The resurgent white elite had already taken control of the city's police force in 1866. On July 30 of that year, the Universal Friends of Suffrage, a predominantly black organization with some white members, had their second meeting at the downtown Mechanics' Institute to draw up proposals for a new state constitution protecting the rights of freedpeople. White supremacists, however, assembled a mob that, together with a special police force made up of former Confederates, started firing at the startled delegates through the windows and along Canal Street. About 40 of the Negroes were killed as they tried to flee, while 160 lay wounded. City officials blamed the "riot" on the black delegates and demonstrators. General Philip Sheridan, the resident military commander, later reported to President Ulysses S. Grant that the alleged "riot" had really been "an absolute massacre by the police. It was a murder which the mayor and police of the city perpetrated without the shadow of necessity."

News of the "New Orleans Riot" incensed the Radical Republicans, led by Thaddeus Stevens, a Vermonter elected to Congress from Pennsylvania, and Senator Charles Sumner of Massachusetts, who had been chafing at President Andrew Johnson's southern sympathies, his easy terms that permitted former Confederates to regain their political status, and his lack of concern for the rights of former slaves. The Republican party swept the congressional elections of 1866, in which adoption of the Fourteenth Amendment was a key issue. On March 2, 1867, Radical Republicans were able to pass a strong Reconstruction Act over President Johnson's veto. It divided the South into five military districts, each under a major general, so that Union troops could protect the rights of freedmen. The act also required each southern state to ratify the Fourteenth Amendment, the charter for equal citizenship for blacks and whites, before it could be readmitted to the Union.

The bitterly fought presidential election of 1868 pitted General Ulysses S. Grant for the Republicans against former New York governor Horatio Seymour for the Democrats. Seymour may have received a majority of the white male vote, but the newly enfranchised black voters in the South helped Grant win the contest. Grant's program, though more moderate than that of the Radical Republicans in Congress, included passage of the Fourteenth Amendment, which finally gave the vote to all (male) citizens, striking down any state restrictions "on account of race, color, or previous condition of servitude."

Despite repeated setbacks, Negroes from the former Confederacy were able to make major advances in what southerners later called Black Reconstruction, or "the tragic decade" between the

1867 Reconstruction Act and the 1877 federal retrenchment by President Rutherford B. Hayes. The progress was uneven, depending on the quality of leadership within each black community and its white friends and enemies, as will be explored in the next chapter. At least since the civil rights revolution of the 1960s, however, historians have rejected the uniformly bleak pro–white-southern picture of the decade presented during the previous century in public school and college texts as well as in films from *Birth of a Nation* to *Gone with the Wind*.

In that unrelievedly gloomy portrayal, southern whites were stripped of their economic and political power, while their uneducated former slaves were turned into the tools of conniving northern agents. The resulting anarchy was exploited by corrupt "carpetbaggers," who had descended on the South to make their fortunes, carrying cheap suitcases stitched together from carpet squares. According to that version, the humiliation of law-abiding folks ended only after white "Redeemers" took hold of the reins of power once more. These monochrome accounts in outdated history books, north and south, scarcely mention the thousands of idealistic northern teachers, nurses, lawyers, and other reformers from the Freedmen's Bureau who had been inspired to make the legal promises of Congress to the freed slaves a reality. Reconstruction is equated in these histories to corruption, not to long-overdue reforms, and little is said about the great injustices that followed the restoration of white power.

Refocusing on New Orleans, we can discern earlier and more thoroughgoing racial progress than in many other southern cities, largely due to the high educational level and leadership ability of its *gens de couleur libre*, as well as to a history of comparative racial harmony and to the city's relatively brief association with the Confederacy. During the Reconstruction decade, for example, black citizens were able to integrate the public schools, and most white parents chose to leave their children in attendance rather than transfer them to private schools. Black leaders found common ground with their counterparts from moderate white groups, at least as long as federal troops and agents helped to avoid yielding the field to extremists. Soon after the coup by white supremacists in 1877, however, squads of toughs invaded the city's schools and forcibly threw the Negro pupils out. Once more, Negro children, who had been denied even a rudimentary education during centuries of slavery on pain of being whipped, were relegated to separate classrooms in dilapidated shape—if they were offered any schooling at all.

As later with the segregated railroad cars, in education, too, former slaves and black Creoles found their facilities allegedly "equal but separate," though, in reality, worlds apart in quality. Before long, racial barriers would spring up in all public accommodations, shutting Negroes out of parks, theaters, restaurants, hotels, hospitals, churches, even city cemeteries. And the renascent party of southern Democrats had already been purging Republican Negroes and their white northern allies—the maligned carpetbaggers—from all levels of government. In Louisiana, one carpetbagger whom we have already encountered was the respected Judge John Howard Ferguson, a Massachusetts native who had gone south after the war, married the daughter of a leading New Orleans attorney, and been elected a state justice, becoming part of the power structure, though evidently respectful of Plessy's attorneys.

Among the less reputable types, Henry Clay Warmoth had come from Illinois as a twenty-six-year-old carpetbagger in 1862, and within three years had been elected by Louisiana voters to be a representative in Washington before the state's formal readmission to the Union. In 1868 Warmoth became the first Republican governor of Louisiana, with Oscar James Dunn, a Negro slave who had purchased his freedom before the war, as his lieutenant governor. Warmoth had appointed Democrats to ensure his reelection in 1870, but a split in the Republican party led to his impeachment two years later. Still, Warmoth, ousted as governor, was able to find a sinecure as a customs collector for the port of New Orleans in 1890.

Dunn had died under mysterious circumstances, reportedly having been poisoned in November 1871 after falling out with Warmoth. Next in line was a new Negro lieutenant governor, P. B. S. Pinchback, the son of a white Georgia planter and a free black woman, who became governor temporarily (for 43 days) in 1872— the first Negro ever to have attained that office in the United States. Despite his white appearance, Pinchback identified himself as a Negro. He had been educated in Cincinnati and rose to an army captaincy under General Butler until he resigned because he felt further army advancement would be blocked by discrimination. Stung by malicious rumors that the Negro agenda included legalizing interracial marriages, Pinchback retorted angrily: "It is false, it is a wholesale falsehood, that we wish to force ourselves upon white people." This capable but controversial figure (because of his ambitious nature) is among the many Negroes prominent during Reconstruction who had been free before the Civil War.

Pinchback had been elected congressman at large and then senator in 1872, but both election claims were rejected by Congress. He was succeeded as lieutenant governor by another wealthy free man of color, C. C. Antoine, who served from 1872 to 1876. Other black officials in Louisiana included P. G. Deslonde, secretary of state from 1872 to 1876; the planter Antoine Dubuclet, state treasurer, 1868–1869; and W. G. Brown, superintendent of education, 1872–1876. These officials, as well as the forty-two black members of the state legislature, generally acquitted themselves very well, surprising observers by assuming "the responsibilities of citizens and leaders" and conducting campaigns with "remarkable" speeches that offered conciliation to former Confederates—whom they would allow the franchise but not yet the holding of office.

If the majority of black leaders rose to the occasion, the newly enfranchised black population—estimated at seven hundred thousand who qualified as voters, out of four million Negroes in the South—found it more difficult to understand and fit into the new political order. The majority, even of the two hundred thousand free blacks, had not been able to obtain any education, so these illiterates were more susceptible to manipulation by white politicians. W. E. B. Du Bois, in a 1910 article, analyzed some of the mistakes during Reconstruction as due to these new citizens having been "ignorant and deceived," but he also concluded that they soon become knowledgeable after establishing schools and joining reformers to fight against corrupt state officials. The net result, Du Bois argued, was "more democratic governments" as free public schools opened and social legislation was enacted. Indeed, many of the new postwar state constitutions were more progressive than their predecessors—for example, removing property qualifications for voting.

In any case, many of these positive steps during Reconstruction were soon reversed. The majority of the fifteen hundred blacks who had held offices in the South were swept out as a purge of voting rolls transformed the substantial numbers of black voters into a tiny remnant. In the space of seven months during 1868, Louisiana experienced "a massive campaign of terrorism by which whites sought to intimidate black voters and compel them to vote the Democratic ticket." In April, Warmoth had received 64,951 votes to win the governorship against 38,046 for his Democratic opponent; in November, the Democratic presidential ticket of Seymour and Francis Preston Blair received 88,225 votes against only 34,859 for the Republicans Grant and Schuyler Colfax. After

Reconstruction ended in 1876, the flood of black voters throughout the South was turned into a tiny trickle, in effect nullifying the Fifteenth Amendment. Registrars turned away Negroes because they were not "grandfathered in" since their ancestors had been slaves, or they rejected them for not passing "literacy tests" that involved impossibly difficult questions about state constitutions, questions that were never put to white applicants. In Louisiana, black voters, who had comprised 45 percent of the electorate, were reduced to 4 percent by 1898.

By the 1890s, members of the committee to overturn the Louisiana railway segregation act had nowhere to turn for relief at the state level. The governor's mansion, the state legislature, and the state courts had long been under the control of Democrats, who no longer showed any respect for the reduced power of black voters. Gone were the Radical Republicans in Congress who had rallied to the cause of freedpeople during Reconstruction, and little thought was given to civil rights by Democratic President Stephen Grover Cleveland, whose attention was focused on lowering tariffs and sending troops to Chicago to break the Pullman Strike of 1894. If there was a faint hope for the black Creole leaders in New Orleans, it was the chance to take their fight to the federal courts, where some of the judges might still be sympathetic to the rights guaranteed to blacks by the Civil War–era amendments.

The U.S. Supreme Court offered some faint hope of putting some of the original fire into the language of the Thirteenth and Fourteenth Amendments, which had been conceived as bulwarks against actions undermining Negro rights by the southern states. True, the Court's last word in 1883, by a vote of 8 to 1, in the Civil Rights Cases had been to deny the right of Congress in the 1875 Civil Rights Act, which was intended to prohibit racial discrimination in inns, public conveyances, and places of public amusement. The five Negroes—predecessors of Homer Plessy in a test case challenging segregation—had protested their individual exclusion from a theater, a hotel, and a ladies' car on a railroad, in New York and San Francisco as well as in Memphis, Tennessee. These plaintiffs argued that the violation of their rights flew in the face of congressional action authorized to enforce the Thirteenth and Fourteenth Amendments.

Justice Joseph P. Bradley, at one time an ambitious railway lawyer from New Jersey, who had been the swing vote in awarding the 1876 election to fellow Republican Rutherford B. Hayes, spoke for the majority in taking a narrow view of these amendments, thereby overturning key sections of the 1875 law. Surely, said Bradley, the Thirteenth Amendment was meant to abolish slavery, not to apply to "every act of discrimination" by individuals as to which "guests" they would entertain. If such acts violated anyone's rights, the injured party could "presumably" turn for recourse to civil suits under state law. An even shakier premise by Bradley was that thousands of free blacks in pre–Civil War days had experienced discrimination, yet there was no legal record that they had ever seen such acts as "badges of slavery"; hence such a claim by the plaintiffs could not be sustained now.

The Fourteenth Amendment seemed more pertinent to the plaintiffs' case, argued Bradley, but he concluded that it was a check on state actions, not on "individual invasion of individual rights." The Constitution does not authorize Congress "to create a code of municipal law for the regulation of private rights." In short, the 1875 Civil Rights Act was unconstitutional. Freed slaves should stop claiming "to be the special favorite of the laws." When it came to social rights, then, the kind involved in access to "public accommodations," Negroes had to look for protection "in the ordinary modes," according to Bradley. That left them only one recourse: to file civil suits for damages in state courts, a hopeless option for black plaintiffs in the South.

One lone justice, John Marshall Harlan, dissented from the 1883 majority opinion after taking several weeks to spell out his reasons. Although Harlan, who grew up in Kentucky, had actually owned slaves and been a member of a racist party called the "Know Nothings," as a justice he had turned into a leading supporter of Negro rights. Indeed, in an authoritative history of black Creoles by Rodolphe Lucien Desdunes, Harlan is identified as a supporter of the New Orleans committee, even a contributor. In the Civil Rights Cases, he painted a very broad view of the Fourteenth Amendment as a legal shield to protect former slaves who had been recently transformed into full citizens of the United States and of their individual states. Far from requiring them to be "special favorites of the laws" in Bradley's loaded term, Harlan countered, the post–Civil War Amendments had been designed to make freedmen "part of the people for whose welfare and happiness government is ordained"—that is, not subject to discrimination. The "social rights" the majority had excluded from protection, Harlan said, were covered by law as much as any other area of public life. They included the right of "a colored citizen to use the accommodation of a public highway, upon the same terms as are permitted to white citizens."

The straw on which Plessy's attorneys fastened their hopes was that Justice Bradley's decision had overturned only the law's application to acts of private individuals, not of state officials. The mistreatment of Plessy, they would argue, was only possible because of the cover of the Louisiana segregation law. Of course, they must also have been buoyed by the knowledge that they had a friend on the Supreme Court—a staunch one—in Justice Harlan, who might become an influential advocate for their cause and perhaps find four of his colleagues to accept the logic of his strong dissent in the Civil Rights Cases. Albion W. Tourgée, a white northern lawyer who had volunteered to steer Plessy's case through appeals up the U.S. Supreme Court, wrote to Louis Martinet, head of the New Orleans defense committee, that he counted Harlan as in their corner; perhaps three others who might be won over; with only a faint chance of persuading a fifth to rule in Plessy's favor.

The New Orleans committee members must have known in September 1891 that theirs would be an uphill fight, but that the odds would be better if white attorneys with experience in such litigation undertook to press this test case than if Louis Martinet stayed in charge. That explains why Plessy's defense was entrusted to James C. Walker at the local level, since he was known as a veteran fighter for racial justice. Walker no doubt had arranged for the bondsman who secured Plessy's release on bail. But the constitutional arguments that Walker presented to Judge Ferguson were coordinated with a senior counsel who had offered his services.

This senior counsel, the legal brain behind the Plessy case, was Tourgée, a colorful Union army veteran from Ohio, who had earned his law degree after being wounded three times in Civil War battles and spending four months as a Confederate prisoner before he was freed in an exchange. Tourgée had returned to the South as an intrepid fighter for the rights of Negroes in 1865, setting up a tree nursery business in North Carolina, then becoming active in state politics and eventually being elected a judge of the superior court. But his outspokenness at Reconstruction meetings to draft a new state constitution and, in court, his dressing down of racist attorneys, brought death threats from the Ku Klux Klan against him and his family. He moved back north, near his homestead in upstate New York, where he achieved national fame as the author of novels, such as *A Fool's Errand*, that were thinly veiled accounts of his own quixotic adventures against the unjust practices of the old South.

Tourgée's network of old friends allowed him to keep abreast of racial conflicts in the South. When he heard about the Louisiana law segregating the railways in 1890, he wrote columns for a Chicago newspaper criticizing it. The New Orleans committee realized that Tourgée had the legal experience and the reputation as a determined fighter against racism that would make him an ideal advocate for their cause. He accepted Martinet's written invitation to become "leading counsel in the case from beginning to end," without fee. His notes and drafts of arguments can be seen today at the Chautauqua County Historical Society near the Tourgée home in Mayfield, New York. It seems clear from these papers that he developed his legal strategy pretty much on his own, with little input from the committee or the lawyers in New Orleans. This may have been due partly to Tourgée's take-charge personality, but it also reflects the fact that the mails at the time could take weeks to traverse the country.

The legal journey of the case began with some initial missteps by Tourgée and his clients. Their first volunteer in the test case was not Homer Plessy but Daniel F. Desdunes, age twenty-one, the son of the Creole historian Rodolphe Desdunes. Like Plessy, Daniel Desdunes was very light-skinned, though his grandparents had come from Haiti; he had been selected to make the irrationality of the segregation law even more obvious. On the morning of February 24, 1892, a few months before Plessy's "sit-in," Desdunes bought a first-class ticket from the Louisville and Nashville Railroad to an out-of-state destination, as he had been instructed. Also in prearranged fashion, a conductor had asked Desdunes to move to the "colored" coach and, when he refused to move, had summoned three policemen who proceeded to arrest him. At that juncture, plans to make this a test case went awry.

In May 1892 the Louisiana supreme court decided in a similar case that the state law segregating railroad cars could not apply to trains destined for another state. The "commerce clause" of the U.S. Constitution, the court declared, had reserved the regulation of interstate commerce to Congress. When that prior case was dismissed, the Louisiana attorney general dropped the prosecution against Desdunes. About two weeks later, the New Orleans committee, after hurried consultation with its lawyers, decided to recruit Homer Plessy, apparently a friend of the senior Desdunes.

This time the issue would be limited to intrastate transportation, with Plessy's trip to take place entirely within Louisiana. The question would no longer concern the federal interstate commerce clause but, simply, whether or not an individual southern state had the legal power to force black passengers into a separate railway car. That would lead to the broader question: could southern states replace the caste system of slavery with a set of legal racial barriers to keep African Americans in a status inferior to whites, despite the constitutional changes after the Civil War that had extended federal protection of basic rights to all citizens?

Before Homer Plessy undertook his fateful journey, the leaders of his black Creole community decided on a desperate strategy. They were about to launch a test case that would almost certainly lose in the trial court and in the state supreme court of Louisiana, because southern judges had been validating all the new segregation laws of the post-Reconstruction era. Therefore, all hopes for eventual success in overturning such a law had to be staked on a favorable outcome from the Supreme Court of the United States.

In the decade immediately following the Civil War, it had been true that the majority of Supreme Court justices had cited key clauses of the Thirteenth and Fourteenth Amendments as ensuring the rights of freed slaves. But by the 1890s, when they would hear this case, that cadre of justices had either retired or died, and only three of their colleagues who had dissented from earlier decisions by seeing the Fourteenth Amendment in a much different light, were still sitting on the Court. The three former dissenters in earlier key cases had been joined by six new justices who, with one exception, endorsed a radically new view of the amendment's purpose. In brief, the majority of Supreme Court justices appeared convinced—contrary to all historical evidence—that the framers of the Fourteenth Amendment had been protecting the rights of corporations, since legally they were "persons," whose property could not be taken by any state "without due process of law."

By this breathtaking leap of logic, the Court had signaled that as a group primarily of former corporate attorneys, it was more concerned with exempting businesses from attempts by some states to regulate wages or working conditions than with shielding former slaves from social restrictions being placed on them in the South. The Court was also reflecting the values of laissez faire and individualism in the Gilded Age, as Mark Twain had named this era in an 1873 novel. One of the period's leading figures, the steel magnate Andrew Carnegie, had written *The Gospel of Wealth* in 1889, justifying the huge hoard of the "robber barons" by advocating its use for the benefit of all humanity. While their parents had fought the bloodiest war in American history over the merits or horrors of slavery, the contemporary generation seemed eager to forget that conflict and, instead, to unite the country for an unprecedented surge of industrialization and development. The role of the South would be to continue contributing the cotton and other raw materials to the industries of the North while it was also building up its own new factories, such as the steel mills of Birmingham, Alabama.

The attorneys for Plessy must have had at least a faint hope that the Court they faced (sans Justice Bradley, who died in 1892) would distinguish the railroad case from the Civil Rights Cases precedent by its obvious grounding in state action against

Louisiana's Negro citizens, which was unconstitutional. They might have relied on Justice Harlan as their advocate among his "brethren," since he had seen the impossibility of disentangling social from legal rights in a meaningful way. The fledgling *Plessy* case involved both social and legal rights, because Louisiana had put its stamp of approval on white prejudice against Negroes. If public discrimination were to be given judicial approval, what good would it do to pretend that the rights of black citizens, such as jury duty or voter registration, enjoyed federal protection?

Extremist groups of the resurgent white elite in the South could nullify such guarantees of "political rights" by using the Klan to threaten Negroes who dared to exercise their civil rights through such actions as registering to vote. A host of bureaucratic tricks, including unequally administered literacy tests or white primaries in one-party districts, would ensure that white political dominance went unchallenged. Rodolphe Desdunes had claimed that Louisiana's adoption of the "grandfather clause" in an 1872 law had, by itself, effectively disfranchised 90 percent of the black population of voting age. Finally, the economic structure of the postbellum South was making it impossible for black farmers to cast off the shackles of a new slavery: that of sharecroppers and tenant farmers who "owed their souls to the company store" until they were buried in segregated cemeteries.

In that light it might seem that Plessy and his attorneys were fighting a hopeless battle. The forces arrayed against them were embodied in a rural South that was reinstituting the caste system for blacks as if the Civil War had never happened, and in an industrial North whose "robber barons" were fixated on profits at any cost. The Radical Republicans who had once championed the antislavery cause were no longer a factor in either Congress or the White House. Could the spirit of their legacy—in federal laws and constitutional amendments—be revived by a new generation of justices on the Supreme Court, who had so far been serving mainly the rich and powerful interests of corporate power? Virtually all the justices were subject to the same willful amnesia that affected presidents and congressmen when it came to recalling key issues such as slavery that had plunged the country into the Civil War. In the late-nineteenth-century rush to return to normality, the reestablishment of the Union and further industrial development were paramount. The rights of Homer Plessy and millions of other blacks who sought judicial confirmation of their full citizenship became forgettable concerns.

# Chapter 2

# RECONSTRUCTION PROMISES
# NEVER KEPT

The New Orleans committee of black Creoles who engineered the challenge to Louisiana's railway segregation law were generally derided by their white neighbors and newspaper columnists. Why did they embark on this costly, protracted, and dangerous project? Their critics saw them as foolish folk tilting at windmills—or, worse, inciting the African American community to overturn the social order after Reconstruction had ended in 1877.

> With malice toward none, with charity for all; with firmness in the right, as God gives us to see the right, let us strive on to finish the work we are in; to bind up the nation's wounds; to care for him who shall have borne the battle, and for his widow, and his orphan—to do all which may achieve and cherish a just and lasting peace among ourselves, and with all nations.

When Lincoln began his political career as a Whig member of the House of Representatives in 1847, he had seemed content to leave slavery alone in the South, as long as it was not extended into the territories of the Northwest in the wake of the 1854

Kansas–Nebraska Act. He voted against declaring war on Mexico, because doing so would extend slavery into the annexed lands; it cost him reelection to a second term in Congress. This policy of halting the spread of slavery to new territories was known as the "Free Soil doctrine" and was distinct from abolition, which demanded an immediate end to slavery everywhere. On October 16, 1854, five months after the Kansas–Nebraska bill was passed, Lincoln made a speech in Peoria, Illinois, denouncing slavery as "founded in the selfishness of man's nature–opposition to it, in his love of justice." Yet he balanced this attack on the institution of slavery with an understanding attitude toward southern slave owners who expected the federal government to help them "reclaim their fugitives" through legislation he said he was ready to support.

In the summer and fall of 1858, Lincoln engaged Stephen Douglas, the senior senator from Illinois, in a series of seven memorable debates to contest the senatorial seat. On June 16, Lincoln launched his campaign with a speech in which he argued that the escalation of the struggle between the pro- and antislavery forces over the preceding five years had led to the crisis that was tearing the nation apart. "A house divided against itself cannot stand," Lincoln said in this historic speech. "I believe this government cannot endure, permanently half *slave* and half *free.*" As the candidate of the new Republican party, which he had joined in 1856, Lincoln made clear in his speech of October 13, 1858, in Quincy, Massachusetts, that he represented men "who think slavery a wrong . . . a moral, a social and a political wrong. We think it is wrong not in confining itself merely to the persons or the states where it exists, but that it is a wrong in its tendency, to say the least, that extends itself to the existence of the whole nation . . . We deal with it as with any other wrong, in so far as we can prevent its growing any larger, and so deal with it that in the run of time there may be some promise of an end to it." Douglas, the Democrat, replied that the future of the issue should be left to the individual states: "If each state will only agree to mind its own business, and let its neighbors alone . . . this republic can exist forever divided into free and slave states, as our fathers made it and the people of each state have decided." Douglas's status quo position gave him the votes to defeat Lincoln in the Illinois senate race, even though it was not a slave state.

Despite the apparent difference between Lincoln's clear stand against the immorality of slavery and Douglas's reluctance to have federal actions interfere with whatever preferences the majority of voters of each state might express, Lincoln was reluctant to endorse specific rights for blacks once they might emerge from slavery. He told a Charleston, Illinois, audience on September 18, 1858, the eve of the Civil War: "I will say then, that I am not, nor ever have been, in favor of bringing about in any way the social and political equality of the white and black races; that I am not, nor ever have been, in favor of making voters or jurors of Negroes, not of qualifying them to hold office, nor to intermarry with white people."

Douglas was generally a supporter of the 1857 *Dred Scott* decision, which denied any constitutional rights to Negroes, although the opinion of Chief Justice Roger B. Taney, speaking for a 7–2 majority, far from bringing closure to the issue as he had intended, only enraged northern abolitionists further and hastened the nation's march to war. Associate Justices John McLean and Benjamin R. Curtis dissented. Curtis would accord Scott federal citizenship, as, when the Constitution was ratified, free blacks had been recognized in some northern and southern states. Curtis also found extensive precedents for congressional action on slavery in the Territories that upheld the Missouri Compromise Chief Justice Taney had overturned. The hostile reaction to his position of

Curtis's fellow justices caused him to resign from the Court and return to practicing law in Boston. (More on the *Dred Scott* opinion in chapter 5.)

Lincoln's position until about and year and a half into the Civil War was that the aim of the conflict was to reunite the country rather than to hold high the antislavery banner. On August 12, 1862, he wrote the abolitionist Horace Greeley, editor of the *New York Tribune* and a Republican party stalwart, "My paramount object in this struggle is to save the Union, and is not either to save or destroy slavery." Only after the Battle of Antietam on September 17, 1862, one of the bloodiest of the war and one that can be considered a narrow Union victory, did Lincoln finally stop vacillating and prepare to publish the Emancipation Proclamation on September 23. Lincoln said, "The moment came when I felt that slavery must die that the nation might live," because he hearkened to "the groaning of the children of Israel, whom the Egyptians keep in bondage." At first, the Emancipation Proclamation was welcomed more in Europe, especially in England, than it was at home, and then only when it became clear that it had not changed the status of a single living slave. A meeting of English workingmen at Manchester congratulated Lincoln on his bold stroke for freedom, and he acknowledged this tribute from workers "suffering . . . in this crisis" (because of its disruption of the cotton trade).

On the proclamation's effective date, January 1, 1863, Lincoln, as the nation's commander in chief, declared that all slaves in any state in rebellion against the United States "shall be, then, henceforward, and forever free." Ever cautious, even at that late juncture, Lincoln was careful not to have his declaration affect slavery in the loyal border states, including Maryland, Delaware, Kentucky, Missouri, and West Virginia. (They took action to abolish slavery, first in West Virginia, in 1863; then in Missouri and

Maryland, in 1864; and in the other states by 1865.) Congress had already abolished slavery in the District of Columbia in April and June 1862. In July, it had also passed the Confiscation Act, declaring that all slaves in Confederate areas under Union Army control were now free, and authorizing the president to recruit "contrabands"—slaves fleeing toward the Union forces—into the army. Lincoln had deliberately refrained from such action, as he was not ready to yield his executive power to the Radical Republicans in Congress, for fear that this might embolden them to pursue harsher peace terms than the ones he had envisioned as part of "presidential reconstruction."

W. E. B. Du Bois concludes his magisterial history of Reconstruction: "The North went to war without the slightest idea of freeing the slave. The great majority of Northerners from Lincoln on down pledged themselves to protect slavery, and they hated and harried Abolitionists. . . . The majority of Northerners before the war were not abolitionists. . . . They attacked slavery only to win the war and enfranchised the Negro to secure this result." Du Bois quotes Lincoln as saying, "Without the military help of black freedmen, the South could not have been won." He adds that Negroes furnished two hundred thousand soldiers in the Civil War who took part in two hundred battles and skirmishes, as well as about three hundred thousand others who assisted Union troops as "effective laborers and helpers." In proportion to the population, Du Bois calculates more Negroes than whites fought in the Civil War. In the final stages of the war, Confederates also had plans to free and arm their slaves, but they held off, realizing that "such actions removed the very cause for which they were fighting." They could scarcely free slaves for the sake of expediency while upholding slavery as a basic tenet of their constitution.

The crucial role played by black Union soldiers had been virtually ignored by historians other than Du Bois at the time he published *Black Reconstruction* in 1935. Indeed, Du Bois had not endeared himself to his colleagues by citing over two dozen of their tracts in his last chapter, "The Propaganda of History," as spouting racist stereotypes. These historians, he said, "believe the Negro to be subhuman and congenitally unfitted for citizenship and suffrage." To cite just two of his examples, William A. Dunning's *Reconstruction, Political and Economic* described the postwar South as a place where "all the forces that made for civilization were dominated by a mass of barbarous freedmen"; James Ford Rhodes's *History of the United States* scoffed, "From the Republican policy came no real good for the Negroes. Most of them developed no political capacity, and the few who raised themselves above the mass, did not reach a high order of intelligence." These were not merely sour grapes from southerners, as Du Bois noted, as even in the North, hundreds of Civil War histories conveyed an "open apology for the Confederacy, in measureless abuse of the Radical figures of Reconstruction." The southern myth had turned into national dogma.

Du Bois argues that not only did many of the freedmen learn how to engage in politics in short order, to educate themselves and their children, and to be a constructive force in their society; but the Radical Republicans in Congress also tried to help them in their transition to independent lives, though the white power-holders in the South frustrated these efforts whenever possible. Certainly the slave owners had done nothing during the Civil War years to prepare their black workers for the future tasks of citizenship; on the contrary, they used any slaves who were impressed into the Confederate military to do only the most menial jobs.

After the war most southern states passed so-called Black Codes in 1865 and 1866, virtually reimposing the caste divisions of the old slave system. Several states decreed that Negroes could be employed only as workers in agriculture or domestic service. Mississippi prohibited black ownership or leasing of rural property, while Negro children had to be apprenticed to white masters. Some states forbade Negroes the ownership of weapons or alcohol. They were generally denied the right to vote, were barred from serving on juries, and kept from testifying in cases where whites were the parties. It was this intransigence that enraged the congressional radicals and led them to impose a military occupation of the South, another step in the escalation of sectional resentments.

The gulf between presidential and congressional plans for Reconstruction widened after Lincoln's death on April 15, 1865, when he was succeeded by his Democratic vice president, Andrew Johnson, a Tennessean who had stayed loyal to the Union after his state's secession. Johnson had begun his working life as a tailor; he owed his ability to read and write to his wife's tutoring. He had served in the state legislature and the U.S. House and Senate before his appointment by Lincoln in 1862 as military governor of Tennessee. Lincoln rewarded him for keeping Tennessee in the Union by accepting him as his vice-presidential running mate in 1864.

As president, Johnson tried to continue Lincoln's Reconstruction policies, but he lacked his predecessor's intelligence, stature, or powers of persuasion. On May 25, 1865, he issued a proclamation offering amnesty to all former Confederates, except their military officers, statesmen, and large landowners—most of whom he then pardoned. He opposed the congressional Radicals' Wade–Davis bill, which Lincoln had refused to sign into law after its passage on July 2, 1864. It would have provided for the appointment of provisional governors in the South until new constitutional conventions repudiated their states' Confederate debts and abolished slavery. President Johnson, once a slave owner himself, had said, "This is a country of white men and a government of white men." He was also against an extension of the Freedmen's Bureau, which had been created on March 3, 1865, but for only the first year after the end of the war. In that short time, hundreds of the Bureau's agents secured labor contracts for former slaves and found new homes for them. The Bureau also helped to set up over a hundred hospitals that gave medical aid to half a million patients, and it distributed more than twenty million rations to needy blacks and whites. In addition, it established over four thousand schools for black children and supervised a reorganized court system.

The Senate had passed a bill by 37–10, sponsored by Lyman Trumbull, the Republican leader from Illinois, to extend the life of the Freedmen's Bureau indefinitely and to empower it to try those accused of racial discrimination in military courts, but the bill failed narrowly, by 18–30, to override Johnson's veto on July 16, 1866. The beleaguered president was awarded this solitary political victory on the grounds that the bill was unconstitutional because of the additional judicial and military powers it would grant the Bureau. A later attempt by Congress did succeed in reviving the moribund Bureau, which lingered on until 1872.

Northern newspapers ridiculed Johnson for being soft on the Confederacy, and his stalemate with Congress over the next year made him increasingly unpopular. Another issue mirroring the rift between the executive and legislative branches was the Reconstruction Act of 1867, discussed later in this chapter, which Congress passed over Johnson's veto on March 2, 1867.

The final issue at conflict was: who had the ultimate power, the president or Congress? Johnson had essentially retained Lincoln's cabinet, although Secretary of War Edwin M. Stanton opposed Johnson's weak Reconstruction policy and aligned himself with the Radical Republicans in Congress. In March 1867, they, in turn, passed the Tenure of Office Act, requiring the president to obtain Senate confirmation before he could remove, as well as appoint, executive officials. In August, Johnson countered by ordering Stanton to resign, without obtaining Senate confirmation. Stanton barricaded himself in his office, and on February 24, 1868, the House impeached Johnson, primarily for flouting the Tenure of Office Act. The Senate trial ended with seven Republican senators voting for acquittal, saving Johnson by one vote and costing them their political careers. Stanton finally resigned in May 1868 and was later nominated to the U.S. Supreme Court by President Grant, but he died before he could take his seat. (It took the U.S. Supreme Court until 1926 to declare the Tenure of Office Act unconstitutional, in a case that concerned the firing of a postmaster, belatedly affirming the president's power to dismiss his appointees.)

When it came to the enrollment of Negroes in the Union army, there was no clear policy enunciated either by the president or by Congress. During Lincoln's time, individual commanders were allowed to improvise their utilization of black troops, with an increasing number following the example of General Benjamin Butler in Louisiana, who had organized "Le Corps d'Afrique," the first Negro army corps, in 1863. They were led by black officers, though Congress set the base pay of black privates at seven dollars a month, compared to fourteen for that of whites. Other early Negro units were the 54th and 55th Infantry regiments recruited in Massachusetts in 1863 from free men in New England, Philadelphia, and St. Louis. The 55th, commanded by Colonel Robert Gould Shaw, took heavy casualties when it joined in the assault on Fort Wagner near Charleston. A monument to Colonel Shaw in Boston, created by Augustus Saint-Gaudens, carries an inscription lauding his men for giving "undying proof that Americans of African descent possess the pride, courage and devotion of the patriot soldier." Despite the outstanding conduct of these units in battle, a number of other Union officers limited black recruits to laboring rather than fighting duties.

of the patriot soldier." Despite the outstanding conduct of these units in battle, a number of other Union officers limited black recruits to laboring rather than fighting duties.

Black veterans of the Union army had been promised rewards they never received, such as farmland on which they could work for themselves and support their families. But where was this land going to come from? An immediate source in prospect was southern plantations that their owners had abandoned. Yet when black refugees were settled on such properties and began to farm, they were frequently evicted after the original owners or heirs pressed their claims. After hostilities ended, restoring the cotton plantations also became a goal of the northern operators of textile mills that had been standing idle. Representative Thaddeus Stevens of Pennsylvania, until his death in 1868 a prime mover in Congress for black rights, advocated a plan to confiscate the plantations of Confederate owners and divide them among freed slaves or northern settlers; yet the scheme was never enacted. We have already seen that General Butler's way of dealing with free blacks on Louisiana farms was to induce them to work for former masters as "compulsory free labor," with military supervision to ensure fair treatment. This semi-free labor system was extended in 1863 to the entire Mississippi Valley.

Under Lincoln the Freedmen's Bureau had been set up as part of the War Department, with General Oliver O. Howard in command, funneling mainly civilian volunteers and funds to southern areas occupied by the Union. Congress had appropriated $17 million for this program. Northern charities joined in the relief effort, contributing an additional $5 million in food supplies to the hungry of all races, plus $3.5 million to establish primary schools. Most schools, though, even at higher levels, were racially segregated because of southern resistance to integrating classes. General Samuel C. Armstrong, the white commander of a Negro regiment, founded the Hampton Normal and Industrial Institute at Hampton, Virginia, in 1886. One of its first graduates, Booker T. Washington, helped to spread the word—welcomed by southern whites—that becoming proficient in manual skills was more vital to Negro advancement than gaining access to theaters and other public accommodations. Washington went on to organize another institute for applied crafts at Tuskegee, Alabama. The original promise of the Freedmen's Bureau, to provide former slaves with "forty acres and a mule," however, was never kept. Instead, their only recourse was, at best, to engage in "sharecropping" or "tenant farming," which left them in perpetual debt to their former owners, who advanced them seed, tools, and other supplies.

An even greater disappointment awaited freedmen who expected to enjoy political equality as a result of the Emancipation Proclamation as well as the Thirteenth, Fourteenth, and Fifteenth Amendments. When Louisiana free men of color met in 1863, they appealed to George F. Shepley, the military governor, to be allowed "to register and vote," but he hesitated because they would have made up the majority of the voting population. He referred them to General Nathaniel P. Banks, the military commander, who refused their appeal, later explaining, "I thought it unwise to give them the suffrage, as it would have created a Negro constituency."

The committee of freedmen sent two Unionists, Jean-Baptiste Roudanez and E. Arnold Bertonneau, as their delegates to plead their case in Washington. On March 10, 1864, they met with Senator Charles Sumner of Massachusetts and Congressman William D. Kelly of Pennsylvania. Two days later they presented a petition for black suffrage to President Lincoln, who was impressed but noncommittal. He urged the new Louisiana governor, Michael Hahn, to consider a limited franchise for blacks if they were educated or had fought for the Union. Lincoln's confidential message asked Hahn to consider "whether some of the colored people may not be let in [to vote], especially those who fought gallantly in our ranks." General Banks called for a state convention in March 1864 to amend the 1852 constitution, but black voting could not command a favorable majority. When Lincoln was asked to instruct the convention, he withheld specifics, merely expressing the hope that the delegates would recognize the Emancipation Proclamation in their document and offer education to young blacks. For the time being, he thought, freedmen should at least have the right to make legal contracts. Characteristically, Lincoln was loath to press for a decision, even one that he had earlier favored.

"Presidential Reconstruction" may have been filled with good intentions, but it took "congressional Reconstruction" to enact a program for action that would truly enforce the rights of freedmen. During the Lincoln era, a radical party caucus was founded by Henry Winter Davis, a native of Baltimore who had helped keep that border state from seceding in 1861 despite its pro-southern sympathies. Though he was censured by the state legislature for his pro-Union views, Davis was once more elected in 1863 to the House of Representatives and became chairman of the Committee on Foreign Affairs. The following year, he teamed with Representative Benjamin F. Wade, the staunch abolitionist from Ohio, to introduce the Wade–Davis bill as a strong alternative to Lincoln's mild Reconstruction plans. Though the bill passed in July 1864, at the end of the congressional session Lincoln simply "pocket-vetoed" it (kept it for 10 days after its passage by Congress without signing it into law at the end of a session). That fall, Davis was finally defeated for reelection, but he selected another Radical Republican, Thaddeus Stevens, to take over his leadership role.

Stevens, born in Vermont and educated at Dartmouth, was an

able orator, like Davis. After establishing a law practice in Gettysburg and Lancaster, he served as a state legislator, noted for a brilliant speech on the "common" school system. He was elected to Congress for two terms, from 1849 to 1853, then again from 1859 to 1868, and became nationally known as a fervent abolitionist and an ardent supporter of equal rights for Negroes. After he was chosen to be chairman of the Ways and Means Committee, he played a central legislative role. In 1864 he also chaired the joint Committee on Reconstruction, which proposed governing the South under army occupation through five military districts. It was Stevens who, in 1868, had brought the charges of "high crimes and misdemeanors" that resulted in the impeachment of President Johnson. Later that year Stevens died, leaving instructions that he be buried in a private Negro cemetery rather than in the segregated white one of his church.

An able associate of Stevens as leader of the Radical Republicans was Senator Charles Sumner, from Massachusetts. After his graduation from Harvard College and Law School, he practiced law in Boston and edited a legal journal. He was appointed by his good friend, Justice Joseph Story of the U.S. Supreme Court, as commissioner of the U.S. circuit court. Then Sumner was elected to Congress, where he opposed the annexation of Texas as a slave state and advocated the withdrawal of U.S. troops from Mexico in 1846. In 1851, as a senator, Sumner became the leader of New England abolitionists, delivering fiery speeches against measures such as the Kansas–Nebraska Act sponsored by Stephen Douglas in 1854, which would have opened these territories to slaveholding and years of strife between pro- and antislavery groups. One of Sumner's speeches, in May 1856, on "The Crimes Against Kansas," was directed at Senator Andrew Pickens Butler, of South Carolina. Two days later, Representative Preston S. Brooks, a relative of Butler's, struck Sumner with his cane so severely that it took him three years to recover from his injuries. As chairman of the Senate Committee on Foreign Relations, Sumner became an influential supporter of Lincoln's policies, especially the emancipation of slaves, and he went further, espousing suffrage and equal rights for freedmen. Though he was not as extreme as Stevens in his civil rights radicalism, Sumner did join his House colleague in the effort to impeach President Andrew Johnson.

Historians have for many years described Davis, Wade, Sumner, and Stevens as ideologues—men who out of personal desires for vengeance against the defeated Confederates lacked the graciousness to offer the conciliatory peace terms of Lincoln and Johnson. These historians, of the North and the South, fail to perceive that the beliefs of such Republican leaders derived from the ethos of equality in the Declaration of Independence—something that cannot be reconciled with southern rationalizations of slavery. It seems obvious that slavery, rather than its abolition, is an ideology, in the sense that it protects vested interests. Yet at least one respected historian, Samuel Eliot Morison, finds Thaddeus Stevens who, embittered by the destruction of his property at Chambersburg by Lee's soldiers in 1863, becomes intent on expropriating the lands of slave owners to distribute them among the freedmen. In light of Steven's lifelong beliefs, it is more plausible to attribute his motives to his consistent support of civil rights than to a sudden impulse at the age of seventy-one to lash out at slavery.

Morison further finds Charles Sumner arguing for Negro suffrage out of his lack of familiarity with freedmen and their faults that, in the writer's opinion, made them ill-equipped for citizenship. Again, Sumner's idealism on equal rights was not the result of a sudden conversation late in his career. In 1849, two years before his election to the Senate, he had eloquently defended the rights of a five-year-old black girl, Sarah Roberts, to attend a nearby white elementary school instead of walking to a distant and rundown grammar school set aside for Negroes by the City of Boston. Sumner's argument before the Supreme Judicial Court of Massachusetts had rested on a clause of the state constitution that all men were created free and equal. That phrase implied that all men enjoyed equal protection of the law, thus barring any form of civil or political discrimination. To separate Negro children, Sumner said, was to "brand a whole race with the stigma of inferiority and degradation." It was especially repugnant to segregate school children, he believed, explaining that it would adversely affect both white and black children later in life.

In a decision that was later to surface as a precedent for the *Plessy* case, Judge Lemuel Shaw, who had acknowledged equality as the great principle of the U.S. Constitution and government, went on to question whether children and adults were each entitled to the same treatment before the law. Further, he denied Sarah Roberts's plea on the grounds that the way she and other individuals were treated "must depend upon laws adapted to their respective relations and conditions." In this case, she had to bow to the regulations laid down by the Boston school committee (the rationality of which Shaw did not go into). Shaw simply endorsed the accepted wisdom that segregation was a good thing for both white and black children. Despite the fact that he lost the case, Sumner's pleading advanced his political career and his reputation as an advocate of equal rights.

Without the support of their friends in Congress, the freedmen would have been fully ensnared immediately after the Civil War in a proto-slave system of the South dominated by the Black Codes. Negroes would never have enjoyed the brief spell of educational, social, and political opportunity they had in the decade of Reconstruction if they had not come under the umbrella of federal protection. If that era had been extended beyond 1876, no doubt some of this progress would have continued and taken root instead of being interrupted by a reversion to the old order that lasted until 1954, with the decision by the Supreme Court in *Brown v. Board of Education.* The energies of southern leaders, black and white, could have been harnessed to economic development rather than to the reestablishment of the former plantation economy based on racial repression. The country preferred "business as usual" to a real Reconstruction that could have modernized the South, starting with the viability of Negro existence there rather than creation of the need for blacks to migrate north to attain respect and economic improvement. The Republican congressional leaders suggested a viable alternative course for the nation, but their major measures were disregarded in the South or struck down by the courts.

At the height of their influence the radicals passed the three 1867 Reconstruction Acts over President Johnson's veto, in effect, finally enacting the Wade–Davis bill provisions. Three years after its pocket veto by Lincoln, it now had real teeth in it. The Acts made readmission of southern states to the Union dependent on newly elected constitutional conventions and legislatures in which Negroes were to vote, as well as on ratification of the Fourteenth Amendment guaranteeing state and federal citizenship and equal protection of the laws to "all persons born or naturalized in the United States." Later, there was also Federal pressure on southern states to adopt the Fifteenth Amendment.

The Acts also divided ten southern states (Tennessee excepted) into five military districts commanded by generals who would take orders from General Grant instead of the president. Unlike the civil administrators who had been governing up to that time, the Union army commanders were given the power to set aside decisions of courts that so far had not been punishing violence against Negroes. The troops also supervised elections for state constitutional conventions, which enacted charters with new bills of rights and eliminated property qualifications for office holders. The white elite boycotted these elections and refused to form coalitions with the newly enfranchised Negroes. The northern troops stayed in their barracks unless called out on a mission, generally averting the hostile acts or formidable appearance of an occupation army. Without protection from them, the night riders of the KKK could well have inflicted terror on Negroes with total impunity.

If President Johnson's feud with Congress can be blamed largely on his southern sympathies and his refusal to budge on measures to bring badly needed help to the four million freed slaves, there was also a secondary, partisan side to the conflict. In the era following Lincoln's assassination, the clash between Congress and the president came to reflect the political ambitions of the parties in Washington as well as their different attitudes toward Negroes. Johnson, the Democrat, was eager to revive his party in the South, just as the congressional Republicans wanted to postpone the enfranchisement of former Confederates because their votes might give permanent national control to Democrats in Congress and the White House. If Negroes were given the vote, however, and these ballots were added to those of fledgling Unionists in the South, Republicans might be ensured long-term political hegemony. While Radical Republicans at times dictated the legislative agenda, they were far from reflecting the mainstream of their party. The fragility of their direction was apparent when key leaders such as Thaddeus Stevens and Charles Sumner left the scene and Republican "liberals" with much more restrained policies toward Reconstruction took over. The post-Reconstruction honeymoon between North and South was based on a union of interests: on the positive side was the benefit to both of a surge in economic development; the negative aspect of their bond was a racism that differed regionally mainly in degree.

The antislavery cause had real resonance mainly in New England, the region that had spawned the first abolitionist organizations, beginning with the American Anti-Slavery Society organized by the Boston editor William Lloyd Garrison in 1833. Its success in that decade was limited to the North, where slavery soon disappeared; but even there, voting and other political rights were enjoyed by Negroes mainly in the New England states. Other northern states generally continued to harbor a racism that on occasion exploded into violence. One of the worst examples grew out of the resentment of young white men in New York City toward their affluent peers who could escape the military draft by paying a three-hundred-dollar fee or hiring a substitute. On July 13, 1863, a mob of these angry men, primarily recent Irish immigrants, set out on a bout of killing and destruction that went on for four days. Their victims were hundreds of Negroes, along with assorted foreigners, on whom these poor whites took out their anger at being forced to serve in a war for the rights of blacks. The property they damaged or looted, amounting to a million dollars' worth, included the homes of antislavery leaders, an orphanage that housed black children, mansions of the rich, and assorted shops and saloons. Finally, to reestablish peace, Lincoln had to divert troops badly needed at the front to New York.

The class-based resentment of men subject to the draft was not restricted to the North. In the Confederacy the legislature had set up numerous categories of exemptions, from conscientious objectors to schoolteachers. But poor white men exploded into rage when plantation overseers were added to this list at the rate of one exempt white for every twenty slaves. Like their northern counterparts, most southern draftees could not afford the price of hiring a substitute for the army, which by the war's final years rose to six hundred dollars. That the Civil War had become a rich man's war and a poor man's fight was a common sentiment on both sides of the conflict. For southern whites who were near the bottom of the social scale, the temptation was to blame their wartime misfortunes on Negro slaves against whose future emancipation they had fought.

W. E. B. Du Bois reminds us that the great majority of southern whites did not own slaves. According to his estimates, in 1860, there were five million or more non-slaveholding whites in the South, and fewer than two million who belonged to slaveholding families. States like Mississippi had been counted among the wealthiest in the nation when the market value of their slaves was appraised, but their collective worth plummeted when this capital asset was struck off the books. Slaveholders who had lost a fortune because of Emancipation tried, unsuccessfully, to obtain compensation from Washington for the loss of their human wealth. After the war, when the "Redeemer" governments enacted segregation measures, the result was a de facto caste system that served to convince the poorest whites that they were innately superior to the most accomplished Negro.

Du Bois, writing in 1935, points out that the role of poor southern whites during Reconstruction was a topic relatively neglected by historians. Yet it was from the ranks of these whites that the forces originated, which, by threats and violence, forced freedmen to abandon the gains they had just won through their ballots. In Louisiana, for example, from 1865 to 1876 governmental leaders were a remarkably integrated group of whites and blacks, of free and slave origin, rich and poor. Forty-two Negroes were elected in 1868 to the first postwar state legislature, constituting about one half of that body; seven of them served in the state senate. The 1868 national election, however, marked the beginning of a campaign of secret threats and assassinations to keep Negroes from the polls; it effectively paralyzed the Republican party in Louisiana. Intimidation and outright fraud affected the outcome of the elections in 1868, 1872, 1874, and 1876. The racist campaign crested in 1876, when it was coordinated by the Knights of the White Camellia (a group founded in New Orleans), the Ku Klux Klan, and an Italian organization calling itself "The Innocents." In Louisiana, the White Camellia, which engaged in violence without KKK-type hoods and paraphernalia, was the most popular of the three.

Some similar factors motivated the Irish immigrants of New York who had brutally attacked Negroes during the 1863 draft riots, and the Italian immigrants of Louisiana who appeared among the lynch mobs there. In both cases the newcomers had high rates of poverty and unemployment. They were susceptible to manipulation by corrupt politicians, because among the intangible rewards they competed for was ratification of their superior racial status and inclusion in a network that offered jobs, housing, and opportunities for assimilation into the ruling class. The perpetrators of racist crimes were generally able to escape judicial punishment, because in the North as well as the South, city police departments and local judges shared their prejudices. In the extreme cases when the national government intervened, it generally restricted itself to temporary measures such as Lincoln's order to Union troops to restore order in New York during the draft riots. In the case of the rigged Louisiana elections, President Grant had asked Congress to take action, which they failed to do. So on three occasions he sent federal troops there to restore Republican candidates to offices from which they had been illegally ousted. Later, he routinely rejected requests from southern states for federal military intervention.

The Ku Klux Klan had originally been organized in 1865 by members of the old white elite in the South to resist what they perceived as threats to their civilization by vengeful Union occupation troops and the Negroes whose rights they protected. They dressed in white sheets, wore masks, rode horses with muffled hooves, and had skulls at their saddle horns, posing as spirits of the Confederate dead returning from the battlefield. Their first leader, "Grand Wizard" Nathan Bedford Forrest, had been an outstanding Confederate cavalry officer who had risen to the rank of lieutenant general in 1865. He was installed at a general meeting of local Klans at Nashville, Tennessee, in May 1867. By 1869 Forrest, evidently aghast at the widespread murders and lynchings being committed by vigilante thugs in the KKK's name, ordered the organization to disband, but some local groups refused to obey him. In 1871 Congress responded to the continuing mayhem by passing the Ku Klux Klan Act, which authorized the president to suppress disturbances by military force, with power to suspend the right of habeas corpus. Grant did put nine South Carolina counties under martial law, but of the more than seven thousand indictments under the Act, few resulted in prosecution because of the reluctance of southern judges and juries to convict those who inflicted violence on freedpeople.

It is crucial to an understanding of the *Plessy* case to fathom the depth of American racism at the time, as lawyers and judges could not help but be affected by it. Except for a relatively tiny band of abolitionists and Radical Republicans from the Northeast, the country subscribed to beliefs in the inferior intelligence of Negroes. Prewar slaveholders had used biblical references and other rationalizations to justify the need for white domination of black laborers "for their own good." Of course, the abolitionists and slaves also drew inspiration from scripture, especially the story of the Jewish exodus from Egypt. Now, in the postwar era, sociologists and other disciples of the new social sciences claimed to provide "scientific" grounds for old prejudices. These theories were both illogical and circular, but they were widely accepted to justify the racial discrimination of the time or, at least, the futility of enacting measures to upgrade the status of freedpeople, who were said to be innately fit only for unskilled labor.

Typical of this genre is Frederick Ludwig Hoffman's *Race Traits and Tendencies of the American Negro*, published in 1896, coincidentally also the year the Supreme Court issued its *Plessy* decision. A German immigrant who worked for the insurance industry, Hoffman was adept at using statistics to make sweeping conclusions about population groups. One chapter of his book sought to prove the dangers of "race amalgamation" (i.e., the consequences of interracial unions). One of the tables cites data from an anthropology journal on the comparative weights of the brains of white, black, and mulatto soldiers. As one would expect from this biased author, the brains of whites were said to weigh an average of 1,424 grams; those of "pure Negroes," 1,331; with those of various degrees of racial mixtures scoring as low as 1,280 grams. Hoffman's conclusion: this proves that "there has been a decrease in vital force by reason of the infusion of white blood." Racial mixing, he asserts, is said to be detrimental to both the white and black partners, with their offspring showing "a lesser degree of resistance to disease and death" than either race by itself.

Other vital statistics from Rhode Island are supposed to show that mulatto women are more likely than blacks to turn to prostitution or concubinage. From these data, Hoffman finds it incontrovertible that "the present physical and moral condition of the colored race" is due to "a low state of sexual morality, wholly unaffected by education."

Hoffman quotes the French writer and diplomat Count Arthur Gobineau as prophesying that "intermixture of different races leads to final extinction of civilization." In his *Essai sur l'inegalité des races humaine*, this demagogic nobleman who had befriended the composer Richard Wagner argued, on a supposedly scientific basis, that humanity "consists of irreconcilably unequal races. The nobler of these can dominate the others; by mixture they can only make themselves less noble." For Gobineau, it is self-evident that the white race is dominant and that its mixing with lower races would doom it to decline. (Gobineau also became an authority cited by the Nazis to support their theory of a superior Aryan civilization.)

Hoffman and his colleagues lent credence to American segregationists, while Hitler's pseudoscience led to the extermination of Jews and other "inferior races" in Europe. In both cases, legislation to achieve racial equality was seen not just as a futile attempt to escape man's genetic destiny but also as a dangerous denial of the need for policies based on eugenics. The circularity of these arguments is that groups of people who were walled off by ghettoes and segregation, with inferior access to schools and mainstream jobs, were then blamed for their low levels of achievement.

Even New England clergymen joined the ranks of opponents to the integration of Negroes in white society. Henry M. Field, a Presbyterian minister from Stockbridge, Massachusetts, toured the South before writing on the "race problem" in *Bright Skies and Dark Shadows*, published in 1890. Field's racism is less obvious than Hoffman's, since he concedes that Negroes had earned their right to live and prosper in America, yet he also relies on an inflexible theory to deny them the choice to sit alongside whites in railroad cars or to have other interracial encounters. Although Field deplores incidents in which "decent and well-behaved" Negro passengers were roughly evicted from railway cars for which they paid full fare, his answer is, "If there be on the part of the whites an unwillingness to occupy the same cars and to sit in the same seats with the blacks, let them be separate; only let equally good cars be provided for both, if both pay for them." His rationale is that it is impossible to enforce a policy that goes against human instinct. "We cannot fight against instinct, nor legislate against it," he writes. "If we do, we shall find it stronger than our resolutions or our laws." This resigned conclusion from Henry Field is particularly relevant to the *Plessy* case; his older brother, Stephen J. Field, was a Justice of the Supreme Court that would hear Homer Plessy's appeal.

Henry Field's self-righteousness and certitude ring false when, in *Bright Skies and Dark Shadows*, he expounds on the lack of black achievements as being in the nature of things. During the 270 years since the first slaves were brought to Virginia, he says, "the negro race has not produced one single great leader." He rejects the idea that their slave status furnished them with a valid excuse. After all, he writes, nearly a century had passed since the North abolished slavery, "and yet the same inferiority [of Negroes] exists." Yet, he asks, "where are the men that [Negroes] should have produced to be the leaders of their people? We find not one who has taken rank as a man of action or a man of thought: as a thinker or a writer; as artist or poet; discoverer or inventor. The whole race has remained on the level of mediocrity." He quotes Theodore Parker, a Unitarian minister from Massachusetts who championed Negro rights yet knew of no black men of wealth in New England—"none eminent in anything, except the calling of a waiter." Field is clearly unwilling to acknowledge the racism that even in the North kept the majority of blacks working in menial jobs and denied them access to white schools and skilled jobs.

The myth of black inferiority also pervaded the supposedly objective work of leading historians. Columbia University professor John W. Burgess wrote in his *Reconstruction and the Constitution* (1903) that "a black skin means membership in a race of men which has never of itself succeeded in subjecting passion to reason." Burgess's disciple at Columbia, William A. Dunning, trained two generations of historians, according to W. E. B. Du Bois, by lecturing on the "mass of barbarous freedmen" and writing with "contempt or silence for the Negro." One of Dunning's premier works on Reconstruction in 1907, *The Tragic Decade*, blamed the travails of southerners on "ambitious northern whites, inexperienced southern whites, and unintelligent southern blacks who controlled the first Reconstruction governments." The result, Dunning contended, was excessive spending on public schools for black children and other instances of waste and corruption, until "reforming Republicans" joined southern Democrats in the 1870s to squelch the "dominant radicals" who had incited racial conflict. (Actually, it was W. G. Brown, the black superintendent of education in Louisiana, who publicly denounced the stealing of funds that had been set aside for schools in 1873.)

W. E. B. Du Bois fought almost single-handedly an academic battle against these historical obfuscators. He was uniquely fit for this prolonged struggle by intelligence, temperament, and a remarkable education. Du Bois, according to his autobiography, was descended on his mother's side from a West African slave who had been forcibly brought to America by Dutch traders in 1730, and was given his freedom after fighting in the Revolutionary War. His father's ancestors were French Huguenots who had come to America in the early seventeenth century; one of them had cohabited with a black woman and brought his two sons to New York. Both families had ended up in Great Barrington, in western Massachusetts, where Du Bois's parents were married, though the father was mostly absent and left the mother to raise William Edward Burghardt on her own. Du Bois says that he experienced no segregation at the local schools and learned to win his teachers' respect by excelling in all subjects despite his family's poverty.

After three years at Fisk University, in 1888 Du Bois won a scholarship to Harvard to study philosophy. Though he was befriended by teachers, including William James, he was not allowed to join the glee club, so he learned to practice what he calls "voluntary segregation." His graduation address on Jefferson Davis won press accolades for his insight and fairness. For his Ph.D. thesis in history, he selected the suppression of the slave trade as his groundbreaking topic; it was published by the university press. Du Bois spent two years on a fellowship in Europe, mainly at the University of Berlin, and then returned to the United States in 1894. Despite his Harvard A.B. and Ph.D.—the first ever awarded to a Negro—no white college would hire him. Finally, Wilberforce University, a black church-related school, offered him a post teaching math and classics. After a year's temporary work as an "assistant instructor" at the University of Pennsylvania researching crime in a black neighborhood of Philadelphia, the teaching post led to a thirteen-year association with Atlanta University. Through his writing, teaching, and convening annual conferences on aspects of black life, he had become in his early thirties a preeminent scholar of the Negro experience in America.

Never one to soften his criticism for diplomacy's sake, Du Bois soon found himself at odds with Booker T. Washington, the president of Tuskegee Institute, whom the white social world had made into the authoritative voice of the Negro community. Du Bois recounts his rebellion against Washington's cardinal virtues—"Thrift, Patience and Industrial Training"—and his advice to Negroes to "learn to dignify and glorify common labor" and to avoid "political agitation." Instead of following this subservient path of adapting to the white power structure, Du Bois called for an end to discrimination in the South. He asked

Negroes to exercise their right to vote and to set their sights on higher education. On July 9, 1905, he assembled fifty-nine black men at Fort Erie, on the Canadian side of Niagara Falls, to found the "Niagara Movement" as a new political force in the black community. It met the following year in Harper's Ferry, a small town in West Virginia famous for the raid in October 1859 by John Brown and a group of abolitionists who captured the federal arsenal there before they were arrested by General Robert E. Lee, convicted of treason, and hanged.

The 1906 meeting in Harper's Ferry was followed by conferences in 1909 and 1910 that led to the formation of the NAACP (National Association for the Advancement of Colored People). Du Bois was director of publications and research and the NAACP's only black officer. He spoke to the May 1909 gathering about the "new slavery" of blacks in the South—deprived of the right to vote, their education limited to vocational schools, and their civil liberties denied. By the time he wrote *Black Reconstruction*, Du Bois had an appreciation for the leading role that free people of color had taken in pursuing their civil rights.

In September 1891, when the black leaders of New Orleans formed the Citizens' Committee to Test the Constitutionality of the Separate Car Law, they must have realized how their rights were being whittled away, year by year, their achievements disparaged by stereotypes of Negroes as constitutionally inferior. If they refused to accept the caricatures of themselves in white newspapers as witless malcontents, they would have to make a last stand in the federal courts. Their oppressors might win, and leave their version of blacks in the history books, but the record of black resistance would eventually surface to present an alternate reality.

# Chapter 3

# CARPETBAGGERS, SCALAWAGS, AND REDEEMERS

When Hillary Clinton was campaigning in fall 2000 for the Senate, one of the most damning terms that her critics could apply to her was "carpetbagger." Mrs. Clinton had lived in several states and the District of Columbia. What was she doing running for office in New York? During the campaign, there was a good deal of fanfare when the Clintons moved to Chappaqua, on the outskirts of New York City, and when the ex-president opened an office in central Harlem. Ms. Clinton crisscrossed the state many times and showed herself to be well acquainted with economic problems in every far-flung locality, evidently to live down the negative image of a carpet-bagger in the original stereotype: a northerner who went south after the Civil War to exploit unsettled conditions and to enrich himself. In its current usage, the term is applied pejoratively to any non-native who pursues a political career in a new district. That reference, however, is simply an appeal to provincialism, since American history is replete with politicians who found it convenient to move to a location more propitious to their elec-toral chances than their home turf. Even the very seat that Mrs. Clinton was seeking had been occupied by such transplanted New Yorkers as Robert F. Kennedy and Daniel Patrick Moynihan.

Kenneth M. Stampp, a leading scholar of the Reconstruction era, points out that the carpetbagger stereotype may have a kernel of truth wrapped in layers of exaggeration. Far from all carpetbaggers, he writes, were the villains portrayed by earlier historians of "the tragic decade" of 1866–1876—men who were poor, ignorant, or corrupt. Some northerners did indeed venture south "in search of political plunder or public office"—and that is how they were all portrayed by the Democratic party at the time. Far from "typical," however, these adventurers were "really a small minority." The others—many of them Union army veterans—came mainly in search of homes and agricultural or business opportunities. Some of them were part of the initial wave of workers recruited by the Freedmen's Bureau in 1865 and 1866: teachers who opened classrooms to Negro children, clergy who helped found African American churches, and others who staffed hospitals and food distribution centers open to needy whites as well as blacks. Their clients may have appreciated these badly needed services, but the average southerner saw carpetbaggers as agents of the punitive clique of abolitionists who wanted to dictate harsh peace terms on the heels of the devastating war. In inculcating former slaves with supposedly dangerous ideas of racial equality in the economic and political spheres, such northerners were viewed as agents of chaos undermining the "southern way of life."

Anybody who made a carpetbagger welcome was seen in the South as a scalawag, another name for a rascal, or even worse, a traitor to his community. It went without saying that such scoundrels were also equated with members of the Republican party who were said to use bribes and other corrupt means to seize power. Once more, Stampp says, it is closer to the truth to depict southerners willing to cooperate with their northern colleagues as practical businessmen who saw their economic future as being dependent on forging national linkages rather than on a reversion to regional isolation. As for corruption, the extent of it during Reconstruction has been greatly exaggerated; here Stampp cites Mississippi, which did not have one political scandal during this era, as the best-governed state of the postwar South. Once the state was compelled to repeal its harsh Black Codes of 1865–1866, which forbade Negroes from leasing or owning rural real estate and maintained sections of the old slave codes, it flourished under Governor Adalbert Ames.

Ames was a native of Maine, the son of a sea captain, an honors graduate of West Point, and a hero of the first battle of Bull Run as a Union officer. He had kept his artillery firing after he had been badly wounded, until he lost consciousness—earning him the Congressional Medal of Honor. He had risen in rank through a series of engagements, including Antietam, Fredericksburg, Gettysburg, and the siege of Charleston, finally attaining the rank of brigadier general, with temporary (brevet) appointment as major general by war's end. He had stayed on as a lieutenant colonel in the regular army occupying South Carolina, taking a year's leave to tour Europe in 1866. On his return, he found himself not entirely agreeing with either the softness of the Johnson policies or the harshness of the Radical Republicans.

Ames set out for Mississippi in 1867 to bring peace and reconciliation to the state. Photographed in uniform, he made a dashing figure, complete with the bushy mustaches of that period. Revolted by the mistreatment of freed slaves, Ames took up their cause: he secured them the right to vote, despite his earlier reservations, and he presided over a military commission that tried a gang of whites who had been murdering black leaders, burning their houses, and driving their families off the land. On June 15, 1868, General Grant appointed Ames provisional governor of Mississippi, replacing a former Confederate general, Benjamin G. Humphreys, who had headed one of the "Johnson governments," set up under the president's authority. At first, Humphreys refused to yield to Ames's authority, and Ames made the conciliatory gesture of offering his rival shared space in the governor's mansion at Jackson. But Humphreys would have none of that, and in a new rigged election he was voted in again. The election had no legal standing, as Congress had not yet qualified the state for readmission to the Union, so Ames had no option but to have his troops escort Humphreys out of the mansion.

Ames tried to restore law and order, though his unit was not large enough to stop recurrent attacks by white extremists on agents of the Freedmen's Bureau and meetings of Republicans or blacks. One of his allies at this juncture was James L. Alcorn, an Illinois native who had come to Mississippi before the Civil War to cultivate several plantations. In November 1868, following the election of Grant to the presidency, one of Alcorn's estates was burned down by the Ku Klux Klan. He had by then identified himself as a Republican.

As part of his task to qualify the state for congressional recognition, Ames launched a program to spark Mississippi's economic recovery and proceeded to purge hundreds of Confederate officeholders from the state rolls. His new appointees included northerners and capable black freedmen. He also reduced the poll tax from $4.00 to $1.50, so that it would be affordable for blacks and impecunious whites.

In the fall of 1869 Democrats and conservative Republicans backed Louis Dent, Grant's brother-in-law, for election as the state's permanent governor. Ames, however, sided with Alcorn, the candidate of the Radical Republicans and the only one likely to take a strong stand against the extremists of the Ku Klux Klan. Though Alcorn protested that as a longtime Mississippi resident he was neither a carpetbagger nor a scalawag, the latter label stuck to him; after all, he was a Republican in the South. Even though only a small force was at Ames's command to provide security at polling places, Mississippians gave a landslide victory to Alcorn, to other Republican state legislators and congressmen, and to the new constitution. In one of his first acts as governor, Alcorn vetoed a bill to make racial discrimination on railroads a crime, because similar laws had caused a backlash in neighboring Louisiana. He did, however, sign a public education compromise bill that neither required nor prohibited racially mixed schools.

In 1870, after the state had been properly readmitted to the Union, Ames was elected by the Republican legislature to the U.S. Senate. Before Ames was officially seated, he had to undergo a critical review by the Judiciary Committee, whose Democratic members questioned his eligibility as a rightful "inhabitant" of Mississippi while serving as its military commander. It took Charles Sumner's personal intervention to amend the committee's negative report and have Ames seated by a vote of 40 to 12. Ames now felt he had the cachet to propose marriage to Blanche Butler, daughter of the controversial military commander of Louisiana, a striking beauty whom he had courted for years. They were married on July 21, 1870, at the Butler family home in Lowell, Massachusetts.

On March 6, 1870, a courtroom shooting in Meridian turned into a "riot," during which about thirty blacks were slain by the KKK. The Senate reacted with an "enforcement bill" to ensure federal protection to freedmen. Ames spoke forcefully for the bill, pointing out that Negroes, a majority of the Mississippi population, were being persecuted for merely trying to exercise their basic civic right by voting. In the meantime, Ames had received word that his erstwhile ally, Alcorn, had removed most of Ames's appointees and, in effect, split the state's Republicans into two factions, moderates and radicals. The remaining radicals supported Ames, but in May 1870 Alcorn, now also a U.S. senator claiming to be a true resident of Mississippi, spoke out against carpetbaggers like Ames, whom he blamed for whatever racial strife existed in the state. Ames held his ground; but Congress, instead of passing the new enforcement bill, ratified Butler's 1870 olive branch to the South: an amnesty bill to remove the Fifteenth Amendment bar on voting and officeholding by former Confederate leaders.

Ames found his Senate service increasingly frustrating. For example, his colleagues overwhelmingly opposed his proposal to stop segregation in the army on the basis of the Fourteenth Amendment grant of citizenship regardless of "race, color or previous condition of servitude." To prove that he still commanded statewide support at home, he resigned his Senate seat in 1873, two years before the end of his term, to pursue the nomination for governor of Mississippi. His rival was the incumbent governor, Ridgley C. Powers, a carpetbagger from Ohio who had joined the Alcorn moderates. With predominantly black support, Ames received the Republican nomination, only to be faced by Alcorn in the general election, running under the newly minted label "Independent Republican." In the political battle between the carpetbagger (Ames) and the scalawag (Alcorn), Ames received approval even from the Democratic press for his persuasive speeches, which helped him to defeat Alcorn in the election by twenty thousand votes.

The two years of the Ames administration emphasized reducing state expenditures, but the governor did not succeed in passing an economic program to provide land for blacks or to eradicate illiteracy. Nor did he command sufficient police forces to curb the rising tide of Klan violence, although he got the legislature to expand the militia and improve its armament. In 1875 Ames made an agreement with Democratic leaders that if they would curb whites engaging in racist violence, he would disband the black militia units that were being blamed for triggering election riots. The Democrats, however, did not abide by their half of the deal. The Democratic state leader, Lucius Quintus Cincinnatus Lamar, had built his political career flaunting his roots as a former plantation owner, Confederate soldier, and, later, emissary in Europe. His grandiloquent oratory helped him gain election to the House of Representatives in 1873. He regularly gave incendiary speeches that incited white mobs to break up meetings of Negro voters.

The Lamar forces intimidated Republican voters, so that one county with a Negro majority was able to deliver only four Republican votes in the early 1870s. After Democrats won majorities in both houses of the state legislature in 1875, they threatened to impeach Governor Ames. He appealed to President Grant for intervention in the rigged electoral situation but was told by the attorney general, "The whole public are tired out with these annual autumnal outbreaks in the South, and the great majority are now ready to condemn any interference on the part of the government." A Senate committee investigated Mississippi's voting and in its report called it "one of the darkest chapters in American history." Without any support from Washington, Ames had little choice but to resign and yield the governor's mansion to the Democratic president of the state senate. The honest and fair era of Mississippi government under Governor Ames was over.

For Ames himself, a long, profitable career lay ahead on his return north, until his death in 1933 as one of the last surviving Civil War generals. After joining his father's flour-milling business in Minnesota, he moved to Tewksbury, Massachusetts, near his father-in-law, and made a fortune investing in real estate, textile mills, and inventive technology. He served as a brigadier general in the Spanish-American War and engaged in the battle of San Juan Hill in Cuba. After the war, in 1898 he scouted out locations for army camps in South Carolina, this time marveling at the hospitality shown him by southerners who had evidently shed their Civil War resentments. (Ironically, Ames was assigned blame for Mississippi's bad government in John F. Kennedy's *Profiles in Courage*, published in 1954, which Ames's daughters protested, although unsuccessfully.)

In the case of Mississippi, at least, this leading carpetbagger and his "scalawag" supporters deserve praise rather than opprobrium from historians. The so-called Redeemers—the old white ruling class that was returned to power in the late 1870s—reestablished a system that denied political access not only to Negro freedmen but also to poor whites. In 1870 the legislature had elected Hiram R. Revels—a pastor from Baltimore who had been chaplain of a Negro regiment and gone with the army to Mississippi, where he served as a state senator—to the U.S. Senate seat formerly occupied by Jefferson Davis, who had become president of the Confederate States of America in 1862. Revels, who had been educated at Knox College, was a Radical Republican and disagreed with Ames's conciliatory state policies. The Senate had challenged the credentials of Revels because they had been signed by Ames, a military officer and not the official governor, but these objections were overruled. After his brief Senate service, Revels became president of Alcorn University, the state school set aside for blacks. Each southern state had its own gallery of rogues and heroes, so the Mississippi example cannot be taken as the rule, but it does show that carpetbaggers were certainly not per se ethically inferior to the Redeemers who succeeded them.

Samuel Eliot Morison, in his sweeping American history text, points out that carpetbaggers went south as entrepreneurs and, incidentally, helped to promote the New South. Two Union army generals from Ohio, John T. Wilder and Willard Warner, were instrumental in launching the ironworks at Birmingham,

Alabama, and Chattanooga, Tennessee. The economist Edward Atkinson advised southern farmers on ways to diversify their cotton agriculture. There were also former Confederate officers such as General James Longstreet, a West Point graduate and a lieutenant general under Robert E. Lee, who were denounced as scalawags for having joined the Republicans in order to steer the party to a more moderate course. After surrendering with Lee at Appomattox Court House in 1865, Longstreet settled in New Orleans. He was appointed ambassador to Turkey in 1880, then U.S. marshall in 1881, and finally U.S. railroad commissioner from 1898 to 1904, rounding out a productive and enlightened postwar career.

The last two so-called carpetbag governments in the South—in South Carolina and Louisiana—lingered on until 1877. South Carolina had no clear winner for the governorship between the Republican candidate, Union general Daniel H. Chamberlain, and the Democratic candidate, Confederate general Wade Hampton, who had even advocated that whites and blacks be registered to vote on equal terms. The 1876 "compromise", by which Rutherford B. Hayes had won an Electoral College majority by promising to withdraw Union troops from the South, decided the issue. On April 10, 1877, when northern troops left Columbia, the state capital, the Redeemers took control of South Carolina's government. Similarly, in Louisiana, the departure two weeks later of Union regiments from New Orleans ensured the return of the prewar white leaders to power in that state.

The turbulent administration of Governor Henry Clay Warmoth was mentioned in the first chapter, but this controversial figure in Louisiana history does not deserve to be treated, as he has been by historians over the years, as the epitome of carpetbag venality and corruption. A much more complex and balanced picture emerges in Richard N. Current's account of Reconstruction history through the interwoven biographies of ten carpbetbaggers. Warmoth seems to have been a figure à la Fielding's Tom Jones—young, good-looking, brash, intelligent, impulsive, and an opportunist repeatedly hoisted on the petard of his own intrigues.

Current describes a typical incident following General Grant's dismissal of Warmoth, a lieutenant colonel, after the battle of Vicksburg, for being absent without leave and for aiding the enemy by inflating the announced number of Union casualties. Warmoth managed to get an audience with President Lincoln, arguing that he had merely been on sick leave and that he had evidence that his figures of Union losses had actually been underestimates.

By mid-1863 Warmoth had been reinstated with full back pay. Two years later he returned to Washington, this time as an attorney for a wealthy New Orleans client who wanted to recover damages for bales of cotton that had been confiscated. At the White House, Warmoth was impressed with the courtesy shown by Lincoln, following his second inaugural address, to the former slave Frederick Douglass. Warmoth also managed to befriend Vice President Johnson in April 1865 during a steamship voyage to the newly liberated Richmond after Lee's withdrawal just before the war's end.

Warmoth, an Illinois farm boy who had earned a law degree one year before joining the Union army, was able to carve out a lucrative legal career in New Orleans after being discharged in early 1865. His best clients were owners of property that had been seized by Union forces, now seeking compensation. General Nathaniel P. Banks, the local Union commander, was an old friend, and he appointed Warmoth judge of a military court, where he did quite a good job, serving for several months as a fair jurist.

After President Johnson named J. Madison Wells provisional

governor, who appointed former Confederates to office, Warmoth turned against Johnson and in September 1865 helped transmute a faction of the Friends of Universal Suffrage, a group trying to secure the vote for freedmen, into the state Republican party. This group selected Warmoth as the state's unofficial "delegate" to Congress, since Louisiana had not been formally readmitted to the Union. Despite his nondescript status, he was welcomed by radical leaders Thaddeus Stevens and Benjamin F. Butler, who had been elected a Representative from Massachusetts after the war. Warmoth would lead the House prosecution in the impeachment of President Johnson in 1868.

To prepare a new Louisiana state constitution, meetings were held in New Orleans from November 1867 to March 1868 at the Mechanics' Institute, the temporary capitol, which on July 30, 1866, had been the site of bloody "riots" against black delegates who were discussing a new state charter. Warmoth influenced the convention to lower the minimum age for governor from thirty-five to twenty-five, which happened to be how old he was. On the second ballot, Warmoth won the Republican nomination over a wealthy black candidate, Francis E. Dumas, who was supported by J. B. Roudanez and his newspaper, the *Tribune* of New Orleans. Warmoth chose Oscar J. Dunn, a Negro house painter, as his running mate for lieutenant governor. Warmoth's campaign was aimed at attracting Democratic as well as Republican voters, and it succeeded in winning majorities both to ratify the new constitution and to elect his ticket by nearly two to one in April 1868.

As the new occupant of the governor's mansion, Warmoth was greeted with death threats from the Ku Klux Klan. White supremacists had been trying to impose segregation in 1867 by setting aside New Orleans streetcars marked by stars for black passengers, but Negroes forced their way into the unmarked cars, and General Philip H. Sheridan, the Union commander, had refused to enforce the segregation order. Now the state legislature's eighty-eight Republicans (which included forty-two black members) at first refused to seat the forty-nine Democrats unless they took an oath never to take up arms against the United States again. After an angry white mob gathered outside the capitol, the Republicans relented and seated the Democrats.

The legislature ratified the Fourteenth Amendment, which sufficed for Congress to readmit Louisiana to the Union and withdraw Union troops. Warmoth saw to it that an old friend from Illinois, William Pitt Kellogg, was chosen as one of the state's U.S. senators, and he made him his spokesman in Washington. As with many of Warmoth's other associates, this bond soon turned to hostility in the volatile climate of Louisiana and national Republican politics.

General Grant, the Republican presidential candidate in 1868, and his running mate, Schuyler Colfax, were opposed by the Democrat Horatio Seymour, with a former Union general, Francis P. Blair, from Missouri, as his vice-presidential nominee. Blair's public letter on the need to end Reconstruction and to "dispossess the carpet-bag State governments," together with the Democratic platform against Republican actions in Congress as "usurpatious, unconstitutional, revolutionary and void," was taken by restive southerners as an excuse to unleash a new wave of racist violence. Warmoth appealed to his friend Senator Kellogg to have Congress reauthorize the former Confederate states to muster state militias that could curb the violence, but a bill to that effect died in a House committee.

Warmoth then wrote to President Johnson to send troops because, Warmoth claimed, lawless bands had already caused 150 murders in Louisiana. Johnson scoffed at the request, but Warmoth's letter gave his enemies a pretext to brand him a slandering carpetbagger. Former Union general Daniel E. Sickles, however, wrote in the October 1868 *Harper's Weekly* that the Mayflower had brought "carpetbaggers" to the New World and that such folks should not be "barred from the South at rebel dictation."

The Louisiana legislature did authorize a militia of 2,500 black and 2,500 white men, at the governor's request, and Warmoth ordered General Longstreet to procure arms for this unit. Then, foreseeing the danger of a race war between the two wings of the militia, Warmoth had second thoughts and shelved the project. He also vetoed a bill that would have punished the owners of steamships, hotels, and other public vehicles and accommodations for not furnishing exactly equal service to white and black customers, out of fear this would incite more racist outbreaks. When the War Department ignored Warmoth's appeals for troops to prevent further extremist attacks on Republican parades and rallies, he set up a police district directly under the command of Lieutenant Governor Dunn, with a force of 130 black and 243 white officers. Warmoth also appealed to Democratic leaders to curb the recurrent violence, but they refused to make any concessions; so he warned his supporters, black and white, not to insist on voting if they were faced with violent threats.

The election on November 3, 1868, turned into a disaster for the Warmoth forces: only 276 of the 18,000 registered Republicans in New Orleans showed up to vote; the threat of violence kept the rest away. The state Republican totals were just half of what they had been seven months before, and the Republican presidential and congressional candidates were all defeated locally. The Democrats had kept up threats and physical attacks until election day, according to a later Congressional committee report, at a cost of 1,081 lives. Warmoth's cautious advice to voters not to risk their lives lost him the support of Lieutenant Governor Dunn and the Roudanez brothers, leaders of the black Creole community. Between the Radical Republicans, who insisted on enacting a full program of civil rights, and the opposing Democrats, who resisted racial progress at every step, there was little maneuvering room for a Liberal Republican maverick like Warmoth.

Did Governor Warmoth deserve charges of corruption that were leveled against his administration by his political enemies? Professor Current's balanced history leaves that an open question, though much of the objective evidence exonerates Warmoth—at least, of having behaved any worse than anyone else in the legally ambiguous circumstances of the postwar South. As Warmoth pointed out in his own defense, there was no state law against paying money for legislative favors, a measure he had urged on unreceptive state lawmakers. He even published the names of dozens of bribe takers, which caused consternation among members of the legislature. In 1871 Warmoth was accused by his opponents of having profited from the state's sale of the New Orleans and Jackson Railroad for one-third of its market value. He responded that the Democrats had previously sold the city's share of this property, and that the Republicans later sold the remainder to private owners who had pledged to make the railway a profitable concern at last. Warmoth also took credit for improvement work on the levees along the Mississippi, which had been deteriorating for years, and for relocating the city's slaughterhouses away from an upstream site that had been polluting the city's water supply. As for his own substantial wealth, Warmoth had begun his local career in a lucrative law practice, then invested in state bonds that had doubled in value. His enrichment no doubt benefited from insider knowledge, though that was no crime at the time.

Warmoth's political power evidently had not diminished when, barred by state law from running for a second term in 1872, he supported the Fusionist ticket (Democrat and Liberal Republican) of John McEnery for governor against William P. Kellogg, the Republican candidate. This time he had appointed registrars in every parish, who were ready to discard any returns that they perceived were the result of intimidation or fraud; but, unlike the 1868 voting debacle, this election proceeded with minimal violence, although the outcome of the governor's race remained in doubt while the rivals traded charges of vote manipulation. The Republicans swept the field—for Congressmen and both houses of the state legislature.

Yet, in what might have become an era of consolidated power for Warmoth, he stumbled into assorted bad luck and contentious allies. He had broken with Oscar Dunn, his lieutenant governor, in favor of an ambitious rival, P. B. S. Pinchback, who was picked by the black state caucus to be the Republican candidate for U.S. senator. Another contender for the Senate seat was the customs collector James F. Casey, who happened to be President Grant's brother-in-law. When Warmoth joined the anti-Casey forces, his old connections to President Grant were jeopardized, and he also became an enemy of what became known as the "customhouse ring," composed of Casey's friends who also had connections to the legislature. After Dunn's sudden death in 1871, Warmoth called a special session of the state senate to elect Pinchback to the lieutenant governor's office, whereupon the customhouse group, which included fifteen state legislators, tried to unseat Pinchback and to impeach Warmoth.

Among Warmoth's previous travails, he had injured his foot in a boating accident, and the infection eventually required amputation of a toe. After three months of recuperation, Warmoth sought a full recovery at a resort in Pass Christian, just across the Mississippi border. While he was there, he received word that Dunn had taken over the governor's office, since Warmoth had officially left the state, and was selecting his own executive staff. When he heard that his opponents were preparing a coup against him in the Republican party committee on August 8, 1872, Warmoth, accompanied by

Pinchback, forced his way into the customhouse despite a company of U.S. troops that tried to bar his way.

The next day, Warmoth gave a rambling speech excoriating his assorted political enemies. This harangue caused some of the targets of Warmoth's wrath to challenge him to a duel, while others prepared to impeach the governor. The grounds were based on Pinchback's unsubstantiated charges that Warmoth, his former patron, had offered him a fifty-thousand-dollar bribe. Warmoth was temporarily saved by the intervention of the militia forces that he had placed under command of General Longstreet.

Ever unpredictable, Warmoth now was prepared to leave the governor's office, which had been provisionally filled for forty-three days during the impeachment period by Lieutenant Governor Pinchback. Warmoth speculated that if he played his cards right and backed the successful candidate to succeed him as governor in 1873, he might be chosen by the legislature to become Louisiana's next U.S. senator. This plan did not work out. At two separate ceremonies on January 3, both the Republican William P. Kellogg and his rival, Democrat John McEnery, were sworn in as governor. President Grant decided the issue by recognizing Kellogg, Warmoth's former ally and now his political enemy, as the proper governor. Neither party had the edge to send a senator to Washington for the next six years, so the post remained vacant.

Louisiana Democrats, under former Confederate general P. G. T. Beauregard, had offered to cooperate with the freedmen in 1873 by recognizing their civil rights, but the following year the Redeemers abandoned this moderate course to renew their racist appeals and violence. The state's White League had a pitched battle with the black militia under General Longstreet and for a few days took over the state government, until they were dislodged.

From his New York hideaway, Warmoth watched these developments and saw the fortunes of the national Republicans plunge.

By 1874 the Democrats won a majority in the House of Representatives for the first time since 1861. He heard that the remaining civil rights measures in Louisiana were being rolled back as schools were resegregated and streetcars marked by stars were once more set aside for black passengers in New Orleans. Warmoth wrote to the *New Orleans Bulletin* reminding readers of the Democratic pledge to protect black civil rights, but the editors responded by trotting out the old stories about Warmoth's reign of corruption. When the state election board belatedly certified that the Republicans had won a majority in the state legislature, the Democrats were convinced they had been swindled yet again. It was to be a Pyrrhic victory for the Republicans, since in two years, President Hayes, in return for his election to the presidency, would abandon all remaining carpetbag governments.

At that low point in his turbulent career, Warmoth was somehow able to shed his carpetbagger past and rebuild his fortunes. After a string of romances that had included the daughters of prominent figures, he picked as his bride Sally Durand, a wealthy jewelry manufacturer's daughter from Newark, New Jersey, and settled at Magnolia Plantation along the Mississippi. There he became a sugar producer and developed a railroad to market his crop. As long as his former carpetbagger friend and later rival William P. Kellogg presided over the Louisiana Republican party and won elections as senator, governor, and representative, Warmoth stayed on the sidelines. When Kellogg retired, Warmoth attended seven Republican national conventions and in 1888 even ran for governor again but lost by a huge margin. For his party services, Warmoth was named two years later by President Benjamin Harrison to be collector of the the port of New Orleans. Ironically, this office had been the base for his political enemies in the "customhouse ring" twenty years earlier.

To his dismay, Warmoth witnessed the promulgation of a new

state constitution in 1898, which reversed the democratic gains of the Reconstruction era. The new document reimposed a property requirement for voting and required a literacy test to register to vote—a requirement that whites could evade by proving that one of their grandfathers had voted. The test was administered in a way that led to the disenfranchisement of virtually all black voters. Warmoth protested the injustice of stripping Negroes of their civil rights, predicting (correctly) that many of them would escape such a regime by moving north.

Warmoth lived to be ninety-one, long enough to witness the rise of Huey P. Long, whose political machine would dominate Louisiana until his assassination in 1935. Long had studied Warmoth's career and looked up to him as a role model. Long's demagogic style, however, was anathema to Warmoth, who in his later years became the personification of a patrician southerner, though one with democratic racial views.

Most histories have portrayed Warmoth simply as a northern adventurer who accumulated a fortune through graft and was unscrupulous in his pursuit of power. In the portrayal by Richard Current, Warmoth emerges as a much more complex figure, combining the political ambitions of a gifted young man with impulsiveness and, periodically, lack of good judgment—altogether not an unsympathetic figure.

Just as the stereotypes of villainous carpetbaggers and scalawags crumble under close examination, so do those of the noble Redeemers. After Reconstruction ended in 1876, much of the leadership in the former rebellious states came from Confederate army veterans and officials. They had also been prominent in the immediate postwar era, when "Johnson governments" had enacted stringent Black Codes that sought to keep former slaves in a perpetually subservient status. Foreshadowing the law challenged by the *Plessy* case in Louisiana, provisions of these codes required racial segregation. In 1865, Florida, for example, had forbidden any black or mulatto to "intrude himself into any railroad car or other public vehicle set apart for the exclusive accommodation of white people," with a breach punishable by thirty-nine lashes. Laws such as this had been annulled by the 1867 Reconstruction Act but periodically reemerged under state authority.

Congress had put in abeyance President Johnson's premature declaration on August 20, 1866, that the "insurrection" of the South was over, "and that peace, order, tranquility and civil authority now exist in and throughout the whole of the United States." For states to be readmitted into the Union and their representatives seated in Congress, their legislatures had to accept the Fourteenth and Fifteenth Amendments guaranteeing the citizenship and equal legal rights of former slaves as well as their right to vote. But Democrats had reconstituted a majority in the House of Representatives in 1874, and by then the delegates of all southern states had been seated and any remaining restrictions on voters because of their Confederate roles had been removed by the Amnesty Act, which had been passed in 1872 when Republicans still controlled the House.

As part of his bargain to secure the presidency in 1876, Rutherford B. Hayes had guaranteed that he would not enforce the Fifteenth Amendment granting the freedmen the vote. The states were left to regulate their own racial relations. In this new climate of legal inattention and denial, no branch of the federal government—president, Congress, or courts—was looking over the shoulders of southern officials who disregarded their constitutional vows by making it increasingly impossible for Negroes to exercise their legal rights and cast their ballots.

The Redeemers restored to power the white elite of the South in ten of the former Confederate states; Texas, the eleventh, was governed in this transitional period by adventurers and politicians out to enrich themselves. In exceptional cases, however, the new state officials did show some concern for the rights of Negroes. One of these exceptions was in Florida, where two of the new governors, Wade Hampton and George F. Drew, promised not to lose ground on the civil rights that had been granted to the freedmen. Despite this pledge, after a brief interlude, segregation also became the law there.

Throughout the South, ordinary people had been convinced for generations that a repressive regime over blacks was essential, because otherwise there would be a race war, with massacres such as the conflict that had followed emancipation in Haiti. (After a century of European colonial rule, Haiti, under the leadership of Toussaint l'Ouverture, had established a republic in 1795. Spain, however, still recognized French rule of all of Hispaniola island, which it had originally colonized, so Napoleon dispatched troops to validate this claim. The French were defeated by Haitian generals Dessalines and Christophe in 1804, when Haiti's independence was officially declared. In the aftermath of independence, many whites were killed and their families driven off the island. After decades of political turmoil in Haiti, in 1864 the United States finally recognized the country's independence, while continuing to interfere in its politics to this day.)

John Hope Franklin alludes to this "nightmarish fear" of southern whites from pre–Civil War days "that the slaves would rise up, slay them, and overthrow the institution of slavery. It had happened in Haiti. Perhaps it would happen here." This recurrent fantasy resurfaced when the war ended, and southerners were sure the dreaded Negro uprising would take place on January 1, 1866. The date came and went without incident, but whites continued to be certain that there had just been a delay and that soon the signal would be given for the freed slaves to murder their former masters and steal their property or burn it down.

In the twisted logic of racism, official discrimination and the free rein given to the Klan vigilantes were necessary deterrents that kept inevitable Negro excesses in check. By the 1890s the registrars who prevented Negroes from voting and the night riders whose random violence terrified Negroes and their dwindling number of white allies constituted two sides of the "redeemed" way of life in the South.

Gordon Allport, in his psychological study of prejudice, finds the mechanism of projection based on stereotyping to be at the core of the concept. To apply Allport's thesis to the case of southern racism at the close of the nineteenth century, abnormal psychology suggests something like paranoia at work. The defeated Confederacy could not bring itself to face the record of two centuries of slavery, throughout which it based its wealth on the exploitation of dark-skinned fellow humans. It rationalized the parasitic system as merely the exercise of white responsibility for uplifting heathens to the level of southern Christian civilization. And it obfuscated the immorality of slavery by a legalistic defense couched in the theory of states' rights and "nullification" of federal laws put forth in the 1830s by John C. Calhoun.

A half-century later, amid the ruins of the postwar South, the elite desperately tried to retrieve its self-respect by laying claim to racial hegemony, the ideology that led to hatred of the northern agents who "manipulated" blacks into asserting claims to equality. The hostility of southern whites against their ubiquitous challengers was then projected onto "enemies"; and who better to fit that role than the former slaves, powerless beings now conveniently perceived as oppressors?

Among the ironies of the dynamic of white fear is that the freedmen displayed very little animosity toward their white overseers during

Reconstruction, even interceding on occasion to restore civil rights to former Confederate officials. And nowhere, not in a single state legislature, did the brief period of black enfranchisement result in majorities of freedmen. Negroes may have dominated the proceedings in some conventions charged with drafting new state constitutions, such as those in Virginia and North and South Carolina, but their goal was mainly to make the system as democratic as possible. Without the admission of all men to the franchise, they were facing an impossible task in assembling a force of pro-Union voters and politicians to advance a progressive agenda to better their lives. Whatever vengefulness was directed at ex-rebels came primarily from a relatively small clique of "Radical Republicans" in Congress, and even they were more apt to spew bitter words than to enact punitive measures against southern enemies.

Like a naive pilgrim, another carpetbagger, Albion Winegar Tourgée, Homer Plessy's future attorney, decided in 1865 to explore the opportunities for a good life in the South. Tourgée appeared in the first chapter of this book as a Union army officer who refused to quit despite his repeated wounds in Civil War engagements. His photograph from that period shows a determined face with a belligerent look, perhaps due to an eye lost in a childhood firecracker accident. He had withdrawn from the University of Rochester before completing his studies but was granted the degree because of his enlistment with the 27th New York Volunteers, as was the custom. He had sustained a serious spinal injury when he was struck by the wheels of a gun carriage after six hours of bloody fighting during the first battle of Bull Run, a rout of the Union in July 1861. He had been discharged from the army with the rank of sergeant, temporarily paralyzed from the waist down, and returned to his father's farm in Kingsville, Ohio, where his school sweetheart, Emma L. Kilbourne, nursed him back to comparative health.

Though not fully recovered, Tourgée reenlisted as a lieutenant with Company G of the 105th Ohio Volunteers a year later. He saw action next in the battle of Perryville, Kentucky, where Union troops pursued the Confederate forces under General Don C. Buell. Here he received a shrapnel wound to his hip that disabled him for another two months.

He had acquired abolitionist sympathies from his New England family, and it is noteworthy that the next major event in his life is that he was court-martialed for refusing to turn over to the authorities a "disobedient" Negro soldier who had helped save his company.

Then, in January 1863 Tourgée was taken prisoner by the Confederates, escaped briefly, was recaptured, and after four months of captivity was at last freed in an exchange. He returned to his Ohio home and married Emma on May 11, leaving her once more in order to fight with Union forces at the battles of Tullahoma, Chickamauga, Lookout Mountain, and Missionary Ridge. During this campaign he applied to join a Negro regiment (he had admired Negro troops who shared their water with him during battles) but was instead appointed a judge advocate with a white unit. However, another accidental injury, and frustration at not being promoted to captain, moved Tourgée to finally resign from the army on December 6, 1863.

Back home, Tourgée resumed his education as a lawyer, in those days generally accomplished by "reading law" while an apprentice to a senior attorney. He was admitted to the bar in short order, by May 1864, and joined a law firm in Painesville, Ohio, while also pursuing his youthful ambition as a writer for a local newspaper.

He eked out a living by teaching temporarily at Erie Academy. But he found no satisfaction in any of these jobs; so when the Civil War ended in 1865, Tourgée wrote to William H. Holden, provisional governor of North Carolina, asking what opportunities there were for someone like himself. Holden's reply was warm: Tourgée would be welcomed there and would find fertile land for sale at bargain prices. Tourgée was drawn by the economic opportunities in the South, by the challenge of assisting the free, if beleaguered, Negroes—and by the hope that a warm climate would relieve the chronic pain he suffered from his war injuries. After scouting out several places in Georgia and North Carolina during the summer, in October 1865 Tourgée decided to move with Emma to Greensboro, North Carolina, where he sensed pro-Union sentiment. He had brought five thousand dollars of his savings to invest in a home and a business.

By then Tourgée had displayed the idealism, stubbornness, and lack of practical sense that would mark his future career as a northern idealist in North Carolina, where his path would be strewn with failed projects. The first was a tree nursery in which he employed Negroes at fair wages because of his belief in racial equality, although that did not endear him to his neighbors. He also practiced law with two partners, but he was inexorably drawn into Reconstruction politics.

Governor Holden, who had been appointed by President Johnson, had called a convention to rewrite the North Carolina constitution as a step in the state's readmission to the Union. This convention had repealed the state's Ordinance of Secession, abolished slavery, repudiated the war debt to the Confederacy, and elected new state officials and members of a future congressional delegation. But when the Tourgée family arrived, North Carolina had elected as its new governor Jonathan Worth, the former state treasurer under the Confederacy, who undid much of Holden's work. Negro leaders had met in October 1865 to ask the legislature for an end to legal discrimination, access to education, and an eventual recognition of their right to vote. The newly elected legislature, however, granted freedmen only the right to file civil suits, denying them the vote and leaving their former masters with the first pick of Negroes as apprentices to tradesmen.

Tourgée objected to this new regime of legal discrimination. In August 1866 he attended a convention of southern loyalists in Philadelphia, where he spoke at length about atrocities against Negroes and white Unionists in North Carolina, pleading for federal intercession. Carried away by his passion, Tourgée evidently exaggerated the number of victims as well as alleging that Negro corpses had been found in a Guilford County pond and that twelve hundred Union soldiers had been forced to leave the state. On his return home he faced a storm of protest, led by Governor Worth's charge that his speech had been "a tissue of lies from beginning to end." Tourgée received a range of threats, from people who would tar and feather him to those who were out to kill him and his family.

Far from changing his ways, Tourgée continued to organize a Union League composed of black and white supporters of Republicanism and radical change. He rode his old horse from meeting to meeting, carrying a pistol for protection. He also continued to publish the *Greensboro Union Register*, which he had launched in November 1866 as the medium of his views, though it was barely able to keep afloat financially. He had hopes of getting a government contract to sustain his publishing venture, but he returned from a lobbying trip to Washington empty-handed. The debts run up by his partners in the nursery business caused him to pull out to avoid bankruptcy.

Then, in the wake of the 1867 Reconstruction Act, Tourgée's fortunes revived. He had split from the Republicans in the camp of former Governor Holden, since their opposition to President Johnson stopped short of advocating the franchise for Negroes. Tourgée was appointed to the local board of voting registrars, earning a badly needed stipend. In September he stood to earn a bit more as one of the two delegates elected from Guilford County to the state convention that would draw up a new constitution. He ran a campaign as the champion of ordinary folks, black and white, against landlords, capitalists, and aristocrats, and won a narrow victory. General Edward R. S. Canby, the Union commander of the Carolinas district, considered Tourgée for a judgeship on the state superior court, but Governor Worth scotched the appointment by referring to Tourgée as a man of "most detestable character" in light of his Philadelphia speech a year before.

Yet Tourgée became an active member of the convention held in Raleigh from January 14 to March 17, 1868, where he was the youngest among the 120 delegates, only 13 of them freedmen. Although he was unable to get the convention to pass a resolution repudiating the Confederate debt, he was able to move on an innovative system of local self-government based on county commissioners, and on a change from appointed to popularly elected judges. His biggest triumph, however, was to have himself named to a three-member panel charged with codifying the laws of North Carolina during the next three years, with a monthly salary of two hundred dollars. For the Tourgée family, this represented a definite reprieve from their recent penury.

Soon there was more good news. While Tourgée had been denied the Republican nomination for a seat in Congress, he had been nominated to a seat on the state's superior court despite Worth's baseless charge that he was not a member of the North Carolina bar. In the April elections, Tourgée won this judgeship by the small margin of twenty-five thousand votes, which entitled him to receive a substantial second salary from the state. He would be hearing cases from a circuit of eight counties, serving a six-year term from 1868 to 1874. By all accounts he acquitted himself as a very fair and reasonable jurist, though his humane decisions were distorted by white supremacists who accused him of being a judge biased in favor of black defendants. A more balanced account, by John Hope Franklin, cites one of Tourgée's harshest critics, who conceded that he was "a most capable judge in all cases where politics could not enter."

Franklin further praises Tourgée for his fearlessness from the bench in denouncing Klan atrocities against Negroes and in castigating attorneys who were rude and insulting to Negro defendants or witnesses. The Klan increased the virulence of its attacks on the judge when a letter from Tourgée to Governor Holden, in which he catalogued recent KKK atrocities against Negroes, became public in the summer of 1870. Even sympathetic biographers such as Olson agree that Tourgée's righteous indignation often got the better of him, such as when he overestimated the extent of white violence and the number of Negro victims.

At last, however, when the Klan's threats broadened to include the lives of his wife, Emma, and their infant daughter, Tourgée began having second thoughts about staying at his post. He weathered attempts to remove him as judge, but after his term expired in 1874, he was relieved to accept appointment by President Grant the following year as a pension agent stationed in Raleigh. In 1878 he began publishing anonymous letters in the *Raleigh Sentinel* and the *Greensboro Patriot*, denouncing his hard-line Democratic enemies for their links to the Klan. He was exposed to more racist critiques when his identity was revealed as author of the novel *Toinette* in 1874, in which a light-skinned slave accepts the role of mistress to her white master until she returns as a nurse after the Civil War and refuses to resume the liaison.

Tourgée lost the pension agency and in 1878 launched a hopeless campaign for Congress on an idealistic platform, including Federal aid to southern education funded through a graduated income tax. In the wake of political defeat, the failure of his assorted businesses, and a new wave of white extremist hostility, Tourgée took his family on a new quest for success in Denver, Colorado. His journalistic and legal ventures did not recoup his fortunes, but he finally achieved national success a few months after his departure from the South when his most popular novel, *A Fool's Errand, by One of the Fools*, was published in New York to general acclaim. John Hope Franklin estimates that sales totaled two hundred thousand, a remarkable total for that time.

To today's readers, the novel is peopled with cardboard characters who do a lot of talking, interrupted periodically by melodramatic turns in the style of *The Perils of Pauline*. What makes it of lasting historical value are the historical asides in which Tourgée recounts true incidents to back up his conclusions: first, that the violence of Reconstruction in the South, far from being a reasonable response to northern military occupation, has its roots in the pre–Civil War era of slavery, when visiting missionaries were whipped for sermons promoting the biblical argument for abolition; second, that the North and South spoke two different languages reflecting their racial views, so that "slavery" was seen by the former as an abomination and by the latter as an essential basis of the southern way of life; third, that achieving equality among blacks and whites was inevitable, and that the only choice for the South was to accept it by stages or have it imposed by force; fourth, that the franchise should not be denied either to former Confederate officers or to freedmen who met minimal literacy and property qualifications; and fifth, that the only way for southerners to attain a morally grounded outlook was through giving them—as well as the freedmen—federal aid for education.

If the reader skips the melodrama, he or she might detect a ring of truth to some of the crucial incidents that are clearly based on Tourgée's personal experience. For example, blacks are terrorized by Klan members, who whip the men merely for seeking economic independence, brutalize the women, and burn down their homes. There are well-meaning southerners who are ostracized because they have been civil to northern white women teaching hundreds of black girls in the community, or because they tried to set up a Negro Sunday school. There is even one rather moderate member of the "Union League" who is murdered for trying to curb the violence of the Klan. Then there are the scurrilous local media that blame such racial violence on the victims, while not a single voice is raised against the racial extremists. Finally, the victims appeal to law enforcement agencies that do not respond, because there have been no eyewitnesses willing to testify against the culprits, or because they know they could never find a local jury to bring in a verdict of guilty against them.

The novel's good reviews in the North enabled Tourgée to break into the upper social strata. He was introduced to James A. Garfield at the Republican national convention of 1880 and invited to work for the presidential nominee. Tourgée later had access to President Garfield and sent him his proposal for massive federal aid to help change southern attitudes, but the assassination of Garfield in 1881 aborted that project. (It also extinguished for decades the hope for a Republican president to provide leadership in civil rights. Garfield was the last chief executive of the nineteenth century to sympathize publicly with the plight of southern Negroes.)

Tourgée spent the next dozen years writing more novels, none of which achieved the success of *A Fool's Errand*, although they enabled him to establish his family at a country house in Mayville, which he called Thorheim, at the shore of Lake Chautauqua in western New York. It was from that hideaway that he directed the legal strategy underlying the *Plessy* case.

A year after the Supreme Court's decision, however, Tourgée gladly accepted an offer from President William McKinley to escape his recurrent financial crises by going to Bourdeaux as the American consul. He remained at that post until his death eight years later, in 1905, at the age of sixty-seven.

Of course, Tourgée's fame faded quickly as the southern version of Reconstruction displaced positive views of Reconstruction in the authoritative histories. Perhaps the most caustic review of *A Fool's Errand* was published by William A. Royall, a Virginia lawyer who had moved to New York. In his "Reply to 'A Fool's Errand,' " Royall accused Tourgée of inflicting "a systematic and well-considered libel upon the people of the South." The fault for the current problems of the South, he said, lay with carpetbaggers like Tourgée. He accused him specifically of having taken thirty-five hundred dollars in 1868 from two notorious railroad promoters, Milton S. Littlefield, a Republican carpetbagger, and George W. Swepson, a native North Carolinian. Tourgée justified this later as a legitimate loan that he had publicly acknowledged and that helped him to buy his Greensboro residence. He had suspended repayments, he said, due to the losses he had suffered in the panic of 1873. Far from doing special favors for the railroaders, as Royall had implied, Tourgée cited the record showing he had worked against state funding for their projects.

It must have been an even worse blow to Tourgée to witness the rising fame of Thomas Dixon Jr., a Baptist preacher from North Carolina who had become a spellbinding lecturer after he moved to New York. Tourgée had once given Dixon some editorial advice, but in 1902 he was shocked to read Dixon's novel, *The Leopard's Spots: A Romance of the White Man's Burden—1865–1900*, an extremely racist version of Reconstruction. This book was to achieve sales of over a million copies and to far exceed Tourgée's works in fame and fortune. Tourgée bitterly denounced Dixon's book and was reported to have burned copies of it in his fireplace, using tongs so that he could avoid touching it. The southern revisionists had twisted and tortured the history that Tourgée had tried to record.

All three carpetbaggers who have been presented as case studies in this chapter left meager legacies despite their best efforts. Adalbert Ames aimed highest, following the ideals of his New England upbringing to wipe out the traces of slavery in Mississippi. When he met stiff resistance from the white power groups, he tried to steer a middle way, to avoid actions that would be taken as further provocations to violence. Henry Clay Warmoth tried to brazen his way to the apex of Louisiana politics and had sporadic successes, both for himself and the Union cause, though his tirades only served to further enrage his political enemies. He lacked the steadiness of Ames and the mature insights of Tourgée.

Albion W. Tourgée was the most political animal of the three—the one who knew that the real issue underlying Reconstruction was whether or not freedpeople would be treated fairly, not the distractions of federalist theory versus states' rights. Of the three figures, he was the most ready to sacrifice his own fortunes to his principles. Despite his many quixotic undertakings, he left behind something of substance: the codified laws of North Carolina as well as writings that capture the social conflicts of the resistant South in the 1860s and 1870s. He was also the architect of the legal strategy for the plaintiff in *Plessy v. Ferguson*, another of his noble failures that would help point the way for future civil rights advocates.

# Chapter 4

# THE "FREE PEOPLE OF COLOR" IN NEW ORLEANS

W e have traced the roots of the *Plessy* case to the history of Reconstruction, the decade that began by raising the hopes of newly freed slaves for economic independence and civil equality but ended by reinstituting the caste system of the old South based on color. Homer Plessy, if he had not heeded those yearnings of his community, would never have undertaken his fateful journey. But before his "carpetbagger" attorney, Albion W. Tourgée, could oversee the legal strategy of this last-ditch effort to stave off racial resegregation, he had to listen to the pleas of not just a single plaintiff but of the committee that had staked its collective fortunes on the outcome of this case.

The Citizens' Committee to Test the Constitutionality of the Separate Car Law did not appear on the judicial stage accidentally. It was challenging the 1890 Louisiana statute requiring that railroad cars must be segregated by race. The committee members were black Creoles, known before the Civil War as "Free People of Color." They were not ready to acquiesce in the infamous "Compromise of 1876," the deal by which southern states cast their electoral votes for President Rutherford B. Hayes in return for his promise to withdraw Union troops from the former Confederate states and not to enforce the Fifteenth Amendment of the U.S. Constitution that was supposed to guarantee freedmen the vote.

Who were these men? They were young and old, led by the sons of the activists of the 1860s—who had tried to shape a democratic government after the surrender of New Orleans to the Union forces in 1862—and by their surviving parents. Except for one other, smaller group in Charleston, South Carolina, they constituted the only free Creole community of color in the United States.

As the Civil War was threatening to bifurcate the nation, the Creole fathers had tried to ensure the birth of a new social order that would shuck off the racial restrictions of the old South: the laws against intermarriage; the exclusion of Negroes from juries and public office; the white monopoly of the franchise; and the color line that kept the races separate in public accommodations as well as in schools, churches, and cemeteries. At that time the Union commander was General Benjamin F. Butler. He had been accused of corruption by the white Louisiana elite, who resented his orders (particularly those that forced wealthy recessionists to set up funds for emergency relief), and it was said of him that he had left New Orleans with "a coffin filled with silver spoons."

Butler had only reluctantly allowed black volunteers to form their own regiments to fight against the Confederacy, because he had been warned of incipient slave revolts initially and did not trust armed Negroes. Taking as his first priority the pacification of restive New Orleans, Butler held off on more radical measures for fear of fomenting a white backlash. He had, however, been in favor of universal male suffrage, regardless of race, taking as his guide the opinion of Lincoln's attorney general, Edward Bates, in November 1862 that free blacks were American citizens. Butler had also allowed Paul Trevigné to edit a biweekly newspaper, *L'Union*, which became the voice of the proud *gens de couleur libre*. By December 1862, however, Butler had been replaced by a much more conservative Union general, Nathaniel P. Banks, who began by trying to placate the white elite.

The original three Union regiments of black troops formed in August 1862 were rarely used in combat. A year later, though, President Lincoln had authorized a New York politician to raise the Corps d'Afrique in Louisiana, since Negro infantry in the Union army had proved their mettle. Hundreds of free blacks, such as the wealthy Francis E. Dumas and C. C. Antoine, became officers of the three so-called Native Guard regiments. They found that their "volunteers," composed primarily of slaves who had fled the plantations by the thousands, needed basic education and military training. The unit chaplains joined other mentors who taught these men, who were eager to learn. In the extended battle for Port Hudson, north of Baton Rouge, in June 1863, the Negro troops proved their courage and took 154 casualties. Their commander, General Banks, praised them for their crucial role in taking the fort. Not long afterward, however, Banks caved in to the prejudices of his white troops and purged black commissioned officers from his Union forces. P. B. S. Pinchback, the northern-educated black who was later to play a key role in the state's Reconstruction politics, was so appalled by this discriminatory policy that he resigned his commission.

The Confederate governor of Louisiana, Henry W. Allen, who was secretary of war under Jefferson Davis, learned of the out-standing performance of Negro troops fighting for the Union; in September 1864, when the supply of southern white recruits was running critically low, Secretary Allen called for the enlistment of Negroes. He was familiar with the initial response of free blacks in New Orleans at the start of the Civil War, when they had formed Home Guard units to defend the state and prevent slave uprisings. Once more, they rose to the occasion by volunteering to defend their homeland. Thomas O. Moore, an earlier governor of Louisiana, had accepted the offer of free blacks on May 12, 1861, to organize a regiment to defend New Orleans. This unit soon grew to three thousand strong, but its white officers kept it from action and limited it to service chores. As the Union army approached, the Negro troops refused to retreat with the Confederate forces; they were caught up in the euphoria of the black population, who were expecting a better future in the wake of liberation. The free blacks among them, however, had mixed feelings, since they knew of the pervasive caste system in the North, which they now expected to extend to the South.

General Banks confirmed the skepticism among the free blacks when he pointedly rejected their request that he consider granting the franchise to black citizens. The black Creoles formed a coalition with chapters of black Masons, whose spokesman was the plasterer Oscar J. Dunn, and with white radicals led by Thomas J. Durant, a Philadelphia-born lawyer who had lived in New Orleans since the 1830s. These three partners conducted a petition drive in January 1864 that gathered a thousand signatures of free black property owners, plus twenty-seven black veterans who had fought under Andrew Jackson against the British in the War of 1812, urging that at least a qualified black electorate be allowed to vote for the state constitutional convention in February. The black Creole leaders were ahead of their time. Even the abolitionist editor William Lloyd Garrison thought it was premature to enfranchise freedmen, which put him at odds with his associate Wendell Phillips, a prominent abolitionist orator, as well as with Frederick Douglass, the former slave who had escaped to Massachusetts, purchased his freedom, and campaigned against slavery as editor of the *North Star*. Faced with this split in Republican ranks, the black Creoles had sent two emissaries to present their case to President Lincoln after being turned away by the military governor of Louisiana, George Shepley.

As has already been mentioned in chapter 2, Lincoln did meet these two delegates—the wine merchant Arnold Bertonneau, who had been a captain in the Louisiana Native Guards (a black unit of the Union army), and Jean-Baptiste Roudanez, a mechanical engineer who had been a cofounder of *L'Union* with his brother Louis-Charles. Lincoln was friendly but noncommittal.

The two emissaries had a more favorable audience with Senator Charles Sumner of Massachusetts and Congressman William D. Kelly of Pennsylvania, persuading them that the franchise should be extended to all blacks, not just propertied freedmen, as was eventually done through the Fifteenth Amendment. However, back in Louisiana the state constitutional convention of 1864 rejected the proposal. General Banks, the force behind the scenes, withdrew Union army support from *L'Union*, making it financially difficult to continue the publication. But the black Creoles refused to be so easily intimidated.

With the backing of Dr. Louis-Charles Roudanez, the staff of *L'Union* was able to continue publishing the first black daily newspaper in the Union states, now under a new name, the *New Orleans Tribune*. Backed by the National Union Brotherhood Association, with Paul Trevigné as managing editor, it soon became a leading organ for civil rights. It campaigned against a bill in the state legislature that would have granted the vote only to those Negroes of a quadroon or lighter shade. Black Creole leaders, even though many of were sufficiently light-complexioned to pass as white, had consistently been against any form of segregation based on skin color. They worked well with some of the group's darker-skinned members on issues such as the campaign against Jim Crow cars. If the leaders drew any invidious distinction against non–French-speaking blacks, it was on social and cultural grounds. Leaders like the Roudanez brothers had been educated at some of the premier schools in France and imbibed the principles of *liberté*, *égalité*, and *fraternité* with their study of the French Revolution. Though some of them may have been slave owners themselves, in the Reconstruction era they found their political interests overlapping those of uneducated freedmen from the plantations.

Segregation would affect Negroes equally, no matter what shade their skin color. Where the black Creoles basically differed from their freedman allies, however, was in their greater air of self-confidence and adherence to principle; former fieldhands were generally ready to settle for crumbs from their old masters or to stop pressing their demands when threatened with violence. The educated Creoles had perfected their diplomatic skills when dealing with whites, using lobbying and negotiating tactics to achieve their aims. At least this is the idealized picture of the *gens de couleur libre* that is painted in some historical accounts.

Quite a contrasting picture was presented by other authors, such as John W. Blassingame, who stressed the limitations of the rights that free blacks enjoyed before the Civil War and that made some of their leaders loath to confront white authorities. In 1860 these Negroes did enjoy the right to sue or be sued in court; but if they did either, they would generally face a court system stacked against them. Some of their property rights were circumscribed; for example, they were not allowed to own liquor stores or racehorses. They had to obtain the mayor's permission to leave New Orleans, or to hold balls, or to found a benevolent society. And if convicted of arson or rape against a white person, blacks could be given the death penalty, unlike whites who assaulted blacks. Even with their special status, *gens de couleur libre* were excluded from areas set aside for whites in jails, theaters, schools, hospitals, streetcars, hotels, and restaurants. Neither were they free to legally marry a white spouse. They were welcome in Catholic churches, even the Saint Louis Cathedral, but kept from attending most Protestant churches except for a handful of Methodist and Baptist congregations reserved for blacks.

Since the organized abolition movement began making forays into the South in the 1830s and news spread of the Nat Turner slave revolt near Norfolk, Virginia, in 1831, at the cost of sixty lives, the white elite of Louisiana progressively deprived free blacks of their traditional rights and forbade their contact with black slaves, for fear of adding their leadership skills to the destructive potential of the restive bondsmen. Black Creoles had to carry passes with them and to observe the nighttime curfew for all blacks. Though the nervous ruling class wanted to constrain the free black population, the fluid urban social structure (white and black customers mingled in neighborhood taverns and brothels) and the multiracial housing patterns of New Orleans undermined such constraint.

The escalating racial restrictions in 1852, however, ended Creole autonomy in the city and induced many young free blacks to emigrate to France, Latin America, or the Caribbean. To some extent, an influx of Negroes from other parts of the South, who were attracted by job opportunities and the chance to gain their freedom, compensated for this exodus.

How can we reconcile such conflicting accounts of black Creoles—either as fearless leaders or as timid accommodationists? To some degree, the former role is the product of chronicles by some of their leaders, such as Rodolphe Lucien Desdunes, who has left one of the few contemporary accounts of this group by a participant observer. It was his son, Daniel, who first defied the 1890 Jim Crow car law in February 1892 by refusing to move from his first-class carriage. As mentioned in chapter 1, Judge Ferguson had dismissed the charges against Daniel Desdunes, because his train had been bound for another state and the Constitution reserved to the U.S. Congress the control of interstate commerce. The accommodationist role attributed to black Creoles has been pieced together from anecdotal documents left mostly by white commentators. The strong self-image of narrators like Desdunes outweighs the impressions of those outside observers who fitted what they saw into stereotypes of obsequious Negroes.

Such contradictory images were recognized by W. E. B. Du Bois as inherent to the problem of black "double-consciousness" in people aware of both their African heritage and their American status as beings considered inferior by the dominant whites. Indeed, as a young man Du Bois had disparaged southern blacks for their internalized sense of inferiority, only to be persuaded by Desdunes that he had underrated the talents of the *gens de couleur libre* in Louisiana. In that case, the community had developed "triple consciousness," fusing their identity as African Americans with more than seventy years of French and Spanish culture. They were indeed multi-ethnic, with an outlook combining African, American, and European values.

Later, in 1907 Desdunes told Du Bois how black Creoles had resisted Americanization throughout their history. As "Latin Negroes" they had a different mindset from "American Negroes." Their ethos of equality had its roots in the French revolutionary tradition as well as in their own experiences as veterans of the army or militia, and in their remarkably high numbers of skilled workers and professionals. The American Negroes, on the other hand, wrestled with underlying problems of identity, as former slaves or their descendants. The white Democrats, Desdunes contended, had been exploiting this split between the groups, denying the equality that Latin Negroes claimed as their birthright and keeping American Negroes from assuming their place as fully fledged citizens.

As a mature scholar, Du Bois countered the white historians whose racist tracts accepted it as gospel that blacks lacked the inherent skills to succeed in the business world. In his history of Reconstruction, Du Bois cites the fact that the free blacks in Louisiana had owned $15 million worth of property by 1860 (though this seems a somewhat inflated figure). The Ricaud family alone could boast of owning four thousand acres and 350 slaves, amounting to a total value of $250,000. In the city most slaves were used for household duties and often ended up being given their freedom. In New Orleans, Pierre A. D. Casenave, a free black, had been the clerk of Judah P. Touro, a wealthy Jewish importer and businessman. Casenave received $10,000 in 1854 as executor and a beneficiary of Touro's estate. He used the money to start up several funeral homes serving mostly white clients, accumulating over $100,000 of equity in this business.

The existence of a vibrant black Creole subculture also disproves the thesis of the "scientific racists" that blacks lacked the genetic makeup and adaptive skills to thrive. From a group of 7,585 in the 1810 census, the free black population had grown to 25,505 in 1840. While it had dwindled to 18,647 by 1860, Du Bois attributes the decline to two causes: emigration out of the region and abroad, and the "passing" of many lighter-skinned Creoles into the white population. Indeed, the two decades of population decline comprised the period in which the rights of free blacks were increasingly restricted. New laws prohibited manumissions (emancipated slaves) to add to their number, others prevented the immigration of new free blacks from other parts of the country to Louisiana, while measures were also instituted to colonize resident *gens de couleur libre* out of the state.

Du Bois and southern black and white historians agree that by the middle of the nineteenth century, talented free blacks from New Orleans had carved out distinguished careers in business, the arts, and the professions. Arthur Estèves, who was later to become president of the Citizens' Committee pursuing the *Plessy* case, owned one of the largest sailmaking businesses in the South. Paul Trevigné, the writer, and an editor of the *New Orleans Tribune*, was a leading member of the committee and had also been a principal of the Catholic Institute for Indigent Orphans, established in 1847. Another committee activist, the lawyer Louis Martinet, had published *The Crusader*, another Negro newspaper published during Reconstruction. Other free blacks could be found in engineering, architecture, and medicine. Their skilled tradesmen included cigarmakers, tailors, carpenters, masons, blacksmiths, stonecutters, and leather workers. It was no accident that Homer Plessy made his living as a shoemaker, since free blacks had come to dominate the curing and tanning of hides and their manufacture into shoes, belts, harnesses, and valises. Plessy's home district, Faubourg Trême, was one of the suburban areas near the original city where free Negroes had bought up plantations in the early 1800s and divided them into small plots for their homesteads. Plessy lived there with Louise Bourdenave, the woman he had married in 1888.

How had such artistic and civic leaders achieved their prominence? Many stood on the shoulders of their fathers' or grandfathers' generation when common-law marriages between Frenchmen and light-skinned women from French colonies in the Caribbean had opened doors to success in Louisiana for their gifted children. Some notable examples are: Robert Norbert Rillieux—whose father was the Frenchman Vincent Rillieux, his mother the free woman of color Constance Vivant—was headed for a brilliant engineering career. After demonstrating his gifts as a young blacksmith, Norbert became a machinist and invented the vacuum pan method of refining sugar that revolutionized the industry in Louisiana. Daniel Warburg, a German-Jewish real estate speculator, married his slave Marie Rose Blondeau, whom he later freed. Their two sons, Daniel and Eugene Warburg,[*] studied sculpture with French teachers and set up a successful enterprise carving marble tombs and statuary. Eugene later went to France and became a noted sculptor. The musician Edmond Dédé had made his name as a conductor and composer in New Orleans before leaving for France to direct the Alcazar Orchestra in Bordeaux. The architect Joseph Abeillard designed many prominent buildings in pre–Civil War New Orleans.

Twentieth-century accounts highlight the sociological consequences of the free black community, with its social space much more conducive to self-expression and advancement than the static world of the slave plantations. The two institutional pillars in pre–Civil War days were the family and the church. Slave families were inherently in danger of disruption, as white masters sold off slaves who would bring maximum prices at auction. Most of the black Creoles managed to maintain stable families, despite their beginnings in the concubinage of wealthy Frenchmen and the light-skinned women, often barely teenaged, whom they courted at the perennial "quadroon balls." These unions were formalized by agreements between the man and the woman's family, specifying the support the man would provide the woman and the property that would be set aside for offspring from the union. Despite legal prohibitions against "miscegenation," there are records of religious ceremonies and civil registrations that evaded the rules.

Although critical writers have characterized these liaisons as a kind of prostitution, the standard seems to have been much more like a common-law marriage, with a mostly monogamous relationship practiced by both parties. In terms of social power, the children who inherited their father's property were destined to become educated for skilled or professional work, equipping them

[*](in French, Warbourg)

to be potential leaders of their community. The most gifted attended private schools and went to France for advanced training. In the city's annals we find the import house of Cecee Macarthy, founded on her inheritance of $12,000, which had grown to $155,000 by the time of her death in 1845. Aristide Mary inherited from his father an entire city block on Canal Street in New Orleans, which enabled him to become a leading planter, political figure, and philanthropist. By 1850 free Negroes with such holdings could boast over $2 million worth of real estate.

Until it was drawn into the post-Reconstruction wave of racial segregation, the Catholic Church in New Orleans was the major force in the spiritual life of white and free black worshippers. This religion, with its tolerant racial policies, was part of the state's legacy of the period from the colonial French and Spanish periods up to Reconstruction. Protestantism penetrated New Orleans mainly after United States rule was established in 1803, and brought in its wake denominational and racial divisions. Under the American influence, Catholic priests had forbidden intermarriage in the later years of the nineteenth century and segregated the originally integrated schools, orphanages, and cemeteries despite resistance from their black parishioners. By the 1880s there had been a wave of expansion in New Orleans parochial schools. The original ten elementary schools and three high schools had multiplied by 1885 to a total of sixty schools, though only five of them accepted black students. Altogether, only about three hundred out of some ten thousand black students attended parochial schools, forcing the remainder to attend public schools. From that time until 1917, however, not a single public high school accepted black students, whose only alternatives were home schooling or parochial school.

When it came to higher education, young blacks were generally limited to the modest educational fare offered at Southern

University or at the small Reconstruction-era Straight University (which in 1935 merged with the city university to form Dillard University) in New Orleans.

The Catholic Church was more than a spiritual home for the majority of free blacks. It was also the hub of a variety of benevolent associations, many linked to black nuns, including the Sisters of the Holy Family, an order founded in New Orleans in 1842, which established a school, church, and orphanage, as well as an old-age home. Another Home for Aged Colored Men and Women was endowed by Thomy Lafon, a wealthy merchant and realtor, who also contributed to the Lafon Orphan Boys Asylum as well as to hospitals and schools. There were other homes for the indigent and orphanages such as the Institution Catholique des Orphelins Indigents, which was opened in 1847 after a prolonged fight over the will of Marie Justine Ciraire Couvent, a former slave who had died a wealthy free woman in 1837. This organization housed a school that employed numerous gifted free blacks as teachers, and many of the school's graduates became prominent civic leaders and businessmen after the Civil War.

By 1860 Protestant missionaries had made some inroads among the black Creoles of New Orleans. There were by then four Methodist churches, with about seventeen hundred members, and two Baptist congregations, with some two thousand black members. Unlike the majority Catholic establishments, these churches were racially segregated from the outset. During Reconstruction, General Banks tried to rely on Baptists and Methodists as a counterweight to the more militant Catholic Creoles. Banks cajoled two Baptist ministers into creating a black newspaper to rival the outspoken *Tribune*, but this effort to divide and conquer the free black constituency did not succeed.

Of course, what was missing from black Creole history by the

1860s was genuine experience in politics. The white citizens of New Orleans may have recognized the artistic or musical talents of their black neighbors, and their business acumen, but they never accorded them the status of fellow citizens who could vote and become government officials. If the free black people of New Orleans appeared in the halls of government, they came not as equals but as supplicants or plaintiffs looking for justice in the courts. Nor did the balance of power shift radically after New Orleans came under Union army control in April 1862. Once more, the black Creole leaders had to plead their community's case to military commandants or provisional governors, who received them with surprise, skepticism, or disdain.

It was not long before these leaders realized that their leverage was negligible. Collectively, they had substantial business and real estate holdings, but their New Orleans population of about eighteen thousand was not numerous enough to decide even local elections—after the Fifteenth Amendment allowed them to register to vote—unless they joined forces with the freedmen who flocked to the city from nearby plantations. But what would be their access to some degree of power?

By 1865, in the third year of Union army occupation, the leaders whose views were carried in the *Tribune* expressed their frustration at being manipulated by self-seeking politicians. President Johnson had announced that his plans for the South did not include providing land or securing the vote for former slaves. Meanwhile, he was granting amnesty to all southerners except for wealthy planters or high officers in the army or government. And soon the majority of this latter group were being granted individual presidential pardons.

In the early Reconstruction years, when the black Creoles and new freedmen had tried to pursue common political goals, there was mutual suspicion about whose agenda would prevail. The

Creole community, composed of people like Homer Plessy and his supporters, embraced middle-class values such as social and civil rights, while the newly freed slaves required the basics— economic survival and access to schools. On some issues there was more of a mutual political dialog between the Creole leaders and the carpetbaggers who were discussed in the last chapter than between the two sectors of the black community whose circumstances varied so greatly.

The leaders in the *Tribune* circle tried to forge links with national coalitions to promote civil rights and advance the cause of the free but destitute former slaves. The National Equal Rights League had met in Syracuse, New York, in October 1864 to adopt a platform for universal male suffrage. This landmark civil rights group brought together 144 black delegates from eighteen states, including Louisiana. The black Creoles of New Orleans made contact with James Ingraham, who served as liaison with the League. In January 1865 they were able to establish a Louisiana branch, with the *Tribune* as its organ.

Newspaper editors appealed to wealthy Creoles to purchase some of the plantations that had been abandoned and to lease them to freedmen, who could farm them as sharecroppers. The Freedmen's Aid Association, formed in February 1865, provided supplies, education, and information to the first independent farmers. By August, Creole leaders of the group, including Jean B. Roudanez and Aristide Mary, had extended loans to several plantations they had managed to rent to farmers. By then, however, the Civil War had ended and the absent white owners came back to reclaim their property. Of the pioneer settlers who were dispossessed, most found refuge in New Orleans, where, lacking literacy and job skills, they worked as laborers or held service jobs from which they were laid off during the periodic economic depressions.

Despite their benevolent work for the freedmen, black Creoles were still trying to maintain their distinct community in one corner of New Orleans, attending Sunday mass and social events while generally keeping their children in schools separate from other blacks who had arrived in the city from nearby plantations. Politically, they still sought to build coalitions to maximize their meager power. In January 1865 they assembled over a hundred Negroes from all parts of the state at a Convention of Colored Men. The meeting planned an action program, which led the group to affiliate with the national Civil Rights League. Later, under the name of the United Suffrage Association (USA), Creole leaders campaigned to secure the franchise for all black men. The *Tribune* group joined the white radicals around Thomas J. Durant to organize the Friends of Universal Suffrage (FUS) on June 10, 1865. This group soon became a recruiting target for Henry Clay Warmoth's National Republican association, which he founded in July.

The black Creoles became aware that the linkages they had made with white radicals had not aggregated sufficient power to stave off the resurgent southern Democrats. The FUS was holding its first convention in New Orleans in September 1865, with Durant unanimously elected its president, when one of Warmoth's black followers proposed that the organization change its name to the Republican Party of Louisiana. After a stormy debate, the motion passed, with Durant's support. Afterward, Warmoth proposed that the newborn party's first official act should be to draft a state constitution providing for Negro suffrage. The motion was defeated after critics questioned the group's authority to adopt such a measure. However, the black Creole leaders joined in supporting Warmoth to be Louisiana's "territorial delegate" in Washington, until the state could be formally readmitted to the Union by Congress.

Warmoth and his faction controlled the state Republican party for the next six years, until his term as governor ended. In order to enact the liberal program he espoused, Warmoth had to fight on two fronts: against the Radical Republicans, who were adamant in pursuing a more extensive program of civil rights, and against the Democrats, who wanted to reestablish the order of the old South. The black Creole leaders came to regard Warmoth with suspicion and to believe that the Radical Republicans could yet succeed.

In April 1868 Warmoth was nominated as the Republican candidate for governor over the *Tribune* group's favorite, the wealthy Francis E. Dumas, who had been a major in the 1862 Union army volunteers. Warmoth selected Oscar J. Dunn, a working-class black, to be his running mate for lieutenant governor, though the Creoles, in a tactical error, did not support the ticket. The mistake caused the standing of the Roudanez brothers to drop and Dr. Louis-Charles Roudanez to retire from New Orleans politics.

The state legislature chosen at that time marked the crest of the program for black power. Nearly 48 percent of the Republicans, who had a two-to-one majority over the Democrats, were blacks, including a group of Creole leaders. Upon Louisiana's readmission to the Union, the 1868 state constitution ratified their agenda: to racially integrate all government facilities, including schools as well as private businesses. Soon, however, Republican power was eroded. In the November 1868 elections, the threats of white racists sharply reduced the number of voters in Republican districts. Warmoth's advice to such voters to think of their safety first, and his 1869 veto of a public accommodations bill, lost him the support of Dunn as well as that of black Creole leaders. Two years later Dunn died and was widely mourned in New Orleans as a principled leader.

Warmoth had the state senate replace Dunn as lieutenant

governor with the northern mulatto Pinckney Benton Stewart Pinchback in the 1872 elections; Warmoth did not foresee that this ally would quickly turn into an enemy, who would temporarily supplant him as governor during his impeachment trial. As a kind of black carpetbagger, Pinchback, the son of a freed woman and a Mississippi planter who had sent him to be educated in Cincinnati, was not fully trusted by Creole leaders. They had distanced themselves from Warmoth for being too ready to compromise with Democrats, and Pinchback had long been his protégé. Both of these men seemed more intent on advancing their own careers than on risking them by taking bold action on civil rights.

Warmoth was forced out of office in 1872. Pinchback agreed to support the Redeemer state constitution in 1879 in return for white agreement to establish the all-black Southern University, not an institution the integrationist Creoles would attend. Lieutenant Governor O. J. Dunn was more attuned to a radical program, but his sudden death on November 22, 1871, removed that potential ally of the Creole faction from the scene.

The black Creoles had become disillusioned with the scandal-ridden state Republican party, but they found no viable alternative. They tried, by nominating their grand old man, Aristide Mary, as the party's candidate for governor in 1872, but he lost to William P. Kellogg, a fellow carpetbagger of Warmoth's from Illinois, who had broken with him after being elected to the U.S. Senate. The Creoles did succeed in having one of their number, C. C. Antoine, a former officer of the Louisiana Native Guards, become Kellogg's running mate as nominee for lieutenant governor. The election was a stalemate, with both Kellogg and his Democratic opponent John McEnery claiming victory. With Congress hamstrung, it took President Grant to decide the issue, in 1873, in favor of Kellogg. Yet in the subsequently deadlocked state legislature, the Democrats managed to strip away most of the civil rights that blacks had gained in the heady days of 1868. Legal segregation again separated black and white children in public schools, as well as passengers on the New Orleans street-cars and city dwellers in other public places, despite protestations by black Creole leaders led by Judge A. J. Dumont.

Feeling betrayed by their Republican allies, these leaders found themselves increasingly isolated while the Democratic party proceeded to restore white rule. Blacks—both freedmen and privileged Creoles—were now behind walls of segregation as an underclass. After the "Compromise of 1876" put Rutherford B. Hayes in the White House, southern Democrats found it unnecessary to show any restraint in placing legal and informal restrictions on blacks, who had lost all hope of securing any protection by the federal government. Blacks who openly resisted the new wave of discrimination encountered threats or open violence by the Ku Klux Klan and other white supremacist groups. Therefore, they mostly kept their radical ideas to themselves.

Fifty black and white Republican leaders who had been split into warring factions for a decade met for dinner at Antoine's restaurant, a landmark in central New Orleans, on January 4, 1879. After the party's crushing defeats in the elections of 1876 and 1878, the Creole leaders had arranged this meeting to overcome their longstanding feuds. Dr. Louis-Charles Roudanez, founder of *L'Union*, had not spoken for over a decade with two of the other prominent guests, former governors P. B. S. Pinchback and Henry C. Warmoth. Now the three political enemies shook hands, but these rivals who had fallen out in good times could not sustain their truce in this era of desperation. Soon after the dinner, mutual recriminations were again exchanged among the factions. In an opening volley, Judge A. J. Dumont, a close ally of Roudanez, attacked the opportunism of Pinchback. Then there were counterattacks from non-Creole blacks and some of the white radicals.

Still, a few of the black Creoles pinned their hopes on a brighter future. One of the most outspoken was Rodolphe Desdunes, who delivered a speech at the funeral of Aristide Mary in 1893. He began by denouncing Pinchback as the type of black politician who was ready to sacrifice principles when it came to his own advancement. In contrast to such American Negroes who were prepared to settle for accommodation with whites at too great a price, Desdunes pointed to "Latins" like Mary and himself. These were Creoles who modeled their lives, he said, on those French radicals of the Revolution, with their credo that "all Frenchmen are equal before the law."

Desdunes had campaigned against the corruption of the Republican party in the state during the 1870s. He had helped to organize the Young Men's Progressive Association while working as a messenger for the U.S. Customs Service, his job for over twenty years. He had also managed to earn a law degree from the racially integrated Straight University. He used his legal training to join in planning a judicial strategy to restore voting rights for blacks after whites had used the "grandfather clause"—exempting those whose grandfathers had voted (i.e., only whites) from rigorous tests for voter registration—and other stratagems to disfranchise them. In 1887 Desdunes had also seen the need for another outspoken newspaper, in the spirit of the defunct *Union* and *Tribune*, that would make a special effort to expose incidents of police brutality against blacks. Louis Martinet became managing editor of this fledgling publication, the *Crusader*, with Desdunes contributing occasional articles. Martinet, like Desdunes a law graduate of Straight University, had been a supporter of Pinchback until he became disenchanted with him because of his patronage network.

On July 10, 1890, the Louisiana state legislature passed the bill that the Creole leaders, under Martinet's leadership, had done everything they could to oppose: it required passengers in railroad cars to be segregated by race. It was now the law. But the Creole leadership was not going to accept it without a fight.

The editors of the *Crusader* had been trying to forge a new coalition of southern black leaders in Washington: the result was the American Citizens' Equal Rights Association (ACERA), which decided to focus on legal challenges against new forms of discrimination in southern states, such as laws against racial inter-marriage and for segregated railroad travel. The American black leaders, tied closely to the Protestant churches they served, found the ACERA program too confrontational, and a general lack of support for it outside New Orleans spelled its premature demise. Desdunes forged ahead and engineered the local founding of a new group to challenge the racist system, using funds he secured from Aristide Mary. It was this Citizens' Committee, assembled in late 1890 and formally established in September 1891, that pooled Creole legal talent with cooperating white attorneys to test individual racist laws.

The committee comprised prominent black Creoles, including Louis A. Martinez, Rodolphe Desdunes, Arthur Estèves, and Caesar C. Antoine. Their first targets were the 1890 Louisiana law segregating railway travel; laws denying black citizens the right to be selected for criminal juries; and those that set up property and literacy qualifications for black men trying to register throughout the South.

The committee first considered launching a boycott of the railroads that made black passengers travel in Jim Crow cars. Then, in September 1891 what become the Citizens' Committee to Test the Constitutionality of the Separate Car Law chose the son of Rodolphe Desdunes, Daniel, to test the segregated railway law. As described in chapter One, on February 24, 1892, Daniel Desdunes bought a first-class ticket on the Louisville and Nashville Railroad, then declared himself legally black despite his virtually white skin. This prearranged protest led, as the committee had planned, to the conductor's calling on three policemen to arrest young Desdunes. The same judge, John Howard Ferguson, who would later hear the case against Homer Plessy dismissed the case against Desdunes, because the state supreme court had ruled in May that Congress had exclusive power to regulate interstate commerce. The committee celebrated its first real victory and recruited Plessy to make another direct assault on the segregated railway law by sending him on a trip within the state in a "whites-only" car.

Rodolphe Desdunes, in his 1911 history of the black Creoles, provides some details about the committee's plan to take their legal battle against the Separate Car Law all the way to the Supreme Court. But Desdunes does not convey with what foreboding the members considered the consequences in the event of a negative decision by the Court; he just complains that the committee got no support from black legislators who had spoken against the bill when it was presented to the legislature. By 1892, he comments acidly, these representatives had become too closely tied to the Louisiana Lottery Company to risk alienating their white colleagues. However, the committee, headed by the businessman Arthur Estèves, he adds, had received letters of support from such prominent whites as Supreme Court Justice John Marshall Harlan and Albion W. Tourgée, who had volunteered to serve as the group's attorney without a fee.

Only in hindsight does this litigation emerge as the final chapter in the history of black Creoles as a unique subculture that had existed for over a century. This subculture had been begun not long after the founding of New Orleans in 1718 by a young French Canadian, Jean Baptiste LeMoyne, Sieur de Bienville, who ordered trees cleared for a site named for Louis Philippe, the Regent of France. In 1722, the colonial court heard the case of a freedman named Laroze for stealing. He was ordered flogged and imprisoned for six years, but he was not deprived of his freedom, evidently a lifelong status. Then, on August 14, 1725, the marriage of two free blacks—Jean Raphael, from Martinique, and Marie Gaspar—was recorded in the New Orleans parish church.

The white pioneers of the settlement were there for diverse reasons. They included nobles fleeing the French Revolution, soldiers from Napoleon's armies, Acadians driven by the English from Nova Scotia and neighboring parts of Canada after French defeats in the French and Indian Wars (1754–1763), salt smugglers, and other convicts deported to clear out French jails. The Acadians stemmed from Huguenots, French Protestants forced to flee after the Edict of Nantes—a guarantee of religious tolerance— was revoked in 1685. Later misnamed Cajuns, they were lured to Louisiana by the colonial government's offer of land, seed, tools, and livestock, but they preferred living in the backwoods bayous to urban life.

The next group of immigrants were the white sugar planters who fled the Haitian slave revolt on the island of Sainte Domingue in the 1790s. They reestablished plantations along the Mississippi delta, creating the demand for imported slaves to do agricultural labor. Other notables from the Caribbean included John James Audubon, the ornithologist, who had first been sent to Europe after his mother was killed in Haiti. The offspring of these French and Spanish settlers created a culture known as Creole, from the Spanish *criollo* and Portuguese *crioulo*, words for native-born (in the New World). They maintained the French language and customs, despite the passing of Louisiana to Spanish dominion from 1769 to 1803.

Until 1730 Louisiana was administered by the Company of the Indies, which imported slaves from its Caribbean holdings or directly from Senegal, West Africa, the successor to the Mali Empire of the fifteenth century. While they were forced to do backbreaking construction work, the slaves were also supposed to be treated fairly. At least those were the dictates of the *Code Noir*, an official catalog of the rights of slaves in 1724: to a Catholic education, to be married in church and have offspring baptized, and to file a complaint in court if they were maltreated. Once freed, Negroes had a range of civic rights—except for voting, holding office, or marrying a white spouse.

The first substantial group to be awarded their freedom were the allies of the French in their war with the Natchez Indians in 1730. When Louisiana was again placed under direct French rule in 1731, other black soldiers were freed for joining Bienville's forces against the Choctaw Indians in 1734–1735, and the Chickasaw in 1739. Other slaves were manumitted by their masters or, occasionally, a few were able to save enough side income to purchase their own freedom.

These were the original members of the *gens de couleur libre*, a term applied strictly to black children who had been born in freedom. Their collective identity was formed after France lost the Seven Years' War to England, and in 1763 the Peace of Paris transferred the colony to Spanish rule, from the French King Louis XV to his cousin, the Spanish King Charles III. For one thing, the importation of slaves from Sainte Domingue was banned; for another, the French of Louisiana began three decades of resistance to their new rulers. With their roots in Haiti severed, Negroes in New Orleans looked to their own Francophone community for support. Finally, the Spanish liberalized the *Code Noir* to make it easier for slaves to attain their freedom, so there was an increase in the number of free people of color as well as in their well-being, especially from the 1760s through the 1790s. Their official census in New Orleans grew to 1,355 by 1802, with a two-to-one preponderance of women, because men often left for work elsewhere.

In the white community, however, the gender difference was in favor of males, because European single women were not attracted by the frontier lifestyle that awaited them. As has been mentioned earlier, the system known as *plaçage*, or common-law marriage between young black women and white men, became common, and the wives as well as the children generally shared in a husband's estate.

Under Spanish rule, additional slaves were imported once more from Africa. The free people of color, who had become assimilated into the prevailing French culture, occupied a distinctly higher status than that of the slaves. They circumscribed their social contact with slaves, since close relationship with or marriage to a slave would result in their becoming *déclassé*. Yet their community was not static. It grew as new groups of slaves received their freedom for service in the militia or army, or by the manumission of their owners, or through loopholes in the slave code, such as their right to petition for freedom after living at least ten years independently of their master.

Their lives became much more restricted after the purchase of Louisiana by the United States in 1803, as the tolerant Latin culture was supplanted by the rules of a Puritanical elite. But on the eve of the Civil War, the essential state of the economy, society, and culture of free people of color was still remarkably good. The variety of their skills and the level of their wealth were unmatched by any other African American community.

The vulnerability of the community was its absence of basic

civil rights. This exposed them to the wavering benevolence of the white elite. When Reconstruction ended, the era of tolerance that had been nurtured for generations—under the French, Spanish, and Americans—came to an abrupt close. Seen in this light, the committee that launched the *Plessy* case was already too late to restore the rights of black Creoles. The walls of racial segregation had been springing up across the South. When the last chinks in those barriers were sealed by the courts, the formerly free people of color would be sequestered in the same ghetto as their newly emancipated brothers and sisters.

# Chapter 5

# *Plessy v. Louisiana:*
## SEARCHING FOR PRECEDENTS

omer Plessy's trial for breaking Louisiana's 1890 railway segregation law was scheduled for June 7, 1892, in Judge Ferguson's state criminal court. Members of the Citizens' Committee to Test the Constitutionality of the Separate Car Law, known as Act No. 111 of the Louisiana legislature, could anticipate that a loss in Judge Ferguson's court would be sustained by the state supreme court in Baton Rouge. The committee's legal gambit was based on getting this defeat out of the way in order to have the case routed directly to the U.S. Supreme Court. After all, local and appellate judges in the state system were subject to regional biases and pressures. They had pledged their loyalty to the Louisiana constitution and their careers depended on the favor of the state legislature, while federal justices could be above all that, at least in theory. Francis Redding Tillou Nicholls, chief justice of the state supreme court hearing the case, was the former post-Reconstruction governor who had signed the segregated railway bill into law in 1890. A graduate of West Point, Nicholls had held a major general's rank in the Confederate army and had first been elected governor as a Democrat in the disputed election of 1876 that ousted Republican Stephen Packard in a coup the following January. Nicholls showed no inclination to recuse himself from the Plessy case, and Plessy's lawyers did not challenge him on bias.

At the state supreme court, decisions were based on common law, statutes, and interpretations of the federal Constitution, including two of the amendments on which Plessy's lawyers rested their case: the Thirteenth Amendment, which abolished "slavery or involuntary servitude" for all but convicted criminals; and the Fourteenth, which provided state and federal citizenship to "all persons born or naturalized in the United States," as well as guaranteeing to them (a) "the privileges or immunities of citizens," (b) "equal protection of the laws," and (c) protection from any state's depriving them "of life, liberty, or property without due process of law."

The Thirteenth Amendment, ratified on December 18, 1865, rejected the majority decision of the Supreme Court in the *Dred Scott* case on March 6, 1857, on the grounds that the Court had not just denied Scott his freedom at the end of an eleven-year legal fight, but had gone out of its way to make slavery a permanent state of noncitizenship, without any claim on constitutional rights. Chief Justice Roger B. Taney, a pro-southern Marylander, had claimed in a racist hyperbole that the Founding Fathers had regarded Negroes as "beings of an inferior order and altogether unfit to associate with the white race, either in social or political relations; and so far inferior that they had no rights which the white man was bound to respect."

If Negroes were second-class humans, as was implied by Taney's decision, they were doomed by the Constitution never to enjoy basic civil rights, such as the right to sue in the federal courts, to move freely from state to state, to have full freedom of speech, to hold public meetings, and "to keep and carry arms wherever they went." If we would allow Negroes to do those things, he claimed, it would inevitably produce "discontent and insubordination among them . . . endangering the peace and safety of the State." The many tangents of this voluminous decision could have been reduced to simply finding that Scott lacked standing to sue in federal court and would have to accept the (negative) judgment of the Missouri Supreme Court.

But Taney had gone out of his way to make *Dred Scott* the first instance in which the Court found a major federal law unconstitutional. That was the Missouri Compromise of 1820, by which Henry Clay had brokered the admission of Missouri into the Union as a slave state in a package deal with Maine as a free state, and set the latitude of 36 degrees, 30 minutes (slightly south of the Mason-Dixon line of 1767) as the dividing line of the Louisiana Purchase. Any future states formed out of land north of that line would be free states; those south of it would become slave states.

Nearly forty years later, Taney claimed that the framers of the Constitution had not authorized Congress to make such broad regulations. His reading of Article IV, Section 2, that "Congress shall have the power to dispose of and make all needful rules and regulations respecting the territory or other property belonging to the United States," was that this power amounted narrowly to the ownership and sale of land in those territories. When it came to slaves, once more Taney stretched the text to fit his southern prejudices. They were not "persons" in the constitutional context, even after they had become free in several states, but remained simply the property of their owners, to be returned to them by states to which they had moved, or if they had been manumitted.

Negroes, differentiated from Indians and other noncitizens by Taney, were the only group of people who would never be eligible for U.S. citizenship. He recognized that some states might have given citizenship to their resident Negroes, but he claimed that such status had no validity anywhere outside that state's jurisdiction, certainly never as a claim on national citizenship. One expert analyst of the *Dred Scott* case, Don E. Fehrenbacher, found Taney engaged in a "gross perversion of the facts," especially when it came to ignoring the rights of free Negroes—such as their entitlement to own property or press suits in court—before the Constitution was drafted in 1787. Further, Fehrenbacher concludes that Taney's unprecedented "judicial invalidation of a major federal statute" was based on "an argument weak in its law, logic, history, and factual accuracy."

The drafters of the Thirteenth Amendment were acutely conscious that they were setting aside Taney's misguided decision, a decision that had helped precipitate the Civil War. They would also extend Lincoln's Emancipation Proclamation of September 23, 1862. Lincoln's edict had promised freedom only to slaves in states that were still in rebellion by January 1, 1863—in practice, of course, only after they came under the military control of Union armies. Lincoln had specified that the Proclamation did not apply to the border states of Delaware, Kentucky, Maryland, and Missouri. It also excluded the area of the South—parts of Louisiana, Tennessee, and Virginia—already occupied by Union troops. The end result was that, contrary to popular belief, the Proclamation, when it was issued, did not actually free any slaves at all. It was a promise of future freedom designed to persuade slaves to come over to the Union side and help win the war.

After slavery had been abolished by the Thirteenth Amendment, however, Plessy's lawyers could argue that vestiges or "badges" of the freedmen's former servitude, such as Jim Crow cars, were also constitutionally banned. As a slap at the Supreme Court for invalidating the Missouri Compromise, the Thirteenth Amendment added a novel clause: "Congress shall have power to enforce this article by appropriate legislation." This language reflects the intention of congressmen who sponsored the

Amendment that it would serve to protect future laws on behalf of the freed slaves that might run afoul of the justices.

A year after passing the Thirteenth Amendment, Congress ratified the Civil Rights Act of 1866, which was drafted to override the Black Codes, to offer an inclusive definition of citizenship, and to safeguard the freedmen's civil rights. President Johnson vetoed the bill on March 27, but it was passed over his veto on April 9, 1866. The Act's central provisions were then given extra protection by Congress against the threat of later erosion and inserted into the newly drafted Fourteenth Amendment. With the abolition of slavery and the broad congressional view of civil rights on the constitutional record, Plessy's lawyers could argue that any "badge of servitude," such as the relegation of freedmen to the inferior Jim Crow cars, could not pass judicial muster.

The more complex of the two amendments just mentioned, the Fourteenth, was the anchor of Plessy's plaintiff's case. If the Thirteenth Amendment had abolished slavery as a precondition to Negro citizenship, the Fourteenth struck directly against Taney's exclusion of Negroes from national citizenship and endowed them with a panoply of civil rights. The third amendment of the set, the Fifteenth, seemed directed specifically against acts of racial discrimination in voting by southern states against Negroes. The Fourteenth was submitted to the states two months after Congress had passed the 1866 Civil Rights Act to ensure that freedmen would be protected against state action by the essence of the Bill of Rights. The amendment had been ratified in 1868 after congressional ire had been aroused when, at the close of the Civil War, the southern states passed Black Codes to restrict Negro rights so that slaves, despite legal emancipation, could in effect be forced again to work at their old plantation jobs. Indeed, ratification of the Fourteenth Amendment had been set by Congress as a condition for states to be readmitted to the Union.

Now, in November 1892 Plessy's lawyers sought to convince the Louisiana justices that their client's "privileges or immunities" had been violated when he was expelled from his seat in the first-class carriage. How could such a law pass scrutiny under the Constitution, they asked, when its evident purpose was to "perpetuate race prejudice"? Although the law's stated purpose was promoting "the comfort of passengers on railway trains," they wanted to know, wasn't its net effect to make racist *whites* feel better but excluded blacks feel inferior? Passengers, no matter what their race, were supposedly equal in being transported to the same destinations, but it must have been obvious to everyone that accommodations for blacks in the Jim Crow cars were far poorer than those for white passengers (although, for some odd reason, Plessy's lawyers did not raise that point except by obliquely asking what guarantee the law offered that the two sets of accommodations would in fact be equal).

The counterargument for the state, submitted by Assistant District Attorney Lionel Adams, was that the case against Plessy did not raise any constitutional questions. The State of Louisiana had the power, under the Tenth Amendment, to exercise so-called police powers, to protect the health, safety, and welfare of its citizens. As for discrimination, Act No. 111 made it equally illegal for a white to burst into the car set aside for Negroes as for blacks to occupy seats in a carriage reserved for whites. If this was indeed an example of legal equality, it seemed deficient in common sense, as no white was likely to want to exchange his or her comfortable upholstered seat for a hard wooden seat in a sooty Jim Crow car. This rationale recalls Anatole France's sardonic comment that "The majestic egalitarianism of the law . . . forbids rich and poor alike to sleep under bridges, to beg in the streets, and to steal bread."

Charles A. Lofgren has minutely examined the conflicting

arguments in the *Plessy* case. In its intermediate stage, as presented to the state supreme court, it was entitled *Ex parte Plessy* (in the interest of Plessy), to be rechristened *Plessy v. Ferguson* en route to the U.S. Supreme Court. Lofgren explicates the logic behind the points that were raised, first by Albion W. Tourgée and James C. Walker in their appeal to Judge Ferguson's rulings, then in their joint "assignment of errors"—a catalog of alleged mistakes in law made by lower courts—in their appeal to the U.S. Supreme Court. In order to persuade that tribunal to accept the case, Tourgée and Walker had to apply for a "writ of prohibition" and a "writ of certiorari." The former was to prevent the actual criminal trial of Plessy from going forward in Judge Ferguson's court; the latter is still the standard route for seeking a hearing by the Supreme Court. One problem with Lofgren's analysis is that it avoids criticizing the legal strategy of Plessy's lawyers, even though some of their points of emphasis or omission seem obvious in the context of leading civil rights litigation.

The Tourgée–Walker brief attacking the law of July 10, 1890, as unconstitutional was divided into eleven sections, which contain a good deal of overlap but do not cite as precedents a sufficient number of similar state decisions on segregated means of transportation to be persuasive. These sections can be grouped around three major points: the first called the Louisiana law a vague and deceptive piece of legislation; the second said it gave unwarranted judicial power to train conductors in determining the race of passengers for the purpose of seat assignments; the third said the law flew in the face of the U.S. Constitution, especially the Fourteenth Amendment.

Tourgée and Walker saw it as a fatal flaw of Act No. 111 that it contained inexact terms, such as "persons of the colored race." This left Homer Plessy and others "in whom color is not discernible" to be assigned to either a white or colored coach depending on the conductor's whim. Their brief listed sixteen conflicting legal definitions of a Negro or mulatto as persons with anywhere from a drop of "Negro blood" to being "one-fourth African." In a South Carolina case, race was "for the most part for the jury to decide by reputation."

Light-skinned Negroes would not be able to tell how they were supposed to fit into the law's black-and-white categories, and if they guessed wrong they could find themselves, at the least, deprived of the value of the first-class ticket they purchased or, at worst, arrested for remaining in a "whites only" seat in defiance of the conductor's order. In either case they would have sacrificed their self-respect or their money and, thus, would have been deprived of their property (or its equivalent) without "due process of law."

In exposing only dark-skinned citizens to such jeopardy, the law also violated the "equal protection" clause of the Fourteenth Amendment, in effect re-establishing the caste system that had prevailed under slavery. Although the lawyers did not emphasize the matter, the Louisiana legislature and court had been acting as if the Civil War had not changed the old order.

The unjust discrimination feature of the law was also reflected in its preferential treatment of black nurses who were allowed to be seated with their white patients or the parent of the mixed-race children in their charge. It dealt much more harshly with racially mixed families, for a white husband had to sit in the white coach while his black wife and mulatto children would have to go to the Jim Crow car. Louisiana law, according to Tourgée and Walker's hyperbole, could be read to "encourage" or at least legalize "miscegenation" by the silence of the legislature on the subject. In what seems an ironic tone, the lawyers then deplore the lawmakers' disregard of a husband's "absolute right to the companionship and society of his wife" by segregating the couple on racial grounds during their train journey. As the brief quaintly put it,

"Thus the bottom rail is on the top; the nurse is admitted to a privilege which the wife herself does not enjoy."

A similar piece of absurdity, Walker and Tourgée charged, was the law's express intent to avoid interracial friction yet to apply the law only to "railroads other than street railroads." Why put physical barriers between passengers by race in the spacious seats of railway coaches yet allow streetcar passengers, no matter what their race, to jostle each other without impediment? It was obvious that "contact between white and colored persons on street railways is more immediate, and many thousand times more frequent." (It was not mentioned in the briefs that black protests had reintegrated New Orleans streetcars in 1867 only after segregated cars had been tried.)

The deceptive nature of the law, according to Plessy's lawyers, was that Louisiana legislators had wrapped Act No. 111 into the specious rationale that it had been written to promote "the comfort of passengers on railway trains." It was obvious, however, that its real purpose was to "legalize a discrimination between classes of citizens based on color." It could not pass scrutiny as a proper law, therefore, since two of its absent features were that it did not apply to all citizens equally and that it did not have a clear and specific import. Tourgée and Walker argued that Judge Ferguson and District Attorney Adams had skirted this issue by shifting the focus to the rights of states and of railway companies. Ferguson had conflated the state's police powers with the right of railroad companies "to adopt reasonable rules and regulations for their protection and for the proper conduct of their business and to designate who shall execute said regulations." No one had mentioned that southern railways had had economic reasons *not* to set up separate Jim Crow cars until they had been pressured to do so by racist lawmakers.

It strikes a reader of the Plessy briefs that their critique of the Louisiana law was not as forceful as it might have been. Instead of confronting the injustice of the segregation laws that multiplied after "Redeemer" governments reinstituted white dominance in the South, Tourgée and Walker strained to come up with unlikely hypotheticals. For example, they asked whether a man and wife on the same rail journey were not being subject to different laws if one of them was planning to visit "many States on the route, the other not to go beyond the limits of the State." If this was a mixed-race couple, they argued, the white partner has "the right to seek and enjoy the society of the other," while the black spouse is allowed to travel only in a segregated coach. The example appears to raise an issue of personal inconvenience rather than a constitutionally grounded injustice. If the justices on this court held matrimonial rights dear, it is doubtful that they were overly concerned with the rights of racially mixed families. The same skepticism applies to the attorneys' plea for the black nurses who were allowed to sit with white children but were then barred from sitting with their own children, who had to be sent to the Jim Crow car.

The second and more forceful phase of the Tourgée–Walker brief focused on the central role of the railroad conductor, who became the state's agent when he determined the race of passengers, assigned them to white or black coaches, and in effect became judge and jury if he inflicted "summary punishment" on someone who resisted his command (in denying him or her the right to travel). This argument was likely to appeal to judges who would be loath to share their powers with railroad conductors, of all people.

Even if a conductor might be trained to follow standard procedures in assigning passengers to seats in carriages designated for whites or blacks, Tourgée and Walker asked, what happened if he made a mistake? How could the state legislature shield the railroad from a civil suit for damages by an aggrieved passenger in such a case? It was a principle established in the common law that a defendant had to be given an opportunity to appeal a decision or to file suit for any damages that he incurred. Yet a passenger who refused to obey the conductor peaceably, as Plessy had done, was automatically charged with a crime, though he had no evil intent and had done nothing bad in itself but merely asserted his "personal liberty" as a basic constitutional right. The attorneys for Plessy asked the Louisiana Supreme Court justices to consider the aggravated wrong done to Plessy when he was jailed before bail had been posted for him. Such "imprisonment of a citizen by authority of a State statute which is repugnant to and in conflict with the constitution," they argued, "is a deprivation of liberty without due process of law."

District Attorney Adams argued that Judge Ferguson had been correct in ruling that Act No. 111 did not deprive Plessy of his "due process" rights, because the law came within the state's recognized authority. In exercising its police powers, he said, Louisiana was rightfully protecting the health, welfare, and morals of its citizens. At least this was true as long as the railroad was providing equal facilities to black and white passengers in their separate coaches. As has been mentioned, Tourgée and Walker had not gone into the specifics of this claim; if they had, the "equal protection" claim of Adams might easily have been exposed as spurious. Their failure to emphasize this clause in the Fourteenth Amendment further allowed the Supreme Court justices to sidestep the issue.

When it came to the law's grant to the railroads of immunity from damages, Lionel Adams had finessed one of the strongest points in Plessy's defense. He simply conceded before Judge Ferguson that the immunity provision was indeed unconstitutional, which the judge had noted in his decision, yet adding that if this invalid provision were canceled from the law the remainder of Act No. 111 could still stand.

The Supreme Court justices picked up on this ruling, putting their own spin on it: that the exemption from damages could apply only if passengers had been correctly assigned to their seats by race. Damage suits could still be filed by passengers who maintained that they had been refused seats because they did not belong to the race assigned to that coach.

Neither version of the faulty provision—Adams's or the justices'—was of help to Plessy, who had never denied that under Louisiana's sweeping definition he was a Negro who deliberately took his seat in the first-class carriage reserved for whites. By his protest, Plessy was risking a twenty-five-dollar fine or twenty days in jail if convicted of breaking the law. As to future plaintiffs in civil suits against the railroads, they were not likely to prevail or to collect substantial damages for their discomfort in Louisiana courts that heard their cases.

The third part of Tourgée and Walker's brief raised the constitutional issue that the segregated train law implied a "badge of servitude" for Plessy, despite the abolition of slavery by the Thirteenth Amendment, and that it violated his assorted rights under the Fourteenth Amendment. Although the attorneys listed all three main clauses of Section 1 of the latter amendment—those protecting citizens against abridgement of their "privileges or immunities"; against deprivation of "life, liberty, or property without due process of law"; and against denial of "equal protection of the laws"—their emphasis was on the first. It seems—with historical hindsight, at least—that they might more profitably have pressed the equal protection and due process claims than those relating to privileges and immunities; the former two, not stressed by Plessy's lawyers, were grounds in subsequent judicial victories for civil rights. While it is not always clear what is meant by "privileges or immunities," or how they could have played a significant role in a case like Plessy's, these two rights appear to be weighty, meaningful, and specific.

Was railroad travel without racial restrictions a "privilege" in the constitutional sense? Prior decisions of the Supreme Court provided little clear guidance. Justice Bushrod Washington, the first president's favorite nephew, who was overshadowed by Chief Justice John Marshall after Marshall joined the Court in 1801, had explicated the phrase "privileges and immunities" in its original usage in an 1823 case. The case had challenged New Jersey's law restricting oystering rights to the state's residents, on grounds of the second section of Article IV of the Constitution, which declared that "Citizens of each State shall be entitled to all Privileges and Immunities in the several states." Justice Washington had found "privileges and immunities" inapplicable. They were, he said, not relevant to such mundane matters but to privileges and immunities "which are, in their nature, fundamental; which belong, of right, to the citizens of all free governments." As an example, he referred to the "the right to institute and maintain court actions." The post–Civil War amendments, particularly the Fourteenth, which provided state and federal citizenship to "all persons born or naturalized in the United States," clearly entitled Homer Plessy to the Article IV "privileges and immunities" as Justice Washington explicated them: "fundamental" and belonging "to the citizens of all free governments."

The phrase "privileges and immunities" was resurrected during congressional debates on Fourteenth Amendment drafts. One of the amendment's movers, Senator Jacob M. Howard of Michigan, a Radical Republican member of the Reconstruction Committee, conceded that "privileges and immunities" in Article IV was too vague a phrase from which to distill a definite meaning. "But it is certain," he added, "the clause was inserted in the Constitution for some good purpose." The plaintiffs in an 1873 suit called the *Slaughter-House Cases* tried to employ "privileges or immunities" to bear on their exclusion from a butchering monopoly in New Orleans established under Governor Warmoth in 1869 after upstream abattoirs had polluted the city's supply of drinking water from the Mississippi River. The butchers who opposed Warmoth's reform law told the Supreme Court that once excluded from the monopoly they could no longer make a living, which they claimed was a property right central to the privileges and immunities guaranteed to United States citizens under the Fourteenth Amendment.

A case brought by white butchers might at first blush seem like an unlikely tangent to a discussion of civil rights, but this case led to the first authoritative reading of the Fourteenth Amendment. On behalf of a narrow 5–4 majority of the Supreme Court, Justice Samuel Freeman Miller, a strong opponent of slavery and long-time friend of Lincoln's, interpreted the amendment quite narrowly. It was intended without question, he wrote, "to establish the citizenship of the negro," but not to "bring within the power of Congress the entire domain of civil rights heretofore belonging to the States." New Orleans butchers could not frame their complaints, then, under the "privileges or immunities" clause.

Miller came to an even more controversial conclusion when he parsed the type of citizenship—state and national—that had seemingly been joined by the Fourteenth Amendment when its opening words declared, "All persons born or naturalized in the United States, and subject to the jurisdiction thereof, are citizens of the United States, and of the state wherein they reside."

According to Miller's opinion, the two types of citizenship, of a state and of the United States, are "distinct from each other," so that only the "privileges and immunities of citizens of the United States . . . are placed by this clause under the protection of the

Federal Constitution." Surely, Miller explained (counter to the historical evidence), Congress could not have intended to "transfer the security and protection of all the civil rights . . . from the States to the Federal government." It is quite another thing for the citizens of a state to seek protection for fundamentals such as the right to acquire and possess property "and to pursue happiness and safety." In those pursuits, Miller added, they must turn, as they always had, to their own state authorities to redress violations of their civil rights; otherwise the effect would be to "degrade the State governments by subjecting them to the control of Congress."

Miller thus ignored the framers of the Fourteenth Amendment, who did indeed intend to bring about a revolution in the federal system, to frustrate the flouting of the rights of freedmen by southern states as Justice Taney had allowed them to do in the pre–Civil War days of *Dred Scott*. At least three of the Amendment's sponsors—Senators George Boutwell, George F. Edmunds and Timothy Howe—criticized Miller's take on the Fourteenth Amendment. Edmunds found that the Court majority had been wrong "in respect both to the intention of the framers and the construction used by them." Howe, even more bluntly, snapped: "The American people would say as they had about the *Dred Scott* case that it was not the law and could not be law." (Differing interpretations of the Fourteenth Amendment are discussed in chapter 6.)

The four dissenting justices were also outspoken in their disagreement with what they deemed to be Miller's misunderstanding of history. Justice Stephen Field quoted Senator Lyman Trumbull of Illinois as enumerating the "very rights belonging to citizens of the United States" by Justice Washington as now embodied in the Civil Rights Act and later in the Fourteenth Amendment. It would be "more tedious than difficult to enumerate them," said Field, but privileges and immunities surely included those rights that "belong to the citizens of all governments." Another dissenter, Noah H. Swayne, castigated the majority of the Court for adding "a limitation that is neither express nor implied" by the text of the Constitution. He saw the majority opinion as flying in the face of the framers and ratifiers of the amendment and thereby turning "what was meant for bread into stone." Justice Joseph P. Bradley scored the majority decision as allowing the states to infringe on "any fundamental privileges and immunities of citizens of the United States." He said that it had been the "intention of the people of this country in adopting that amendment to provide National security against violation by the States of the fundamental rights of citizens."

The *Slaughter-House Cases* were not used as a precedent by Tourgée and Walker in their briefs before the Louisiana Supreme Court, because that decision was the first in a series that curtailed freedmen's rights under the Fourteenth Amendment. The case would resurface in their argument before the U.S. Supreme Court in 1896, however. At that time, Plessy's attorneys had to face the emasculated version of Negro rights that the majority of justices had endorsed in the *Slaughter-House Cases*. They would have to devalue that precedent by citing cases at odds with it. Otherwise, it would be hard to maintain that Plessy's exclusion from a first-class carriage was a deprivation of a basic right derived from his national, rather than his state, citizenship. By then, none of the justices who had ruled on the *Slaughter-House Cases* were still sitting, the only exception being Justice Stephen J. Field, one of the original four dissenters.

In the meantime, however, Field had become a stalwart advocate of property rights against regulation by the states, at the expense of the rights of freedmen. Field's theory of inherent "natural" rights did not include those of Negroes, as shown by his dissent in an 1880 case in which the majority rejected a Virginia judge's claim that he had the individual power to refuse to summon Negroes for jury duty. For Field, the Court was sanctioning an unwarranted interference by Congress in state judicial conduct, as expressed in the Civil Rights Act of 1875, because he did not consider jury service a constitutionally protected right.

That a majority of the Court had endorsed jury duty as one of the basic political rights deserving federal protection under the Fourteenth Amendment had little practical significance. Unless a state official publicly announced the exclusion of Negroes from jury lists, it was easy to achieve the same result in a more roundabout way and thereby avoid a suit in federal court. Soon after Reconstruction, grandfather clauses, discriminatory literacy tests, poll taxes, and other ruses were used throughout the South to disqualify blacks who wanted to register as voters. When jurors were selected from voter lists, the inevitable outcome was all-white grand and trial juries. As Judge Loren Miller has shown in his survey of Supreme Court decisions on Negro cases, the system of all-white juries through the 1960s signaled to southern whites, including police officers, that they "could maim and even kill Negroes without fear of prosecution" in criminal cases, while juries in civil trials "guaranteed success for the white exploiter" as well.

There was another case that was cited repeatedly by Tourgée, although its effect had been to deny federal protection to Negro victims of a white mob in Louisiana. This 1875 decision of the Supreme Court, *Cruikshank v. United States*, stemmed from a wave of violence in the wake of the disputed 1873 election for governor that was mentioned in chapter 3. Before President Grant decided the standoff between William P. Kellogg and John McEnery in favor of the Republican Kellogg, angry Democrats unleashed a series of attacks on "carpetbaggers" like Henry Clay Warmoth and on Negro voters. The worst outbreak occurred in Colfax in Grant Parish (a town named for Grant's vice president, Schuyler Colfax) at Easter time, when a white mob killed about a hundred black men who had been attending a political meeting—a number far exceeding the number of victims in the New Orleans "riot" of 1866. Three of the killers were indicted and convicted under the 1870 Enforcement Act of Congress, to implement the Fourteenth Amendment, specifically for lynching two of the blacks and interfering with their "right and privilege to assemble together." Section 6 of the Act had forbidden conspiracies to deny the constitutional rights of any citizen, and the freedom to assemble was part of the First Amendment.

The Supreme Court unanimously decided the case on March 27, 1876, with Chief Justice Morrison R. Waite writing a decision that essentially let the murderers go free. Waite, a disciple of Roger B. Taney when it came to favoring states' rights in cases involving freed slaves, found that the indictment had been defective. It had not literally cited the infringement of rights under federal, as distinguished from state, citizenship as it might have if the Negro assembly had been held "for the purpose of petitioning Congress for a redress of grievances." Waite added insult to injury by finding it "even more objectionable" that the white killers had been charged with depriving "the lives and liberty of persons without due process of law." The federal government, he said, could not punish a conspiracy to falsely imprison and murder anyone, since those were charges reserved for state authorities to invoke.

Justice Waite and his brethren ignored the history of slavery in Louisiana as well as the realities of the disadvantaged lives of freedmen after they lost their federal protection at the end of Reconstruction. Waite claimed that "the right of the people peaceably to assemble for lawful purposes existed long before the adoption of the Constitution of the United States. It was not, therefore a right granted by the Constitution." The obvious fact was that Negroes had never enjoyed such a right in Louisiana prior to the passage of the Fourteenth Amendment and the acts passed by Congress to enforce it. As to the right of citizens not to be deprived "of life or property without due process of law," Waite asserted that "this adds nothing to the rights of one citizen against another. It simply furnishes an additional guaranty against any encroachment by the states upon the fundamental rights which belong to every citizen as a member of society." In other words, if the Ku Klux Klan attacked Negroes while the police turned their backs—or even gave the green light to the attackers—it did not constitute the kind of public state action that mandated a federal response. Yet by sending the victims of racist attacks back to their state courts to seek justice, the Court was— given the realities of "Redeemer" rule in the South after 1876— sending them on a fool's errand.

For Plessy's attorneys to sprinkle citations to *Cruikshank* into their appeals brief without comment seems futile, unless they wanted to prick the conscience of justices who had left the victims of white racist violence without a judicial remedy. Perhaps they were trying to imply that it was time to make amends by giving the Court's cognizance to the rights of Homer Plessy to use his first-class ticket without "being thrown into prison for refusing to abide by the decision of a railway conductor." Of course, they also wanted to underline that the *Plessy* case was basically different from *Cruikshank*, in that the conductor was acting de facto as an agent of the State of Louisiana. The connection between the authorities and the perpetrators of the "Colfax Massacre" was not as blatant.

Plessy's attorneys cited some state court decisions to show that regulations that purported to be racially neutral but did in fact result in discrimination had been overturned on Fourteenth Amendment grounds. In California, for example, a San Francisco ordinance of June 14, 1876, had decreed that all male prisoners in the county jail should have their "hair clipped to a uniform length of one inch from the scalp." In the case of *Ah-Kow v. Nunan*, a state court had ruled that that ordinance was "directed expressly against the Chinese" (because of their pigtails) and, therefore, constitutionally invalid.

For some unknown reason, Tourgée and Walker did not cite a decision much closer to home. Louisiana had passed a law in 1869 that empowered common carriers to adopt rules and regulations regarding passenger service in the state, "provided said rules make no discrimination on account of race or color." A Negro woman named Josephine DeCuir had tried to buy a first-class ticket on an interstate boat for a local (intrastate) trip from New Orleans to Hermitage, Louisiana. When she was told the staterooms were reserved for whites, Mrs. DeCuir bought a second-class ticket but took possession of a first-class cabin nonetheless. After the staff of the steamship threw her out of the cabin, she sued for damages, as the law allowed. Indeed, a jury awarded her one thousand dollars in damages, and the verdict was upheld in the Louisiana courts.

In 1878 Chief Justice Waite, for a unanimous Supreme Court, ruled that the state courts had been wrong. In *Hall v. DeCuir*, Waite found that Louisiana had wrongly tried to regulate interstate commerce, a subject reserved to Congress by the Constitution. Even though Mrs. DeCuir's voyage was intrastate, the ship was proceeding afterward to Mississippi. Thus, while the state "purports only to control the carrier when engaged within the state, it must necessarily influence his conduct to some extent . . . throughout his voyage." Justice Waite did not bother to ask whether Congress's failure to act on the matter might not have indicated that it was delegating some of its power to Louisiana under the state's police power over intrastate travel. He was more concerned with any offense to white passengers: "A passenger in the cabin set apart for the use of whites without the state must[,] when the boat comes within, share the accommodation" with black passengers. Waite concluded, "If the public good requires such legislation, it must come from Congress and not from the states."

Justice Nathan Clifford, in a concurring opinion, emphasized the need to observe racial customs that amounted to the doctrine later known as "separate but equal." It is an interesting aspect of this case that in 1869 the same state could find that racially segregated travel amounted to discrimination; then, in 1890, to define equality as inherent in segregated railway coaches.

If an abrupt shift in the political winds in 1876 could spell a transition to new racist "customs," there was also a strange air of inconsistency in Supreme Court opinions on the state regulation of commerce. Tourgée and Walker cited *Louisville, New Orleans & Texas Railway Co. v. Mississippi*, decided in 1890, although the majority opinion appeared to undercut Plessy's case. Mississippi had passed a law in 1888 requiring railroads to provide "equal, but separate, accommodation for the white and colored races." The state prosecuted the railroad for failing to provide separate coaches and the courts assessed a fine. At first the case seems like a mirror image of *Hall v. DeCuir*, as both Louisiana and Mississippi had poached in the area of interstate commerce, the former by requiring integration, the latter segregation, of the races. Yet Justice David Josiah Brewer, speaking for a majority of seven, found a way to uphold the Mississippi statute. He agreed with the state's supreme court that this law regulated only intrastate commerce, despite the fact that it required the railroad to add a Jim Crow car when a train entered the state.

Brewer's ruling rested on the state court's earlier holding that the law only affected the intrastate segment of the route, based on his reading of the interstate commerce clause of the Constitution, without touching on the Fourteenth Amendment. He was careful to point out that he was not ruling on whether passengers were being subjected to "choice or compulsion," just on "whether the state has power to require separate accommodations for the two races." The state had such power, said Brewer, though he left open the question of whether Negro passengers could be forced to use the Jim Crow car.

In one of his refreshing flashes of realism, Justice John Marshall Harlan cut through the obscurantism of the majority, saying "I am unable to perceive" how the Louisiana law "is a regulation of interstate commerce" and the Mississippi law "is not." Though Harlan was able to persuade only one fellow justice, Joseph P. Bradley, to join him in dissent, it was remarkable nonetheless, for Bradley had been the author in 1883 of the decision in the *Civil Rights Cases* that had invalidated key sections of the 1875 Civil Rights Act and declared that freedmen could no longer be considered "the special favorite of the laws."

The argument on Plessy's behalf before the Louisiana Supreme Court seems, on the whole, rather hastily written. Part of the fault may lie with the poor state of communications in that era, when it could take weeks for Tourgée and Walker to receive each other's letters. It may also be that both of the attorneys expected to lose at the state level before they could petition the U.S. Supreme Court to hear their case. If Plessy's lawyers won, the state's attorneys would not have the same option of seeking review to finally settle the issue.

The first document filed for the state was a rebuttal to Plessy's charges by Judge Ferguson himself. The judge claimed, incredibly, that at the time of the arraignment he had no way of learning whether "Homer A. Plessy was a white man or a colored man, or that he belonged to the white race or to the colored race." Yet the court file contains a sworn statement by detective C. C. Cain, the arresting officer, that Plessy's offense had consisted of "remaining in a compartment of a coach . . . to which by race he did not belong, to wit, a compartment . . . assigned to passengers of the white race." Since Cain's statement was included in District Attorney Adams's "information," it seems disingenuous of Ferguson to pretend that he was unable to tell that Plessy was a Negro. In any case, the judge found Act No. 111 "a good and valid statute of the state of Louisiana," which Plessy was charged with violating. Nor did Ferguson find the case to "raise any question under the Constitution and laws of the United States."

Lionel Adams, the district attorney, supported Judge Ferguson's decision that Plessy's trial should proceed. His brief to the state supreme court outlined four grounds for the constitutionality of the segregated railway law: first, the state's police powers permitted the racial segregation of trains without running afoul of the Thirteenth and Fourteenth Amendments; second, these amendments were expressly designed to protect *political* rights of freed slaves, such as voting, not assorted "social rights"; third, Act No. 111 did not discriminate against Negroes, because it provided equal rules and punishments for whites who might want to sit in the "colored car"; and fourth, a series of state and federal court decisions had held in similar cases that it was legal to enact segregation in schools as well as on trains and ships.

Of course, Adams did not point out that Plessy was the first person to be charged with a crime because he refused to obey a state law requiring segregated seating on "a public conveyance." As for Tourgée and Walker's objection to the railroad conductor making what amounted to a judicial determination of race, Adams asked what alternative there was. Surely, to organize a judicial tribunal on a train to determine the race of every complaining passenger "would be impracticable—in fact, almost impossible." He cited as precedent the case of *Logwood v. Railroad Co.* heard in

1885 by a federal circuit court in Tennessee. Judge Hammond instructed a jury in that case not to award Mrs. Logwood damages for being seated in a Jim Crow car. That court had approved the conductor's role in seating a passenger by race, and also allowed that the railroad was not required to furnish exactly equal accommodations to black and white travelers. Hammond had said, "Equal accommodations do not mean identical accommodations." How unequal the black and white coaches actually were on Plessy's trip was never explored by either set of attorneys. Adams merely shrugged off any discomforts in the Jim Crow car with, "All travelers have to submit to some discomforts and inconveniences and should not be too exacting."

In the Plessy case before the Louisiana state supreme court, a dispute arose between the parties regarding a state's so-called police power. Tourgée and Walker failed to see how segregating railway seats had anything in common with the accepted power of states to promote the health, welfare, or morals of their citizens. For Adams, the State of Louisiana had every right to adopt a law "to promote the comfort of passengers on railway trains." Segregating the races, he implied, avoided potential conflict, although there had been no reported incidents of fights breaking out on trains between black and white passengers.

A student of the Constitution may be amazed at how much authority states assumed under the Tenth Amendment, which seems like no more than an afterthought to the Bill of Rights. The Tenth Amendment simply states: "The powers not delegated to the United States by the Constitution, nor prohibited by it to the States, are reserved to the States respectively, or to the people." During the economic surge after the Civil War, the police power of states was interpreted by the Court as the limited regulation of businesses "affected with a public interest" rather than primarily the enacting of state rules establishing racial segregation. Yet as protective as these justices tended to be of private business interests, even narrower was their view of federally protected rights of workers or racial minorities; the Court's outlook would not change until the New Deal revolution, three decades into the next century.

In making the case for the Louisiana law, District Attorney Adams did not fully develop the legislature's rationale in having to exercise its police power by racially segregating railway passengers. He mentioned similar statutes that had been upheld in other southern states, but this was done in a haphazard manner; it was as if he were winking at the justices about what they all knew—that segregation laws had been proliferating in the post-Reconstruction South. If such legal barriers had little to do with the general health and safety, who would complain if any addition to the "welfare" of white citizens was "balanced" by the subtraction of Negro rights? Was there really any need to go into the necessity for such measures? The five members of the state supreme court fulfilled Adams's expectations when they issued a unanimous decision against the claims of Homer A. Plessy on December 19, 1892.

Justice Charles E. Fenner, who seemingly has no other claim to historical fame, disposed of the *Plessy* case in a somewhat cavalier manner. He reduced the eleven points of Tourgée and Walker's brief to one question: Could the segregated railway law of 1890 apply to Negro passengers in light of the Fourteenth Amendment? Fenner said that all other points, such as charging that the Thirteenth Amendment prohibited "badges of slavery" represented by Jim Crow cars, had already been ruled out by prior judgments of state supreme courts or the U.S. Supreme Court as extending "only to the subject of slavery."

For Fenner, the only thing left to decide was whether "the statute in question establishes a discriminatory distinction between citizens of the United States" based on race. If it had done that, Fenner conceded, the law would be "obnoxious to the

139

fundamental principles of national citizenship," namely, to the rights guaranteed to all United States citizens by the Fourteenth Amendment. Then, to test the fit of this amendment to the case, Fenner paradoxically reached back to two decisions by state courts in the North that predated the ratification of the Fourteenth Amendment in 1868.

The first of Fenner's precedents was *Roberts v. City of Boston*, decided in 1849 by Lemuel Shaw, chief justice of the Massachusetts Supreme Court. Shaw had upheld the status of the segregated schools in Boston, under the state constitution, against the criticism of the abolitionist Charles A. Sumner. In that case, five-year-old Sarah Roberts had to walk past five elementary schools that denied her admission because she was a Negro. The Boston school committee would let her attend only the rundown Smith Grammar School, which had been reserved for black children. More than forty years later, Fenner quoted Shaw's eccentric opinion that racial prejudice would not be caused by segregating the schoolchildren, since "this prejudice, if it exists, is not created by law and [probably] cannot be changed by law." In taking his segregationist cue from Boston, Fenner chose to ignore the fact that the Massachusetts legislators had passed a law *ending* school segregation just six years after the *Roberts* decision.

In his second precedent, Fenner cited an 1867 decision by the Pennsylvania Supreme Court that a railroad's own rules requiring racially divided cars for its passengers were not really discriminatory. Justice Daniel Agnew came to this conclusion in *West Chester and Philadelphia Railroad Co. v. Miles* not from consulting his copy of the Constitution but from the Bible: "To assert separateness is not to declare inferiority in either. It is simply to say that, following the orders of Divine Providence, human authority ought not to compel these widely-separated races to intermix." In other words, in Agnew's views God meant for blacks and whites to keep their distance, just as in previous centuries slaveholders had cited scripture to rationalize their superior wealth and power.

As for the 1890 Louisiana law, Justice Fenner agreed with District Attorney Adams that Louisiana was justified in this "exercise of the police power." To wit, the state lawmakers had been correct in their view that "separation of the races in public conveyances . . . is in the interest of public order, peace and comfort." Fenner did not specify who was thus comforted or discomforted. He simply found the law not to be discriminatory, because it would apply equally to Plessy and other Negroes in whites-only cars and to the hypothetical white person who might try to sit in a Jim Crow car reserved for blacks.

# Chapter 6

# THE FOURTEENTH AMENDMENT "CONSPIRACY"

Were the justices of the Louisiana Supreme Court suffering from historical amnesia when they denied that the state's segregation of railway cars did not run afoul of the Fourteenth Amendment of the U.S. Constitution? Had they forgotten that the drafters of the amendment, notably Representatives Thaddeus Stevens of Pennsylvania and John Bingham of Ohio, specifically tried to embody in it the letter and spirit of the 1866 Civil Rights Act? Finally, did the justices even obliterate from their memories why the Civil War had been fought? Many students have had a problem interpreting the 1892 decision in *Ex parte Plessy*. It seems anachronistic, since it rests on precedents set in state courts before the war, when southern states felt free to defy acts of Congress. The war had settled the issue; federal law had supremacy over states' rights.

We have already scanned the abrupt switch from postwar Reconstruction policies to the restoration of white elite rule in the former Confederacy. Before analyzing how the Supreme Court reacted to the appeal in *Plessy v. Ferguson*, we have to sketch in the revival of the theory of states' rights, which seems mainly due to underlying economic causes. Like the "Gilded Age" to which Mark Twain's 1873 novel lent its name, the 1890s was an era of intellectual, esthetic, and cultural innovation. It was fueled by the rapid expansion of the nation's economy, specifically the northeastern industries that by the eve of World War I would be out-producing the rest of the world in oil and steel, setting the pace in methods of mass production, and establishing the United States as a world power. Southern agricultural products and raw materials were indispensable for what became known as the "second industrial revolution."

The political forces radiating from Washington to the state capitals became aligned with property owners who commanded giant corporations and boasted of being able to have officials, from state judges to congressmen and presidents, do their bidding. They were called "robber barons" by the Midwest farmers who could not afford to pay the railroads' exorbitant rates to ship their produce to market.

One of their number, Jay Gould, began his career as an ambitious clerk in a country store in Roxbury, in upstate New York. Then he turned leather merchant and surveyor, using his savings to purchase land along the Delaware and Lackawanna Railroad. He was only twenty when he became involved in financial speculation on Wall Street. Ten years later, in 1868, he gained control of the Erie Railroad from Cornelius Vanderbilt. He attempted to corner the gold market, using inside contacts in Washington, in concert with financiers James Fisk and Daniel Drew. The scheme caused the panic of "Black Friday"—September 24, 1869—which before it became a disaster was checked by President Grant, who released enough government gold to stabilize the market. When public protests forced Gould out of his directorships in 1872, he moved west, buying up stock in the Union Pacific and three other railroads known as the "Gould system." Gould reflected the cynicism of his fellow plutocrats when he boasted that he was rich enough to "hire one half of the working class to kill the other half."

Gould's cohorts—coal and iron magnate Andrew Mellon, oil baron John D. Rockefeller, steel industrialist Andrew Carnegie, and other self-made millionaires—endowed foundations and universities to enhance their reputation. For Carnegie, who wrote *The Gospel of Wealth* in 1889, wealth was to be used for the benefit of all humanity. Many social science scholars at the endowed institutions elaborated on the theories of "social Darwinism," which celebrated the superior abilities of their benefactors as well as the inherent defects of the lower classes and "inferior races."

It was this clique of the super-rich—the one percent of the population who owned more than half of all the property in the country—that hired the lawyers who persuaded the Supreme Court justices that a novel "conspiracy theory," so they asserted, disclosed the hidden meaning of the Fourteenth Amendment, the text of whose first section seemed clearly designed to protect the former slaves who had been given their freedom by the Thirteenth Amendment on December 18, 1865. It read:

> All persons born or naturalized in the United States, and subject to the jurisdiction thereof, are citizens of the United States and of the State wherein they reside. No state shall make or enforce any law which shall abridge the privileges or immunities of citizens of the United States; nor shall any State deprive any person of life, liberty, or property, without due process of law; nor deny to any person within its jurisdiction the equal protection of the laws.

The opening sentence on citizenship had been added from the House floor. The rest of the section had been drafted by Congressman Bingham, because he felt it would, for the first time, "protect by national law the privileges and immunities of all citizens of the Republic and the inborn rights of every person within its jurisdiction whenever the same shall be abridged or denied." Senator Jacob M. Howard of Michigan agreed with Bingham that "the great objective of the first section of the amendment is . . . to restrain the power of the States and compel them at all times to respect these great fundamental guarantees." Howard concluded by seeing in that section "a direct affirmative delegation to Congress to carry out all the principles of all these guarantees, a power not found in the Constitution."

Another member of the joint committee that drafted the amendment was Roscoe Conkling, a New York Republican boss who was elected to the House in 1858 and to the Senate in 1866. In 1876 Conkling had accumulated sufficient power in his New York stronghold to mount a campaign for the party's presidential nomination, if not for himself, then to secure a third term for President Grant. Conkling was stymied by James G. Blaine, who supported the eventual winner, Hayes, and four years later his successor, Garfield. Conkling, who would became the author of the "conspiracy theory" to find arcane meaning in the Fourteenth Amendment, had succeeded in changing only one word of it: "person" for "citizen" in the last two clauses of the first section. This was to become his secret legal weapon ten years later.

At the time, Conkling explained that "many of the larger States now hold their representation in part by reason of their aliens." That was a far cry from his later position, that the word "person" would allow corporations (as legal "persons") to receive federal protection from state regulation. Conkling, a close friend of President Grant and part of his spoils system, had the distinction of turning down both a nomination by Grant in 1873 to be Chief Justice of the Supreme Court, and the post of Associate Justice— after the Senate had confirmed his nomination by Chester A. Arthur in 1882. Conkling had been defeated by Hayes in the struggle for control of federal appointments in the states, which became a presidential prerogative.

But Conkling was reelected by the New York legislature to the Senate in 1880, where his circle included Thomas Platt, the state's junior senator, as well Chester A. Arthur, the vice president, and New York governor Alonzo B. Cornell, son of the financier who founded Cornell University. Arthur and Cornell had extended Conkling's power base by controlling the New York customs house. Conkling claimed Garfield had promised him patronage rights in return for his support in Garfield's presidential bid, and when Garfield denied this, Conkling resigned from the Senate in 1881 in pique. (Arthur became president in September 1881 after Garfield's assassination.) The *New York Times* suggested at that time that Conkling backed off the Supreme Court deal because the position paid too small a salary and did not carry any patronage. Indeed, after moving to Manhattan, Conkling made a small fortune in the private practice of law—not a mean achievement for someone who had passed the bar after "reading law" in a Utica, New York, law firm.

Conkling's specialty became the defense of railroad companies against state taxes and regulations. He was determined to reverse the restrictive view of the Fourteenth Amendment that a Supreme Court majority had taken in the *Slaughter-House* Cases of 1873, when Justice Miller had refused to apply the "privileges or immunities" clause to the disgruntled New Orleans butchers who claimed it protected their property rights from a state monopoly. Even a "most casual examination of the language of these amendments," namely, the Thirteenth, Fourteenth, and Fifteenth, he said, would reveal "the one pervading purpose lying at the foundation of each . . . : we mean the freedom of the slave race, the security and firm establishment of that freedom, and the protection of the newly-made freeman and citizen from the oppressions of those who had formerly exercised unlimited dominion over him."

The Court's hands-off policy on state regulation of property had been reaffirmed in 1877, in *Munn v. Illinois*, a case brought by an independent warehouse operator against the Illinois "Granger law." (The Grangers—Midwest farmers fighting excessive charges by the railroads for carrying and storing their produce—had established rate control laws in Wisconsin, Minnesota, and Iowa as well.) Chief Justice Morrison R. Waite, speaking for a 7–2 majority, upheld the state's rate-setting power on grain elevators. Such a statute was within the state's police power, according to Waite. Further, it did not violate the due process clause of the Fourteenth Amendment, since "when private property is invested with a public interest," the property ceases to be private and is properly subject to regulation. It was up to the legislature, not the Court, to determine what kind of regulation was permissible.

Justice Stephen J. Field filed an angry dissent, joined by Justice William Strong. Field based his opinion on an expansive reading of the due process clause of the Fourteenth Amendment. His extreme defense of inalienable property rights became known as "substantive due process," because it flowed from a belief in the inherent rights of property holding and use, protected from regulation by the states. It had an almost mystical quality, though Field did anchor it in the Fourteenth Amendment, with its protection of life, liberty, and property. In his *Munn* dissent, Field attacked the majority's sanction of Illinois grain storage controls as leading the way to an "invasion of private rights, all property and all business . . . held at the mercy of a majority of its legislature." A law that claimed to protect hard-pressed farmers was, in his opinion, "nothing less than a bold assertion of absolute power by the state to control at its discretion the property and business of the citizen, and fix the compensation he shall receive."

When Conkling entered the fray, the way to an expansion of judicial power had already been pointed by the American Bar Association (ABA), which was established in 1878. Judge Thomas McIntyre Cooley, of the Michigan Supreme Court, another advocate of laissez-faire, had argued for greater safeguards against the "radical ideas" that were behind the expanding power of state constitutions and laws. Cooley wanted these barriers to be twofold, a proper application of the Constitution and "natural law," a rather fuzzy concept by which judges would protect the rights of property owners against state regulation. Despite the colonial history of the United States, with broad-based state power to fix prices, Cooley read into the "due process" clauses of the Fifth and Fourteenth Amendments a ban on the restriction of property rights. In 1881 the ABA launched a campaign to unshackle property from government restriction, even if ownership was exercised by monopolies or trusts.

In September 1882 Conkling presented a startling argument to the Supreme Court on behalf of the Southern Pacific Railroad, which had been assessed taxes by San Mateo County, California. He called the taxes discriminatory and contrary to the "due process" clause of the Fourteenth Amendment. How could this be when just nine years previously, the Court in the *Slaughter-House* Cases had ruled that this clause had been designed to protect the rights of freedmen?

Conkling, the respected lawyer and power broker who had been a member of the Joint Congressional Committee, virtually pulled a rabbit from his hat. He revealed for the first time that this committee had kept a handwritten journal, a musty old book that he waved in front of the justices. He read what he said were quotes that he claimed proved Congress had been reacting to unnamed "individuals and joint stock companies . . . appealing for congressional and administrative protection against invidious and discriminating State and local taxes." The framers of the amendment had "planted in the Constitution a monumental truth to stand foursquare to whatever wind might blow." Congress and the states that ratified their handiwork "went to the trouble of so amending the National Constitution as to forbid, and as far as they could to prevent, the very thing which boisterous agitation drove California to do." The "persons" of the Fourteenth Amendment, then, were not primarily the freedmen that everyone had taken as its subject so far, but the giant incorporated businesses under their guise as legal persons.

The justices did not question the existence of the journal or Conkling's interpretations of its ambiguous phrases. He had twice declined a seat on the Supreme Court, so they accepted what he said. They also succumbed to his version of constitutional history in a series of decisions at the close of the nineteenth century. By May 1886 a unanimous Court upheld the California state ruling that taxes could not be assessed by the county or state against fences erected on the property of the Southern Pacific and Central Pacific Railroads. Although the narrowly based decision did not formally respond to the constitutional questions raised by the lawyers, Chief Justice Waite's explanation revealed how closely the justices had come over to the Conkling "conspiracy theory." Waite said that there was no need to decide "whether the provision in the Fourteenth Amendment to the Constitution which forbade a state to deny any person within its jurisdiction the equal protection of the Constitution, applied to these corporations. We are all of the opinion that it does."

How did the Court's adoption of Conkling's distorted view of the due process clause affect the protection sought by African Americans under the Fourteenth Amendment? By 1896, when it would consider the claims of Homer Plessy, the Court had ruled on 150 cases brought under that amendment. But only 15 of them, just 10 percent, concerned state action against Negroes. It is simple to assess the relative chances of the pro bono lawyers for these plaintiffs and the leading attorneys for businesses. The shift from concern for the rights of freedmen in 1868 to the rights of corporations against state regulation in the 1880s and 1890s did not bode well for Plessy.

Not only had the language designed to safeguard the new black citizens of southern states been usurped by corporations, but the Court's personnel had shifted markedly during that time. Seven of the nine justices who had decided the *Slaughter-House* and *Munn* cases had resigned or died by 1890. Only Stephen J. Field, staunch defender of property rights, lingered on, joined in 1888 by his nephew David J. Brewer, who shared his uncle's philosophy. The new justices had been drawn predominantly from the same business circles that now sought federal protection for their property. The corporate attorneys who appeared before them were preaching to the choir, while those pleading cases of discrimination against Negroes faced a far more skeptical audience than they had during Reconstruction.

If it seems preposterous to accuse Roscoe Conkling of hoodwinking the Supreme Court justices, who were predisposed to swallow his "conspiracy theory" of the Fourteenth Amendment, there is solid scholarship behind the charge. In 1938 Howard Jay Graham torpedoed Conkling's claims in a *Yale Law Journal* article that cited chapter and verse from the arguments in the *San Mateo* case. Conkling's argument was a farrago of a few real citations from the joint committee journal, with misquotes and assumptions of what might have been on the mind of its members when they used specific words to suggest broader connotations. Graham found passages of Conkling with the flavor more of fiction than fact. For example, he said, "Those who devised the Fourteenth Amendment may have built better than they knew. . . .

To some of them the sunset of life may have given mystical lore." After analyzing the speech and comparing it with what has been discovered in the journal's text, Graham concluded that Conkling "suppressed" pertinent facts and misrepresented others. In effect, he "deliberately misquoted the text of the [joint committee's] Journal and even arranged his excerpts so as to give his listeners a false impression of the record and his own relation thereto."

A look back at a speech given by Conkling twelve years before his inventions in the *San Mateo* case reveals how far he moved from his original position in defense of Negro rights. On February 20, 1870, he spoke to the Senate on "Constitutional Amendments—Powers of States." His anger had been aroused by the attempt of New York to rescind its ratification of the Fifteenth Amendment, apparently at the behest of Democrats in the legislature. Conkling first attacks such a tactic, since retraction is not a power included in the constitutional clause on amendments. Then he denounces the Confederate states for their March 1861 conspiracy when they tried to demolish the federal system by adopting their own charter, with *"each state acting in its sovereign and independent character"* [italics in original].

Conkling skips next to the draft riots in New York City when, "duped and imbruted [i.e., degraded] thousands rioted in blood," even burning down a Negro orphanage, when they succumbed to rumors that "the colored people of the South, if their chains were broken, would sweep like a black wave over the North . . . to compete with white labor and cheapen its wages." Now in Conkling's home state new misinformation spread by Tammany had aroused a panic that the white electorate would be swamped by Negro voters "against whom the way to the ballot box has long been barred." But what, Conkling asks, do the four million voters in New York have to fear from the votes of seven or eight thousand Negroes?

Conkling appears here as an advocate for civil rights, using a "strict construction" argument to ratify Negro voting rights. Later, he would turn his rhetoric to defend corporate property rights with a fanciful interpretation of constitutional text. One common feature of these two positions is that they both inveigh against so-called states' rights, in favor of national protection for Conkling's causes. In both cases he also omits part of the historical record that would undermine his case. In the 1870 speech Conkling makes retraction of a state's ratification seem a novel affront to the essence of the Constitution. Yet, as his audience no doubt knew, when the states were asked to ratify the Fourteenth Amendment, at least three states—Oregon, Ohio, and New Jersey—rescinded their earlier approval. Final ratification achieved the necessary two-thirds margin only after Congress had exerted pressure, such as not seating senators in opposition, and even more blatantly, overriding the refusal to ratify by the southern states (except for Tennessee) through passage of the Reconstruction Act. This statute had declared that "no legal state governments" existed in the ten recalcitrant states, then instituted military control that would be removed only after they had adopted new state constitutions providing for black suffrage, and finally had their new state governments ratify the Fourteenth Amendment before they could send representatives to Congress again. Those coercive means ensured adoption of the amendment at last.

The first scholarly attempt to sift the records of Congress in order to divine what the authors of the Fourteenth Amendment really had in mind was by Horace Edgar Flack, a scholar at Johns Hopkins University, in 1908. While Flack's monograph lists voluminous passages from congressional debates, it is more concerned with whether the amendment's authors were fully conscious of the revolution their words implied in federal–state relations than whether their hidden meanings intended to extend to corporate property. It was clear to Flack that the Radical Republicans who staffed the joint committee were fully aware that the Bill of Rights was inadequate to the task of protecting freedmen from the repressive actions of southern states. In one of Chief Justice John Marshall's last decisions, *Barron v. Baltimore* in 1833, he had ruled against the claim of a wharf owner that Baltimore's diversion of a stream had taken his "property without just compensation," violating the Fifth Amendment. Retreating from his earlier strong federalism, Marshall here found the Bill of Rights intended to restrict only the federal government. When it came to violation of citizens' rights by states, plaintiffs would have to look to their state constitutions and courts.

Flack does find a minority of Republicans, representatives of the border states, plus Congressman Bingham of Ohio, opposed to the broader provisions of the 1866 Civil Rights bill, because they suspected that its grant of "rights and privileges" was so broad as to be unenforceable. But the bill was passed, even overriding President Johnson's veto (by 33 to 15 in the Senate, 122 to 41 in the House), though some Republican newspapers thought it was unconstitutional in forcing equal access for Negroes to schools, hotels, churches, and theaters. Two weeks after the Civil Rights Act was adopted, according to Flack, there were several incidents in which Negroes tried to gain access to accommodations previously reserved for whites. Since Flack does not give citations, just newspaper reports, it is not possible to gauge to what extent these early test cases succeeded in paving the way for Plessy. Among several railway cases was one in which two freedmen tried to buy tickets to a sleeping car from Washington to New York but were kept out after white passengers said they would leave the car if the Negroes were admitted; another Negro in Baltimore wanted a ticket to ride on the York Road in a railway car but was "compelled to the front platform where colored persons were allowed to ride."

When the mysterious journal of the joint committee was finally published in 1914, according to Graham, B. B. Kendrick edited the handwritten notes to convince historians that Conkling's "conspiracy theory" had been justified. This was seemingly corroborated by remarks of Representative Bingham, a former railroad lawyer, in which he used "person" to stress the need for "equal protection in the rights of property." Kendrick's version even convinced Charles A. and Mary R. Beard to adopt the "conspiracy theory" in their noted 1927 work, *The Rise of American Civilization*. It evidently fitted their preconceptions that economic and social factors were the mainsprings of American history. It took until 1937 before the Supreme Court, under New Deal pressure, abandoned the mystical notion that "natural law" and "substantive due process" cast a special protective aura around private property.

There was a much simpler explanation than the "conspiracy theory" for the use of the word "person" in the Fourteenth Amendment: it had been used (twice) in the Fifth Amendment, with its catalog of individual rights. James Madison had intended the Bill of Rights to offer protection against actions by both federal and state authorities, but in 1833 Chief Justice Marshall had concluded that the first ten amendments restricted only the former, since the state conventions ratifying the Constitution had insisted on them to furnish "security against the apprehended encroachments of the general government." Only gradually, during the twentieth century, was there a process of so-called incorporation: applying the guarantees of the Bill of Rights not just to the federal government but also to limit state and local authorities. The means has been the due process clause of the Fourteenth Amendment. Some of its framers in 1866 had suggested that the "privileges or immunities" clause would convey such basic rights. Though there was no direct contradiction by representatives and senators, some of them refrained from addressing the point or expressed seemingly contradictory views.

In any case, it became clear to the Supreme Court justices at the centenary of the Fourteenth Amendment in 1968 that this "document of human freedom lay dormant" during much of its life; in William J. Brennan's words, "It was employed instead as a weapon by which to censor and strike down economic regulatory legislation of the States."

Justice Abe Fortas speculated on what might have been the amendment's impact "if Justice Miller had voted the other way in the *Slaughterhouse* [*sic*] *cases* and thereby turned the majority around," instead of emasculating the "privileges or immunities" clause. In the *Santa Clara County* case of 1886, Fortas also saw Chief Justice Waite's surprising announcement—that corporations were the "beneficiaries of the equal protection and due process clauses"—as linked to the Court's curtailment of the amendment's scope for "the Negroes or Freedmen."

Chief Justice Earl Warren cited several cases that undercut the amendment's design "to make national citizenship paramount to state citizenship, to confer national citizenship upon the newly free slaves, and to secure for the former slaves the equal enjoyment of certain civil rights." Warren singled out the *Civil Rights Cases* and *U.S. v. Harris,* both 1883 decisions, as examples of the "state action doctrine" by which the Court limited the impact of congressional action under the Fourteenth Amendment to only "correct or nullify state laws or acts of state officials or state agents" that conflicted with its provisions. The effect, Warren said, was to posit that the amendment had not changed the "state–federal constitutional balance." The Court was thereby reverting to pre–Civil War federalism and, in Warren's view, wrongly interposing the Tenth Amendment for the states' rights bias of the justices.

Behind the judicial wrangling about what may have been the ambiguous promises of the Fourteenth Amendment, there is a counterpoint argument about so-called states' rights. At an obvious level, the amendment was the first shot in a constitutional revolution against the powers of states to infringe upon the rights of citizens without being held to account by the federal government. If this was its general tenor, the text was specifically directed at the eleven southern states that were imposing restrictions on the rights of Negroes. The amendment certainly had the potential, though only fully realized nearly a century later, to have federal courts and other officials intercede for a persecuted minority. It was ironic that, instead, corporations seized upon the word "person" in the due process clause to envelop their property with safeguards against state regulation— only in that case it was not the victims of southern racism but Midwest farmers and, later, eastern industrial workers whose grievances were ignored in federal court.

Even in the shift of emphasis from Negroes to corporate clients, it is apparent that there is no simple negative correlation between judicial pleas under the Fourteenth Amendment and assertions of state sovereignty under the Tenth. The relationship is more of a multifaceted dialectic, depending on the power of the party raising the claims, the historical phase of state–federal relations, the reigning philosophy of the Court, and other factors. To bring this concept down to the real world of *Plessy v. Ferguson*, Tourgée and Walker had to consider that their client, a Negro fighting a wave of southern segregation, was in a position of powerlessness; that the 1890s were in an era of assertiveness by the southern states when it came to exerting their police powers; that the Court had shifted the impact of the Fourteenth Amendment from the rights of freedmen to those of corporate property owners, yet that states' rights, as such, were being circumscribed by a series of Court decisions against price and rate setting by Midwest and western counties and states.

Looking at the context in which the Fourteenth Amendment was passed, we find strong, if not conclusive, evidence that at the end of the Civil War the historical tide of Negro rights was cresting, and the amendment's supporters sought to put a protective shield around the rights of freedmen in their new status as national citizens. Thirty years after the Fourteenth Amendment's passage in 1866, the *Plessy* decision marked the point at which the tide had turned, and judicial support for the rights of black Americans ebbed for much of a century, until the first stirrings of the civil rights movement. The picture is much more complicated when we analyze the drafting and early history of the Tenth Amendment.

In the 1780s members of state conventions considering ratification of the Constitution made numerous demands that it include a strong statement that what had not been expressly granted to the national government would be "reserved" for the states. James Madison, together with his fellow Federalists Alexander Hamilton and James Wilson, at first argued that such a clause was unnecessary since it seemed obvious; as Wilson put it in 1787, "everything which is not given, is reserved." Madison's response to the state legislators calling for the Tenth Amendment was that it was "superfluous." He said, "I admit that they [safeguards] may be deemed unnecessary; but there can be no harm in making such a declaration."

In *The Federalist Papers* Hamilton explained that adding a bill of rights might be "unnecessary," possibly even "dangerous." In the United States, unlike Great Britain with its charters, the people were in charge, and by defining certain rights such as "liberty of the press" someone might get the wrong idea that the press could be restricted in yet undefined ways. The conventions in several states, however, did not accept this argument. With "Antifederalists" spreading fears of a potentially dictatorial central government, the outcome hung in the balance. Massachusetts, New York, and, most of all, Virginia, tied their ratification to last-minute promises of a future bill of rights.

In October 1788 Madison, hard-pressed in his own race as congressman from Virginia, listened to the counsel of Thomas Jefferson and publicly announced his support for adding "essential rights" to the Constitution. True to his word, Madison introduced an initial list of seventeen amendments at the first session of Congress on June 8, 1789, most of them taken from the Virginia Declaration of Rights. He shepherded them through committees that reduced the number to twelve, of which the final ten received approval by the required three-fourths of the states on December 15, 1791.

It was not long before the first "states' rights" conflict erupted. Fearful of the radical ideas spread by the French Revolution, the Federalists under President John Adams had passed the Alien and Sedition Acts in 1798. These laws made it a crime for "any person" to "write, print, utter or publish . . . any false, scandalous and malicious . . . writings against the government of the United States . . . with intent to defame" it. About two dozen critics of the government were arrested and several editors given fines and jail sentences. That same year, Madison, in Virginia, and Jefferson, in Kentucky, drafted resolutions to "nullify" such excessive actions of the federal government. These resolution became moot when, in 1800, Jefferson was elected to the presidency. Using the arrest of newspaper editors who supported him as a campaign issue, he let the Alien and Sedition Acts lapse without further prosecutions. In 1964 Justice William Brennan, for a unanimous Court, struck down laws that punished statements critical of public officials unless actual malice could be proven. He also said that 166 years after its promulgation it was time to acknowledge that the Sedition Act was no longer valid.

If Madison and Jefferson occupied a position that became known as "strict constructionist" when defining limits to the powers of the national government, Hamilton's view was "loose constructionist," and his argument ultimately won over President George Washington when he signed the bill establishing the Bank of the United States in 1791. Congress at first followed Jeffersonian strictures and refused to renew the bank's charter in 1811, but after five years of economic turmoil, Congress reversed itself and chartered the Second Bank of the United States in 1816. Several states, including Maryland, showed their opposition to the charter by taxing the bank's branches. The bank's cashier, James McCulloch, refused to pay the state tax, and when the Maryland courts upheld the tax law, the case was appealed to the Supreme Court.

In 1819 Chief Justice Marshall, for a unanimous Court, delivered a classic opinion, essentially endorsing Hamilton's rationale. While chartering a bank was not among Congress's powers as specified in the Constitution, it had not been forbidden either. As Marshall parsed the Tenth Amendment, it permitted "incidental or implied powers" to be exercised by Congress through the clause giving it power to "make all Laws which shall be necessary and proper for carrying into execution the forgoing Powers." Finally, the "supremacy clause" of Article VI prohibited Maryland from taxing an agency of the federal government. Marshall said that the undermining of federal agencies had not been intended by the people when their representatives ratified the Constitution: "They did not design to make their government dependent on the states."

The charter of the Second Bank of the United States lasted until 1836, when President Andrew Jackson vetoed its continuation because he accused it of meddling in the election of 1832 and of establishing a banking monopoly. That year he had split with John Caldwell Calhoun, a fellow South Carolinian who took states' rights to an extreme. Previously, Congressman Calhoun had been an ardent nationalist, a leading advocate of fighting Great Britain in the War of 1812. His causes had been the strengthening of the army and navy, building roads to connect states, protective tariffs, and, incidentally, renewing the national bank's charter—all issues that he opposed after joining the Jacksonian cause. The unprecedented resignation of Calhoun as vice president in 1832 allowed him to return to South Carolina, where he had a large plantation. He was instrumental in calling a state convention to strike down the so-called Tariff of Abominations in 1828, and its even steeper rate in 1832, through his novel theory of nullification.

In short, Calhoun argued that a state that believed an act of Congress was harmful to its interests could simply reject its enforcement. It was as though he had leapfrogged back to the government in operation before the Constitution was adopted in 1789, with its Articles of Confederation—a kind of United Nations where delegations of states met to make policy but (like permanent members of the Security Council) could exercise a veto if they disagreed with any or all of the others. He expounded a theory that majority rule in the United States was a "fiction," and that minorities could be protected only if they could form a sectional bloc to stop domination by the national government.

After he returned to the Senate in 1833, Calhoun, through mediation by Henry Clay, accepted a compromise on his disagreement over tariffs. However, until his death in 1850 he responded to the abolition movement by defending slavery in the South. Without basic legal protection of regional interests, Calhoun felt, the dynamic expansion of the North would usurp the federal system.

Of course, Calhoun's strategy—of nullification and, if need be, secession—became the doctrine of the Confederate States of America and was enshrined in its constitution in February 1861. Indeed, most historians find the resulting inability of the Confederacy to follow a common policy rooted in this flawed theory of individual state sovereignty. In any case, it would seem that the outcome of the war should have discredited Calhoun's anachronistic theories; but they reappear, in modified form, in the post-Reconstruction programs of the southern states. From the perspective of Plessy's lawyers, the professed right of Louisiana to set up a segregated system of railway travel—combined with the more extensive racial barriers mushrooming throughout the South—undercut the constitutional rights of Negroes to the full benefits of national citizenship.

The concept of states' rights has a central place in federalism, but only if it is balanced by national supremacy when laws conflict, as maintained by Justice Marshall, who never overturned a federal law because of a state's challenge. Throughout the early history of the states' rights doctrine, it became increasingly linked with the property interests of the South, whether concerned with banking, tariffs, or slavery. The northern mercantile and industrial forces were generally behind a strong national government.

Despite a growing sentiment in favor of abolition, northern states never resorted to nullification to defy the Fugitive Slave Law of 1793; instead, many of them passed "personal liberty laws" to protect their free black populations from being kidnapped, while on the whole enforcing the return of runaways, as required by Article IV of the Constitution. There were local incidents of what may be called civil disobedience, of refusing to yield runaways to slave catchers, but the abolitionists relied on the justness of their cause to win national support as they fought to gain new territory for emancipated slaves. Some of the most extreme abolitionists, such as Captain John Brown of the Kansas militia, fought pitched battles when necessary, as Brown did in his raid on Harper's Ferry in 1859. General Robert E. Lee and his marines captured Brown, who was convicted of treason on December 2 and hanged, becoming a martyr in the North.

Chief Justice Roger B. Taney has already been described as an apologist for slavery in the *Dred Scott* case. As successor to John Marshall on the Court, and a fervent Jacksonian, Taney was also known for his expansive interpretations of states' rights. He and a majority of justices based a series of decisions in 1837 on their broad definition of "police powers, which permitted states to alter the charters of corporations, to deny entry to impoverished immigrants, and to establish state banks that could issue notes used as currency." These were not merely abstract concepts for the Court; they accorded with the belief of the justices that individual states could serve as testing grounds for the country's technological development and commercial expansion.

However, Taney's belief in the rights of slave owners took precedence not just in *Dred Scott* but also in the 1842 case of *Prigg v. Pennsylvania*. Edward Prigg, a professional catcher of runaway slaves, had forcibly taken a Maryland slave named Margaret Morgan and two children (one of them born in Pennsylvania) back to her owner, after a local justice had refused to swear out the certificate of removal required by the Fugitive Slave Act of 1793. Many northern states, having abolished slavery, ignored this federal law that required the return of escaped slaves to their owners. They used their state laws to require a jury trial for fugitives, or to forbid state officials to assist in their capture.

Pennsylvania, one such state, then indicted Prigg under its 1826 personal liberty law. Justice Joseph Story's decision found the Fugitive Slave Act not only constitutional but also based on the Constitution's fugitive slave clause, which he termed "a fundamental article, without which the Union could not have been formed." (Story was mistaken, in that the wording in Article IV had been added as an afterthought, with almost no discussion, at the Constitutional Convention.)

For Story, *Prigg* presented no real problems. A slave owner must "have the right to seize and repossess the slave, which the local laws of his own state confer upon him as property." Like other key sections of the Constitution, the fugitive slave clause of Article IV had been a matter "of compromise of opposing forces and opinions." Ultimately, this provision was intended to "secure to citizens of the slaveholding states the complete right and title of ownership in their slaves." Though not expressly given the power to enforce this clause, Congress could legally act, because "where an end is required, means are given, and where a duty is enjoined, ability to perform it is contemplated. . . ." After the Fugitive Slave Act had been passed, Congress had in effect preempted the field, since "Congress, if constitutional, must supersede all state legislation upon the same subject." So the Pennsylvania "personal liberty law" was unconstitutional.

Was there any consideration by the Court for Margaret Morgan and her two children, who had been forcibly taken from freedom back to slavery? Only a slight loophole—not for her, but for others who might be in her shoes. Story, a Massachusetts native who had adopted the nationalist bias of his mentor Marshall, allowed recaptured slaves one small chance: state officials, including judges, should enforce the federal law requiring the return of fugitives, but the national government could not force them to do so, since it lacked the power to make state authorities do its bidding. It was this "out" that impelled Taney to add a rather stinging concurrence and a partial dissent to the opinion.

First, Taney incorrectly described Story's opinion as barring state officials from enforcing the Fugitive Slave Act. Then he criticized it for blocking state enforcement legislation, even though Story had only said that such laws could not go beyond the scope of the federal law. Taney argued that it was the duty of states "to protect and support the owner when he is endeavoring to obtain possession of his property within their respective territories"—actually the thrust of Story's opinion, too.

The Court seems to have dealt with the fate of three human beings with as little concern as if they had been stolen pieces of somebody's household furnishings instead of kidnapped fugitives. It also ignored the increasing moral outrage of abolitionists in the North after Pennsylvania enacted its "personal liberty law" against forced seizures of slaves in 1826. Only one independent justice, John McLean of Ohio, dared to dissent from his colleagues and say that he would have sustained Prigg's conviction on kidnapping charges in state court, on the grounds that under its police powers the state had a right to require claimants to first apply to a magistrate for a "removal order" to prevent "the forcible abduction of persons of color." McLean, a self-taught and not very distinguished jurist, did have a grasp of reality that was lacking in his more learned colleagues. He was later one of the two dissenters in the *Dred Scott* decision.

The *Prigg* opinion did not became a landmark Supreme Court decision, because it did little to settle the slavery controversy. Northern states bridled at the decision and passed stronger laws to protect the rights of runaways. Southerners still had sufficient leverage to have Congress enact a much stricter Fugitive Slave Law in 1850, which closed the loophole left by Story.

The 1850 act did force state officials to bow to federal magistrates to order the return of fugitives—indeed, simply on the basis of an affidavit sworn by someone who claimed to be a slave's owner or representative of the owner. The new act set steep fines and jail terms for anyone helping to rescue a fugitive, and runaways were not allowed to testify on their own behalf or request a jury trial. Yet the abolitionists grew bolder in perfecting the "underground railroad" that offered protection to slaves who escaped to shelters in northern states and Canada. Despite the liability of one thousand dollars that federal marshals faced if they lost the slaves they were returning, the marshals at times permitted their captives to be "liberated." More than nine hundred fugitives were returned under the act between 1850 and 1861; however, as many as ten thousand slaves escaped during the same period, according to southern claims. Between fifteen and thirty thousand fugitive slaves were estimated to be living openly in the North in the 1850s, representing over a million dollars' worth of missing "merchandise" to their masters. In Harriet Beecher Stowe's *Uncle Tom's Cabin*, which sold over a million copies, the novel's title character is sold by a slave trader to the villainous Simon Legree and is then murdered by his new owner for not renouncing his Christian beliefs. The novel stoked the flames that would lead to the violent sectional conflict a decade later.

When Albion Tourgée was preparing the case for Homer Plessy, he knew that, oddly enough, of the justices whom he was going to try to persuade that the Fourteenth Amendment had set a new standard of national citizenship and basic rights, most of them had returned to a predilection for the Court's pre–Civil War view of the states' sweeping police powers. The northern ardor for Negro rights had cooled. Reconciliation with the South was now seen as essential for the country's economic development. Only one justice had maintained steadfast in his conviction that the promises of Reconstruction should have been kept but had not been; he had himself been a slave owner who had witnessed the excesses of that system of exploitation.

# Chapter 7

# EN ROUTE TO THE SUPREME COURT

John Marshall Harlan never forgot an incident that occurred when he was a small boy accompanying his father, James Harlan, to a Sunday church service in his hometown of Frankfort, Kentucky. On the main street they passed "a company of slaves that were being driven to the 'Slave Market' in a neighboring town. The able-bodied men and women were chained together, four abreast, proceeded [*sic*] by the old ones and the little 'pickaninnies,' who walked unbound."

"This pitiful procession," as Malvina Shanklin Harlan, John's wife for over fifty years, later recounted, "was in the charge of a brutish white man, belonging to a class which in those days was called 'Slave-drivers,' because their duty was to drive gangs of slaves, either to their work or to the place of auction. Their badge of office was a long snakelike whip made of black leather, every blow from which drew blood.

"The sight stirred my father-in-law to the depths of his gentle nature. He saw before him the awful possibilities of an institution which, in the division of family estates, and the sale of the slaves, involved inevitably the separation of husband and wife, of parent and children; and the dreadful type of men which the institution developed as 'Slave-drivers' seemed to my father-in-law to embody the worst aspects of the system."

The indignant James Harlan walked up to the slave-driver and, shaking a forefinger in his face, said, "You are a damned scoundrel. Good morning, sir." Then father and son continued on to church. Young John always remembered that his father, "like some Old Testament prophet seemed to be calling Heaven's maledictions upon the whole institution of Slavery." It was also, for the boy, "the nearest thing to 'swearing' that he ever heard from his father's lips."

Malvina's memoir did not find a publisher during her lifetime; only eighty-five years later did it catch the attention of Justice Ruth Bader Ginsburg, who shepherded its publication. It was edited by historian Linda Przybyszewski, who had studied it in the Harlan Collection of the Library of Congress and realized its value as a key to Justice Harlan's "enigma": "How a former slaveholder and an opponent of emancipation came to support the legal equality of blacks." Indeed, the anecdote of James Harlan's confrontation with the slave-driver (more likely, a slave trader) makes sense only if understood in the context supplied by Professor Przybyszewski, namely, that both the elder and younger Harlan were themselves slaveholders "who condemned the cruelties of slavery." The father owned some two dozen slaves, eight of whom the son inherited. There is evidence that the father, at least, engaged in buying and selling slaves, though such memories were evidently expunged from the family saga in order to present James as a benevolent patriarch of both his children and the black members of his household.

Malvina Harlan, who had been brought up by an Indiana family with abolitionist beliefs, was at first horrified to move into the slave-owning household of her father-in-law. But in her writings she romanticizes the intimate connections between the Harlan family and the slaves who shared their joys and tragedies. Malvina expresses surprise to find that all the slaves were "carefully looked after, not only physically but morally. . . . The close sympathy existing between the slaves and their Master or Mistress was a source of great wonder to me as a descendant of the Puritans, and I was often obliged to admit to myself that my former views of the 'awful institution of slavery' would have to be somewhat modified." These feelings, expressed after her husband's death in 1911 and deleting any mention of the family's buying and selling of slaves, were likely retouched to enhance the Harlan image.

The true history of John Marshall Harlan's development into the Supreme Court's earliest and most outspoken champion of Negro civil rights does not evolve in a straight line; it takes a zigzag route, from early racist and xenophobic values to a kind of conversion, politically and perhaps religiously, in his mid-thirties. It does not present the stereotypical picture of an egalitarian, whose lone dissents on the Court seem, through some sort of prophetic gift, to be fifty years or more ahead of their time. It is perhaps more revealing to follow the career of a young man from a border state who moves from the parochial economics of a slave society to the mature values of politics on the national stage at a time when the country had become stratified by wealth and race. It would follow that he could revive the ethos of equality under the protection of the federal government that prevailed in the early days of Reconstruction.

In October 1893 Albion Tourgée, Plessy's lawyer, wrote to Louis Martinet, who had organized the test case in New Orleans, that their appeal faced an unfriendly reception from the Supreme Court justices. Five of them, Tourgée surmised, were "against us," and four of their number would "probably stay that way until Gabriel blows his horn." Only one justice, clearly Harlan, was "known to favor the view we must stand upon." Ten years before Tourgée wrote this letter, Harlan had commanded national attention by his dissent from the other eight justices in the *Civil Rights Cases,* as described in chapter 1.

Justice Harlan had announced his dissent in the *Civil Rights Cases* from the bench, but we now learn from his wife's memoirs why it took weeks for him to file his written opinion. Malvina Harlan recalls that her husband had stumbled upon a quaint ink-stand in the office of the Marshal of the Supreme Court, which turned out to have belonged to Roger B. Taney, who had used it in writing his *Dred Scott* decision. Harlan had been given the ink-stand by the marshal, but then the wife of Senator George Pendleton of Ohio had fancied it as a memento of Taney, her great-uncle; in a moment of gallantry, Harlan had offered it to her. Before it could be delivered to Mrs. Pendleton, however, Malvina squirreled it away among her own treasures. When she saw that her husband's conflicting thoughts were blocking him from writing his overdue dissent, Malvina presented him with her hidden trophy—and the classic words of the opinion flowed from Taney's inkwell. Harlan's inspiration came after his memory had been jogged by Taney's characterization of Negroes as "beings of an inferior race," hence "altogether unfit to associate with the white race, either in social or political relations." Since ratification of the Fourteenth Amendment, Harlan pointed out in his dis-senting opinion, the situation had radically changed.

The amendment, Harlan wrote, transformed "all of that race, whose ancestors had been imported and sold as slaves, at once, into the political community known as 'People of the United States.' They became, instantly, citizens of the United States, and of their respective States." Here Harlan parted company with his robed brethren. Where they saw the congressional effort to pre-vent discrimination in inns, theaters, or trains as a prelude to enacting "a municipal code for all the States, covering every matter affecting the life, liberty, and property of the citizens," Harlan said, "Not so." He defined access to public accommoda-tions not as a matter of "social rights" but as "civil rights" that afforded legal protection against discrimination. Social rights, in his opinion, which *were* properly beyond government control, had to do with purely personal relations that people were free to conduct as they wished. Civil rights, however, concerned legal rights, such as the use of a "public highway" and the inns and conveyances along it. To Harlan, the administrations of such public places (often under state licenses) should not be permitted to practice racial discrimination any more than a post office or a courtroom could. (This was a view deemed extreme in 1883, yet it was essentially adopted by a unanimous Court in 1964 when it decided *Heart of Atlanta Motel v. United States*, upholding the 1964 Civil Rights Act and its public accommodations section.)

Harlan's dissent received a lot of national attention, and the favorable letters and newspaper articles about it found their way into a scrapbook that was stored with his papers in the Law Library of the University of Louisville. Tinsley E. Yarbrough, the author of one of the most extensive Harlan biographies, lists several of the positive responses. Justice William Strong of Connecticut, who had abruptly resigned from the Supreme Court in 1880, told Harlan that after reading his "very able opinion—the best you have ever written," he was no longer sure that the majority had been right. "The opinion of the Court, as you said, is too narrow—sticks to the letter, while you aim to bring out the spirit of the Constitution."

Strong had been a limited supporter of Negro legal rights, especially opposed to excluding Negroes from juries, which he had termed as "practically a brand upon them, affixed by law; an assertion of their inferiority, and a stimulant to that race prejudice which was an impediment to securing to individuals of the race that equal justice which the law aims to give them." However, in another 1880 case he had ruled that the absence of Negroes, no matter how systematic or obvious, was not per se a violation of the

Fourteenth Amendment. Southern states had used this hint of a loophole to exclude Negroes from juries without openly declaring that they were doing so.

Another of Harlan's former colleagues, Noah H. Swayne, a rather mediocre justice who had resigned in 1881, wrote Harlan that he had read the *Civil Rights Cases* dissent "through without laying it down for a moment" and considered it among the "greatest" opinions in the Court's history, sure to make "a profound and lasting impression upon the Country." Even Roscoe Conkling, by then a veteran supporter of civil rights, told Harlan that he had read the opinion "not only with admiration, but with surprise at its strength of position." Frederick Douglass, who had escaped slavery in Maryland in 1838 to become a leading abolitionist, praised Harlan's "heroic stand . . . in defense of liberty and justice." He found it especially remarkable coming from a native of a "slave state" and its "moral vapor," who now found "the courage to resist the temptation to go with the multitude."

As the Harlan family now basked in the justice's fame, little was heard of his earlier, less enlightened views. In his youth John Marshall Harlan had adopted the Whig party view of Henry Clay, a close friend of his father's; it was to try to find a middle way between North and South by adopting a gradualist approach to emancipation while trying to preserve the Union. By 1854, with the Whigs in decline, Harlan, in his early twenties, joined the Know-Nothing party, an anti-Catholic and xenophobic group that derived its name from the response members were supposed to give when asked their motives and purpose, "I know nothing." Harlan gave rousing speeches in the cause of this party, advocating states' rights and racism. Under the party label, he won his first election in 1858 as county judge.

On the eve of war, Harlan, determined to keep Kentucky from joining the Confederacy, joined the Constitutional Unionist party

Newly freed slaves. Back Row: Wilson Chinn, Mary Johnson, Robert Whitehead. Front Row: Chas. Taylor, Augusta Broujey, Isaac White, Rebecca Huger, Rosina Downs. Credit: Schomburg Center for Research in Black Culture; photographer: George H. Hanks, 1863

**above and right:** Drawings of the so-called "riot" of New Orleans on July 30, 1866, when a white mob and police attacked Blacks who had met to draw up a new state constitution. Credit: Prints and Photographs Division, Library of Congress

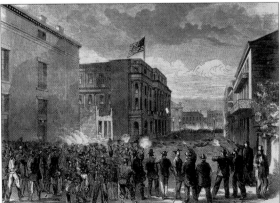

Thomas Nast's "This Is a White Man's Government" (Sept. 15, 1868) depicts Democratic presidential candidate Horatio Seymour (right) joining hands with the Confederacy (center) and an Irish voter depicted with weirdly simian features (left), to prevent the Negro from reaching the ballot box. Credit: Schomburg Center for Research in Black Culture

"THE FIRST VOTE."—DRAWN BY A. R. WAUD.—[SEE NEXT PAGE.]

Freed slaves voting for the first time, following passage of the Fifteenth Amendment in 1870. Credit: Prints and Photographs Division, Library of Congress

A typical one-room black school in the South. Credit: Schomburg Center for Research in Black Culture

On the steps of Supreme Court, May 17, 1954, in Washington, D.C., Mrs. Nettie Hunt attempts to explain the court's decision ending racial segregation in public schools to her daughter. Credit: Schomburg Center for Research in Black Cultures

Southern blacks waiting to go north. About 1.5 million blacks left to look for job opportunities between 1910 and 1930. Credit: Schomburg Center for Research in Black Culture

Thurgood Marshall, head of the NAACP legal department and chief attorney for the plaintiffs in Brown v. Board of Education, 1954.

A "Jim Crow" sign on a southern movie theater with segregated seating. Credit: Schomburg Center for Research in Black Culture

An 1872 Currier & Ives engraving shows the first African Americans elected to Congress after the Civil War. Left to right: Senator H. R. Revels (MI), Representatives Benjamin S. Turner (AL), Robert C. De Large (S.C.), Josiah T. Walls (FL), Jefferson H. Long (GA), Joseph H. Rainy (S.C.), and R. Brown Elliot (S.C.). Credit: Library of Congress

A young cotton farmer on a plantation in the Mississippi Delta plowing a field near Clarksdale. Credit: Prints and Photographs Division, Library of Congress

Justice John Marshall Harlan who wrote the dissenting opinion in Plessy v. Ferguson. Credit: Handy Studios, Collection of the Supreme Court of the United States

Justice Henry Billings Brown who wrote the majority opinion in Plessy v. Ferguson. Credit: Parker Studios, Collection of the Supreme Court of the United States

Albion W. Tourgée, the lawyer from upstate New York who served as senior counsel for Homer Adolph Plessy. Credit: Chautauqua County Historical Society, Westfield, N.Y.

*Ignorance and neglect are the mainsprings of misrule.*

Albion W. Tourgée

The 1896 Supreme Court that decided the Plessy v. Ferguson case. From left to right: Edward D. White, Henry B. Brown, Horace Gray, Stephen J. Field, Melville W. Fuller, John M. Harlan, David J. Brewer, George Shiras, Jr., Rufus W. Peckham. Credit: Collection of The Supreme Court of the United States

An advertisement for the East Louisiana Railroad Co. from a New Orleans publication, 1900. Homer A. Plessy was arrested on one of its "White Only" carriages. Credit: The Historic New Orleans Collection

The crew of a railroad train leaving New Orleans in 1887. They had to enforce the state segregation law. Note Black adolescents on lower right. Credit: The Historic New Orleans Collection

(the successor party to the Whigs). After the South seceded in 1861, Harlan chose to defend the Union as colonel of the Tenth Kentucky Volunteers. In 1863, however, after he had been recommended for promotion to brigadier general, Harlan resigned his commission. The ostensible reason was the need to take on his family's leadership after his father's death that February, but some biographers have found an underlying motive in Harlan's disillusionment with President Lincoln's policies.

The record does show that Harlan denounced the abruptness of Lincoln's Emancipation Declaration and in 1864 campaigned for Democratic nominee George B. McClellan and against Lincoln's reelection. At least up to this point, Harlan had hitched his political career to the biases of his Kentuckian audience, which was quite hostile to attempts by Union troops in the state to requisition the property of slaveholders and, in 1865, to enforce the Thirteenth Amendment abolishing slavery. McClellan carried only three states, but Kentucky was one of them. The able speeches of the formidable six-foot-three Harlan, laced as they were with racist jokes and criticism of the Union troops, helped him, at age thirty, win election as a Constitutional Unionist to the office of state's attorney general. Party switching was not uncommon in this border state that was just emerging from the Civil War.

By 1868 Harlan had shed his provincial outlook and made his fateful switch to the Republican party. This was a sharp ideological turn for an ambitious thirty-five-year-old lawyer who had been, up to that point, appealing to the southern sympathies of his neighbors. It would clearly involve personal costs, as Harlan learned when he was defeated for governor in 1871 and 1875. What, one wonders, was the moment of truth that caused him to admit to his critics that his past stands against emancipation, foreigners, Catholics, and Negro civil rights had been wrong?

Harlan never spelled out the reasons for his political conversion, but among them must have been his abhorrence at the growing number of Klan-related attacks against Negroes; his close relationship with a new, Republican law partner; and his realization that as a maverick from a border state he could fill a prominent role in national Republican ranks. He had also grown stronger in his Presbyterianism, and the Presbyterian Church had condemned slavery and supported emancipation nationally.

The Ku Klux Klan had been spreading through Kentucky, and Harlan had been asked to file suit against a white man who had beaten an eleven-year-old Negro girl so badly, when she was slow getting dressed for work, that she became blind and crippled. Harlan's law firm was also approached by a client who reported that the Klan had been behind a mob attack on Negroes who had tried to vote in the August 1870 election in Harrodsburg. After being threatened with a massacre if they persisted in their attempts to register at the courthouse, the Negroes had sought federal intervention which, under President Grant, was notable by its absence. After a rash of such incidents, thirty thousand Negroes fled north. These racist outbreaks must have shaken Harlan's faith in the benevolence that he had—in his father's house—thought to be the benchmark of white–black relations.

One of the Klan's major critics in Kentucky happened to be Benjamin H. Bristow, a former Union army colonel like Harlan, who had been appointed Assistant U.S. Attorney in the state. Bristow joined the Harlan law firm in 1870 after four years of filing indictments against Klansmen and securing twenty-nine convictions in federal court. He left shortly thereafter for Washington to become the first Solicitor General of the United States, representing the government before the Supreme Court. In 1874 Grant appointed him secretary of the treasury. Bristow helped persuade Harlan that federal prosecutions were needed to protect Negro rights and to keep the Klan, which had reached a modus vivendi with the state's Democrats, in check.

Harlan's friendship with Bristow also served as a link to the Grant administration and an entree into Republican national politics. Harlan had been considered the dark horse for the vice-presidential nomination in 1872, after losing the governor's race in Kentucky the year before. In 1876 he headed the state's delegation to the Republican national convention, intending to support Bristow for president.

Bristow had become a national figure for his single-minded attack on corruption, especially his exposé in 1874 of the "Whiskey Ring," a number of Grant's high officials who had defrauded the government of whiskey tax revenues. But on the eve of the convention, Bristow notified his supporters that he was reluctant to enter the fray, and soon James G. Blaine, the Speaker of the House, took the lead. Harlan now played a crucial role, withdrawing Bristow's nomination and throwing the state's votes to Ohio governor Rutherford B. Hayes, who became the candidate and, eventually, president.

We have already noted the disputed election of 1876, when Samuel J. Tilden, the Democratic governor of New York, seemed to have won, until a Republican-stacked commission gave Hayes a one-vote edge in the Electoral College on March 2, 1877. In April, Hayes appointed Harlan to a five-member commission that was sent to Louisiana to decide which candidate had won that state's governorship—Republican Stephen B. Packard or Democrat Francis R. T. Nicholls. As part of the "Compromise of 1877," Hayes, on the advice of the commission, withdrew the Union troops that had been backing Packard, effectively yielding the office to Nicholls, despite his Confederate army service. The reward for Harlan's services, especially his role in ensuring that Hayes received the Republican nomination, was not long in coming.

President Hayes first offered Harlan the prestigious appointment of ambassador to Great Britain, but Harlan turned it down as not in his line and unaffordable in his economic circumstances. Next, Harlan and his old associate Bristow were both interested in a Supreme Court vacancy that had opened up with the resignation of Justice David Davis of Illinois, who wanted to run for the Senate. The White House rejected Bristow as being filled with presidential ambitions that might pose a problem. This opened the door to Harlan, whose political value was that he had southern roots and strong Republican loyalties.

First, he had to run the gantlet of the Senate Judiciary Committee, where critics dug up his vintage views against emancipation and the Civil War amendments; that antagonized some of the remaining Radical Republicans as well as Roscoe Conkling, who had become an embittered foe of Hayes for "stealing the presidency." Harlan's honesty in explaining his conversion to Republicanism, and a flood of bipartisan testimonials to his abilities, finally won him confirmation by the Senate on November 29. The maverick Kentuckian could now be content with the lifetime tenure and steady, if limited, income that came with a seat on the Court ($10,000 at the time), which also assured him of the independence to make rulings as his mind and ethics dictated. Here, he felt, he could make his mark on history.

By the time Albion Tourgée and the New Orleans supporters of the *Plessy* appeal were sizing up their chances with the Supreme Court after their preliminary loss in the Louisiana courts, Harlan had become the only justice with an avowedly liberal stand on civil rights. Those long odds against them are among the reasons that the lawyers allowed the appeal process to creep along for another four long years. When Plessy had taken his fateful journey, the

Republican Benjamin Harrison was president after having defeated the incumbent Democrat Grover Cleveland in the Electoral College although having lost the popular vote. Tourgée speculated that a more radical Republican might appear in the White House in 1893, one who would perhaps add another justice of Harlan's leanings to the Court. But that was not to be. Cleveland, after four years out of office, won the 1892 election, and the Court's complexion grew increasingly pro-business and anti–civil rights, while the country became reconciled to the segregated social system that was now a fact of life in America.

Cleveland's second term began with bank failures and an industrial depression. The hard-pressed farmers and industrial workers turned to populist leaders for relief. But Thomas E. ("Tom") Watson, first elected to Congress from Georgia on the Farmers' Alliance ticket in 1890, had built the Populist party to displace the southern "Bourbon" elite so he could build his own career. Instead of forming an alliance of poor black and white farmers, all of whom were suffering from excessive bank and railroad rates, he decided to whip up the region's racism and become the most powerful politician in the South.

Watson described Booker T. Washington as "bestial as a gorilla" and excoriated Catholics, Socialists, and Jews in his demagogic speeches. Other rabble-rousers exploited rural poverty throughout the South, getting state conventions to adopt new constitutions that disfranchised Negro voters. The 130,334 registered Negro voters in Louisiana in 1896, for example, had been whittled down to 1,342 in 1904. And southern legislatures during this era passed a blizzard of Jim Crow laws. A parallel horror was a wave of lynchings, which reached a crest of 155 black murder victims in 1892. (There was a total of 2,522 Negro and 702 "other victims" between 1889 and 1918. The "others" were generally victims of extralegal justice in the West.) Mainstream populists, represented by figures such as William Jennings Bryan, became a segment of the Democratic party on issues such as using "free silver" from the West as an alternative to the national gold standard.

The increasingly pro-business Supreme Court, with the sole exception of Harlan, did not offer Tourgée the receptive forum he had anticipated he would have by delaying the case. The Court was headed by Melville W. Fuller, who came from an old New England family and had briefly attended Harvard Law School, making him the first chief justice with academic legal training. He had supported Stephen Douglas against Abraham Lincoln and later expressed sympathy for the South during the Civil War. After moving to Illinois from Maine, Fuller worked for Chicago's largest bank, which was owned by his father-in-law. He became wealthy through his commercial legal practice and real estate investments. President Cleveland named him to succeed Chief Justice Morrison Waite, who had died in March 1888, because Fuller shared the president's views (for sound currency and against protective tariffs), and Cleveland also hoped that Fuller might swing Illinois to the Democrats in the November election. During his tenure, Fuller became known for dubious opinions: invalidating the federal income tax (though the result was overturned by the Sixteenth Amendment), and finding the Sherman Antitrust Act not applicable to the Sugar Trust because manufacture for sale was not deemed "commerce." Fuller also announced his belief that the Fourteenth Amendment had produced "no revolutionary change," hence was of little use to Negro victims of discrimination.

Most of the other justices, with the exception of Harlan, also espoused a strong pro-business interpretation of the Constitution. Edward D. White, the one justice from the South, had grown up as the son of wealthy Louisiana sugar planters and had therefore undoubtedly used slave labor. During the Civil War, he was captured and briefly held prisoner by Union forces. Then he read law and became a lieutenant of Governor Francis R. T. Nicholls, who had signed the state's railroad segregation bill into law. White was appointed by Nicholls to head the state supreme court and, in 1888, to fill a vacancy in the U.S. Senate, where he served until 1894. His preoccupation was to protect domestic sugar growers. He even delayed taking his seat on the supreme court for several weeks so he could include sugar among the goods protected in the Wilson–Gorman Tariff Act. White's questionable contribution to constitutional law was adding the word "unreasonable" to the restraints on trade prohibited by the Sherman Antitrust Act.

By this sleight of hand, he succeeded in ruling for Standard Oil as only exercising a "reasonable" monopoly, which was not against the law, at least as interpreted subjectively by the Court.

When the *Plessy* case came up for decision in 1896, both the longest-serving justice and the most recently appointed one were known as committed defenders of property rights, under the theory of so-called substantive due process, which went beyond the words of the Constitution to enshrine the Adam Smith vision of a free marketplace managed by an invisible, benevolent hand. As championed by Justice Stephen J. Field, this subjective concept allowed the Court to strike down state regulations of business that were not considered "reasonable."

Field had grown up in New England, the son of a Congregationalist minister, and, after reading law with his brother David Dudley Field, practiced in New York. In 1849 he had followed the Gold Rush to California but made his money through legal fees and real estate speculation. After serving on the California Supreme Court, Field was named to the U.S. Supreme Court in 1863, soon becoming known for poorly grounded dogmatic opinions, which have not stood the test of time. In 1880, for example, he had filed a dissent to *Ex parte Virginia*, a case in which a Virginia judge had refused to include Negroes on jury panels, and in which the majority upheld an enforcement act by Congress that ensured that Negroes would not be excluded. States had the right to limit whom to seat on juries, Field had said. Since states had excluded women as well as men over sixty-five, why not Negroes? he asked. Further, he defined jury duty as a political right, while the Fourteenth Amendment "extends only to civil rights." Congress had no business, he concluded, to "exercise coercive authority over the judicial officers of the States." Determined to surpass the thirty-three-year tenure of the great John Marshall, Field refused to consider stepping down, even after Justice Harlan, on behalf of his colleagues, diplomatically asked him to do so. Field disliked Presidents Cleveland and Harrison too much to let them appoint his successor, and so he lingered on, a white-bearded troglodyte, until 1897, doing little work.

The most recently appointed justice who would hear the *Plessy* case was Rufus W. Peckham, a successful corporate attorney from New York who was serving on its court of appeals when he was named to the Supreme Court by President Cleveland in 1895. Previously, the appointment of Peckham's brother Wheeler to the Court had been derailed by David Hill, the New York senator who in 1889 headed the state's Democratic party machine. Peckham, who had called a New York law regulating grain elevators "vicious in its nature and communistic in its tendency," soon became a leader of the Court's conservatives. As a variant of substantive due process, he developed an extremely broad view of freedom of contract, which he used to invalidate a New York law that had set hours and health conditions for bakery workers. Notwithstanding dissents by Harlan and Oliver Wendell Holmes, Peckham refused to concede that the baking trade could ever be considered unhealthy—despite the state legislature's unanimous passage of the law.

Another conservative justice was David J. Brewer, born in Turkey to missionary parents and then raised in privileged circumstances. With a degree from Albany Law School, Brewer had moved to Kansas, serving on that state's highest court from 1874 to 1884, then on a federal circuit court. Appointed to the Supreme Court by Benjamin Harrison in 1890, Brewer, a nephew of Justice Field, was an avowed admirer of capitalism, no matter what its inequities might be. In 1895 he wrote the opinion *In re Debs*, upholding the railway union president's conviction for disobeying a sweeping injunction against support of the Pullman workers' strike. Workers had struck when George M. Pullman had lowered their wages, literally, to the starvation level.

President Cleveland had ordered his attorney general to obtain an injunction against the union for obstructing the railroads and holding up the mail. He also sent federal troops to Chicago in 1894, although Illinois Governor John Peter Altgeld had protested that the state government had not asked for federal intervention. Eugene V. Debs had tried to mediate, then ordered railwaymen not to move the Pullman cars. He was arrested and convicted, under the Sherman Antitrust Act, of "restraint of trade," despite the injunction.

Brewer's opinion affirmed Debs's six-month sentence for obstructing commerce on grounds that included threats to the property rights of railroad companies. Court injunctions became the standard way for corporations to squelch labor troubles, a practice that continued until the New Deal. After the *Plessy* decision, Brewer upheld a Kentucky law that prohibited Berea College, a private institution, from offering racially integrated classes; he also found no federal grounds to interfere when a gang of armed whites forced blacks off their lumbering jobs in Arkansas, since it involved only " individual" as opposed to state actions. In both cases Harlan wrote eloquent dissents (see chapter 9).

The justices sitting in 1896, again, with the exception of Harlan, also came to the Court with wealth, either inherited or acquired. Justice George Shiras Jr. was the son of a wealthy Pennsylvania brewery merchant. He had graduated from Yale College and briefly attended its law school. He had stayed aloof from the state's Republican party politics in order to concentrate on a thriving corporate law practice. President Benjamin Harrison appointed Shiras to the Supreme Court in 1892, despite his thin judicial and public service experience, because he filled the right geographical slot and was independent of the anti-Harrison party faction in Pennsylvania. Shiras occasionally showed glimmers of independence in a few due process cases, but he generally sided with the majority in striking down state and federal regulatory laws.

Justice Horace Gray came from a Massachusetts family that had suffered temporary business reverses; after studying law at Harvard, he began a successful legal career as a court reporter with the state supreme court. In 1864 he became the youngest justice of that court, and in 1873 its chief justice. His appointment to the Supreme Court in 1882 by President Chester Alan Arthur was facilitated by an old classmate, Senator George F. Hoar. Gray showed reluctance to follow his conservative colleagues in using "substantive due process" as a device to limit state actions. At the time of *Plessy*, Gray had written few notable opinions and, in a contentious court, relatively few dissents. Two years later, however, he expanded the concept of citizenship in the Fourteenth Amendment to include Chinese, who had been excluded on the basis of an 1882 act. Using common-law rules, Gray said that members of *all* ethnic groups, including Chinese, could base their citizenship on birth in the United States.

Rounding out the justices from whom Plessy's lawyers could expect little was Henry Billings Brown, the son of a prosperous Massachusetts businessman, whom Chief Justice Fuller selected to draft the *Plessy* decision. After being graduated from Yale University and studying some law there and at Harvard, Brown had moved to Detroit, where he married the daughter of a wealthy lumber trader and began to specialize in admiralty law. During the Civil War, he hired a substitute to serve in the Union army, as the law allowed. His Republican party activities earned Brown an appointment to a county court, then a post as assistant United States attorney and, in 1875, the United States District Court judgeship for eastern Michigan. His contacts with important people brought Brown to the notice of President Benjamin Harrison, who appointed him to the Supreme Court in 1890.

On the Court, Brown was protective of business and property rights, though not as extremely so as some of his colleagues. He generally wrote opinions that legitimated the social conditions and precedents of the day. What must have been even more disturbing to the partisans for Plessy was Brown's express belief that "respect for the law [is] inherent in the Anglo-Saxon race." His biographer sums up Brown as "a privileged son of the Yankee merchant class, . . . a reflexive social elitist whose opinions of women, African Americans, Jews, and immigrants now seem odious, even if they were unexceptional for their time."

In short, from Tourgée's point of view, all the justices but Harlan would have appeared to be disinclined to accept a reading of the Fourteenth Amendment that would be favorable to Plessy's case, although the relative tolerance of Gray and Shiras when ruling on the rights of Asians may have given him a glimmer of hope. The remaining justices, led by Fuller, Field, and White, had built careers on protecting corporations from state and federal regulations through a concept of "due process" shorn of its origins in the racial equality platform of 1868. What chance, one wonders, did Negroes have to expect their rights to be validated by a Court that was fixated on economic laissez-faire doctrines emblematic of the republic?

Thirteen years before it was to act on the *Plessy* case, the Supreme Court had ruled on the *Civil Rights Cases*. In 1883 Justice Joseph Bradley had declared the 1875 Civil Rights Act unconstitutional, with its provisions for public accommodation without racial discrimination. "It would be running the slavery argument into the ground," Bradley had scoffed, "to make it apply to every act of discrimination which a person may see fit to make" as to whom he can refuse a seat "in a coach or cab or car, or admit to his concert or theater, or deal in other matters of intercourse or business." The Thirteenth and Fourteenth Amendments could apply only to the official actions of states, not to those of private persons. Otherwise, Bradley warned, Congress could write the municipal codes to every citizen's "rights of life, liberty, and property."

This was the same Justice Bradley who in 1873 wrote a notorious concurrence to the majority opinion excluding a woman, Myra Bradwell, from practicing law in Illinois. It is the "natural and proper timidity and delicacy which belongs to the female sex," he had written, that "evidently unfits it for many of the occupations of civil life. . . . The paramount destiny and mission of woman are to fulfill the noble and benign offices of wife and mother. This is the law of the Creator."

Now, Bradley's 1883 decision sharply narrowing the impact of the Thirteenth and Fourteenth Amendments cast its shadow on the 1896 case.

As has been mentioned, there was a key difference: the earlier discrimination had supposedly been inflicted by private persons and businesses, while now it was Louisiana's official law that decreed segregation. But for the plaintiffs in both cases, the effect was the same: the wife of Richard A. Robinson, the earlier Negro passenger who had not been allowed to take her seat in a white "ladies car" in Tennessee because of a railroad regulation, had the same response as Homer Plessy when he was denied his seat in the first-class carriage because of state mandate. They both felt abashed at being ordered to Jim Crow cars and protested the infringement on their civil rights. Two of the justices sitting in 1896—Field and Gray—had been in the 1883 Court majority; a third, Harlan, had of course written his stirring dissent. But two former justices—William Strong and Noah H. Swayne—who had commended Harlan for this dissent, had long retired.

When Tourgée plunged ahead with the case, he must have felt that an experienced ally would be indispensable, given the odds. He recruited Samuel F. Phillips, an old friend from Reconstruction days in North Carolina. In 1883 Philips had argued on behalf of the five plaintiffs in the *Civil Rights Cases* before the Supreme Court, though in a losing cause. He had also served as solicitor general, the federal government's chief counsel, and stayed on in Washington to practice law. Phillips is listed as co-author of the first brief for *Plessy*, with F. D. McKenney, another Washington attorney, who seems to have played a minor role in preparing it.

The first part of Phillips's brief recounted the facts of the case, stressing that Plessy had undertaken his journey "respectably and plainly dressed," clearly "not intoxicated or affected by any noxious disease." Nonetheless, in part two Phillips said that a conductor was required by state law to assign passengers to separate cars for their respective races; any passenger who refused such an order became liable for a fine of twenty-five dollars or "imprisonment in the parish prison for not more than twenty days." The third part contains the constitutional basis for Plessy's appeal:

first, the law violated the Fourteenth Amendment by abridging Plessy's "privileges or immunities" as a citizen of the United States. Whatever difference might exist "between white and colored citizens," it is not proper to give it the "force of law," thereby injuring Plessy by unequal treatment.

Second, the "discrimination . . . is along the line of the late institution of slavery, and is a distinct disparagement of those persons," amounting to what Phillips termed a "taunt [i.e., injury] by law."

Third, though the state law provided allegedly equal accommodations to both races, any physical equivalence doesn't matter. From a Negro's viewpoint, "the white man's *wooden* railway benches . . . would be preferred to any *velvet* cushions in the colored car [italics in the original]."

Fourth, what confronts a citizen of Louisiana is that, by law, he is assigned to "either a superior or inferior class of citizen," both being "offensive" and a hindrance to free travel because they smack of a servitude abolished by the Thirteenth Amendment.

Fifth, Phillips cited two precedents: one in which a Mrs. Catherine Brown was ejected from a white car for her refusal to sit in a colored car on her journey from Alexandria to Washington, and won fifteen hundred dollars in a civil suit; another in which a state was prohibited from taxing a passenger's interstate travel. Neither seemed more than only tangentially related to the *Plessy* case.

A second brief, by Tourgée and his New Orleans associate James C. Walker, essentially recapitulates their arguments in the Louisiana courtrooms. They raise basic questions not covered by the 1890 segregation law: How can it classify all railway passengers into blacks and whites when people like Homer Plessy, as "octoroons," have "color . . . not discernible in their complexion"? If the conductor exercises his delegated power of assigning seats, isn't he assuming the authority of a judge? Why was "no remedy for wrong" to passengers provided in case the conductor made a mistake? Did Homer Plessy's seven-eighths-white ancestry not amount to "property," of which he was being "deprived without due process of law," in violation of the Fourteenth Amendment?

Tourgée and Walker's brief also charges that the Louisiana law "imposed a badge of servitude" on Plessy and "perpetuates the distinction of race and caste," contrary to the Thirteenth and Fourteenth Amendments. But the heart of their brief is to argue that the Fourteenth Amendment created an entirely novel definition of citizenship. National citizenship was meant to become "paramount and universal," henceforth, state citizenship was "expressly subordinate." Americans, including newly freed slaves, who acquired national citizenship were thereby guaranteed "*equality* of right" as well as "*the free enjoyment of all public privileges.*" States, such as Louisiana, were officially "ousted of *all control over citizenship* [italics in the original]." It was a bold argument, though Tourgée had apparently not found judicial or legislative sources to buttress it.

Neither did Tourgée directly confront the conclusion of the Louisiana Supreme Court that segregation laws like this were merely "following the order of Divine Providence"—that is, separating the races as God had intended. He might have pointed out that this was just a veneer to cloak the judges' own prejudices. Why, he might have asked, revert to the segregation scheme of the southern slaveholding era, when integration after the Civil War had been generally accepted by the people, as provided in Louisiana law for rail and steamship travel in 1869? Couldn't that decade when black and white children attended the same schools in New Orleans, and their parents traveled together peacefully, have been seen as a sign of God's will? Perhaps the iconoclasm needed to raise such questions was deemed improper court procedure at the time.

There was no lack of self-assurance in the Supreme Court briefs for the State of Louisiana. Milton J. Cunningham, the attorney general, began by announcing that the sudden notice from the Court had not given him time to write new briefs, so he had just reprinted the opinion of the state supreme court, since Justice Charles Fenner had "thoroughly covered the grounds presented in the case." Those rehashed arguments simply denied Plessy the protection of the Thirteenth Amendment, because Bradley, in the *Civil Rights Cases*, had found that being refused service in public accommodations did not fasten upon a person "any badge of slavery." Then, the Fourteenth Amendment was said to apply only "when States attempt by legislation to establish an inequality in respect to the enjoyment of any rights or privileges." But the state law used the established criteria of race, whereby Negroes were so classified if in any degree they were "descended from African ancestors."

So conductors were not using discretion, since "any man must know the difference between a Negro and a white man." Any disputes on that score could be resolved by a court. No inequality could be established by Plessy, because the law punished transgressors equally who would not go to their racially segregated cars, whether black or white.

Finally, Cunningham quoted the state court as saying that the case was simply an application of recognized "police powers." The court's arguable conclusion: anyone insisting on "thrusting the company of one race upon the other" would just exacerbate the repulsion between them.

The second brief for the state had been prepared by Alexander Porter Morse, a Washington attorney who specialized in appellate cases. Morse focused more sharply than Cunningham on a key argument: that prior decisions by federal courts had set very broad limits on a state's "police powers" when they had been challenged by persons asserting their rights under the Fourteenth Amendment. Morse cited an 1885 case upholding a San Francisco ordinance limiting the business hours of laundries despite its disproportionate effect on Chinese owners. In that case, he argued, the justices had given wide latitude to a state "regulation designed not to impose unequal or unnecessary restrictions upon any one, but to promote, with as little inconvenience as possible, the common good."

How was any good to the public promoted by the Louisiana railway segregation law that applied to railroads but not to streetcars? Most of the state's blacks, Morse claimed without substantiation, lived on farms, so their rail journeys portended the "danger of friction from too intimate contact," presumably with white farmers. In cities, however, white and black populations were more evenly balanced, and they shared " a more advanced civilization." Hence, on streetcars there was less "danger of friction" than on trains. (This dubious distinction would surely puzzle anyone who has experienced taking crowded city buses or subways, as opposed to roomier trains.)

The numerous precedents cited by Morse do not conclusively settle the novel question raised by Plessy's lawyers: whether or not a state could constitutionally *require* racial segregation to be imposed by a private company. But the earlier cases do show parallel instances in which states set up separate public schools for white and black children; even Congress had allowed District of Columbia schools to operate that way. Further, federal judges had not raised major objections based on the Fourteenth Amendment when segregation had been extended to other facilities. The national trend had clearly been running for the kind of "equal but separate law" that Plessy was now challenging.

In only one of Morse's precedents, *Strauder v. West Virginia*, mentioned earlier, had the Supreme Court taken a firm stand against state curtailment of Negro rights. In 1880 Justice William Strong had said, for a Court majority of 7 to 2, that the Fourteenth Amendment had been "adopted to assure the enjoyment of civil rights that under the law are enjoyed by white persons." In ruling against the blatant exclusion of Negroes from criminal court juries, Strong had decreed that state laws "shall be the same for the black as for the white" citizens, with both entitled to "stand equal before the laws of the States." Specifically, Negroes were supposed to be protected from "discrimination . . . against them by law because of their color"; they were to be shielded from "legal discriminations, implying inferiority in civil society," that put them in a position inferior to whites. Then why did Morse refer to this opinion? It was clearly his intent to differentiate it from the situation in *Plessy*. *Strauder* dealt with the civil rights of former slaves who would now enjoy the rights derived from their citizenship under the Fourteenth Amendment, such as voting or serving on juries, under federal government protection.

But when it came to the area of so-called *social* rights, Morse left the controlling power in the hands of state authorities under their "police powers." In his narrow reading of the Fourteenth Amendment, the only prohibited state actions were those proved to be "unreasonable." Plessy, he contended, had not established either that the railroad had assigned him unequal "accommodations . . . on his proposed passage," or that he had been subjected to "discrimination . . . as a passenger on account of his color." In Morse's opinion, Plessy had not shown that the "colored" car to which he was directed was worse than the white car, or that the state's "discrimination" did not apply "equally to white as to colored persons."

In case Plessy's lawyers raised facts about the clearly poor quality of Jim Crow cars, Morse was ready with a broad definition of "equal": "*equal accommodations* do not mean *identity* of accommodations [italics in the original]." In other words, racially segregated railroad cars—or hotels, theaters, and other "places of public amusement"—could legitimately be set up by states as long as they were more or less equal. The obvious differences between white and black railway cars were well known; indeed, the only similarity was that they were both headed in the same direction. Morse was evidently counting on the justices to ignore the demeaning impact of the inferior facilities into which Negroes were being forced by the states. Congress and the executive branch had already tacitly accepted the renewed caste system of the South. Now the Court was being asked by the State of Louisiana to indulge in the same hypocritical pretext for segregation: that racial barriers would make everyone feel more comfortable, so segregation was a legitimate state option no matter what the authors of the Thirteenth and Fourteenth Amendments clearly intended. The portentous decision of the justices in the *Plessy* case, though they could not have divined it at the time, would determine the relationship between blacks and whites in the United States for decades to come.

# Chapter 8

# THE DECISION COMES DOWN

O n April 13, 1896, the *Plessy* case was scheduled to be heard before the Supreme Court of the United States. Albion W. Tourgée planned to travel from his home in Mayfield, New York, to join his old friend Samuel F. Phillips in presenting oral arguments to the Court against the law segregating black and white railroad passengers. At least two sources agree that Tourgée did appear, although one Washington newspaper column hinted that he said it "was another fool's errand" (the title of his 1879 novel about Reconstruction). James C. Walker, Tourgée's New Orleans associate, begged off because of illness, and Louis Martinet had too little notice to reach Washington in time. As a spokesperson for the constitutionality of the law, Milton J. Cunningham, the Louisiana attorney general, had asked to be excused by the Court. His place was taken by Alexander Porter Morse, the native Louisianan mentioned earlier who had become a busy Washington lawyer specializing in federal appeals.

The Supreme Court met in the old Senate chamber, which it had occupied since 1860 when its basement quarters in the Capitol had been turned into a law library. The renovated chamber had a long table at which the justices sat, with a row of green marble columns behind them. For visitors, there were benches fitted with red velvet cushions—though it is unlikely that many of the seats were occupied, as *Plessy* was not attracting national attention. The justices did not have offices, just a conference room on the lower floor next to the library where they could exchange views on the case; they would have to draft their opinions in their studies at home. Court clerks and other officials were crowded into adjacent rooms.

We do not know exactly what the attorneys said to the Court, because oral arguments did not begin to be recorded until the 1950s. Albion Tourgée, however, transcribed his forty-four-page argument, which can be found among his papers at the Chautauqua County Historical Society. Knowing that he would be limited, as each side was, to approximately thirty minutes, Tourgée did not restrict himself to the reasoning used by Phillips in his brief—that the segregated railway act infringed on Plessy's "privileges and immunities," which were basic rights derived from the national citizenship that he enjoyed thanks to the Fourteenth Amendment. Instead, Tourgée launched a broad frontal attack on segregation as incongruous with the underlying principles—the *ethos*—of the United States. Whatever he lacked in the way of precedents, Tourgée tried to make up for with a radical interpretation of citizenship as granted to Negroes in 1868.

Tourgée was certainly talking the language Harlan had used in his dissents, but it may have gone right over the heads of the eight conservative, pedestrian justices. He tried to unmask the Louisiana law as an exercise of "white class privilege," which the legislature disguised by camouflaging its bias, specifically using the "equal but separate" seating provisions to give an appearance of "impartiality." Tourgée admitted that he was raising a new point on appeal, not so far "alluded to in any of the briefs," namely that the Louisiana law was "designed to discriminate against the colored citizens" and tends to "reduce them to a dependent and servile condition." Therefore, the Court should reverse the Louisiana courts, "no matter whether the relator [appellant] is white or black."

Instead of applying equally to all citizens, Tourgée argued, the law punished two separate crimes: the crime committed by black citizens who refused to enter a "colored" car or to leave a "white" car, and the crime of white citizens who refused to leave a "colored" car or enter a "white" car. The intended effect was unequal, Tourgée argued, since "the real object is to keep Negroes out of one car for the gratification of whites." The converse was not true, because it did not disturb "a colored passenger" to be joined by whites. The logic of segregation, he added, operated in only one direction: for the "special privilege" of a "class or race claiming superiority." Never in history, claimed Tourgée, had the weaker group asked to be fenced in. Inevitably, "A race or class claiming superiority . . . desires to see its exclusiveness crystallized into law." Hence, "The claim that this act is for the common advantage of both races . . . is farcical." Since the law was rooted in inequality rather than universality, Tourgée contended that it could not be fairly applied to Plessy, because—in Tourgée's picturesque phrase—"no man can be hanged with a rotten rope"; it violated a basic rule of law as well as the equal protection of the Fourteenth Amendment.

To compound the law's inequities, Tourgée focused on its vagueness as it affected people like his client, Homer Plessy. A law's provisions are supposed to be clear and specific. First, he asked, how were passengers who are unable to read—one-third of all Louisiana citizens—supposed to realize that they were entering the wrong car, particularly if they happened to be the only occupants? Second, a passenger with "one-eighth or one-sixteenth colored blood" may not have known whether he was "a white man or colored." He was not told his racial identity by law; indeed, this was a question that "science is totally unable to solve." And "common repute" may have given him yet another answer. So the law that made it a crime for a man to be "in a car to which he did not by race belong" stated "a conclusion, *not a fact* [italics in the original]." Yet the decision was left in the hands of a railway conductor, not a judge.

The Louisiana Supreme Court agreed with Plessy's counsel that the statute had wrongly exempted the railroad or its employees from liability if a passenger was assigned incorrectly to a car by race. But any such damage suit, Tourgée contended, was likely to bring the wronged party only "nominal damages," probably the amount of his fare. In the meantime, the conductor had the legal right to have a passenger ejected from the train. How was the offended person supposed to counter such peremptory action, which deprived him of liberty and property (and, perhaps, the losses sustained by the interruption of his trip)? In the legal language of the time, Tourgée also considered such a man's reputation as "property"; in the case of a white man, to be forced to sit in a "colored" car would be worse than suffering leprosy—it would leave a lifelong stigma. Tourgée asked the Court whether the law really expected each passenger in Louisiana "to carry a certified copy of his pedigree" to prove his right to sit in the car set aside for members of his race. What recourse, he asked the justices facetiously, would they leave the citizens of Louisiana injured by the separate car law, other than to flee the state?

Then Tourgée sketched the Negroes' place in American history so that the Fourteenth Amendment could be seen as an essential part of the Constitution rather than in the circumscribed form in which it had previously been presented to the Court, which had grudgingly validated only such aspects of the amendment as voting rights and jury duty. He began by citing "all men are created equal," from the Declaration of Independence (though that document, preceding the Constitution by eleven years, had never been accepted by the Court as its guide). Tourgée conceded that the Constitution seemed to have been drafted "to perpetuate slavery," but he argued that the relationship between the states and their citizens had been profoundly altered by the Civil War.

Before the war, Tourgée pointed out, American citizenship had been enjoyed only by whites. Afterward, a recast definition of citizenship in the Fourteenth Amendment offered an expanded list of rights—in a "classless" fashion—to everyone, regardless of race. In antebellum days the federal government had been charged with the "protection of slavery"; for example, it pursued fugitive slaves and returned them to those persons who were their legal owners under southern state law. When Congress and the states adopted the Fourteenth Amendment, however, the government's role changed from protecting the rich to safeguarding the rights of the "poor, weak and despised." Hence, Tourgée challenged the justices to apply the amendment's protection "to secure equality of right to all against the fear of state interference." He urged them not to relapse into their more accustomed role as protectors of "wealth [and] political power"— namely, the status quo.

Tourgée offered a broader vision of the Fourteenth Amendment than as existing merely "for the benefit of colored citizens"; that interpretation would make it appear that states were left in control of their citizens' rights. Instead, he told the Court the amendment should be seen as putting restrictions on the rights of states that had seceded. Its revolutionary intent was to create new definitions of both state and federal citizenship, with the latter paramount. Tourgée was asking the Court to reject the 1873 majority opinion of Justice Miller in the *Slaughter-House* Cases, who had read the amendment's second sentence in a very limiting fashion. In Miller's parsing, the sentence in question—"No State shall make or enforce any law which shall abridge the privileges and immunities of citizens of the United States"—provided protection of the plaintiffs' rights only as citizens of the United States, not as citizens of their state. Hence, only a few basic national rights were to be safeguarded by Congress, while the broad spectrum of state-controlled rights were off limits to federal jurisdiction. Without reference to the intent of the amendment's framers, Justice Miller had arbitrarily left persons seeking redress for violation of their state-related civil rights with only the time-honored recourse of going to state courts. By 1896 it was clear that such tribunals, in the southern states at least, were less than useless to plaintiffs in civil rights cases.

For Tourgée to have a chance at winning over the justices, he had to persuade them that the Fourteenth Amendment did not simply put a new gloss on traditionally defined citizenship; it fundamentally changed the state–federal balance. First, he contrasted the "old" citizenship with the "new," noting that United States citizenship had been based only on "race or descent [from United States citizens]", and in the federal system each state could define the "conditions and limitations of its own citizenship," which was not organically linked to national citizenship. The ratification of the Fourteenth Amendment in 1868, however, recast citizenship as "the right of all persons born (or naturalized) in the United States." Therefore, Tourgée argued, the amendment "created a new national citizenship" that guaranteed to everyone, irrespective of race, "all the rights, privileges and immunities" shared by all; state citizenship became "incidental" with the automatic grant of United States citizenship upon birth (or naturalization) to everyone residing in every state. States still exercised jurisdiction in their spheres, Tourgée concluded, but the federal government assumed a "final and exclusive . . . supervisory right" to decide "in all matters pertaining to Equality of rights, privileges and immunities" that justice had been done. In short, Tourgée's view of the revised Constitution made it imperative that the Court rule in favor of Plessy and not send him back to Judge Ferguson's court in New Orleans for a racially biased verdict.

Where Tourgée had tried to overpower the justices with a revived vision of equal rights in the language of the Radical Republicans who had erected the legal framework of Reconstruction, Alexander Porter Morse merely had to bring them down to earth, to the realities of 1896, twenty years after the end of that era. Notes for Morse's oral arguments have not been preserved, but it is apparent from his and Milton Cunningham's briefs that the advocates for Louisiana thought that precedents, and the restrictive judicial reading of the Fourteenth Amendment at the time, were on their side.

Most of Cunningham's brief simply quoted the text of Justice Charles Fenner's decision on *Plessy* by the Louisiana Supreme Court. Fenner had cited decisions, mostly from northern state courts in pre–Civil War days, to show that segregation based on race prejudice had been considered to be in the natural order of things. Morse's brief was also sprinkled with decisions that he said had more recently approved state-ordered segregation. However, only one of these precedents had dealt with legislated segregation— an 1889 decision of the Mississippi Supreme Court—and even that decision had not ordered separate seating of passengers by race but merely validated a state order to railways to provide such segregated cars.

Perhaps Morse, as an experienced litigator before the Supreme Court, was gambling that the justices were not likely to quibble about his catalog of precedents, even though he was stretching them to encompass the novel features of Louisiana law. Nor was he expecting the Court to bother researching the intention of the men who had framed the Fourteenth Amendment when he argued that they had surely not intended to interfere with the right of states to segregate all kinds of facilities, including public schools and railroads. The justices no doubt realized that with rare exceptions their recent rulings had diminished the civil rights of Negroes. For example, while the Court had ruled against West Virginia in 1880 for excluding Negroes from jury service, later rulings had let stand all-white jury judgments as long as they had come about not by law but by circumvention, such as by means of de facto white voter registration lists.

The members of the Court at the time *Plessy* was heard had not hesitated to overturn state regulations when they touched on the property of corporations; only Justice Harlan had protested strongly when states had used so-called police powers to condone discrimination, even violence, against Negroes. In Morse's make-believe world, which a majority of the justices shared, Negroes had been constitutionally chartered as voters and jury members, and they could take any infractions of their rights to their state courts for redress. Louisiana could force them into separate rail-road cars, no matter how inferior the cars were in reality, based on the fiction that whites and blacks would be punished equally for crossing the color line. How likely was it that a majority of the Court would rediscover the true intent of the Fourteenth Amendment, given its late–nineteenth-century mutation into a protection of property rights? Could the justices transcend the pervasive racial prejudices of their time? Or would they simply rehash Justice Fenner's biased opinion from the Louisiana Supreme Court?

The first news from the Court was that the *Plessy* decision would be made by eight justices rather than nine. Justice David J. Brewer had recused himself without giving any reason; there does not seem to have been an obvious conflict of interest, so it is hard to tell how Brewer might have voted. He had generally conservative leanings (noted in chapter 7) in favor of property rights, but was also willing to let states segregate schools and be allowed not to intercede when a gang of whites forced black workers off a job in Arkansas. Yet he had also dissented in cases where the Court had denied Chinese citizens access to federal courts to present their claims for citizenship.

Brewer's absence was probably of little concern to Plessy's attorneys, but they must have had few grounds for optimism when they learned that the opinion had been assigned to Justice Henry Billings Brown. Brown was known for his general support of the police powers of the states, because he felt that state policies were close to the "wishes of the citizens as they may deem best for the public welfare."

On May 18, 1896, nearly four years after Plessy's fateful interrupted railway journey, Justice Brown finally announced the opinion of seven of the justices, with Justice Harlan in dissent. His opinion is prolix and turgid, mixing facts with racial prejudices. It (1) begins by outlining the facts of the case, then (2) deals dismissively with Plessy's claim that the law violated his rights under the Thirteenth Amendment. It reserves the bulk of its logic for a series of inquiries: (3) how did the Fourteenth Amendment apply to efforts by states to require segregation, (4) what could be learned from precedents in this area, (5) why a state's police powers could extend to racially segregating railway travel, and (6) whether integration could be achieved by laws. Following are synopses of each of these sections, with italicized commentary.

(1) Brown's opening offers a straightforward summary of the 1890 Louisiana law requiring "equal but separate accommodations

for the white and colored races," with railway officers charged "to assign each passenger to the coach or compartment used for the race to which such passenger belongs (also referred to as Act No. 111)." The penalties for passengers refusing such assignments—both fines and imprisonment—are then recounted. Brown also mentions the law's loophole: that "nothing in this act shall be construed as applying to nurses attending children of the other race."

Then, Plessy is identified as a passenger who "was assigned by the officers of the company to the coach used for the race to which he belonged, but he insisted on going into a coach used by the race to which he did not belong." Yet his indictment never stated what "was his particular race or color." Only in his lawyers' petition for appeal was it stated that Plessy "was seven eighths Caucasian and one eighth African blood; that the mixture of colored blood was not discernible in him, and that he was entitled to every right, privilege and immunity secured to citizens of the United States of the white race. . . ."

*Even this factual account is replete with legal fictions. For example, the prosecutor's "information," serving as an indictment, was open about Plessy's standing as a Negro under Louisiana law (noted in chapter 1). Everyone in Judge Ferguson's courtroom knew that this was a test case in which Plessy had refused to move to the Jim Crow car. If he had not made the point to the conductor that he was a Negro, how would the authorities have known that Plessy was deliberately breaking the segregation law? That Plessy deliberately broke the law must have been especially obvious if "the mixture of colored blood was not discernible in him." Brown has made Judge Ferguson into a symbol of blindfolded justice who dealt evenhandedly with someone protesting segregation while seemingly unaware of the defendant's racial classification. This illusion of legal and judicial equality allows Brown to accomplish a twofold purpose: (a) to satisfy the requirement of the*

*Fourteenth Amendment for "equal protection of the laws," and (b) to camouflage the law's racist premise by pretending that the state only desired to reduce endemic racial friction by setting up barriers under its police powers.*

(2) Brown continues by cavalierly disposing of Tourgée's argument that, among other things, the Louisiana segregation law pins a "badge of servitude" on Plessy and other Negroes. He does not meet that claim head-on, but simply asserts: that Act No. 111 "does not conflict with the Thirteenth Amendment . . . is too clear for argument." By his narrow reading of the amendment, Brown interprets it only as a prohibition of "slavery and involuntary servitude . . . a state of bondage; the ownership of mankind as chattel." Louisiana was not putting Plessy into chains, according to Brown, so why all the fuss? He does not accept Tourgée's concept that forcible segregation amounted to "a badge of servitude." All that the Louisiana railway act had done, says Brown, is to imply "merely a legal distinction between the white and colored races," part of their obvious differences, without any "tendency to destroy the legal equality of the two races, or to reestablish a state of involuntary servitude."

Brown then buttresses this finding by reference to two key decisions, the *Slaughter-House Cases* and the *Civil Rights Cases*. In the former, according to Brown, the Thirteenth Amendment was "said . . . to have been intended primarily to abolish slavery"; in the latter, Justice Bradley had said, "It would be running the slavery argument into the ground to make it apply to every act of discrimination. . . ." Further finessing Tourgée, Brown concludes that he understands that the Thirteenth Amendment has not been "strenuously relied upon" by the plaintiff . . . "in this connection."

*Thirty years after the abolition of "slavery" or "involuntary servitude," it was possible for judges like Brown to consider these concepts as relics of the past. Yet any common usage of such terms, as in a dictionary, goes beyond mere ownership of men as chattel to extend the terms to include being under the control of others. If Brown had had the least empathy for people like Plessy, he might have understood their feeling of abasement when they were pushed into dirty, crowded Jim Crow cars. Yet Brown's verbal sleight-of-hand in legitimating racial "distinctions" that are not inherently discriminatory betrays his obtuseness. As Bernard Schwartz has put it in his history of the Supreme Court, "The device of holding a group of people separate—whether by confinement of Jews to the Ghetto, by exclusion of untouchables from the temple, or by segregation of the black—is a basic tool of discrimination." To call the status of persons who wall off others equal to that of ghetto-dwellers is an exercise in hypocrisy or self-delusion.*

*Brown's citations are likewise suspect. The* Slaughter-House Cases *found "the one pervading purpose" of the Thirteenth, Fourteenth, and Fifteenth Amendments, which it lumped together, as "the freedom of the slave race, the security and firm establishment of that freedom, and the protection of the newly-made freeman and citizen from the oppressions of those who had formerly exercised unlimited dominion over him." Justice Miller's wording here is expansive rather than restrictive. In the* Civil Rights Cases, *Justice Bradley did indeed overturn the 1875 Civil Rights Act, designed to implement the Thirteenth and Fourteenth Amendments, because he feared Congress would otherwise venture into "a code of municipal law for the regulation of private rights." Bradley, a railroad lawyer from New Jersey, had ensured the 1876 election of fellow Republican Rutherford B. Hayes to the presidency when Bradley served as a member of the nearly deadlocked 1877 electoral commission.*

*In a strange reading of pre–Civil War history, Bradley found that— in the North, at least—Negroes had enjoyed the same rights as whites to frequent hotels and restaurants; therefore, they could not now claim that discrimination by private businesses was a "badge of [the] slavery" barred by the Thirteenth Amendment. But Bradley was careful to distinguish purely individual actions without state support, for which criminal courts were the remedy, from "civil rights which are guaranteed by the Constitution against State aggression."*

*Brown cites only Bradley's restrictive language concerning discrimination suits against private firms, not his positive reference to federal recourse against state actions. He thereby blurs the difference between the allegedly private wrongs by theater owners and the like in that case and the state-mandated segregation in* Plessy. *This is Brown's way of making it appear that* Plessy *doesn't really present a novel constitutional question. To no one's surprise, Brown also totally ignores Harlan's strong dissent in the* Civil Rights Cases, *which found that discrimination in public accommodations by any state or individual under state authority violated the Thirteenth Amendment by inflicting "a badge of servitude," and the Fourteenth by violating not just "social" but "civil rights" of American citizens.*

(3) Brown next inquires how the Fourteenth Amendment applies to this case. He uses a literal, limited reading of its first section: to establish Negro citizenship, and to protect American citizens generally from having their "privileges or immunities" curtailed by "hostile legislation of the States." Yet this translates only into enforcing "the absolute equality of the races before the law," without otherwise keeping states from making "distinctions based upon color." Thus, "absolute equality" is limited to the realm of the ballot box and the courtroom, not touching anything in the sphere of so-called social rights. The range of rights that Brown seeks to exclude from legal protection is quite extensive, from the integration of schools and other facilities to interracial marriages.

Brown considers any discrimination in the social sphere exempt from judicial enforcement, because it is "in the nature of things" that constitutional protection could "not have been intended to enforce social as distinguished from political equality, or a commingling of the two races upon terms unsatisfactory to either."

Such a concept derives from the somewhat mystical idea of natural law or, in its late-nineteenth-century incarnation, "substantive due process," which leaves judges to divine the justice of laws without considering the impact of their decisions on those who feel they have been victimized.

Brown states that, far from being subjective, he has used the standard of reasonableness. He would not have let stand laws that would have directed "white men's houses to be painted white, and colored men's black," or that would have ordered people of each race to walk upon opposite sides of the street. Such extreme examples, from Phillips's and Tourgée's briefs, would have been unreasonable—not "enacted in good faith for the promotion for the public good" but "for the annoyance or oppression of a particular class."

*The organic evolution of rights in Brown's view scarcely allows for a change in basic attitudes and practices, such as was contemplated by the authors of the Fourteenth Amendment. Brown goes on to select cases from pre–Civil War days to illustrate the inherent distaste of whites in America for permitting Negro children to attend their public schools or to sit alongside them in trains or other "public accommodations." Things are the way they are because people want them to be that way. Brown appears to be unapologetic for the circularity of his argument: that he, as a judge, ostensibly without prejudice, is legitimating a system of institutionalized racism; and further, that by telling Negro plaintiffs he cannot do anything about their manifold social rights, he is relegating them to a ghetto existence in which their "equal political rights" become meaningless.*

*Brown goes out of his way to blame the victims of discrimination for their own plight: he claims that plaintiffs like Plessy have it all wrong, that if there are such malcontents who feel "that the enforced separation of the two races stamps the colored race with a badge of inferiority," it is their own fault. Nothing in the words of the Louisiana legislature shows such intent; therefore, any sense of abasement comes "solely because the* colored race chooses to put that construction upon it." As long as southern legislators camouflage the racist intent of their laws, Brown implies, the practice of state-run segregation passes the scrutiny of federal courts. Southern states can even use racial "distinctions" in their statutes and not be accused of "discrimination."

In Brown's world, Negro plaintiffs who have been denied their rights to equal treatment in many phases of their lives are told, inferentially, that they are not being "reasonable." By the standard of judges like Brown there are only blacks and whites, so Plessy and other people of mixed race are in limbo. Brown disagrees with Tourgée that any mixed-race plaintiffs can claim damages to their reputation: if they are really black, Brown contends, they cannot be deprived of "property" for being in the Jim Crow car, since they are "not lawfully entitled to the reputation of being a white man"; if they are really white, however, they may have "action for damages against the company" for being deprived of "so-called property." Overall, Brown is rather dismissive of claims based on such insubstantial matters as reputation, especially from Negroes, whom he chastises for having too negative an attitude.

Finally, the standard Brown uses for "reasonableness" turns out to be the state legislature's "reference to the established usages, customs and traditions of the people, and with a view to the promotion of their comfort, and the preservation of the public peace and good order." Brown seems totally unconcerned about the race-based premise of this standard. The customs and traditions are those of the white elite in the post-Reconstruction southern states. The concept of comfort and sense of public peace also reflects the view from the top, not the bottom, of the social pyramid. To legitimate the established order, Brown simply disregards the Fourteenth Amendment and its panoply of civil rights. The discomfort and abasement of Negroes counts for little in Brown's scheme of things—as admittedly was true of most Americans in the 1890s.

(4) Justice Brown cites a long list of cases, mostly from state

courts, as his guideposts in how far the police powers of Louisiana should extend when it comes to segregating railway travel. Two of these cases, *Roberts v. City of Boston* (1849) and *West Chester and Philadelphia Railroad Co. v. Miles* (1867), were mentioned in chapter 5 in connection with the rationale for the Louisiana Supreme Court's decision in *Plessy*. Brown explains why he reaches back so far, to the time before the ratification of the Fourteenth Amendment, for precedents: both Massachusetts and Pennsylvania had in their state constitutions' language in references to equality that was similar to that later used in the federal amendment. Still, Brown was doubtlessly aware that the *Roberts* decision was so controversial that in 1855 the state legislature overruled the Boston school committee by integrating public schools in Massachusetts. Brown must have agreed with Justice Shaw's odd comment that since law was not the cause of segregation, it could not be its solution. He may also have bought into the Pennsylvania court's conclusion that racial separation was immutable, though Brown did not attribute it to God's design as much as to the social science of his day. A leading school of sociology considered popular "folkways" as the substratum for social institutions, and that rationale well served status quo justice like Brown's.

Brown also used as precedents two contradictory Supreme Court decisions: *Hall v. DeCuir* and *New Orleans & Texas Railway Co. v. Mississippi*. Mrs. DeCuir had won a state judgment of one thousand dollars for being denied a first-class cabin on a boat sailing between two Louisiana cities; in 1877 the Supreme Court had reversed by holding that the 1869 Louisiana law forbidding "discrimination for race or color" in transportation was potentially an invasion of Congress's power to regulate interstate commerce in that the boat's ultimate destination was out of state. In 1890, however, the Court had upheld an 1888 Mississippi law

fining a railroad for not providing racially segregated accommodations, despite Justices Brewer and Harlan's dissent that the circumstances in the two cases were identical. The Court majority in
the latter case held that the Mississippi law was intended to apply
only to intrastate commerce, though trains did cross state borders.
Of course, Brown found the 1890 decision "much nearer and
indeed, almost directly in point" to Plessy's circumstances. One
obvious difference was that the Mississippi law had not ordered
Negro passengers to be forced into separate cars, as the 1890
statute had in Plessy's case.

Justice Brown's opinion included a potpourri of state court
decisions in the areas of transportation and education, though
the incidental contact of railway passengers and the more intimate relationship of schoolchildren differed greatly in impact.
Some commentators have pointed out that none of these cases
furnish Brown with a clear precedent of the situation he faced
in *Plessy*, especially since many of the decisions date from
pre–Civil War days, and none deals with state-enforced racial
segregation of passengers.

Charles Lofgren has found that an 1883 New York appellate
court opinion, *People v. Gallagher*, may have had a major influence on Brown's thinking. In that case the court had denied that
a law could establish racial equality in public schools. Such "laws
which conflict with the general sentiment of the community
upon which they are designed to operate," the judges said, could
not work. The New York court also said that it was in "the
nature of things" that "many social distinctions lay beyond the
reach of law"; indeed, that attempts "to enforce social intimacy
and intercourse between races" tended to be self-defeating, by
tending "only to embitter the prejudices . . . which exist between
them, and produce an evil instead of a good result." In an afterthought the court claimed that "a natural distinction exists"

between white and black races "which was not created, neither can it be abrogated, by law."

*Brown seems to have been intent on giving legal standing to the segregation laws that had been mushrooming across the South at the time. He refused to recognize that Louisiana's involvement in prosecuting Homer Plessy represented a novel feature in the evolution of constricted interpretations of the Fourteenth Amendment. He therefore stretches the relevance of anachronistic holdings from other state courts, many predating the amendment's passage. He also delights in showing that pro-segregation holdings could be cited from many northern states, where Negroes enjoyed very limited rights before the Civil War. Against such a backdrop of pervasive discrimination, the Louisiana treatment of Plessy might not seem to be particularly reprehensible; it could, in Brown's perspective, even be seen as "reasonable."*

*Another weakness in this section of Brown's opinion is that a comparative critique of the precedents he cites is nearly impossible; he cites cases that uphold discriminatory education laws in Ohio, Missouri, California, Louisiana, New York, Indiana, and Kentucky, but does not describe any of their relevant laws. The same is true of the dozen cases, nine of them from southern states, allegedly based on "similar statutes for the separation of the two races upon public conveyances." We do know that they were* not *all discriminatory; the 1869 Louisiana law mentioned above, for example, required common carriers to "make no discrimination on account of race or color." In any case, the Supreme Court is not bound by state court decisions.*

*When Brown discusses court-approved school segregation, he obfuscates. "Similar laws," he claims, "have been enacted by Congress under its general power of legislation over the District of Columbia." As has been mentioned, Congress provided local options to District schools on whether to segregate or integrate their students, but Brown makes it appear that segregation was mandatory. Lofgren also notes that Brown excluded those precedents by state courts that had overturned "separate-but-equal*

*schooling," particularly the decision by the Iowa Supreme Court in 1868
that found "racially segregated schools" not only "a violation of the spirit
of our laws" but tending "to perpetuate the national differences of our
people and [to] stimulate a constant strife, if not a war of the races."
Moving even further from Plessy's circumstances in a Jim Crow car, Justice Brown mentions the judicial acceptance of "laws forbidding the intermarriage of the two races," based on an Indiana court decision.*

(5) Since the preponderance of state court cases Brown cites led to
court-approved segregation, he has no problem placing the
Louisiana railway segregation law in the province of legitimate
state police power. It appears to him not only "a reasonable regulation" but also one that is in accord with "the established usages,
customs and traditions of the people, and with a view to the promotion of their comfort, and the preservation of the public peace
and good order." The reasonableness standard is not explained as
it applies to *Plessy*; it is employed by Brown simply because he
takes it as a given that the Court will concede "a large discretion"
to acts of the state legislature.

As for a state legislature's proper employment of its police
power, besides being reasonable it must, according to Brown, fulfill three other conditions: it must effect "such laws as are enacted
in good faith, for the promotion for the public good, and not for
the annoyance or oppression of a particular class." It seems easier
for Brown to judge when police power is transgressing than to
define its scope. For his negative example, he selects the case of
*Yick Wo v. Hopkins*, in which a unanimous Court in 1886 had overturned a San Francisco ordinance that licensed laundries if they
were approved by a city board. Two hundred Chinese laundry
owners, including Yick Wo, were denied licenses, and their
attorney contended that the ordinance had violated their rights
under the Fourteenth Amendment. The opinion by Justice

Stanley Matthews stated that San Francisco had gone beyond the traditional police power to regulate the use of property. Its ordinance was found to constitute "class legislation" and, according to Brown, had been "a covert attempt . . . to make an arbitrary and unjust discrimination against the Chinese race." Brown found none of those prohibitions to apply to the Louisiana railway law.

*Brown's justification for the segregation of Louisiana railway passengers merely echoes Justice Fenner's opinion in the state supreme court. At least at this remove, it is clearly a view reflecting both judges' bias in favor of white elite privileges. Despite its pretense at being evenhanded in punishing trespassers of both races who venture into each others' compartments, the law gives comfort only to the whites in the first-class carriages. It is not based on any record of breaches of "the public peace and good order" during the preceding era when railways had been integrated by law. So there are certainly grounds, which Brown ignores, for questioning the "good faith" of the legislature in forcing Negroes into Jim Crow cars. Only by twisted logic can the law be seen as promoting "the public good" and not annoying or oppressing "a particular class." It is ironic that Chinese laundry owners in San Francisco were given the full protection of the Fourteenth Amendment by the Supreme Court, but that the Negroes, for whom the Constitution was specifically amended, were denied those rights.*

*In 1896 six of the nine justices who had ruled for Yick Wo in 1886 were no longer on the bench. The pro-business orientation of the later Court made its majority hostile to state regulations such as abuses of police power, but quietist, except for Justice Harlan, when it came to challenging racially discriminatory state laws. As long as the laws discriminated against Negroes in a covert fashion (as San Francisco was said to have oppressed the Chinese plaintiffs), they could be found reasonable exercises of police power. It would take until the mid-twentieth century for the Yick Wo decision to be used as a precedent and for Brown's opinion in Plessy to finally be rejected.*

(6) If Plessy was not going to have his claims accepted by Justice Brown, when, if ever, could Negroes expect to enjoy the equality under the laws that they had been promised by the Fourteenth Amendment? Justice Brown, who had evidently taken an interest in contemporary social science theories, took a leaf from the works of Yale professor William Graham Sumner, who held that laws could be effective only if they were grafted onto existing "folkways." Brown rejects Tourgée's revolutionary call for a judicial interpretation of the Fourteenth Amendment that would hearken back to its authors' intent of fully protecting the rights of Negroes as full-fledged American citizens. That argument, he notes, "assumes that social prejudices may be overcome by legislation, and that equal rights cannot be secured to the negro except by the enforced commingling of the two races. We cannot accept this proposition. If the two races are to meet upon terms of social equality, it must be the result of natural affinities, a mutual appreciation of each other's merits and a voluntary consent of individuals."

Then Brown proceeds to inflate Plessy's plea for civil treatment while a train passenger in Lousiana into a global program to uproot racial prejudice. "Legislation is powerless to eradicate racial instincts or to abolish distinctions based upon physical differences, and the attempt to do so can only result in accentuating the difficulties of the present situation. . . . If one race be inferior to the other socially, the Constitution of the United States cannot put them upon the same plane." Brown's response to Plessy's request for truly civil treatment is that he must first wait for southern whites to change their negative attitude toward sitting alongside Negro passengers. Perhaps, in Brown's timeline, that day would come after whites had grown to appreciate what Negroes had accomplished since Emancipation. In 1896 that day was indeed approaching—but without the force of laws and courts, only at glacial speed.

*It is such extraneous comments, or* obiter dicta *as they are called by judicial commentators, that make Brown seem to be adding insult to Plessy's injuries. He subscribes to a doctrine of Negro inferiority, at least on the social stage, and shrugs his shoulders. Plessy and other blacks are told not to turn to their legislators or judges to free them from discrimination, but to their white neighbors and state government officials. But what if those whites came under the spell of racism, spread by the Ku Klux Klan and other white supremacist groups? Too bad for the blacks, Brown implies, since only narrowly defined "political rights" are the concern of the Court. In his blurred view of history, nothing fundamental has changed in southern society as a consequence of the Civil War or the postwar amendments and laws. If the Black Codes from slave days have reappeared as Jim Crow laws, that must be a symptom of deep-rooted customs, which are based on obvious physical differences (in the face of Plessy's white appearance!).*

*As William Graham Sumner averred in his static social theory (which parallels his economic doctrines of free trade in an unfettered sphere), folkways (the term he coined to refer to habitual group responses) endure from generation to generation because they are efficient. Only after the group has decided that some folkways enhance collective welfare do they become mores, which are then turned by the state into laws. In this view of human nature, members of a society are largely unconscious of how their behavior has been shaped by such folkways, but it is in their best interest to follow the dictates of their culture. Justice Brown adapts Sumner's rationalization of the status quo to profess that it would be futile, even harmful, to attempt to change a culture by means of laws and judicial opinions that try to shape behavior.*

*Like many other such ideological models with pretensions to scientific accuracy, Sumner's (and Brown's) sweeping theory does not concern itself unduly with contradictory facts. Richard Kluger, for example, has pointed out that transportation practices in the South were far from uniform at the time. Instead of "established usages, customs and traditions of the people," which Brown sees as uniformly justifying segregation, "in many places, second-class coaches had long been shared by white and colored passengers." Indeed, in seven of the eight southern states with segregated transportation laws at the time of* Plessy, *those laws had been in force for only eight years or less. The passage of the Fourteenth Amendment indicates that Congress intended to forcibly reverse the South's return to institutionalized discrimination against Negroes. By ratifying the hypocritical Louisiana law, which cloaked its racism with the eyewash of "equal but separate" provisions, Justice Brown and his six colleagues defaulted in their role as protectors of citizens' constitutional rights. Only one justice, John Marshall Harlan, in his dissent, correctly assessed the harm done by the* Plessy *decision as equivalent to the decision in* Dred Scott, *which validated inherent Negro inferiority.*

The majority decision legitimated segregation, which, albeit in covert form, can be said to persist to this day. Justice Harlan's dissenting opinion is only a bit shorter than that of the Court majority, but its brilliance took a half century to be discovered and begin to be implemented. Harlan would not settle for the "separate but equal" camouflage his colleagues used to conceal discrimination. Instead, he responded to Tourgée's challenge: to carry the intent of the Thirteenth and Fourteenth Amendments into all facets of public life to achieve true equality.

Harlan's opinion, like Brown's, begins by outlining the facts of the case, but with a sarcastic spin. For example, after stating the law's exception to allow "nurses attending children of the other race" to accompany their charges, Harlan adds that no such waiver is provided for a white man who needs "to have his colored servant with him in the same coach" for health reasons, or for a colored maid who wants to attend her white employer and risks imprisonment for "zeal in the discharge of duty." He sets up his premise for dissenting by calling such a crime as Plessy's the result of Louisiana's regulating "the use of a public highway by citizens of the United States solely upon the basis of race." If railroads are, as shown by over half a century of common law and American precedent, "in trust for the public," then no racial distinctions can be allowed to affect the state's provision for their use. Here Harlan devotes a paragraph to explaining that people generally have their "pride of race," but the expression of such feelings cannot be permitted to undermine the rights of fellow citizens.

Then Harlan accepts Tourgée's history of the Thirteenth and Fourteenth Amendments as fundamentally revising the definition of citizenship. They guaranteed to Negroes full equality before the law, as well its negative corollary, "exemption from legal discriminations, implying inferiority in civil society." The Thirteenth Amendment banned not only outright slavery but also "any burdens . . . that constitute badges of slavery or servitude." It was followed by the Fourteenth Amendment, which "added greatly to the dignity and glory of American citizenship." Harlan cites a series of decisions in which the Court overturned state laws that excluded Negroes from jury panels, based on the awareness that now "all citizens are equal before the law."

Next, he deconstructs the Louisiana law, with its equal-race formula. "Every one knows," says Harlan, that this statute intends "not so much to exclude white persons from railroad cars occupied by blacks, as to exclude colored people from coaches . . . assigned to white persons." Of course, people can travel in any company they like, and government cannot prevent a white man and a black man from choosing "to occupy the same conveyance on a public highway" without infringing on "the personal liberty of each." Using examples from Tourgée's brief, Harlan asks what is to prevent states with such power from keeping whites and blacks from walking on the same side of the street, or even from sitting on the same side of a courtroom. Even more absurdly, why couldn't they have separate railway accommodations for Protestants and Catholics? The majority opinion rejected such outcomes as "unreasonable," but Harlan says that all laws must be presumed reasonable as long as legislatures seek germane ends through law. It is not the place of courts to adjudge such reasonableness of laws, but rather to adjudge their constitutionality.

Then Harlan exhibits that "pride of race" that he earlier assumed to be the right of all. He contends that the "white race" is undoubtedly "dominant . . . in prestige, in achievements, in education, in wealth and in power." And so it will "continue to be for all time," but only if it observes the constitutional command of "liberty" for all. In that view, "there is in this country no superior, dominant, ruling class of citizens. There is no caste here. Our Constitution is color-blind, and neither knows nor tolerates classes among citizens. In respect of civil rights, all citizens are equal before the law. The humblest is the peer of the most powerful." These phrases have a Lincolnesque ring, yet they evidently reflect Harlan's religious beliefs and even his family's history as slaveholders. A certain amount of pride in one's achievements may be justified, but when it becomes excessive—and is used to demean others—it is sinful and hurtful to both parties. That is the syllogism underlying his dissent.

Harlan uses the remainder of his remarkable opinion to berate his seven colleagues in the majority. He predicts that their "judgment . . . will, in time, prove to be quite as pernicious as the decision made by this tribunal in the *Dred Scott case*." Justice Taney in that case denied to the descendants of "Africans who were imported into this country and sold as slaves" their right to protection under the Constitution. Instead, he termed them "a subordinate and inferior class of beings" without "rights or privileges but such as those who held the power and government might choose to grant them." That opinion led to the Civil War, and the *Plessy* decision is likely to "stimulate aggressions . . . upon the admitted rights of colored citizens" as well as encouraging states "to defeat the beneficent purposes" of the Constitution by such laws.

What have the sixty million whites to fear from "the presence here of eight million blacks?" Harlan asks. Instead of laws, like the Louisiana statute, that foster "race hate," he urges state and national governments to promote peace by recognizing the right to "civil freedom" for all. Here Harlan broadens the meaning of "civil rights" to include the entire public sphere, not just the political rights of voters and jury members. Railroad travel does not confer "social equality," Harlan contends, between members of different races any more than would having them sit together in a jury box or vote by integrated lists. Again, there is a religious ring to Harlan's conclusion, that "the thin disguise of 'equal' accommodations for passengers in railroad coaches will not mislead any one, nor atone for the wrong done this day." The separate cars or "partitions" required by the Louisiana law make no more sense than would erecting such barriers to separate "black and white jurors."

Harlan concludes with his vision of the new page in the country's history that has been turned by the enactment of the Civil War amendments. Before this era, "race prejudice was, practically, the supreme law of the land." The precedents cited by Justice Brown date mostly from that earlier period, "when colored people had very few rights which the dominant race felt obliged to respect." Therefore, Brown will not take the trouble to review those earlier opinions by state courts. If other states follow Louisiana's example, "the effect would be in the highest degree mischievous." Slavery may have been abolished, but Harlan fears that states may now seek to pass "sinister legislation . . . to place in a condition of legal inferiority a large body of American citizens, . . . constituting a part of the political community called the People of the United States."

John Marshall Harlan became one of the longest-serving justices on the Court; but during his thirty-three years of service, out
of the 16,826 cases that he heard, this opinion was to stand out as
a beacon to guide civil rights adjudications throughout the second
half of the twentieth century.

# SEGREGATION WITHOUT JUDICIAL RESTRAINTS

T
he *Dred Scott* decision in 1857 was a bombshell, unloosing a nationwide storm of protest that led inexorably to the Civil War. Northern abolitionists bridled at Chief Justice Roger B. Taney's invalidation of the 1820 Missouri Compromise, by which Congress had tried to set geographical limits to the spread of slavery. Speaking for the Court majority, Taney had also gone out of his way to read African Americans out of the Constitution. As "beings of an inferior order . . . altogether unfit to associate with the white race . . . and so far inferior, that they had no rights which the white man was bound to respect," they could never lay claim to citizenship, even when they had been freed under state law. The only rational explanation for the opinion of those seven justices is that they reflected the entrenched southern point of view. Slave owners' rights to their slaves as "an article of merchandise and traffic" had been taken for granted since at least a century prior to the Declaration of Independence; by endorsing its immutability, the justices hoped to settle the slavery issue and avoid the secession of the South. Taney was espousing the dogmatic faith in slavery that he had imbibed from his tobacco-growing family of Maryland aristocrats.

The *Plessy* decision, by way of contrast, failed to arouse national passions or protests. Yet in this decision, too, a majority of the Court skipped recent history to patch together what seemed a formula to avoid incipient regional conflict. The seven justices who assented to the decision had ignored the actions of the president, Congress, and the states during—and following—the Civil War and the adoption of the Thirteenth, Fourteenth, and Fifteenth Amendments that had been its result. They also frustrated the claims of another African American plaintiff, Homer Plessy, whose suit might have led to truly equal rights for himself and eight million of his newly recognized fellow citizens. The decision by Henry Billings Brown, of New England merchant stock, reflected his social Darwinist credo in which Anglo-Saxons were seen as natural pillars of a lawful society. Like his colleagues in the Court majority, Brown had had little if any contact with blacks in their educational, professional, or social pursuits. It is ironic that the plight of southern blacks was clearly seen only by Justice Harlan, a former slave owner himself, who warned his colleagues to avoid planting "the seeds of race hate . . . under the sanction of law." As Taney had left Dred Scott and his family's fate to the mercy of his master, so Brown told Homer Plessy that in effect he could enjoy most of his rights only with the acquiescence of his capricious white southern neighbors. Plessy's feelings of degradation by the Louisiana railway statute, according to Brown, were simply due to his negative attitude—seeing himself victimized because he "chose to put that construction on it." The Court's baffling conclusion to the case was that laws and courts were "powerless to eradicate social instincts"; yet it issued an opinion that in effect gave judicial sanction to white racist impulses.

The *Plessy v. Ferguson* decision caused scarcely a ripple when it was announced on May 18, 1896. The next day's *New York Times* relegated it to page 3 of its second section, where it was in company with the railroad news. The *Times* briefly reported the

Court's validation of the Louisiana segregation law for railroad travel, noting merely two of the grounds on which the opinion was based: that the law applied only to a railroad operating entirely within the state (so did not involve the interstate commerce powers of Congress), and that the cited precedents included federal and state laws permitting the establishment of "separate schools for children of the two races." While the law was covered by the state's police power, the *Times* story added, it was also said to be the object of Justice Harlan's "very vigorous dissent," since "he saw nothing but mischief in all such laws."

A dozen contemporary accounts of the Court's action on *Plessy* were collated by historian Otto H. Olsen. The decision was hailed by the *Daily Picayune* in New Orleans, which boasted that by now, "there are similar laws in all the States which abut on Louisiana and, indeed, in most of the Southern States." Consequently, it proudly announced that "this regulation for the separation of the races will operate continuously on all lines of Southern railway." (Of course, that admission put the lie to the state's claim that it was only regulating intrastate commerce, because in the South segregation laws followed a traveler across state boundaries. Congress did not attempt to assert its constitutional primacy in this area, taking nearly a century after it passed the 1875 Civil Rights Act before it timidly reentered the field in 1957 to establish a Civil Rights Commission.) The New Orleans newspaper concluded that if the law went beyond equality to the "common" distribution of rights, "there would be practically no such thing as private property, private life, or social distinction, but all would belong to everybody who might choose to use it. This would be absolute socialism, in which the individual would be extinguished in the vast mass of human beings, a condition repugnant to every principle of enlightened democracy."

This racist sentiment is echoed by a commentary in the

*Dispatch* of Richmond, Virginia. "Some colored people make themselves so disagreeable on the cars," says this writer, "that their conduct leads white men to ponder the question whether such a law as that of Louisiana is not needed in all the Southern States." There are no specifics on the allegedly offensive behavior of Negro passengers. The writer appears happily surprised that such a law stood "the test of the courts" and predicts that the "legislatures of other Southern states" will follow Louisiana's example.

Indeed, *Plessy* was seen throughout the South as an invitation to treat African Americans virtually as lepers. Laws quarantined drinking fountains and toilets by race. Negroes were forbidden to eat at white restaurants and luncheonettes. They had to use separate hospitals when they were ill and, after they died, find their final rest in black cemeteries. Florida and North Carolina prohibited white children from using textbooks that had been touched by blacks. Alabama even made it a crime for blacks and whites to play checkers together. In Mississippi, blacks and whites had to use separate phone booths. Any Negro who inadvertently crossed the color line could expect to be severely punished.

By the end of the decade, which was also the beginning of the twentieth century, all eleven southern states and some border states were adopting laws that put up barriers not only on trains but in public schools, libraries, parks, theaters, and hotels. Tennessee, Florida, Mississippi, Texas, Alabama, Kentucky, Georgia, and Arizona had passed railway segregation laws prior to 1892; after *Plessy* they were joined by South Carolina (1898), North Carolina (1899), Virginia (1900), Maryland (1904), and Oklahoma (1907). Before 1896 a Negro passenger who took a train from Philadelphia to Indiana could not be forced to change to a Jim Crow car while crossing Maryland and Kentucky, despite their segregation laws, because the Constitution had reserved to Congress the power to control interstate commerce. By 1898, however, a Tennessee court ruled that even interstate passengers could be forced into segregated cars, given the spread of Jim Crow laws throughout the region. And the plight of African Americans was even worse than the legal picture indicated, because informal barriers were more pervasive, extending de facto to northern churches and public accommodations.

The reaction to *Plessy* in the northern media, however, was generally negative, especially in Republican newspapers. The *Republican* in Springfield, Massachusetts, shrugged off the decision as something to be expected in the South, "where white supremacy is thought to be in peril," a region where such laws "may be expected to spread like the measles." It asked, mockingly, "Did the southerners ever pause to indict the Almighty for allowing negroes to be born on the same earth with white men?" The *New York Daily Tribune* found the majority decision in *Plessy* "unfortunate," and agreed with "the strong dissenting opinion of Justice Harlan, who says there is no more reason for separate cars for whites and Negroes than for Catholics and Protestants."

The newspapers in Rochester, New York, divided along political lines, with the Democratic *Union Advertiser* seeing the Court as ruling not by expediency but simply on the grounds of "state power," with each state entitled to regulate "railroads within its own territory." The Republican *Democrat and Chronicle* deplored the Court's "concession to one of the lowest and meanest prejudices to which the human mind is liable . . . against people of a specified race and color." It took the occasion to deplore a Florida law against teaching "white and colored children together" that had recently led to the arrest of "several Northern gentlemen and ladies" who taught in a church school in Orange Park. Some Republican papers stayed true to their abolitionist roots. Democrats, supportive of Grover Cleveland, their first elected president since the Civil War, leaned toward the "Solid South," which had become the bedrock of their party.

The bitterest denunciations of *Plessy* could be found in Negro newspapers. The *Weekly Blade* of Parsons, Kansas, termed the "Democratic majority" of the justices such a disgrace it proposed that the nation "put an end to the infernal, infamous bodies," like the Court. The editor was aghast at the legitimation of the "Louisiana 'Jim Crow' car law." He concluded, "Justice Harlan was the only one on that bench with grit enough in him to utter a protest against this damnable outrage upon a race that for more than 275 years labored under the yoke of bondage, but in 30 years of partial freedom has reached the very gate of the nation's most noble." It should be noted that this editor was mistaken about the Court's "Democratic majority." In 1896 only Justices Stephen J. Field and Edward D. White were Democrats.

Most pro-business Republicans had also abandoned the cause of civil rights and after the Spanish–American War in 1898 were increasingly advocating "white power." Following the annexation of Hawaii, that war, under President William McKinley, added eight million more "colored subjects" from Cuba, Puerto Rico, and the Philippines to the population of the United States. What had been launched as a struggle against the cruelties of Spanish rule in Cuba, despite a last-minute compromise offered by the Queen of Spain, turned into the extension of American business and political influence. When the "liberated" Filipinos showed little eagerness to accept United States dominion, their insurrectionist leader Emilio Aguinaldo and his guerrillas were pursued and finally captured, after fierce battles, by American troops.

Some leading intellectuals justified the new colonial theory in broadly racist terms; they included John William Burgess, a political scientist at Columbia University; Alfred Thayer Mahan, a historian at the Naval War College; and Albert J. Beveridge, a constitutional scholar who was elected to the U.S. Senate from Indiana. On the opposite side were such public figures as Mark Twain, William Jennings Bryan (twice defeated by McKinley), and Carl Schurz, as well as members of the Anti-Imperialist League. Schurz had fled to America after the failure of the Revolution of 1848 in his native Germany. He befriended Lincoln, rose to the rank of general in the Union army, then became a newspaper editor, was elected to the Senate from Missouri, and later, appointed secretary of the interior, serving from 1877 to 1881.

The *A.M.E. Church Review* framed its critique in moral terms. This Negro church organ saw the Supreme Court intent on denying any Negro rights except "to sit upon juries and to vote" and envisioned that other civil rights would be dismissed "if the prejudices of large numbers of the white race are thwarted." Only Justice Harlan was described as foreseeing "greater evils . . . by validating laws made in hate than can result from standing upon the broad grounds of right and humanity." The writer affirmed the Christian belief that in the sight of God, "all the nations of the earth" are equal, for "in Christ Jesus there is neither Jew nor Greek, bond nor free, Scythian or Barbarian."

Other voices from the African American community were also raised against the *Plessy* decision. The most muted criticism came from Booker T. Washington, whose address to the Cotton States and International Exposition at Atlanta, Georgia, on September 15, 1895, had evoked praise from whites for its program of black self-improvement grounded in manual labor. A year before the *Plessy* decision, Washington had seemed to accept racial separation "in all things that are purely social," like the fingers of a hand, in his metaphor. Yet, two months after the Court had spoken on *Plessy*, he wrote in a Boston journal that the decision might be "good law, but it is not good common sense." He argued that "colored people do not complain so much of the separation . . . as of the fact that the accommodations, with almost no exceptions, are not equal, still the same price is charged. . . ."

Washington made it clear that he was not lodging a complaint "against the white man or the 'Jim Crow Car' law," but that "such an unjust law injures the white man, and inconveniences the negro." In an echo of Justice Harlan's admonishment to whites that by denying full citizenship to Negroes they were undermining the egalitarian basis of the Constitution, Washington argued, on moral grounds, "the injury to the white man" by his unjust actions "is permanent." In a lynching a Negro might suffer "physical death," but the white perpetrator faced "death of the soul."

A more pointed critique was crafted by Charles W. Chesnutt, one of the first important African American writers of fiction. His parents had been "free people of color" in North Carolina who had moved to Ohio but relocated to Fayetteville, North Carolina, after the Civil War. In 1887, Chesnutt moved to Cleveland to study law, was admitted to the bar, and then became a writer of published stories, novels, and a biography of Frederick Douglass. He became a friend and editorial associate of Albion Tourgée, and in an undated speech (ca. 1911) in the archive of Fisk University, he discusses "The Courts and the Negro." He finds the *Plessy* opinion "as epoch-making as the *Dred Scott* decision." He recoils especially at Justice Brown's dismissal of segregation as stamping Negroes "with a badge of inferiority . . . solely because the colored race chooses to put that construction upon it." Chesnutt comments, "I have never been able to see how a self-respecting colored man can approve of any discriminating legislation. To do so is to condone his own degradation. . . . If discrimination must of necessity be submitted to, it should meet no better reception than silence. Protests were better still." The ruling, he says, extends segregation in the South "as completely . . . as the business of daily life will permit."

It seems remarkable that among the varied commentators on the *Plessy* decision, not a single one focused on the effect it had on the plaintiff, Homer Plessy, and his black Creole community. Plessy, whose suit had stopped his original criminal trial in its tracks, now had to appear once more before Judge John H. Ferguson in New Orleans's state criminal court. On January 11, 1897, nearly five years after his arrest for sitting in a first-class carriage for "whites only," Plessy pleaded guilty to violating Louisiana's 1890 railway segregation law; under the law's terms, he could pay the fine of twenty-five dollars or go to jail. He chose to pay the fine. The defense committee that had supported his legal challenge to the statute had spent over $2,700 dollars on court costs. The remaining $160 in its treasury was distributed to local charities. There were six dollars left to send as a testimonial to Albion Tourgée, who had worked so long without pay. Plessy chose to return to his work as a shoemaker and appears to have led a relatively happy, long life with his family before he was buried in the Catholic cemetery of St. Louis on Basin Street in New Orleans. His memorial is shared with others, in one of the layered graves above ground that are customary in this city, which floats above the Mississippi River.

There are no special words on Plessy's tombstone to honor him and no landmarks named for him, though his moment of courage has earned him a place in history. His example of committing civil disobedience to what he considered an unjust law served to inspire protestors sixty years later at the dawn of the civil rights era. On December 1, 1955, Rosa Parks, another seemingly ordinary person, refused to be moved by force, thereby setting off another major legal confrontation. Plessy cast a shadow into the next century.

As for Plessy's community, after the formerly "free people of color" found themselves crowded in with the multitude of freed slaves in fenced-off enclosures, it lost its vitality. The once-tolerant social world of New Orleans soon ejected Negroes not only from trains but also from schools and public accommodations. The state law's formula of "equal but separate" had been reshuffled by the Supreme Court into "separate but equal." Charles S. Johnson has shown that neither phrase represents reality. In transportation most trains would not admit black passengers to Pullman sleeping cars, dining cars, or club cars. When baggage and mail cars were added behind the locomotive, a Jim Crow car invariably followed (or was de facto half of the baggage car). Its dingy interior, lack of heat or carpeting, and filthy toilet were a far cry from the quality coaches designated for whites. Nor was there complete racial separation, since whites who smoked or drank, as well as shackled prisoners accompanied by guards, were routinely found in the Jim Crow car. Ray Stannard Baker relates that during the early 1900s, "No other point of race contact is so much and so bitterly discussed among the Negroes as the Jim Crow Car." In 1944 Swedish sociologist Gunnar Myrdal found that the Jim Crow car was still "resented more bitterly among Negroes than most other forms of segregation."

As if the Jim Crow car wasn't demoralizing enough, there were the train stations Johnson describes after four decades of segregation, with separate entrances and waiting rooms for Negroes and small, dirty toilets when there were any at all. By the 1940s second-rate quarters also awaited intercity bus travelers, who were often seated in the back of the vehicle—if there was room after whites had occupied the front seats. Negroes could expect to wait outside, while whites were admitted into waiting rooms, often with segregated lunch counters. The enforcement of these laws varied somewhat from state to state and town to town. In Birmingham, for example, streetcars had partitions clamped on the back of the seats to indicate the race of passengers for whom they were reserved. In New Orleans, steamboats and trains had "whites only" sections, as did, eventually, the front seats of streetcars.

In Houston and Atlanta, some white taxi drivers refused to take black passengers. When plane travel became common, a few airlines tried to exclude or segregate black passengers; later, integrated seating became generally accepted, although airport lounges remained segregated. The system was a crazy quilt, and it was suffused with an arbitrary set of rules—state laws and local ordinances—clearly intended to make Negroes feel like pariahs. To escape the trauma of such demeaning travel, they scraped money together to buy automobiles, in which they could maintain their dignity. Thus cars came to occupy a central role in African American culture.

What had been quite a liberal society in Louisiana during Reconstruction, by the turn of the century accepted the segregation system of the Deep South. In 1868 the state had adopted a constitution that no longer required racial separation of public school children; in 1870 it had repealed the law that prohibited racial intermarriage. But by 1894, in Louisiana white and black "concubinage" had become a crime again, and the state's 1898 constitution, like those of sixteen other states, segregated public schools. Louisiana's state colleges for Negroes offered graduate-level education that was clearly substandard. In one scholar's words, "Integrated schools, whites felt, would humiliate them because such schools represented an admission of the Negro's equality. . . . Segregated schools were a recognition of the superiority of the white race."

In 1890 there had been seventeen Negro legislators who protested Louisiana's passage of the railway segregation law. Even in 1896 there were still 130,334 registered Negro voters in the state. Then, in 1898 the new constitution offered permanent voter registration by September 1 to men, under a so-called grandfather clause, if they had been entitled to vote in any state on January 1, 1867, or if they were the son or grandson of such a person and at least twenty-one years old. This law permitted whites to register without having to demonstrate educational and property qualifications or pay a poll tax. By 1904 the number of Negroes registered to vote had dropped 90 percent, to 1,342. Black voters, who in 1896 had constituted a majority of those registered in twenty-six of Louisiana's parishes, were in the minority everywhere by 1900. As a result, African Americans no longer had the votes to elect local, state, or national representatives to speak for their interests.

The black Creoles of Louisiana tried to salvage their self-respect by moving to more tolerant societies in Southern California, Mexico, or the Caribbean. A number of the octoroon types were able to pass easily as whites. Some of the rest remained, though not a sufficient number to maintain their unique culture. In New Orleans for a time, Creoles clustered in the downtown area "below Canal Street," separated from so-called uptown blacks by neighborhood as well as by cultural and religious allegiances. By the mid–twentieth century, highway construction crowded out many of the Creole residents in the Seventh Ward around Claiborne Avenue. They drifted to more outlying areas on the eastern side of the city. The pressure to go north or west, out of the Deep South, was social, political, physical, and economic.

Negroes were regularly embarrassed in daily encounters throughout the South at that time, while traveling, shopping in stores, trying to find restaurants that would serve them or churches that welcomed them, and visiting parks, theaters, and other places of amusement. They found discrimination at their place of work, while looking for schools and universities to attend or send their children to, and in professions they wanted to enter;

they were also barred from housing in districts under "restrictive covenants." After an initial phase of acceptance by Populists in the 1890s, they had been shut out of the political system; they faced barriers when trying to register to vote; they were excluded for decades from running in "white primaries" by Democratic party bosses who ran their party like a private club. It took until 1964, and the adoption of the Twenty-fourth Amendment, to ban the poll tax.

The wave of lynchings referred to earlier—mob killings—that had claimed over a hundred victims a year by the 1870s reached a high of 235 annually in 1892. In September 1895 the *Daily Picayune* in New Orleans treated a Mississippi lynching almost as a joke, then headlined one in Memphis, Tennessee, "Justice Was Done." Soon afterward the same paper reported the lynching of a Negro in Shreveport for "attempted rape," and another in Hammond, Louisiana, for robbery, commenting that the community felt "that summary justice is necessary as a lesson and warning." Several other lynchings in the state were described later that year in the *Picayune* in gruesome detail, though few of the victims were rumored to have committed rape. Lynchings were not limited to the South. In 1908, soon after W. E. B. Du Bois had held a meeting of his two-year-old Niagara Movement in Springfield, Illinois, the home of Abraham Lincoln, a race riot erupted. It took five thousand militiamen to put it down. Two Negroes were lynched, seventy others were injured, and two thousand blacks had to flee the city. An article about the violence by an outraged southern writer, William English Walling, influenced Mary White Ovington to help organize the 1909 meeting in New York that gave birth to the NAACP.

Up to that time, the only organization to raise an alarm was the Anti-Lynching League, formed by Ida B. Wells, an African American teacher, writer, and speaker from Mississippi, who conducted a personal crusade in the 1890s to expose the falsehoods behind these racist murders. Fleeing from Memphis after her newspaper office was burned down, Wells was cheered at appearances in England, but congressmen turned a deaf ear to her calls for an anti-lynching law.

It was noted in chapter 2 that the Ku Klux Klan and similar white racist groups, such as the Knights of the White Camellia in Louisiana, sprang up across the South in the 1860s and 1870s primarily to frighten Negroes from asserting political power and to intimidate their "carpetbagger" and "scalawag" allies. The outlandish masks and sheets of the KKK were originally meant to symbolize the spirits of the Confederate dead, but soon they served as the disguise of secretive murderers. At a meeting in Nashville, Tennessee, in 1867, former Confederate cavalry general Nathan Bedford Forrest assumed the title of "Imperial Wizard"; he saw himself as the head of an informal force organized to keep order during lawless times. However, within two years Forrest realized that he lacked the power to discipline individual "Klaverns" (Klan chapters) of self-appointed vigilantes. He resigned, but the Klansmen, resentful poor whites and angry plantation owners who had lost millions of dollars of their slave "property," continued their rampages.

Congress passed a "Force Act" in 1870 and a "Ku Klux Klan Act" in 1871 (also known as Enforcement Acts or "Force Bills"), but despite hundreds of indictments there were very few convictions. When the last Union troops left the South in 1877, Negroes were defenseless. They developed a response of public submissiveness to ensure their survival, and few dared to antagonize the Klan by trying to register as voters. In the wake of *Plessy*, when segregation became the rule, there was little need for the Klan, and it began to fade away; violence against Negroes, however, continued to be endemic.

In its second incarnation, the Klan was revived on the eve of America's entry into World War I as a national group no longer limited to the South, with an initial rally in 1915 at Stone Mountain, Georgia, led by William J. Simmons, a former minister. The Klan now assumed the ideological trappings of the mid–nineteenth-century Know-Nothing party, denouncing Catholics and Jews as well as Negroes. It exploited the militant patriotism of a nation at war and preached a fundamentalist brand of Protestantism. It suppressed attempts by Negro veterans of World War I to claim equal rights as their due when they returned home. By the 1920s the Klan was able to mount a march of ten thousand in Washington, D.C., and it played a major role in the 1922, 1924, and 1926 elections on the local, state, and congressional levels. It controlled state governments not only in the South but also in northern states such as Indiana and Oregon, and had considerable influence in New York, New Jersey, Maine, and Pennsylvania. Affiliates of the Klan succeeded in indicting and convicting the mayor of Indianapolis and the governor of Indiana.

Racist violence abated during and after the 1930s Depression but still claimed fourteen-year-old Emmett Till as a murder victim in August 1955 for allegedly whistling at a white woman. He was forcibly taken from his uncle's house, severely beaten, then shot, and his body thrown into the Tallahatchie River. Though a Mississippi jury found two white men accused of the killing not guilty, the men later confessed to a magazine interviewer.

There was a full-fledged KKK resurgence in the 1960s to counter students demonstrating for access to schools, to attack "freedom riders" trying to integrate bus travel, and to repress black voter drives in the South. A Klan-related conspiracy was found responsible for the 1964 murder of three civil rights workers—James Chaney, Andrew Goodman and Michael

Schwerner—in rural Mississippi, but only after an indictment in federal court using the 1870 Act.

Benjamin R. Tillman, a South Carolina governor whose racist campaign won him a seat in the U.S. Senate in 1895, said "to hell with the Constitution" if it interfered with the lynching of rapists. "Pitchfork Ben," as Tillman had been called for his truculence, combined his populism with race baiting. But only a sixth of lynch victims were ever accused of rape, and the truth about these and other assorted rumors that inflamed lynch mobs will never be known. In addition to the officially recorded (low) number of lynching victims between 1882 and 1964—4,700, according to Tuskegee University studies—a pervasive fear affected African Americans throughout the South that any minor slight might lead to retribution by white night riders who would be protected by a code of silence.

The lives of southern Negroes were also cut short by the segregation of most white hospitals, which excluded Negroes except perhaps for first aid in emergency cases such as auto accidents. In the 1930s one black woman was diagnosed with appendicitis in a Birmingham clinic but denied treatment. She told an interviewer that the nurse "talked to me worse than she would have if I had been a dog. I walked out." Prompt, courteous medical care of black patients by white doctors and nurses was far from the norm. In Dalton, Georgia, Juliette Derricotte, an internationally known educator, was refused emergency care after a serious automobile accident, and died. These cases were typical of the inferior care available to black patients throughout the South.

Since Negroes who remained farmers had been forced into a system of sharecropping, the bulk of their crops was claimed by their white landlords. Their advance "loans" for seeds and tools, as well as food and supplies from the company store, left them with annual debts generally exceeding their meager profits.

Others who farmed rented land—so-called tenant farmers—were rarely able to acquire ownership of their small plots. Exploited economically; denied decent education and housing; treated as an inferior caste in stores, churches, courtrooms, and public accommodations; blocked from voting and serving in public office— Negroes asked themselves, why stay in the South? The indignity of Jim Crow cars may not have been the main impetus to migrating north, but the segregated facilities in the wake of *Plessy*, reinforcing a sense of lost dignity and an inability to advance, must have made it easier for many Negroes to decide to leave their old homes in the South.

The first pioneers who left for Detroit, Chicago, New York, and other northern cities wrote back to their relatives that a better life awaited them. Although they found discrimination in the North as well—in schools and housing and in the workplace— at least there blacks were able to vote and to be heard in the halls of justice. They began to be elected to public office in Chicago, Detroit, Cleveland, Philadelphia, and New York City, and even once more to take seats in Congress. More than a million Negroes joined the "Great Migration" north between 1910 and 1930. At both ends of the trek, there were profound cultural effects.

The migrants came from the isolated "black belt" communities and were now exposed to urbanization, first in southern towns and cities, then in enclaves in the North. The demographic changes were profound: from 1890 to 1930 the rural black population increased only 12 percent, while its urban component increased 251 percent. In just one decade, 1910–1920, the Negro population increase was 50 percent in New York, 67 percent in Ohio and Illinois, and 251 percent in Michigan, where black workers flocked to the Detroit auto plants. The old caste system was left behind by migrants, who could now attend integrated public meetings and amusements, schools, and workplaces. After achieving higher levels of literacy, urban residents could better express their common problems and lobby for improvements. In New York during the 1920s, Negro writers contributed to the flowering of poetry and novels in a cultural movement known as the Harlem Renaissance, which expressed black pride in art, music, and literature.

Of course, black southern migrants were not received with tolerance by the white residents of every northern city. In 1917 there was a race riot in East St. Louis, Illinois, that resulted in the deaths of thirty-nine blacks and eight whites. In 1919 another riot began in Chicago when a Negro boy crossed an imaginary racial line in the water at a Lake Michigan beach and was stoned until he drowned. The subsequent three weeks of violence claimed the lives of twenty Negroes and sixteen whites, with additional hundreds injured. Another riot erupted in Washington, D.C.

In 1943, in the midst of World War II, a race riot cost the lives of thirty-one men and women in Detroit. One report said that whites blamed blacks for starting the attack on some white men, but a more correct version was that the police, most of them transplanted southerners, were responsible for shooting the majority of the victims. Twenty-five Negroes were killed, all those arrested were black, and it was Negro property that had been burned.

The difference between such riots and a lynching, however, was that Negroes in the North offered direct, collective resistance when attacked. Increasingly, the riots also mixed racial with economic issues—for example, the food riots in 1933 in Harlem. In Detroit there was frustration by Negro workers who encountered business and trade-union hostility when they competed for skilled jobs.

With the advent of World War II, however, the government

began to recruit black as well as white workers for defense industries, although the armed forces continued to practice segregation. There were separate Negro units in the army, generally with white officers, while the navy kept Negro recruits to "mess duties," and the marines accepted no blacks at all.

During the migration of southern Negroes, northern and border-state cities often passed ordinances that established racial segregation either by district, or block by block. Louisville, Kentucky, framed its 1914 ordinance in the language of *Plessy*, making it an equal crime for blacks and whites to occupy a building in a block that had a majority of residents of the other race.

In order to test this law in a prearranged civil case, Robert Buchanan, a white man, sold a lot in his predominantly white area to William Warley, a Negro; the sale was contingent on Warley's being able to build a house on the lot, which would violate the ordinance. Buchanan and Warley prearranged the scenario that would lead to a civil court case: Warley applied for a permit to build on Buchanan's property, and as they had anticipated, his application was rejected by the City of Louisville because it violated the 1914 ordinance. Because Warley could not build on the lot, he was not obligated to pay for the property; but to challenge the ordinance, Buchanan sued him for payment in civil court.

Both at the local trial and on appeal to the state supreme court, Buchanan was told that the segregation ordinance was constitutional under the state's police power. The sale agreement was therefore void. If Negroes had to reside in less attractive sections of the city, the state justices said, nothing stopped residents from beautifying them; wealthier Negroes who were also shut out of areas reserved for whites ought to help "their less fortunate fellows . . . and thus, in the end, it [the law] will justify that enlightened civic spirit by which it is demanded."

In 1917, with the NAACP defending Buchanan's challenge to the law and enforcement of his sales contract, the case reached the Supreme Court, which unanimously found the ordinance unconstitutional under the Fourteenth Amendment. Justice William R. Day's opinion stated: "Colored persons are citizens of the United States and have the right to purchase property and enjoy the use of the same without laws discriminating against them solely on account of color." Despite the existence of racial hostility among neighbors, said Justice Day, its "solution cannot be promoted by depriving citizens of their constitutional rights and privileges." The decision was an early victory for the NAACP.

Noble as Justice Day's sentiments were, white property owners found a loophole: the use of so-called restrictive covenants in property deeds, whereby purchasers bound themselves not to sell to Negroes, Orientals, or Jews. These supposedly private agreements maintained residential segregation for another three decades. Challenges to such agreements were rejected by state appeal courts: in Missouri by extending the *Plessy* precedent from railway travel in 1917, and in Michigan by adapting some of the *Plessy* language, that "the law is powerless to eradicate racial instincts or to abolish distinctions which some citizens draw on account of racial differences in relation to matters of purely private concern." In an initial Supreme Court review of such restrictions in the District of Columbia in 1926, all the justices joined in a narrow reading of the Fourteenth Amendment as limited to state action. Justice Edward T. Sanford denied that such contracts between private individuals amounted to government action that deprived persons of liberty or property without due process of law.

Where such discreet means were not effective in keeping Negroes walled off in ghettoes, racist whites often took the law into their own hands, while the police in northern cities generally looked the other way. In Chicago, around 1917, white residents began organizing to keep Negroes from renting or buying property in the "white" parts of the city. During the next four years, white racists set off fifty-eight bombs, averaging "one race bombing every twenty days for three years and eight months," according to the Chicago Commission on Race Relations. Two Negroes were killed in the explosions and many other people were injured, including white realtors who had sold or rented property to Negroes in white residential areas. Only two suspects were ever arrested by the police; one was released after two days, and the other was freed on bond for a year without a trial date.

One of the most insidious ways the *Plessy* ruling was used to subvert the future progress of Negroes was the decision's explicit connection to "separate but equal" schools. By the early twentieth century, there were seventeen southern and border states with segregated educational systems. From the time the first slaves were brought to America in 1619 until slavery was abolished in 1865 by the Thirteenth Amendment, slave owners—to bolster their own myth of racial superiority—had forbidden their slaves to educate themselves, even through reading the Bible, on pain of corporal punishment. The few who did learn to read and write had to do so in secret. After Emancipation, freed slaves flocked to the schools opened by volunteer women who went south during Reconstruction with the Freedmen's Bureau. As has been noted, Negro children had attended integrated schools in New Orleans in accord with a court order in 1870, at a time when most white parents, to save money, had taken their children out of white private schools and sent them to public ones. After barely a decade of remarkably peaceful integration, however, white extremists forcibly expelled black children from public schools in Louisiana, and segregation in schools soon became the law across the South.

Schools for black children were ostensibly "separate but equal," though in most rural areas their conditions were particularly abysmal. Pupils of several grades were often crowded into one room, and they were perennially short of textbooks and other equipment. Their teachers were paid substantially less than white teachers, and very little in state funds was spent on school buses for black pupils. During agricultural seasons when the need for labor was high,  no effort was made to enforce truancy rules for black children working on the farm. Only a small percentage of such children were able to attend segregated colleges, where standards were lower than in white state universities.

Attempts by a few idealists to swim against this tide were rudely quashed, as is shown by the example of Berea College, a private Christian school founded by the American Missionary Association in 1854 in the Kentucky mountains, which began admitting students without regard to race after the Civil War. By 1904 Berea had 735 white and 174 Negro students when, despite the school's best efforts to follow its religious mission without state aid, the administrators found themselves running afoul of a new state law specifically designed to put an end to interracial education. The law prohibited teaching Negro and white students at "any school, college or institution" unless it taught students "of one race or color" at a "separate and distinct branch" at least twenty-five miles away. Berea College was, accordingly, found in violation of this law and assessed the one-thousand-dollar fine.

The Kentucky Supreme Court ruled against Berea on appeal, though it found the distance required for a separate racial branch "unreasonable." But the crux of the law was sustained, because it aimed at the "preservation and purity of the races," which the court was sure had been intended by God. The court also said that interracial associations would lead "to the main evil, which is amalgamation," followed in short order by "illicit intercourse" and then "intermarriage." In addition, the court told Berea that

"Its right to teach is as the state sees fit to give it," so that Kentucky had the right, unilaterally, to change the college's charter from merely teaching "all youth of good moral character" to never having black and white students in the same classroom.

When the case was heard by the Supreme Court in 1908, Justice David J. Brewer (who had also ruled against Homer Plessy) went the last mile in the cause of states' rights. He sidestepped the main issue of the case—the rights of black students who had been barred from the main campus of Berea College—to focus entirely on Kentucky's power to radically change the school's charter. It did not seem to Brewer (and six other justices) that the charter was substantially impaired by the state's requirement that the school separate students, either by time or space. That was an inherent right of states over corporations, he said, avoiding the question of whether it was also a right regarding individuals such as Berea's teachers and students. Kentucky's attorneys had made it clear in their brief to the Supreme Court that outright racism was at the heart of their case, saying, "If the progress, advancement and civilization of the twentieth century is to go forward, then it must be left, not only to the unadulterated blood of the Anglo-Saxon-Caucasian race, but to the highest types and geniuses of that race."

Justice John Marshall Harlan, joined by Justice William R. Day, wrote an angry dissent. He asked the other justices, "Have we become so inoculated with prejudice of race that an American government, professedly based on the principles of freedom, and charged with the protection of all citizens alike, can make distinctions between such citizens in the matter of their voluntary meeting for innocent purposes simply because of their respective races?" He called the Kentucky statute "cruel and inconsistent with the great principle of the equality of citizens before the law."

Further, Harlan cut through the logic of Brewer's approval of state regulation of corporations while leaving open the legitimacy of controlling individuals, by asserting that the state legislature clearly sought to limit both when it banned "the teaching of the two races together." Also, contrary to the state's claim that it had sought to prevent forcible racial mixing, Harlan spelled out the free nature of the students' choice. He said that when pupils "of whatever race" choose "with the consent of their parents or voluntarily to sit together in a private institution of learning, no government, whether Federal or state, can legally forbid their coming together for such an innocent purpose." He also saw God as not behind racial separation, since "instruction to others" was a divine gift for "beneficent purposes and may not be interfered with by Government, certainly not when not harming" public morals or safety. Education, he concluded, was not a social but a civil right that enjoyed constitutional protection. If private schools could be segregated, why not Sunday schools or even sitting together in the "same Christian church"? Harlan had no doubt that even in the absence of corporate boards, voluntary groups or persons would not be allowed by Kentucky to teach white and black pupils together. Indeed, this soon became the law in Kentucky, as well as in Georgia, Oklahoma, and other southern states.

Harlan's fellow justices and other legal scholars treated him with little respect during his nearly thirty-four years on the Court; they taunted him, calling his disagreements a case of "dissent-ary." Oliver Wendell Holmes, himself known for forceful dissents in free-speech cases, derided Harlan, saying, "He had a powerful vise, the jaws of which couldn't be got nearer than two inches to each other." In the *Berea College* case, however, Holmes disagreed with Brewer's reasoning but concurred in the result, leaving states free to forbid interracial associations even on blatantly racist grounds.

While Holmes supported the theory that the Fourteenth Amendment "incorporated" the Bill of Rights as applicable to the states, he took a very limited view of civil rights, approving of southern restrictions on Negro voting rights as well as laws against the right of tenant farmers to break their contracts. His Boston Brahmin outlook also biased Holmes in favor of social Darwinist doctrines; in 1927 an opinion he wrote upholding a Virginia law for the sterilization of "mental defectives" contained the snide phrase "Three generations of imbeciles are enough."

Despite Justice Holmes's disdain for Harlan's intellect, Justice Henry Billings Brown, the author of the majority opinion in *Plessy*, paid Harlan a significant posthumous tribute. In 1912, a year after Harlan's death, Brown conceded in a law review article that Harlan may have been right after all in his broad interpretation of the Thirteenth and Fourteenth Amendments. "There is still a lingering doubt," wrote Brown, "whether the spirit of the amendments was not sacrificed to the letter, and whether the Constitution was not intended to secure the equality of the two races in all places affected with a public interest. It is somewhat remarkable that the only dissent emanated from the only Southern member of the Bench." Further, Brown admitted that by hindsight Harlan "had assumed what is probably the fact, that the [Louisiana] statute had its origin in the purpose, not so much to exclude white persons from railroad cars occupied by blacks, as to exclude colored people from coaches occupied or assigned to white persons."

It would take another half-century for Harlan's broadly based view of civil rights to be accepted by the Supreme Court. In that interim, progress at what seemed like a snail's pace was being made in individual cases that had been brought, with the help of NAACP lawyers, to show that the supposedly equal accommodations of a segregated society were far from exhibiting the equality they claimed in the statute books.

# Chapter 10

# THE WALLS BEGIN TO CRUMBLE

The first half of the twentieth century was not a propitious time for civil rights—in the courts, in Congress, or in the White House. In the South, the Jim Crow system continued to demean African Americans, while their basic political rights—voting and jury service—were denied to them, either blatantly or through subterfuges. Northern patterns varied, ranging from fairly open access to public accommodations to informal exclusion, but at least the growing black population could freely register to vote and attend public schools. Nevertheless, informal segregation kept black students out of the best high schools and colleges, which kept them out of the occupations and corporate positions a good education led to. In Congress, southerners who were elected from "solid" Democratic districts and states accumulated the seniority and committee chairmanships that gave them the power to block reforms, such as anti-lynching bills. Congressional Republicans gave occasional lip service to civil rights in order to satisfy their Negro supporters, but rarely put their words into action.

African Americans did not find much support from the occupants of the White House either. When President Theodore Roosevelt invited Booker T. Washington to dinner on October 18, 1901, there was a storm of protest, mainly from the South, even though Roosevelt previously supported white supremacist Republicans and even Democrats. When he toured the South in 1905, most Negro leaders, including W. E. B. Du Bois (but not Booker T. Washington), condemned the president for his failure to criticize Negro disenfranchisement. After an August 1906 riot in Brownsville, Texas, for which the Negro Twenty-fifth Regiment was officially blamed (in spite of the soldiers' gallant fighting in Cuba during the Spanish-American War), Roosevelt dispatched an inspector to Texas. Relying solely on the inspector's report, the president, hoping to win favor in the South, peremptorily ordered the men of three companies of the Negro Twenty-fifth to be dishonorably discharged.

The 1908 Republican platform's grandiloquent words endorsed "equal justice for all men, without regard to race or color," but William Howard Taft, on a presidential campaign tour in 1909, assured southerners that he saw no constitutional problem in having Negroes kept from voting. In 1912 Woodrow Wilson became the first Democrat since Cleveland and the first southerner since the Civil War to be elected president. On the eve of the election, Wilson had assured Negro leaders that he would promote "the interests of their race in the United States," which earned him the support of Du Bois, but he soon reneged on this promise. Wilson extended Taft's orders segregating Negro employees in most government departments, even though Congress balked at enacting a bill to adopt this as official policy. Wilson declared that World War I would make the world safe for democracy, but Negro candidates were trained to be officers in separate army camps, troops were segregated, and most Negroes were not permitted to join combat units.

Southern congressmen had been working during this period to

legislate discrimination against Negro government employees. Representative James B. Madden of Louisiana had proclaimed in 1914 that the United States was "a white man's country," that a Negro was congenitally "a misfit when in authority even over his own race," therefore, it would be "unjust" to have him occupy a position over a Caucasian. Representative Martin B. Madden, a Republican of Illinois, however, fought hard against such discriminatory bills. In 1914 and 1916 an able witness against such bills was Archibald H. Grimké, the first black graduate of Harvard Law School. Like his brother, Francis, a pastor of the Fifteenth Street Presbyterian Church in Washington, Archibald had been born of a mixed-race mother who had been a slave, and a white father who had owned the children and their mother but freed them.

In March 1914 Archibald Grimké had tangled with Representative Martin Dies of Texas (later to be notorious for his investigations of "un-American Communist activities") at a hearing of the House Committee on Reform in the Civil Service. Grimké had led off by declaring that "you cannot separate the colored people in the government service without humiliating them." Then he rejected Dies's contention that "one of the races must be the ruling race. Both cannot rule, and the Negro race as rulers is unthinkable." Dies then responded, "We have solved the question in the South and white supremacy is a fixture." Grimké stood his ground, telling the Congressmen, "In fifty years everything is going to be changed." He added that through their taxes "the colored people of the South support their own schools and much more besides." He concluded by saying that Negroes in the civil service objected to these bills, without exception.

Another typical legislative battle in 1914 pitted southern Democrats against an amendment to an agricultural extension funding act by Republican Senator Wesley L. Jones of Washington to equalize moneys going to white and black land-grant colleges and agricultural experiment stations. The attack was led by James K. Vardaman of Mississippi, a notorious segregationist, who began by professing his "love" for Negroes and for his "old black mammy." Senator Vardaman then commented that the Negro "does not vote much in Mississippi but I really think he votes more than he ought to vote, if he votes at all. I do not think that it was ever intended by the creator that the two races should live together upon equal terms." Jones's bill was defeated, with all but two Democrats voting against it.

In this era it was only sporadically that the Supreme Court responded to the pleas of Negro plaintiffs, especially after John Marshall Harlan's death in 1911. But more and more, after a 1914 challenge to the states' "grandfather clauses" and literacy tests, lawyers from the fledgling NAACP made their presence felt in courtrooms. Before looking at their initially minor victories, it is appropriate to consider the historically significant role played by Harlan, a man who received little honor in his own time.

Until recently, the tendency for biographers of Justice Harlan has been to cast him in the role of a prophet when it came to race relations, a jurist whose solitary voice in dissent would eventually become accepted by a majority of the Supreme Court. The work of Linda Przybyszewski cuts through such romantic retrospection. She demystifies Harlan as indeed a remarkable man when it came to outgrowing his early southern prejudices, yet one who still shared the attitudes of his southern contemporaries who believed in maintaining social distance between blacks and whites.

Harlan could hold seemingly contradictory beliefs; for example, he believed that the civil rights of Negroes granted in the Fourteenth Amendment should be expanded to cover the full scope of public accommodations, yet he accepted segregation in public schools as well as state laws against racial intermarriage. Even in his stirring *Plessy* dissent Harlan refers to the "dominant" racial position of whites, though he predicates this status in the future on their completely fair treatment of blacks. He saw himself as exercising a paternalistic role toward his family's slaves, and his wife even romanticizes the justice's black "court messenger," James Jackson, as someone who shared the couple's joys and griefs like a member of the family. Inconsistent as Harlan may have been in his beliefs, however, he was moved, perhaps by his deep Christian faith, to expound on the obligation of whites to be caring and compassionate toward blacks.

In the *Berea College* case Harlan denounced the racism of the Kentucky legislature as "cruel and inconsistent with the great principle of the equality of citizens before the law." He even invoked God, whose injunction to humans to teach each other was, he contended, beyond the state's power of contravention. But he shied away from extending the right of black and white students to learn together in public schools, concluding with: "Of course what I have said here has no reference to regulations prescribed for public schools, established at the pleasure of the State and maintained at public expense."

Przybyszewski attributes Harlan's reluctance to include public schools in the sphere of constitutionally protected racial integration to an awareness that white churchmen had questioned whether Berea's tolerant policy might not lead to racial intermarriage or, as it was called at the time, "miscegenation." Indeed, in 1882 Harlan had joined in a unanimous Supreme Court decision that let stand an Alabama law punishing adultery by a mixed-race couple more harshly than by a same-race couple. At Berea, Harlan recognized that the college administrators controlled the dating rules of their students, but younger schoolchildren would not be under such close supervision. Alternatively, Harlan's restraint could be attributed to the fact that he had studied the record of the adoption of the Fourteenth Amendment, which showed that the framers had not expressed their intent clearly on its application to public schools. The same lack of historical guidance would confront the Court when it returned to the issue in 1954.

It has been even more difficult to explain Harlan's decision for a unanimous Court in the 1899 case of *Cummings v. Richmond County Board of Education*, three years after *Plessy*. A Georgia county had closed a Negro high school, diverting the money to Negro elementary schools, but kept a white high school open. The attorney for the black parents had argued that racial segregation was "the vice in the common school system of Georgia," but his formal brief addressed the narrower question, whether the white high school should be closed as well until an equivalent facility was available for Negroes. The Court ruled against granting an injunction against the white high school, since it involved educational decisions that should be left to the states. It found no "clear and unmistakable disregard of rights secured by the supreme law of the land," which might have justified federal intervention. Harlan dodged the larger issue of segregated education, saying, "We need not consider that question in this case. No such issue was made in the pleadings." The Court's rule that it could not address a constitutional question unless it had been raised in the original record gave him a way to avoid confronting the inherent injustice of school segregation. The legal establishment acted as if the Court had confirmed segregation in public schools and referred to the *Plessy*, *Berea*, and *Cummings* decisions, even though none of them had squarely faced that issue.

In the post-Harlan Court the NAACP faced generally unsympathetic justices, who, at most, endorsed the form of equality but not the substance. That is evident in the case of *Guinn v. United States*, which was argued with two companion cases in 1913, all dealing with "grandfather clauses" that southern states used to restrict Negro voting by making it contingent on literacy or property qualifications that were waived for persons (and their sons or grandsons) eligible to vote on a certain date when only whites could register. There was no such clause in the constitution of Oklahoma when it was admitted to statehood in 1908, but an amendment in 1910 added the requirement that the prospective voter had to be able to read and write any section of the state constitution, with the proviso that the condition did not apply to those who were citizens on January 1, 1866 (i.e., before ratification of the Fifteenth Amendment giving Negroes the vote). The Republican U.S. District Attorney John Emory brought criminal charges against state election judges Guinn and Beal for denying the vote to a Negro who did not qualify under the clause, because the Republicans' chances depended on the black vote. The two judges were indicted under the 1870 Ku Klux Klan Act and convicted of conspiracy for denying a citizen the "free exercise of any right or privilege secured to him by the Constitution or laws of the United States." The Oklahoma Democratic party provided lawyers for the judges.

At the Supreme Court's hearings, Moorfield Storey, a Boston attorney who had been Charles Sumner's secretary, represented the NAACP as a friend of the court, to argue that the Oklahoma clause was unconstitutional. The NAACP side also had the support of the Justice Department, since President William Howard Taft realized that he needed the votes of Negro delegates to secure the party's nomination for a second term. Chief Justice Edward D. White, the Louisianan who was an associate justice during the *Plessy* case, wrote an opinion for a unanimous Court finding the grandfather clause an invalid breach of the Fifteenth Amendment. Except as a symbolic victory, this decision had little impact, since the former states of the Confederacy had allowed the dates of their grandfather clauses to lapse. They would now discriminate against Negro voters by less blatant administrative means that would escape judicial scrutiny for a long time.

One of these means was for southern states to prohibit Negroes from voting in primary elections. In the post-1896 South, the only election that counted was the Democratic party primary. Therefore, when Negroes registered to vote as Democrats, Texas enacted a law in 1923 that baldly declared: "In no event shall a negro be eligible to participate in a Democratic party primary election in the State of Texas." Lawyers from the NAACP backed the suit of Dr. L. A. Nixon of El Paso to challenge this law on the basis of the Fourteenth and Fifteenth Amendments. The latter would appear to be the obvious grounds for rejecting the law, since it prohibits discrimination in "the right of citizens of the United States to vote." However, enigmatically, Justice Oliver Wendell Holmes, for a unanimous Court in 1927, found it sufficient to rest overturning the Texas law on the Fourteenth Amendment, because its equal protection clause prevented racial classification by law. By not simply using the Fifteenth Amendment, Holmes avoided ruling on the more basic issue—whether Negroes could be prevented by state action from voting in a general election.

The Democratic party of Texas had not been involved in the 1927 suit, so it felt free to use a loophole in the decision. The Texas legislature had passed a law later in 1927, stating that "every political party in the State through its State Executive Committee shall have power to prescribe the qualifications of its own members and shall in its own way determine who shall be qualified to vote. . . ." Accordingly, members of the party executive committee limited the right to vote in primary elections to "all white Democrats who are qualified under the constitution and laws of Texas."

Dr. Nixon's lawyers returned to court. This time, in 1932, the Supreme Court justices divided 5 to 4, with Justice Benjamin N. Cardozo's majority opinion narrowly holding that the proper decision-making body of the Democratic party was the state convention, which had not delegated its authority to the executive committee. Hence, it was the state's action that had caused Dr. Nixon's disenfranchisement. Cardozo followed the earlier Holmes opinion: exclusion from the primary election violated the equal protection clause of the Fourteenth Amendment.

The four dissenters joined the opinion of Justice James C. McReynolds, formerly President Wilson's attorney general, who naively viewed the Texas Democratic party as a group of private individuals who were free to exclude anyone they chose. As long as there was no outright state interference, this party, financed by its members, could select candidates freely. A state party was like a private club, the four dissenting justices said, so Texas had not discriminated against Dr. Nixon, who presumably could form his own Negro party if he desired. They totally disregarded the state's close regulation of election procedures as evidence that the primary was a public, not a private, act. In any case, the result of this second case was that Texas repealed all primary election laws, leaving the Democratic party convention free to exclude Negroes. The charade of southern white primaries as privately run affairs was allowed to continue until 1944.

Because jury lists were generally drawn from registered voters, Negroes in the South also found themselves facing biased judges and prosecutors and juries not of their peers. Only when a criminal case was heard in flagrant violation of due process was an occasional appeal heard by the Supreme Court.

One of these rare cases was *Moore v. Dempsey*, which has wider historical interest. It originated in Phillips County, Arkansas, where Negro tenant farmers found themselves hard-pressed by white plantation owners who never gave them an accounting of their outstanding debts. A World War I Negro veteran named Robert L. Hill had begun to organize a Farmers Progressive Household Union, in 1919, in order to improve conditions for tenant farmers. White farmers began circulating rumors that the union's members were assembling weapons for a violent uprising. On September 30 a local deputy sheriff and a railroad policeman began shooting at a Negro church in the village of Hot Spur, where the union was meeting. Several of the Negroes as well as Deputy Charles Pratt were killed that night, which led to seven days of clashes, leaving a total of some two hundred Negroes and five whites dead.

The sheriff had sworn in three hundred white deputies, whose thirst for vengeance was allayed only after the state governor called for five hundred troops to restore order. The governor also ordered an investigation by a local white committee that on October 7 blamed the violence entirely on a "deliberately planned insurrection of the negroes against the whites." The committee staved off a white mob that was threatening reprisals against black farmers only by promising that the Negro ringleaders would be legally charged, convicted, and executed.

Indeed, an all-white grand jury indicted six Negroes on October 29, and they were tried five days later. A white attorney was unable to see his clients, who within minutes were convicted by an all-white trial jury that had not heard a single defense witness, and sentenced to die in the electric chair. More convictions were obtained against dozens of other Negroes on testimony of witnesses who later reported being beaten with chains to make them "confess." Frank Moore, one of the condemned men, applied to a U.S. District Court for a writ of habeas corpus, contending that a lynch mob was ever present to deal with any recalcitrant juror or any defendant who might have been acquitted.

When the judge denied that he had jurisdiction in the case, NAACP lawyers took an appeal to the Supreme Court. In a 6-to-2 decision, Justice Holmes, on February 19, 1923, ordered the district court to hold a habeas corpus hearing and to investigate the facts alleged in Moore's petition. "If in fact a trial is dominated by a mob," said Holmes, "so that there is a departure from due process of law," and "if the state supplying no corrective process carries into execution a judgment of death or imprisonment based upon a verdict thus produced by mob domination, the state deprives the accused of his life or liberty without due process of law." Justices McReynolds and George Sutherland, in their dissent, argued that the judgment of state courts should be respected in criminal trials. They also contended that the Court should not have departed from a 1915 case in which habeas corpus had been denied to a Jewish man who was accused of murder in Atlanta and eventually killed by a lynch mob, despite an eloquent dissent by Holmes and Chief Justice Charles Evans Hughes against "lynch law."

The facts in the Arkansas case were even more outrageous, in that the American Legion post and two civic associations were on record as opposing lenient treatment of the accused Negroes, citing a "solemn promise" made to them by "leading citizens of the community that if the guilty parties were not lynched, and let the law take its course, that justice would be done and the majesty of the law upheld." Further, members of the investigating committee had publicly declared that they had prevented a lynching only on the promise that the accused Negroes would be condemned to death by the courts after the trial. The flimsiness of the prosecution case may also be gauged by the fact that no new trials were ever held, and the accused had sentences commuted or were simply released to leave the area. Still, the *Moore* case served as a small signal that habeas corpus writs could be used in federal courts to challenge state court convictions obtained by violations of constitutional rights.

By 1930 segregation in the South was worse than ever. Although the Klan had been declining since the economic depression had focused interest on more basic survival issues for

blacks and whites, Negroes had to play their stereotyped sub-
missive roles in order not to provoke white hostility. As the last-
hired on industrial or service jobs, they were often the first to be
laid off. The *Plessy* ruling was supposed to be a bow to states'
rights, since interstate commerce had been constitutionally
reserved as the domain of Congress, yet there were few challenges on these grounds. A Kentucky case in 1910 did raise the
issue of the state's requiring travelers from other states to switch
to Jim Crow cars when they crossed the state border, but only
Justice Harlan dissented from the majority opinion supporting
the railroad. In that ruling, Justice Joseph McKenna, son of Irish
immigrants, claimed that accommodations had been equal,
although the facts contradicted that conclusion. Then he justified
segregation of interstate passengers because Congress had not
specifically prohibited it. He concluded: "Regulations which are
induced by the general sentiment of the community for whom
they are made and upon whom they operate, cannot be said to
be unreasonable." This was more of the *Plessy* ruling, that constitutional law had to follow "folkways." From the time of
Harlan's death in 1911 until the 1930s, there was no justice left
to dissent on behalf of civil rights.

Yet change did finally come, as all branches of government
reacted to the economic crisis that led to the election of President
Franklin D. Roosevelt and the enactment of his New Deal. One of
the catalysts of change in civil rights was the NAACP, which had
made merely token appearances in courtrooms since its founding
in 1909. Its first African American secretary and cofounder was
James Weldon Johnson, a lawyer better known for his contributions to literature. He was succeeded in 1930 by the dynamic
Walter White, a blond, light-skinned Negro from Atlanta, who
helped steer the organization to a more ambitious program: "a
large-scale, widespread, dramatic campaign to give the Southern

Negro his constitutional rights, his political and civil equality. And to give the Negroes equal rights in the public schools, the voting booths, on the railroads and on juries in every state where they are at present denied them, and the right to own and occupy real property."

Since little support could be expected from Congress or the White House, the NAACP set its sights on expanding its legal staff to take the battle to the courts. The program was at first entrusted to Nathan Margold, but when he left in 1933 to become an attorney for the Department of Labor, it was passed on to Charles H. Houston, a Harvard-trained lawyer who was dean of the Howard University Law School and mentor to a generation of civil rights lawyers. Before that program could be implemented, however, a sensational criminal trial in Alabama preoccupied the entire nation, from the media to the Supreme Court. This was the case of the "Scottsboro Boys," which eventually reached the Supreme Court three times, as *Powell v. Alabama* in 1932 and as *Norris v. Alabama* and *Patterson v. Alabama* in 1935. Some of the lessons of this case were to give new direction to the nascent civil rights movement.

The explosive nature of the case was due to its touching on the stereotyped bugaboo of segregationists: black men accused of raping white women. Even the hint of such an accusation had sufficed to trigger off hundreds of lynchings in the South. Now, on March 25, 1931, on a freight train from Chattanooga, Tennessee, nine black teenagers were forcibly stopped in Jackson County, Alabama, and accused at first of the assault and attempted murder of six white youngsters whom they had fought with and thrown off the train a short time before. While they were in the county jail in Scottsboro, the young black men, ranging in age from thirteen to nineteen, found themselves identified as rapists by two white women, Victoria Price and Ruby Bates, who had hopped the freight to look for work after they'd lost their jobs in a textile mill.

Many conflicting claims were made during the ensuing trials, but it seems creditable that the young black men told the truth when they said they had never seen the white women before encountering them in a police lineup. Afterward, some of the black men confessed that as soon as they heard this new charge they thought it was tantamount to a death sentence. "I knew if a white woman accused a black man of rape, he was as good as dead," said Clarence Norris years later. "All I could think was that I was going to die for something that I had not done."

Indeed, it was almost a miracle that the dozens of armed white men who had taken the accused men off the train had not killed them that night. It took quick thinking by M. L. Wann, the county sheriff, who had made an urgent call to Benjamin Meeks Miller, the Alabama governor, who in turn summoned the National Guard to surround the prison in Scottsboro. Twelve days after the arrest, four different juries heard the two women tell how all nine of the defendants had held knives to their throats, torn off their clothes, and raped them. One of the white boys, a friend of Victoria Price, appeared briefly to confirm her story. A doctor testified that he had found old evidence of sexual intercourse but no injuries when he examined the women.

Judge A. E. Hawkins had appointed six local lawyers to be defense counsel; then he replaced them with Stephen Roddy from Chattanooga, who showed up, he said, just informally at the request of the boys' parents. When Roddy protested he was not prepared to be sole counsel, the judge invited an inept local attorney to join him; they had only thirty minutes to confer with their clients, called no witnesses, and allowed one defendant, Clarence Norris, to testify that he had seen all the others rape the women without touching them himself. A defense motion for a change of venue was denied, as was a plea to remove the case of an under-age defendant to juvenile court. The trial, in a courtroom packed with angry whites, took four days, with eight defendants found guilty and later sentenced to death. Only the case of Roy Wright, the thirteen-year-old, was declared a mistrial because the jury could not agree on whether to follow the prosecution's recommendation to impose the death penalty.

After news of this hasty trial reached the country, a trial that had demonstrated little regard for the rights of the young, uneducated black teenagers, a tug-of-war ensued among protest groups that wanted to file appeals, and among critics—including Albert Einstein, Thomas Mann, and H. G. Wells—who wrote letters to the Alabama Supreme Court and governors from all corners of the world. The American Civil Liberties Union sent Hollace Ransdall, a young journalist and teacher, to investigate. Her extensive report described the crowd of about ten thousand who flocked to the village of Scottsboro to witness what she called "a legal lynching." She also learned that both of the women "victims" had the reputation of having supplemented their scanty mill work wages by prostitution, with white and black clients alike. The ACLU board could not agree to publish Ransdall's report but provided copies of it to others, including the NAACP, which began to fight with lawyers from the Communist Party of the United States over the right to represent the boys on appeal.

Communist lawyers from the International Labor Defense, headed by George Chamlee, a mercurial Chattanooga attorney, were first on the scene and impressed the eight prisoners with their sincerity. Throughout the summer of 1931, NAACP delegates, led by Walter White, tried to change the boys' allegiance, but by the end of the year the boys' parents persuaded them to trust the Labor Defense. Their initial appeal, to the Alabama Supreme Court, resulted in a 6-to-1 verdict supporting the fairness of the trial, with Chief Justice John C. Anderson dissenting, although the court granted one defendant, Eugene Williams, a new trial on the grounds that he was a juvenile when the crime was committed. The defense briefs had argued that the trial had violated the defendants' due process rights under the Fourteenth Amendment because of the inadequate time to prepare their defense and obtain counsel, as well as the exclusion of Negroes from the grand jury that had made the indictment. At the behest of the Labor Defense, the Supreme Court agreed to review *Powell v. Alabama*, and it issued its remarkable decision on November 7, 1932.

Justice George Sutherland, despite his reputation as a staunch conservative, spoke for the seven justices who found that the trial of the Scottsboro boys had violated the due process clause of the Fourteenth Amendment, namely its guarantee of a fair criminal trial. Specifically, the defendants had been denied the right to counsel because of the judge's failure to appoint an attorney for these indigent parties. "Whether requested or not," Sutherland said, the trial court should assign counsel "in a capital case, where the defense is unable to employ counsel, and is incapable of making his own defense because of ignorance, feeble mindedness, illiteracy, or the like."

The two dissenters were Justices James C. McReynolds, a southerner, and Pierce Butler of Minnesota, known for his conservative views in free-speech cases. Butler's opinion rested on the doctrine of states' rights. He pointed out that the trial had followed Alabama laws and that the state's supreme court had found no procedural violations. He was concerned that the majority opinion of his brethren constituted "an extension of federal authority in a field hitherto occupied exclusively by the several states." Indeed, that had been their intention.

This was a landmark decision, the first time that the Supreme Court required state courts to provide counsel to indigent defendants—not as a general rule, but at least in cases where it would affect the fairness of the trial. In subsequent cases the Court held that the *Powell* rule applied to state cases involving capital punishment and to others where fairness was in the balance, as opposed to federal cases in which the Sixth Amendment was taken to ensure the right to counsel of all defendants facing serious criminal charges. Because of their economic circumstances, southern Negroes would be among the major beneficiaries of this decision. In the Scottsboro case it meant that the eight convictions were void and that Alabama would have to conduct new trials.

This time a change of venue was granted to the defendants, to Decatur in nearby Morgan County. In the intervening four months, the NAACP again tried to pry the Labor Defense lawyers from the case, offering, as new counsel, to bring the celebrated Clarence Darrow out of retirement and to team him up with another distinguished lawyer, Arthur Garfield Hayes. After some waffling, the defendants decided to stick with their old legal team. In January 1933 the Communist party was able to deflate accusations that they had undertaken the defense only to let Alabama make martyrs out of the Scottsboro boys for ideological reasons. The Labor Defense coup was to hire (without pay) the most famous criminal attorney in the country, Samuel Leibowitz, who had defended seventy-eight clients accused of first-degree murder and obtained seventy-seven acquittals and one hung jury. He was a graduate of Cornell University and its law school, and had made a brilliant career by combining flamboyant cross-examinations of shaky witnesses with an entertaining style when addressing juries.

Leibowitz had made it clear to the Labor Defense people that he did not share their political or economic views. He also had never been in the South before, and thought he would be able to win the case by appealing to the "great heritage of honor" of the white citizens of Alabama. He was soon disabused of this illusion when he called his first witnesses in the second Scottsboro trial, on March 30, 1933, in order to argue that the indictment was defective because Negroes had been excluded from the rolls of the grand jury and the next trial jury. Some of the leading white citizens candidly admitted that not a single black had ever been called to serve because, in their opinion, all blacks lacked good judgment and couldn't be trusted. Then John E. Knight Jr., the state's attorney general, went after black witnesses who had been called by Leibowitz to demonstrate that as prominent citizens they would be qualified jurors. The judge ruled that the defense had established as fact that Negroes had been excluded from juries—grounds for future appeal—but, nonetheless, the trial of the first defendant, Haywood Patterson, would proceed.

While Leibowitz was unable to shake Victoria Price's story of her alleged rape, he got Lester Carter, a young white man whom she had denied knowing, to testify that he had accompanied Price and Ruby Bates, had sex with them, and gotten off the train with the women after the fight between the black and white youths. But the biggest surprise was the appearance of Bates for the defense. She corroborated Carter's account and admitted concocting the rape story at Price's behest in order to avoid a charge against the white boys under the Mann Act for crossing state lines for immoral purposes. Bates admitted she had told the fabricated story that Price had concocted at the first trial. Nonetheless, after being told by a prosecutor to refrain from a verdict "bought and sold in Alabama with Jew money from New York," the jury found Patterson guilty and sentenced him to death. Two months later, Judge James E. Horton shocked the courtroom, where he had been hearing motions from the defense for a new trial, with his finding that the proof of Patterson's guilt was inadequate because the weight of the evidence was on the side of the accused; he also ordered a new trial (which cost him reelection two years later).

The third trial was held on November 20, 1933, again in

Decatur, but only after prosecutors had managed to have Judge Horton replaced by William Callahan, a man without a bachelor's or a law degree, who was known for his racist views. Again, Leibowitz managed to have the record reflect that jury rolls were predominantly white, though a dozen blacks had been added since March, as a defense expert found. Judge Callahan routinely granted the prosecution's objections, particularly those made to the testimony that had shown flaws in the initial testimony of Price and Bates. He also denied key defense motions, such as a one-day delay to allow a deposition to be taken from Bates, who had just undergone an operation. In record time the jury found Patterson guilty and again sentenced him to death. A second trial of Clarence Norris began the next day and ended in the same way on December 6, 1933—with a conviction and a death sentence.

Appeals in both cases were denied by the Alabama Supreme Court, but trials of the other Scottsboro boys were suspended until the U.S. Supreme Court could rule on defense objections. This time, on April 1, 1935, the justices were unanimous in reversing the verdicts because of the convincing defense evidence that Negroes had been systematically excluded from the grand jury that had indicted Norris and from the trial jury that had convicted him. The opinion, by Chief Justice Charles Evans Hughes, began by looking at affidavits of the Alabama jury commissioners claiming that they had not been able to find a single Negro, of the 8,311 in Morgan County, who had the required "integrity and character" to serve on a jury. "We find it impossible to accept such a sweeping characterization of the lack of qualifications of Negroes in Morgan County," said Hughes, adding that he could find no mandate, given the Fourteenth Amendment, for "this long-continued, unvarying and wholesale" practice. He therefore ordered Alabama prosecutors to start anew with fresh grand jury indictments and trials.

Incredibly, Jackson County now did find two Negro farmers qualified for the grand jury, one of whom sat on the panel that returned new indictments on November 13, 1935, against the eight young men who had now been imprisoned for more than four and a half years—since March 1931. Accordingly, a fourth trial of Patterson began on January 20, 1936, again before an all-white jury, because none of the dozen Negroes whose names had appeared on the jury rolls were selected. This time Leibowitz had complained that the Communist party was exploiting the case, so a new Scottsboro Defense Committee had been cobbled together at the behest of Socialist leader Norman Thomas and Roger Baldwin of the American Civil Liberties Union. Leibowitz served as senior counsel, assisted by Clarence Watts, a local attorney. Despite their objections, Judge Callahan ruled against all their attempts to present evidence to show that Price's reported rape could not have happened. The judge's biased charge to the jury replayed the script of the previous trial. To no one's surprise, the jury returned a guilty verdict after eight hours; but because one juror held out against the death penalty, this time the sentence was seventy-five years in prison.

The defense and prosecution lawyers could not agree on how to present medical testimony at the trial of the other accused men, so the men were temporarily sent back to the Birmingham jail. But a short while later, outside Decatur, one of the defendants, Ozie Powell, was slapped by one of the deputies, Edgar Blalock. Powell slashed him across the throat with a hidden penknife, only to be shot in the head by the sheriff. Both Blalock and Powell recovered, though the latter was left with permanent brain damage.

Eventually, in July 1937 four of the accused were tried again and once more found guilty, with Clarence Norris sentenced to death for the third time, Andy Wright to ninety-nine years in prison, Charlie Weems to seventy-five years, and Ozie Powell to twenty years for his assault on the deputy after the rape charge against him was dropped. Then, Assistant Attorney General Buddy Lawson announced that the state would drop charges against four other defendants—Willie Roberson, Olen Montgomery, Eugene Williams, and Roy Wright—because the first two had offered plausible alibis and the last two were only twelve and thirteen years old at the time of the incident and had already served six years. Leibowitz was jubilant at what he termed a miracle.

It took another six years for the state pardon board to free Charlie Weems in 1943, Andy Wright and Clarence Norris in 1944, and Ozie Powell in 1946. Haywood Patterson escaped from prison in 1948, and was arrested in Detroit in 1950, but after Michigan Governor G. Mennen Williams refused to extradite him, he finally had Alabama's charges against him dropped. Samuel Leibowitz was named a judge in Kings County Court (Brooklyn) in 1941 and, later, a justice of the New York Supreme Court.

The protracted story of the Scottsboro boys is hardly a tribute to the opportunity Negro defendants had to find justice in southern courts. Despite objective proof of their innocence, these defendants were repeatedly convicted by judges and juries and spent many years under terrible conditions in prison. Still, it was a time of incipient change, beginning with the lynching atmosphere in an Alabama courtroom in April 1931 and, in a sense, ending when Governor George Wallace invited Clarence Norris to his office in December 1976 and signed a final pardon for Norris's breach of parole thirty years earlier. By that time, even the segregationist Wallace had come to realize that he needed the four hundred thousand black voters registered in his state.

For the first time since the 1870s, the Supreme Court that had intervened in the case abandoned its deferential role toward state misadministration of justice in civil rights cases and was able to stop the execution of these hapless defendants. The justices had spoken out, however, only when they had faced a clear breach of fairness in a murder trial that made it necessary to affirm the due process of law guaranteed by the Fourteenth Amendment, particularly when it came to assuring defendants an adequate defense with sufficient time to prepare for trial. The Court had also upheld the need for grand and trial juries to be chosen without blatant racial discrimination. These were only modest inroads into the southern system of white-run segregation, but they were a significant prelude to more dramatic changes to come.

If the system is viewed as combining social and legal aspects, it is possible to see a causal link between the partitions in railroad cars and the two-tiered justice of the courts. When the Negroes of Louisiana were excluded by law from decent accommodations on railroad cars, they could sense that they would lose other rights, too, from voting and jury service to decent schools and medical care. The white elite was turning citizenship into the privilege of a private club, with membership open only to those without a "drop of black blood." People like Plessy and the black Creole members of his defense committee were no longer respected for their achievements but were forced into the stereotypes of racist ideology.

The judges upheld the tenets of this faith, yet they were not entirely insulated from the social upheavals of the New Deal period. Somewhat reluctantly, President Franklin D. Roosevelt moved to change accepted southern practices, particularly when the exigencies of World War II arose. Yet Negro soldiers were allowed to join combat infantry units only after the Battle of the Bulge in December 1944, and on the eve of a war against the racist regime of Hitler, Negro groups turned the public's attention to the discrimination in employment that had kept black workers in unskilled farm jobs when they were needed in the defense industry.

On June 25, 1941, President Roosevelt, by Executive Order

8802, established the Fair Employment Practices Committee, to ensure that government agencies would include in contracts with private industry provisions against discrimination by race, color, creed, or nationality. The FEPC, as it became known, was given powers to investigate reports of discrimination and to take remedial steps, as well as to make recommendations to the president on further steps against discrimination in the war industry. The measure was resisted in the South; even in other parts of the country, some unions began to resist fair employment laws passed by the states. Postal clerks went so far as to use the Fourteenth Amendment to claim that their union, limited to Caucasians and American Indians, had the right to defy a New York order to integrate their membership. In 1945 the Supreme Court rejected this argument, saying, "It would be a distortion of the policy manifested in that amendment which was adopted to prevent state legislation designed to perpetuate discrimination on the basis of race or color."

In 1941 a newly created Civil Rights Division in the Justice Department challenged the venerable white primaries that southern states had used, with the Court's blessing in 1935, to exclude Negroes from political parties' supposedly private process of selecting their state candidates. The federal lawyers brought a test case against Louisiana election commissioners charged with altering and falsely counting primary election ballots in violation of federal civil rights laws. The Supreme Court ruled that Congress had the constitutional power to regulate primaries when they were used to choose candidates for federal office, and that citizens had the right to have their votes properly counted when that right was violated by private or state action.

Two years later the NAACP used this precedent to attack the 1935 *Grovey v. Townsend* decision, which had upheld discrimination by the Texas Democratic party as a private act beyond constitutional protection. The NAACP sponsored Lonnie Smith in a suit against S. E. Allwright, a Texas election judge who had refused to issue him a primary ballot in the 1940 election. Under the logic of the *Classic* decision, Justice Stanley F. Reed said in 1944 that the negative rulings against Smith could not deter federal courts from judging for themselves whether Texas policy was due to private or state factors. He said that despite the contrary opinion of the Court nine years before, it was now apparent that state laws governing the primary system of parties makes "the party which is required to follow these legislative laws an agency of the state. . . . This is state action within the meaning of the Fifteenth Amendment." In short, the precedent was overruled. Justice Owen J. Roberts, the lone dissenter, complained that such an abrupt reversal by the Court would tend to promote disrespect for its rulings. Even without the blessings of the Court, however, the exclusion of Negro voters continued in the South for another twenty years through such devices as "literacy tests," biased against black applicants, and the poll tax, until that was outlawed by the Twenty-fourth Amendment in 1964.

While it was unusual for the Court to reverse itself so quickly, it had happened before, when Franklin Roosevelt had brought a new reform spirit to the judiciary; he had also appointed seven new justices between 1935 and 1944. They tended to share his liberal spirit, particularly after he had threatened to "pack the Court" with additional justices in February 1937 after it had overturned several crucial New Deal laws. Though the country met the threat with a storm of protest, Justice Roberts joined four other justices in March to give future New Deal acts a 5-to-4 majority—the so-called switch in time that saved nine. Nonetheless, the president was following a "southern strategy" to win congressional approval for his program, and that meant little progress on civil rights. While Eleanor Roosevelt was much more outspoken—for example, in her backing of anti-lynching bills as well as in her support for the four Scottsboro boys still in prison—her husband's excessive caution in this field angered Walter White, the executive secretary of the NAACP, and other black leaders.

On the eve of World War II the NAACP leaders sent out a call for a "March on Washington for Jobs and Freedom." Some of their key demands, on July 1, 1941, were "for the integration of Negroes in the armed forces" and "for the abolition of Jim Crowism in all government departments and defense employment." Three days before the scheduled march, which was supposed to culminate in a rally of a hundred thousand at the Lincoln Memorial, the White House prevailed on A. Philip Randolph, president of the Brotherhood of Sleeping Car Porters, to cancel the event. To defuse Negro anger Franklin Roosevelt appointed a black man, Dean William Hastie of Howard University Law School, to a post in the War Department and promoted another black, Colonel Benjamin Davis, to brigadier general, the highest rank that had been attained by a black officer in the army. Roosevelt used a similar strategy of tokenism to pacify Jewish leaders when they proposed increasing immigration quotas after reported Nazi persecution in Germany. When Roosevelt asked Negroes and Jews not to embarrass him by protests while he promised to keep working behind the scenes for their cause, they felt they couldn't say no to the president.

Again in the midst of another world war, Negroes put on their country's uniform only to be met by segregation in army camps and racist harassment by southern fellow soldiers who, despite the Negroes' complaints, went unpunished. There was also a general lack of federal intervention during the so-called race riots in northern cities. Thirty-one men and women were killed in a Detroit racial confrontation in February 1943, for which Negroes were officially blamed, although one investigative reporter found twenty-six of the victims to have been black, shot by racist police officers.

The wartime United States presented a mixed picture of Negro progress. Black and white workers labored side by side in the defense industry and the military, and black families enjoyed a general economic upturn. But after their shifts were over, the workers went to their respective racial enclaves, worshipped separately, were segregated in theaters, parks, hotels, and restaurants, and, at least in the South, blacks kept to their Jim Crow accommodations because of the constant threat of violence. The Supreme Court justices had intermittently condemned blatantly unfair discrimination against Negro voters and outright injustice for black defendants. It would be another decade after the end of the war, however, before the Court would wrestle with the anachronism of the *Plessy* ruling: separate but equal.

# Chapter 11

# *Plessy* FINALLY MEETS ITS MATCH

The *Plessy* decision seemed to apply only to a specific situation: the Louisiana law of 1890 racially segregating passenger trains. However, as has been noted, the Supreme Court's "separate but equal" ruling was applied during the next decades to justify racial barriers in all aspects of life, literally from cradle to grave: colored hospitals for babies, segregated schools for children, job discrimination for adults, fenced-off parks, partitioned public accommodations and churches for families, and, finally, segregated cemeteries. The "Jim Crow" caste system was rooted in the South, but its tendrils extended into the border states and even into much of the North. Despite the legal formula—"separate but equal"—everyone knew that there was no real equality for Negroes; nonetheless, the highest court in the land had established the constitutionality of separateness. Who would dare to challenge it?

The preceding chapter reviewed the sporadic victories of the nascent NAACP after it was founded in 1909. Its few staff attorneys managed to find federal judges who recognized the violations of the Fourteenth Amendment's guarantees of "due process" and "equal protection" in cases involving segregated housing ordinances and, in the South, restrictions on Negro voter registration and jury service selection. By 1914 news of these initial successes brought new members to the organization, which by that time had fifty branches throughout the country. In 1930 the NAACP, under the leadership of Walter White, decided to focus its energies on representing southern Negroes in the courts to gain them their constitutional rights: "equal rights in the public schools, in the voting booths, on the railroads and on juries in every state . . . and the right to own and occupy real property." From 1910 to 1930 more than a million Negroes had joined the Great Migration north, which gave rise to an urban middle class; the nine million who stayed in the South were predominantly farmers, on land that belonged to whites.

The NAACP used Negro newspapers to spread the word about its new focus on racial equality in the South and in 1935 named as its new legal director Charles H. Houston, a brilliant graduate of Harvard Law School, where he had been a protégé of Justice Felix Frankfurter. Houston had then practiced law for five years until his appointment in 1929 as dean of Howard University's law school. During his years at Howard, he had raised the standards of the law school and attracted students such as Thurgood Marshall who would become advocates for equality in voting, transportation, and, most important, education.

Houston's first test case was that of Lloyd L. Gaines, a resident of Missouri and graduate of Lincoln University, its state school for Negroes. He had applied for admission to the state university's law school, which rejected him because it accepted only white applicants. Missouri law provided that if a Negro resident could not study a subject at Lincoln University, the state would pay the student's tuition for a course equivalent to Missouri's in an adjacent state. The state courts agreed that such an offer provided Gaines with equal protection of the law, but he appealed to the Supreme Court in November 1938 for a writ of mandamus, which would order S. W. Canada, the registrar of the University of Missouri, to grant his admission at its law school.

Six of the justices agreed that Gaines had not been treated with equality by the State of Missouri. In an opinion written by Chief Justice Charles Evans Hughes, the Court pointed out that white residents could study law in Missouri, while blacks had to go to another state. Other aspects of the state's segregated higher education met with the Court's approval, since it seemed to provide separate but equal facilities according to the *Plessy* formula. The two dissenting justices, James C. McReynolds and Pierce Butler, protested that the majority opinion would force the state to either abandon its white-only law school or disrupt the "accepted practice" of having racially separate schools. Missouri upheld its tradition by quickly opening a separate law school for black students; meanwhile, Gaines had abandoned his attempt to become an attorney.

Ten years later, in 1946, a parallel case was brought by Ada Sipuel, who had been denied admission to the University of Oklahoma law school. In January 1948 a unanimous (unsigned) opinion of the U.S. Supreme Court found that the state was required to provide her a legal education "in conformity with the equal protection clause of the Fourteenth Amendment." Two weeks later, Sipuel, under her married name, Ada Fisher, was back in state court seeking a revised order directing her admission to the law school. The court did direct the university to enroll her, but only until the state might establish a separate school for Negroes. She then asked the Supreme Court to have her admitted without any conditions, but in February 1948 the justices ruled that her original case had failed to raise the issue of whether a separate Negro school was illegal under the Fourteenth Amendment. This left the *Plessy* "separate but equal" rule intact; but because Oklahoma did not choose to set up a law school for blacks only,

Mrs. Fisher was duly enrolled in the state law school and later admitted to the state bar. Ironically, the state's failure to establish a separate law school for blacks resulted in de facto integration.

In 1950 the NAACP brought two more cases against segregated higher education in the South. In the first, George W. McLaurin, a sixty-eight-year-old black teacher in Oklahoma, had applied to take a graduate course in education at the University of Oklahoma because it was not offered at the black state school, Langston University. After a federal court ordered McLaurin's admission, he was indeed admitted, but under the state's strict segregation rules: the university erected what amounted to a one-man ghetto for McLaurin. He was given a seat in an anteroom next to the classroom (later modified to a seat behind a rail marked "Reserved for Colored"). In the library he had to use a special upstairs desk behind a screen (later altered to a separate table on the main floor). In the cafeteria he was told to eat at a separate table at times different from other students (later, he was just seated apart from white students at regular mealtimes).

A unanimous Supreme Court, through an opinion of Chief Justice Frederick M. Vinson, found that the school had impaired McLaurin's "ability to study, to engage in discussion and exchange of views with other students and, in general, to learn his profession." Consequently, the decision read, these strictures "deprive him of his personal and present right to the equal protection of the laws" under the Fourteenth Amendment. Once admitted to the school, he "must receive the same treatment at the hands of the state as students of other races."

If the Supreme Court had removed the invisible wall around McLaurin because it prevented his fully obtaining an equal education, what would it do with the state of Texas, which had set up a separate school for one Negro student to study law? In the second case brought before the Court in 1950, a postal clerk named

Heman (sometimes erroneously cited as Herman) Marion Sweatt had applied in 1945 to be admitted to the University of Texas Law School in Austin. When the university rejected him, Sweatt sued, naming its president, Theophilus Painter, as the defendant in a case called *Sweatt v. Painter.* In December 1946 a state court postponed the trial to give the state time to open a separate Negro law school the following year. In 1947 the "colored law school" opened in Houston; it consisted of two black lawyers as faculty in two rented rooms. The state appeals court heard Sweatt's argument that this was radically inferior to the white law school. A second version of the black school was then offered to Sweatt, this time in three rented rooms opposite the state capitol in Austin, with three part-time instructors from the all-white school. For obvious reasons, this was still not acceptable to Mr. Sweatt.

In the next legal round, Sweatt was represented by the NAACP's special counsel, Thurgood Marshall, head of the organization's Legal Defense and Educational Fund, which had been established on October 11, 1939, as a "nonprofit organization" to take advantage of new tax laws favoring private donations. When Marshall arrived in Texas for Sweatt's trial, he said, "I think we've humored the South long enough. . . . This is going to be a real showdown fight against Jim Crow in education."

Testimony before the Texas court revealed that the whites-only law school and the one proposed for Negroes occupied two totally different worlds. The former had 850 students, 16 full-time professors, a library of 65,000 books, moot courts, a law review, a branch of the national law school honor society, and a network of alumni prominent in their profession. The black law school had by then been assigned 4 part-time faculty to teach its one prospective student in basement quarters, with most of its 10,000 library books still on order. The May 1947 trial in Austin took five days, with the state attorney general, Price Daniel, pitted against

Marshall and his associates, James M. Nabrit, a professor at Howard University Law School, and W. J. Durham, an attorney from Dallas. Daniel tried to prove that Sweatt had initially agreed to attend the classes in Houston until the NAACP had talked him out of it.

Marshall presented facts to demonstrate the inequality of the two schools. His expert witnesses were eminent educators who showed that the proposed Negro law school would lack the interchange with other students that was essential in legal training. The NAACP legal team also argued that segregation in higher education was not a reasonable policy, and that in this case Negro lawyers would be ill prepared to practice in a profession dominated by white lawyers and judges. Still, as was expected, the Travis County court held that the black school would offer Sweatt "privileges, advantages and opportunities for the study of law substantially equivalent" to those enjoyed by the white students at the University of Texas Law School. During the three years that it took for the case to go through state appeals before it reached the Supreme Court, the State of Texas had enhanced the Negro law school—by 1950, it had five full-time professors, a moot court, and a larger library—but not enough to persuade Heman Marion Sweatt to enroll.

Thurgood Marshall knew that the Supreme Court, if confronted with irrefutable facts, might turn the lost battles of the *McLaurin* and *Sweatt* cases in state courts into a winnable war against legal segregation. Consequently, the NAACP briefs went beyond arguments for the admission of Negro students to white graduate schools: they also challenged the rationale of *Plessy* in justifying the feasibility of "separate but equal" education. Their main thrust, however, was to show the inherent inequality in the Oklahoma and Texas graduate schools between facilities offered to black and to white students. An amicus brief by nearly two hundred law professors, led by Thomas I. Emerson of Yale, challenged *Plessy* head-on by questioning the use of any racial "discrimination" or "distinction" in law, in the face of the equal protection clause of the Fourteenth Amendment. Of even greater weight was an amicus brief by the Justice Department, which came to an analogous conclusion. On the side of the Texas attempt to justify the existence of its segregated pygmy of a law school were eleven other southern states filing their amici briefs on the basis of the venerable fifty-four-year-old precedent of *Plessy*.

The Court that was weighing decisions in the *McLaurin* and *Sweatt* appeals was known to the NAACP to be quite cautious when it came to civil rights. It was headed by Frederick M. Vinson, who had been appointed by President Harry S. Truman in 1946 because of his experience as a congressman from Kentucky, a judge on the U.S. Court of Appeals for the District of Columbia, and, following a series of other posts in the Roosevelt administration, secretary of the treasury. Vinson presided over a divided Court, with conservatives Robert H. Jackson, Felix Frankfurter, Harold Burton, and Stanley Reed equally balanced against liberals William O. Douglas, Wiley Rutledge, Frank Murphy, and Hugo Black. When Rutledge and Murphy died in 1949, Truman had replaced them with Sherman Minton, who had served alongside Truman as senator from Missouri, and Tom Clark, an attorney general from Texas. It seemed that the conservatives were in the ascendency when they were joined by Minton, and they could often count on the pragmatic Vinson as well.

Richard Kluger's research of the evolution of the twin decisions, following a conference of the justices in May 1950, shows that the chief justice was taking a narrow approach in the draft that he had assigned to himself. Justice Frankfurter sent Vinson a memo to show that he agreed with the moderate tenor of the draft as well as with Justice Reed's suggested changes. Frankfurter found that the evolving opinion was aimed at "the desired result without needlessly stirring the kind of feelings that are felt even by truly liberal and high-minded Southerners. . . . It seems to me desirable now not to go a jot or tittle beyond the *Gaines* test. The shorter the opinion, the more there is an appearance of unexcitement and inevitability about it, the better." Then he added one more restrictive wording—to change the phrase "These are handicaps to an effective education" to "These are handicaps to graduate instruction." Even Justice Black, the leading liberal on the Court, promised not to dissent from the Vinson draft in order to aim at a unanimous opinion on this controversial issue.

The June 5 session of the Court disappointed only the NAACP lawyers when the Court rested its rejection of the Oklahoma and Texas segregated systems on a strict comparison of offerings for black and white students. As has been noted, the virtual quarantine of George McLaurin at the University of Oklahoma obviously and unquestionably deprived him of any exchange with white fellow students. For Heman Sweatt, it was equally clear that the regular school for whites was "superior," despite the last-minute tinkering to make the black law school appear equal. Here Vinson added a new factor, that of intangible differences: "the University of Texas Law School possesses to a far greater degree those qualities which are incapable of objective measurement but which make for greatness in a law school." He included as examples the "reputation of the faculty, experience of the administration, position and influence of the alumni standing in the community, traditions and prestige."

Vinson's conclusion was that even if more tinkering with faculty and books were to improve the image of the school set aside for Negroes, it would still be clearly inferior. Especially in studying for the profession of the law, he said, "Few students . . . would choose to practice in an academic vacuum." No cosmetic changes could conceal the fact that the proposed black school, Vinson added, excludes "85 per cent of the population of the State," namely, those "lawyers, witnesses, judges and other officials" with whom Sweatt would have to deal in his legal practice. Because in the segregated school Sweatt would be deprived of the legal equality guaranteed by the Fourteenth Amendment, he should be admitted to the university law school.

Yet Vinson shrank from taking the next logical step: to find *any* segregated education unconstitutional for the same inherent reasons. There was no need, he found, to reexamine *Plessy v. Ferguson* "in the light of contemporary knowledge respecting the purposes of the Fourteenth Amendment and the effects of racial segregation."

This failure of judicial leadership meant that only the two specific individual plaintiffs benefited in Oklahoma and Texas from the ruling. Other states of the solid South could pretend that their racially segregated graduate schools still passed legal muster, at least until a black student would go to the time and expense of taking them to court with a bill of particulars. The NAACP saw that it would soon exhaust its limited resources in the struggle it had undertaken. Its cadre of attorneys realized how gargantuan an attack would be required to end segregation in the public schools—which, for black children in more than eleven thousand districts, mostly in the South, were patently inferior. White children generally enjoyed modern buildings, school buses, sports programs, better-paid teachers, and new books and equipment. Black schools were often located in run-down shacks, with inadequate books and supplies, and teachers who were very poorly paid and had been licensed under marginal standards.

The chief strategist for directing the NAACP's limited resources toward opening schoolhouse doors to millions of black children was Thurgood Marshall, a veteran of numerous desegregation lawsuits around the country. Marshall was born on July 2, 1908, in West Baltimore, Maryland, to a father who worked as a waiter on railroad dining cars and a mother who taught in a segregated elementary school. The courses Marshall chose in high school seemed to show that he was following his mother's wish that he study to be a dentist.

As a teenager, he took a summer job with his father as a waiter on the Baltimore & Ohio Railroad. When he first reported for work, the chief dining-room steward gave him his uniform, a white jacket and a pair of black pants far too short for the six-foot-tall young man. Marshall asked for a longer pair. "Boy," said the steward, "we can get a shorter Negro to fit these pants a lot easier than we can get new pants to fit you. Why don't you scrunch down a little more?" Marshall needed the job to pay for his education, so, as he later recalled, "I scrunched." His self-deprecating humor was to stand him in good stead later, when he had to keep up a brave front during his courtroom appearances before segregationist judges.

In public school, and later at Lincoln University, a college for black men in Pennsylvania, Marshall had a knack for getting into trouble. He cut a lot of his college classes, then spent a good deal of time playing cards. In his sophomore year he was suspended for hazing freshmen—in particular, for shaving their heads before they could join his fraternity. Marshall acquired a reputation as a playboy, but he finally settled down enough to earn a B average and, in 1930, to receive his degree with honors. Despite his shaky start at Lincoln, he decided to study law. After he was turned down at the segregated white law school of the University of Maryland, he enrolled at the all-black Howard University Law School. In order to save money by living at home, he got up every morning at 5:30 to catch the train from Baltimore to Washington.

Marshall's talents as a budding lawyer were soon recognized by several of his professors at Howard, including Charles H.

Houston, the school's dean, and William Henry Hastie, who was to become the country's first black federal judge. In 1933, after Marshall graduated first in his class, Houston recruited him to join the NAACP, first as special counsel, then as director of the Legal Defense and Educational Fund. During his twenty-five years with the NAACP, Marshall achieved twenty-nine legal victories against discrimination in education, housing, transportation, electoral politics, and criminal justice. By 1950 Marshall had been able to move the Supreme Court to admit, in the *McLaurin* and *Sweatt* decisions, that in addition to quantitative differences between graduate programs for black and white students, segregation imposed "intangible" burdens on blacks, who were unable to associate with their white colleagues and thus had to settle for an inferior education, which was reflected in the lower prestige accorded to degrees from segregated black schools.

The NAACP was ready to use the logic of the graduate school decisions to turn the spotlight on state-supported public schools, in the hope that what had been apparent to the Court in the cases of a few lawyers or educators would be just as convincing when the justices dealt with millions of schoolchildren. Two years after the opinions in *McLaurin* and *Sweatt*, five such cases percolated up from trial courts in Kansas, Delaware, Virginia, South Carolina, and the District of Columbia—the first four under the Fourteenth Amendment and the last under the Fifth Amendment. But it would be another two years before the Supreme Court was ready, in 1954, to issue an opinion that would affect public education throughout the country.

Shortly after the decisions of June 5, 1950, a conference of NAACP lawyers and staff had agreed with Marshall that it was time to push for an all-out end to segregation in education, and the group's board of directors had approved the plan. While they would continue to work through state and federal courts to desegregate universities and graduate schools, the Legal Defense Fund attorneys would now focus on arguing in federal courts that segregated black public schools were inferior and that the system itself violated the "equal protection" standards of the Fourteenth Amendment.

One of the NAACP's initial clients in this campaign was Oliver Brown, father of seven-year-old Linda Carol. She had discovered in 1950 that she was not allowed by Topeka city law, under the local option system of the State of Kansas, to attend the Sumner School, a school for white children, even though it was only a ten-minute walk from her home on First Street. At the time, she could scarcely have imagined that a lawsuit bearing her name would make United States history. The Browns, who lived in a mixed ethnic neighborhood, had received a notice telling them how to register their children for fall classes. Oliver took Linda to the nearby school and left her outside while he went to the principal's office. When he came out a few minutes later, Linda saw that he was quite upset. The notice had not mentioned that the Sumner School was for whites only, and therefore Linda and her two sisters would have to enroll elsewhere.

As Oliver Brown told Judge Walter A. Huxman in June 1951 at the federal court that heard the case of *Brown v. Board of Education of Topeka*, it was dangerous for Linda to walk six blocks through heavy traffic, then take a school bus to the Monroe School reserved for black children. In order to reach the school so far from her home, she had to leave her house at 7:40 A.M., then walk between the train tracks on First Street to get to the bus stop. The bus frequently came late, leaving her on the corner in the cold, rain, or snow. If the bus was on time, it got Linda to the school a half hour before the doors opened at 9:00 A.M., so she would be forced to wait outside, often clapping her hands or jumping up and down to keep warm. Brown explained that he had joined the

NAACP suit because he wanted his daughter to avoid these hardships by attending her neighborhood school, a safe seven-block walk away.

Linda Brown was only one of eight Negro children whose cases were heard in Topeka, presented by NAACP counsel Robert L. Carter and his associates, who included Jack Greenberg; but because Linda's surname was first alphabetically, the related cases were subsumed under "Brown" as the plaintiff. The trial was at times tedious, as both plaintiff and defense lawyers tried to establish minutiae that would provide grounds for later appeal. But there were moments of simple drama, as when Silas H. Fleming, the father of two boys, was explaining how long their bus trip to a Negro school was, compared to the two-block walk to the nearest white school. In the midst of this testimony, Fleming said he would like to tell the court why he had joined the lawsuit. Greenberg was aghast: would Fleming blurt out something embarrassing?

Instead, Fleming explained that it was not the material differences between the schools that had motivated him. It wasn't a matter of better lunches or more qualified teachers at the white schools. His point was "that not only I and my children are craving light—the entire colored race is craving light, and the only way to reach the light is to start our children together in their infancy and they come up together."

Among the expert witnesses called to testify to the harmful effects of segregation was Dr. Hugh Speer, an education professor at the small campus of the University of Kansas City. Under cross-examination, he was asked if black children wouldn't be upset to be outnumbered fifty to one by whites in an integrated school. Dr. Speer told the court he was sure they would be fine, based on the experience of ten black students in an elementary "demonstration" school of 210 children that he had observed. He and his assistants had witnessed "that these children are very happy, very well adjusted, and they are there voluntarily." It was just like jumping into the water for the first time, said Speer: kids adapted quickly. If sent to formerly all-white schools, a black child would "have the opportunity to learn to live with, to work with, to cooperate with, white children who are representative of approximately 90 percent of the population of the society in which he is to live."

The record also included the strong testimony of Louisa P. Holt, a sociologist at Kansas University who had formerly been associated with the famed Menninger Foundation. When the federal court ruled against the NAACP in *Brown v. Board of Education of Topeka*, based primarily on the *Plessy* precedent—that is, the substantial equality of the separate facilities—it included in its "Findings of Fact" Ms. Holt's conclusion: "Segregation of white and colored children has a detrimental effect upon the colored children. . . . A sense of inferiority affects the motivation of a child to learn. Segregation with the sanction of law, therefore, has a tendency to retard the educational and mental development of Negro children and to deprive them of some of the benefits they would receive in a racially integrated school system." The NAACP knew that despite its expected loss in Kansas, such a finding would serve to confront the Supreme Court with the dilemma of how to square such facts with the 1896 abstraction of "separate but equal."

Even if the local option law of Kansas did not entail statewide segregation, the racial division of public schools throughout the South admitted of no exceptions. In South Carolina, for example, the state constitution decreed that "no child of either race shall ever be permitted to attend a school provided for children of the other race." Unlike the attempt by Kansas to portray black schools as equal to white, in rural Clarendon County, South

Carolina, there was no question that black schools were markedly inferior. Black children attended run-down, ramshackle school-houses, some with just one or two teachers, with crowded class-rooms, and without libraries, lunchrooms, or playgrounds. Blacks made up about 70 percent of the county's population, but at last count, in 1938, a third of them grew up illiterate.

By 1950 few black children had more than a fourth-grade edu-cation. Indeed, black children also had to overcome economic barriers to pursue an education; they were generally expected to help their families farm, hence they were taken out of school for months at a time during the planting and harvesting seasons. White children also had better than a 4-to-1 financial advantage, receiving $179 per capita for their education in Clarendon County, as opposed to $43 per black child. Levi Pearson, one of the local black farmers, had tried to challenge the inequities of the system in 1947, focusing on the rickety buses that often broke down when they took his three children nine miles to their seg-regated school. But a court in Charleston threw out his suit on June 8, 1948, because of a technicality: Pearson lacked legal standing, because his property was within the border of one dis-trict, while his children went to school (albeit because they were forced to) in an adjacent one!

In March 1949 the Pearsons and a few other black residents of Clarendon County went to the state capital, Columbia, to meet with Thurgood Marshall to see if the NAACP would fight for the educational rights of their children. Pearson recounted the pres-sure he received from his white neighbors who wanted to frighten him from pursuing this legal course: every bank and store had cut off his credit, so he was unable to buy supplies for his farm; the lumber mill refused to pick up his logs when he cut down his trees; and his crop rotted when white farmers would no longer lend him a harvester. Marshall's challenge was that in order to bring a test case, the Pearsons would first have to assemble nineteen other plaintiffs; if they acted as a group, white intimidation tactics could no longer work. Within eight months the twenty plaintiffs assembled—no longer simply to find better school buses, but to secure a decent education for their children. They knew they were risking their livelihood; as tenant farmers, they could be kicked off their land.

The new lawsuit was called *Briggs v. Elliot*, since Harry Briggs was first in the alphabetical order of plaintiffs, while R. W. Elliot (some sources have his name as R. M. Elliott) was the school official of Clarendon County. White retribution was not long in coming. Briggs was a navy veteran who farmed five acres and also worked as a mechanic at a gas station. His wife had a job as a chambermaid in the town of Summerton and took care of their five children. As he later recalled, "The white folks got kind of sour. They asked me to take my name from the petition." When the gas station owner asked him if he knew what he was doing, Briggs replied, "I'm doing it for the benefit of my children," only to be fired on Christmas Eve for taking this stand. Mrs. Briggs told her employer that she would not persuade her husband to drop the suit, only to be told that this was the last week she would be needed. Other black parents who participated in the lawsuit also found themselves out of work and pushed off their farmlands.

Thurgood Marshall pursued a three-pronged legal strategy. First, he wanted to establish the obvious qualitative differences between the black and white schools of Clarendon County. Second, he would challenge the constitutionality of the South Carolina laws decreeing school segregation, claiming they violated the "equal protection" clause of the Fourteenth Amendment. Third, he would bring psychological evidence to show that the intangible factors of segregation had further harmful effects on Negro children.

Marshall's chief witness in the risky endeavor was Kenneth B. Clark, a young professor of social psychology at the City College of New York who had earned his Ph.D. at Columbia University after his undergraduate years at Howard University, where he had been an activist. In a projective experiment with black children, Dr. Clark and his wife had conducted tests of the children's perceptions and attitudes, using black and white dolls. When he gave his doll test to the children at the Negro elementary and high school at Scott's Branch, two-thirds of the pupils chose the white doll as the "nice" one and the black doll as the "bad" one. This proved, according to Dr. Clark's testimony, that segregated schools caused a black child to have "basic feelings of inferiority, conflict, confusion in his self-image."

The Clarendon County school board had produced as its expert witness E. R. Crow, superintendent of schools at Fort Sumter. Crow claimed to have heard from "Negro school administrators" that they would "prefer to have schools of their own race." Under cross-examination by Marshall, however, Crow was unable to recall the name of any of these sources. Nor could he find evidence to back up his prediction that "the public schools of the state would be abandoned" if the courts ordered them to be integrated. This was a far cry from the testimony of the Kansas defense expert, Paul E. Wilson, who had been asked in the *Brown* trial what the results of integration in that state would be. "In perfect candor," he had answered, "I must say to the Court that the consequences would probably not be serious."

The NAACP legal team of Thurgood Marshall, Robert Carter, and Spottswood W. Robinson III made an overwhelming case before the three judges of the federal court in Charleston; but three weeks later, on June 21, 1951, Judge John H. Parker, joined by Judge George B. Timmerman, used the *Plessy* precedent to justify their shrinking from overruling "three quarters of a century" of segregated educational practices. Despite the evident shortcomings of black public schools, Parker stated that he believed the differences between white and black schools were bound to disappear because the state legislature had just authorized a $75 million school bond issue. Then, Governor James F. ("Jimmy") Byrnes undercut the NAACP case when he announced that the bulk of that money would be spent on improving the quality of black schools; his promise had satisfied any concerns two of the judges may have had. They gave Clarendon County six months to report what progress had been made in bringing black schools up to state standards. If the system of segregation was ever to change, Judge Parker said, "This is a matter for the legislatures and not the courts."

Only Judge J. Waties Waring disagreed, in a stinging twenty-page dissent. He said that if racial prejudice was ever to be eliminated, it had to be in early childhood, not in graduate school. In short, "Segregation in education can never produce equality and is an evil that must be eradicated. . . . The system of segregation in education adopted and practiced in the state of South Carolina must go and must go now. *Segregation is per se inequality* [italics in the original]." Having made his solitary stand, Judge Waring soon afterward left the state to live out his years in New York.

The NAACP case in Virginia followed the same essential course as South Carolina's, except that the three-judge federal court was unanimous in upholding segregated schools as the product of neither "prejudice nor caprice" but simply a time-honored way of following "the mores" of the state's residents, good for Negroes and whites, besides abiding by the segregation clauses of the state constitution. The logic seemed to echo the majority opinion in *Plessy*, where the justices had bowed to alleged folkways. The Virginia case was launched by the NAACP, under Spottswood Robinson's direction, after students at a black high school in Prince Edward County went on strike in April 1951 to protest that their enrollment had far outrun the facilities of the old building, yet the school board had stalled repeatedly to replace the tarpaper shacks for the overflow with a modern structure. The case was named *Davis v. County School Board* because the first plaintiff's name alphabetically was Dorothy Davis, a fourteen-year-old daughter of a local farmer. Like South Carolina, Virginia had decided to counter the suit by a last-minute appropriation of funds to the county board for the long-delayed new black high school.

The fourth case to be appealed to the Supreme Court came from Delaware, a border state that had adapted its institutions to the segregated ways of its southern neighbors. Yet by the 1950s it was one of the border states eager to admit the true disparities between its white and black educational institutions. A local NAACP activist lawyer named Louis L. Redding teamed up with Legal Defense Fund attorney Jack Greenberg in 1950 to win a suit in state chancery court ensuring admission of black students to the previously all-white University of Delaware, because the state college designated for Negroes was markedly inferior.

A year later, the same legal team faced the same judge, Collins Seitz, to prove that a black high school in a Wilmington suburb as well as a one-room schoolhouse in rural Hockessin were both far below state standards. Once more the NAACP was able to supply psychological experts to put into the record their data showing that segregated schools had a harmful effect on students. In his April 1952 decision, Judge Seitz agreed with the experts that racial separation created lifelong mental health problems for Negro children. He also acknowledged the higher quality of nearby white schools and ordered them, for the first time in U.S. history, to admit the eleven children who had brought suit. But he concluded that it was beyond his powers to overrule the "separate but equal" doctrine of *Plessy*, leaving that issue for review by the Supreme Court.

The fifth case brought by the NAACP against segregation in public schools originated in the District of Columbia. Since the District was governed by Congress, not a state of the Union, its residents were not covered by the Fourteenth Amendment with its guarantee of equal protection for citizens of the states, so they had to assert their rights under the due process clause of the Fifth Amendment instead, though that was difficult in the face of congressional action. Southern congressmen made sure that blacks went to the city's segregated black public schools. For years, protests by Negro parents had been led by a barber named Gardner Bishop, who eventually secured the legal help of civil rights pioneer Charles Houston, by then an NAACP adviser. During his final illness, in April 1950, Houston told Bishop to take the cases to James M. Nabrit Jr., a Howard University law professor and a top graduate of Northwestern University Law School. Bishop took Houston's advice.

In the fall of 1950 Bishop had tried to enroll a group of eleven black students from run-down, overcrowded schools in downtown Washington to the brand-new John Philip Sousa Junior High School, with a six-hundred-seat auditorium, a playground with seven basketball courts, and forty-two sparkling new classrooms: despite the school's underenrollment, its principal had turned them away because it was for "whites only." When Bishop next took the students' case to the board of education, the superintendent of schools explained that he was sorry but he was just following the laws of Congress. One of the boys who had to start the school year at decrepit Shaw Junior High School was Spottswood Bolling Jr., while C. Melvin Sharpe was president of the District board of education, lending their names to the suit, *Bolling v. Sharpe*.

Instead of basing his argument on qualitative differences between white and black schools, Nabrit tried a radical strategy: attacking the congressional acts as "bills of attainder," that is, laws that in defiance of Article I of the Constitution inflicted "punishment without a judicial trial" on black children, condemned to an inferior education because of their skin color. He also argued that segregated schools were not "reasonable," as the law demanded, and that they had not worked for the benefit of the community.

In his presentation to the U.S. District Court, Nabrit said that the Bolling case should be decided in accordance with the conditions of the time, which differed from the times when the Bill of Rights and the Fourteenth Amendment had just been adopted: "What schooling was good enough to meet [the children's] constitutional rights 160 or 80 years ago is different from the question what schooling meets their rights now."

Despite Nabrit's ingenious but unprecedented arguments, in April 1951 U.S. District Court Judge Walter M. Bastian ruled against Spottswood Bolling and the other children. He pointed out that they had not established the specific ways in which their schools were said to be inferior, so that—unlike judges in various states—he could not order them to be improved. The judge accepted the finding of the board of education that black students had adequate schools available to them in the District. Finally, he cited Supreme Court precedents, going back to *Plessy v. Ferguson* in 1896, that had approved separate but equal facilities; therefore, he could not rule against the express will of Congress.

Just as James Nabrit was preparing his case for appeal to the circuit court, however, the Supreme Court intervened. By 1952 the justices had become aware of the similarities in the five cases from Kansas, South Carolina, Virginia, Delaware, and the District of Columbia, all of which had exposed the harmful effects of segregated schools on black students. They resorted to a seldom-used rule to speed up the process of appeals by skipping the U.S. Court of Appeals, which they could do for cases "of such imperative public importance as to justify the deviation from normal appellate processes and to require immediate settlement in this Court." Despite the air of exigency, however, it would take two more years of maneuvering before the justices could settle the question, whether the fictions of *Plessy* could survive the light of the social realities of mid–twentieth-century America.

In December 1952, under the umbrella of *Brown v. Board of Education*, the Court held a round of oral arguments. By their questions to Legal Defense Fund lawyers, the justices signaled that they agreed it was time for a critical review of segregated schools. Is there evidence, asked Justice Stanley F. Reed, that segregation impaired the "ability to learn" of black children? Yes, said Robert L. Carter, the fund's attorney. Was "there a great deal more to the education process, even in the elementary schools, than what you read in the books?" Justice Harold H. Burton wanted to know. "Yes, that is precisely the point," replied Carter. Justice William O. Douglas spelled it out when he said that "education is different" from other forms of segregation, since *Sweatt* and *McLaurin* had shown that beyond comparisons of facilities, "things we cannot name are more important to the students" yet are missing in segregated schools.

Paul Wilson, counsel for the State of Kansas, expressed alarm that if the Court were to overrule *Plessy* it would tell twenty or so states that they had been wrong in basing their laws on that case for so long. But Justice Burton didn't flinch at that possible outcome. Today's state courts and legislatures, he commented, were operating under different social and economic conditions from those of the South seventy-five years before, when the Jim Crow laws had been adopted. Only Justice Felix Frankfurter appeared alarmed: since the score of states practicing segregation extended into the North, he mused, was it really the Court's job to reverse such long-established practice and to rule against every example of "man's inhumanity to man?"

Thurgood Marshall, the NAACP's senior attorney, pointed out that in *Briggs v. Elliot* psychologists had indicated that segregation destroyed a black child's self-respect and "stamped him with a badge of inferiority." Could the justices condone the way the South Carolina court had ignored such mental injuries? Justice Frankfurter said he could not accept such theories, which amounted to "natural law," as ground for making a sharp break with history and declaring that segregation "is bad." Marshall offered an alternative argument: if a state distinguished in its laws between black and white citizens, it must have a "reasonable" purpose—not just to extend privileges to whites. This seemed to satisfy Frankfurter, who said, "I follow you when you talk that way."

After this round of arguments, the justices met to ascertain whether they could find common legal ground for a decision that all of them could support and that might persuade the opponents of school integration. At this conference, Chief Justice Vinson appeared hesitant to adopt an order to desegregate all of the nation's public schools, as well as reluctant to overrule *Plessy*'s "separate but equal" formula outright. With the Court divided, the justices postponed a decision and ordered the lawyers on both sides to comb the historical record to determine the intentions of the framers of the Fourteenth Amendment on the school question.

Then, on September 8, 1953, Vinson suddenly died. In a fateful appointment, President Eisenhower named Earl Warren, longtime governor of California, to succeed him. Whatever Warren lacked as a legal scholar he more than made up with political skills, especially the ability to reconcile opposing parties. He was determined from the outset to jettison *Plessy* and to stop sending Negro children to inferior schools.

When the Court reassembled, the NAACP lawyers would have to disclose to the justices the meager fruits of their intense research: that the historical evidence about the views on education of the men who had written and adopted the Fourteenth Amendment was inconclusive. The NAACP would have to argue that public schools had assumed a much more central role by 1953 than they had had in 1868. But even without definitive evidence, Thurgood Marshall told his associates, he thought he could win on other points—a "nothing to nothing score" on historical grounds "means we win the ball game." The NAACP lawyers also felt that if the Court ruled in favor of Linda Brown and the dozens of other children, it would have to let them attend white schools within a year, for to do otherwise would rob them of their constitutional rights and permanently damage them.

First, the NAACP team had to counter the briefs defending segregated schools. Segregation's major defender was John W. Davis, at the age of seventy-nine a nationally known lawyer who had argued 149 cases, a record, before the Supreme Court. Davis had served in Congress and as solicitor general under Woodrow Wilson; in 1928 he had been the Democratic candidate for president. When Governor Byrnes asked him to take South Carolina's case, Davis agreed to do so without pay, accepting only a silver tea service from the grateful state legislature.

Judging by his arguments, Davis seems to have grossly underestimated Thurgood Marshall's persuasive force. Davis rested his case on stare decisis, the principle of following precedent, as well as on the implicit powers of the states under the Tenth Amendment. *Plessy v. Ferguson* Davis claimed, was a precedent "so often announced, so confidently relied on, that it passes the limits of judicial discretion and disturbance." When challenged by Justice Burton as to whether racial relations had not changed so much in the interim as to affect segregation laws, Davis replied, "Changed conditions cannot broaden the terminology of the Constitution." Then he tried to soften the states' rights argument by claiming that localities could respond to parents' wishes more readily than

Washington; surely he concluded, the Supreme Court didn't wish to sit as "a glorified Board of Education for the state of South Carolina."

In rebuttal, Marshall said that it was not legislatures bending to the will of the majority but "this Court" that would be the proper forum to define "individual rights of the minority people." For the justices to act would only be an extension of their logic in the 1950 *Sweatt* and *McLaurin* decisions, in which black graduate students had been afforded "equal protection," taking crucial "intangible" factors of school prestige and student psychology into account. Indeed, after these two cases, border states, including Kentucky, Arkansas, and West Virginia, had integrated graduate schools without a legal contest. For Davis, however, forcibly integrating schools would lead to destructive results, with racial "miscegenation" sure to follow. As for Dr. Clark's "doll tests," even more northern black children than southern ones seemed to have a "confused self-image," as shown by their preferring to play with white dolls. Yet Davis could cite no psychologist in favor of segregation.

Milton Korman, who argued the case for the District of Columbia, echoed Davis in painting a picture of black children happier in their separate schools, which provide "a receptive atmosphere." Instead of encountering racial hostility, he said, their Negro teachers could impart "colored folklore" as an essential part of their culture. "I got the feeling yesterday," said Marshall in his final rebuttal, "that when you put a white child in a school with a whole lot of colored children, the child would fall apart or something. Everybody knows that is not true. Those same kids in Virginia and South Carolina—and I have seen them do it—they play in the streets together, they play on their farms together, they go down the road together, they separate to go to school, they come out of school and play ball together. They have to be separated in school."

After the first round of arguments, Justice Frankfurter suspected that at least four justices would have voted to uphold segregated schools; therefore, he persuaded the others to postpone a decision for a year. At that time, he hoped, the NAACP lawyers could present more convincing legal grounds for integrating schools. Justice Douglas, in his autobiography, claimed that the vote in December 1952 would have gone 5 to 4 for segregation. When Chief Justice Vinson died in September 1953, Frankfurter expressed relief that the Court might become united in its decision on *Brown*. He is reported to have said, "This is the first indication I have ever had that there is a God." Frankfurter blamed Vinson for having allowed feuds to fester among the justices, bringing the Court into disrepute. When the new chief justice, Earl Warren, surveyed the southerners on the Court (Hugo Black, from Alabama; Tom C. Clark, Texas; and Stanley Reed, Kentucky), he at once realized how difficult it would be to support a decision integrating public schools for someone "born and reared in that part of the nation where segregation was a way of life and where everyone knew the great emotional opposition" that integration would arouse.

Warren was extremely circumspect when it came time to deal with the *Brown* case again. He sounded out his colleagues without revealing his own views for at least four months. In the meantime, he let Black, the senior justice, preside over the Court's conferences for several weeks until he could comfortably take over. When Warren asked the others their opinions, he refrained from asking for a vote, so that they would not feel boxed into clashing positions. Perhaps Warren's best means of persuasion was his skill at male bonding, finding interests that he shared with them, such as baseball, playing cards, or fishing, until they really formed a team called—at first disparagingly, then with respect—"the Warren Court."

It is not clear why Warren so single-mindedly pursued the goal of school integration. Despite his crusade, when he was California attorney general, to put Japanese Americans into detention camps, he recalled having gone to school with black classmates. For his three terms as governor, his chauffeur had been Edgar Patterson, who later remembered being asked to relate what it had been like to grow up as a Negro in the South: "and then I used to tell him about some of the things that happened in New Orleans, the way black kids felt."

Another crucial factor for Warren, an intensely patriotic man, may have been his awareness that Soviet propaganda in the Cold War capitalized on American discrimination against Negroes. This theme would also have struck a chord with other justices and may explain why they finally overcame their initial reservations to rally round their chief, who kept stressing their duty to their country.

The final round of arguments in *Brown v. Board of Education* was scheduled for three days in December 1953. What guidance could be derived from the framers of the Fourteenth Amendment? First, for the NAACP, Spottswood Robinson said the "broad purpose" of the amendment had been to end segregation and achieve equality in all fields, including education. He quoted one representative from the congressional debates in 1866 who specifically wanted schools to be included. Justice Frankfurter responded that one congressman's comment did not satisfy him that states had been directed to admit black children to white schools.

Thurgood Marshall then shifted the perspective to the present, arguing that it was up to this Court to put an end to segregated schools, even though Justice Robert Jackson said he still harbored doubts about courts stepping in where Congress had failed to act. In his summation, Marshall eloquently declared that school segregation implied "an inherent determination that the people who were formerly in slavery . . . shall be kept as near that stage as possible, and now is the time . . . that this Court should make it clear that this is not what our Constitution stands for."

John Davis, the attorney for South Carolina, said that the authors of the Fourteenth Amendment had never intended "that it would abolish segregation in public schools." Indeed, the "equal protection" clause had never been meant to lead to interracial schools, as the federal government's authorization of segregated schools in the District of Columbia showed.

More significant for the justices was the appearance of J. Lee Rankin, Assistant Attorney General of the United States, who had been asked to state the views of the executive branch. He said, "It is the position of the Department of Justice that segregation in public schools cannot be maintained under the Fourteenth Amendment." Since the amendment's framers had never stated their intent to preserve school segregation, it was the Court's prerogative to strike it down. However, in line with President Eisenhower's known concerns about southern resistance to integration, Rankin suggested that a year might be needed to enforce a plan, "school district by school district," supervised by local judges.

On December 12, 1953, with the last oral arguments still ringing in their ears, the justices assembled for a conference. Warren told his colleagues that the old doctrine of "separate but equal" could no longer be justified, because it implied the inferiority of Negroes. A majority agreed with him, but there were a few holdouts, so Warren urged them to talk with each other for another month or two until they could achieve a consensus.

By early March 1954 all but two of the justices agreed to rule against segregated schools as unconstitutional. One of the last to be persuaded was Justice Reed. Warren told him, "Stan, you're all by yourself in this now. You've got to decide whether it's really the best thing for the country." Justice Jackson kept insisting that he would write a concurring opinion that qualified his agreement. But then on March 30 he suffered a heart attack. Warren visited him in the hospital, sharing drafts of the opinion he had been writing. Finally, with a minor change, Jackson also signed on and even, to Warren's dismay, "insisted on dressing and coming to the Court for the announcement."

That day came on Monday, May 17, 1954, when Earl Warren electrified the courtroom by announcing that *Brown v. Board of Education* had been decided. He delivered a short, powerful opinion, deliberately written in language that ordinary citizens could comprehend. The crucial passage read: "We conclude that in the field of public education the doctrine of 'separate but equal' has no place. Separate educational facilities are inherently unequal." Warren rested his opinion on two basic grounds: First, since adoption of the Fourteenth Amendment in 1868, when there were hardly any public schools in the South for Negro children to attend, public education had increasingly held a central place to the extent that now such education had become "the very foundation of good citizenship." Second, a look at the psychological evidence had shown, as the Kansas court had noted, that segregated education "has a detrimental effect upon the colored children . . . as denoting the inferiority of the Negro group." (The controversial "footnote 11" cited eight such studies.)

In short, states that operated racially segregated schools were found to violate the "equal protection" guarantee that the Fourteenth Amendment had extended to all citizens, with special emphasis on newly freed slaves. The *Plessy* doctrine was scrapped as anachronistic: at least when it came to "public education, separate but equal has no place."

What about Spottswood Bolling and the other black children in the District of Columbia? Warren admitted that the District's status was different from the states' because the Fourteenth

Amendment did not apply to it, but he argued that the due process clause of the Fifth Amendment achieved essentially the same ends. Essentially, black children were being deprived of "liberty . . . without due process of law"—that is, their freedom to attend schools of their choice was being denied them. "Segregation in public education is not reasonably related to any proper governmental objective"; therefore, it was "an arbitrary deprivation" of the liberty of "Negro children of the District of Columbia." Warren deemed it "unthinkable" that the federal government could have "a lesser duty" than the one just imposed on states: to no longer maintain segregated public schools.

What was left dangling was exactly how the opinion was to be enforced. That would require another round of arguments and briefs by October 1. The justices clearly had not been able to agree on a formula to put their bold opinion into action, and they were testing the waters to see what the southern reaction to *Brown* would be. The Court also needed to hear again from the Justice Department, because in the end it would be federal officials who would have to police enforcement in thousands of school districts. At the time, no one could have predicted how many years it would take until some of the children who had been named in the original suit—as well as millions of others—would finally gain entry to the schools that southern states had kept reserved for whites only. But first there was a general mood of celebration in the North, and among southern Negroes.

# Chapter 12

# FIFTY YEARS OF INTEGRATION: HALF MEASURES AND HALTING PROGRESS

The second half of the twentieth century began with the *Brown* decision, hailed as the dawn of a new age in black–white relations, only to be followed by a decade of southern resistance. By the 1960s young, new leaders, dissatisfied with the slow pace of progress, formed militant civil rights groups to register African American voters in the South and to break down other racial barriers. President Lyndon B. Johnson pushed the 1964 Civil Rights Act through Congress, guaranteeing federal enforcement of voting rights, school integration, equal employment opportunities, and the desegregation of public accommodations. It was the strongest such measure since Reconstruction. The Supreme Court supported plaintiffs who asserted their rights under the act's provisions; but after Earl Warren's retirement in 1969, Warren Burger, his successor as chief justice, presided over a Court that proceeded much more cautiously.

In 1986 President Ronald Reagan appointed William H. Rehnquist, the most conservative member of the Burger court, to be the new chief justice. As Justice Robert H. Jackson's law clerk in 1952–1953, Rehnquist had written a memo sharply disagreeing with Thurgood Marshall's argument that "a majority may not deprive a minority of its constitutional right." To the contrary, he wrote, "In the long run, it is the majority who will determine what the constitutional rights of the minority are. . . . I think *Plessy v. Ferguson* was right and should be re-affirmed."

The current group of justices has espoused a "new federalism," with greater power ceded to the states, and a narrower reading of the Fourteenth Amendment that upholds the granting of benefits only to minorities who can prove they have been victims of intentional discrimination. Since the 1978 *Bakke* decision, it has been clear that affirmative action programs are illegal if they involve quotas, yet racial factors have been allowed to be considered in university admissions insofar as they contribute to "diversity." The present Court has weighed a challenge to the diversity-based admissions programs at the University of Michigan and its law school; the programs are opposed by President George W. Bush as illegally employing quotas but backed by a coalition of advocates as an essential tool to achieve a diverse student body.

In the fifty years since *Brown v. Board of Education* there has been an arc, from public recognition of long-standing discrimination against Negroes and its need for legal remedies, to the current skepticism in the country toward granting further benefits to minorities, particularly in education and employment. Idealists point to the need to relieve African Americans of unequal burdens— as evident in their disproportionate rates of poverty, chronic illnesses, school failures, and, especially among young men, jail sentences—and skeptics tout the need for a "merit system," focusing on zero-based individual achievement without regard for disparities in opportunity. The cliché of a level playing field—a requirement of fair competition—is used by reformers to argue the need for more progress in ensuring fairness, as well as by conservatives who are generally satisfied with the way things are.

In the current debate, the long historical perspective of

blacks—in which years of slavery and subsequent discrimination far exceeded the relatively short period of equal rights—is pitted against the perspective of whites, who judge how much has been achieved in civil rights during their own lifetimes. What is inadequate in the eyes of one group is seen as excessive by the other. Given the present conservative political climate in Congress, the White House, and the courts, it has become increasingly unlikely that new measures will be taken to improve the plight of those citizens who may not be able to achieve any degree of enfranchisement without the help of legislators, jurists, and members of the executive branch of government. There is little doubt that the rich and powerful in our society have an easier time gaining access to their legislators and winning favorable verdicts in the courts, yet justice demands that this reality be offset by concern for the poor and powerless. It is up to those who have sworn to uphold the Constitution of the United States to see to it that basic rights, opportunities, and material help are available for a community whose least advantaged members tend to be black and Hispanic. Otherwise, are we not in danger of regressing to the *Plessy* era, when the less powerful were granted only the illusion of equality? If it is imperative to balance the interests of the society's socioeconomic classes, how can this be achieved?

The delayed implementation of *Brown v. Board of Education* is a lesson in the doggedness of entrenched power holders in resisting challenges to their status and privileges. Only when the material costs of their further resistance outweighed their privileges did members of the southern elite begin, with delays at every step, to open their school doors to black children. And in the long run, federally engineered integration did lead to better-financed schools for everyone. Curiously, educational integration eventually reached higher levels in the South than in the North, where "white flight" from inner cities to their suburbs resulted in new residential patterns that separated the races. In the fight against court-ordered busing of schoolchildren, northern parents raised the banner of "neighborhood schools" to maintain the qualitative edge of facilities for white children—in wealthy areas with ample tax funds—over underfunded, substandard inner-city schools.

The outlines of these future patterns were not apparent when the Court announced its *Brown* decision in 1954 and when it wrestled for another year with what would become known as *Brown II*, the issuance of an order to implement school desegregation. The morning after *Brown I*, the *New York Times* ran a banner headline: "High Court Bans School Segregation." The *Washington Post* celebrated the occasion by calling *Brown* "the most important [opinion] on racial relations since the Supreme Court ruled before the Civil War that Dred Scott, a Negro slave, was not a citizen." Yet, in the same issue of the *Post*, Governor Herman Talmadge of Georgia scoffed at the decision, saying it had reduced the Constitution to "a mere scrap of paper." More disturbing, Senator James O. Eastland of Mississippi vowed that the South "will not abide by nor obey this legislative decision by a political court. We will take whatever steps are necessary to retain segregation in education."

At the Supreme Court, the NAACP attorneys argued that no matter how unpleasant it might be for southern whites, all schools should be opened to black children by the fall of 1955, with integration completed a year later. Lawyers for the southern states countered with briefs that sketched in lurid colors how passionately white parents would resist the Court's order, and argued the need for an extended timetable to permit each school district maximum freedom to adjust the order to its circumstances.

In the last round of oral arguments in April 1955, Emory S. Rogers, the replacement for John W. Davis, who had represented South Carolina in *Brown v. Board of Education* until his death a few weeks before, managed to arouse the anger of the normally even-tempered chief justice. Rogers said that white parents will not "send their children to the Negro schools." Warren countered, "It is not a question of attitude; it is a question of conforming to the decree." Surely, Warren added, Rogers was not asserting that school districts would fail to "make an honest attempt to conform to this decree." No, said Rogers, "let us get the word 'honest' out of there." "No," answered Warren, "leave it in." Unfazed, Rogers insisted, "I would have to tell you that right now we would not conform. . . ."

In the end, Warren came to be persuaded by Herbert Brownell Jr., the attorney general, who had once more been asked to present the government's brief (which was taken as reflecting President Eisenhower's caution in not imposing a rigid timetable on resistant southern districts). Brownell proposed leaving the enforcement of *Brown* (*Brown II*) to federal district courts, where judges would be able to gauge how to adapt the Supreme Court's order to local conditions. The government could expect "popular hostility," said Brownell, but that should not provide an excuse "for a failure to end school segregation. Racial segregation in public schools is unconstitutional and will have to be terminated as quickly as feasible." Ultimately, Justice Frankfurter suggested that Warren incorporate a phrase used by Justice Oliver Wendell Holmes many years earlier in a dispute over pre–Civil War debts between Virginia and West Virginia: "With all deliberate speed."

The justices assembled for a final conference on April 16, 1955, with John Marshall Harlan, the grandson of his famous namesake, taking the place of Justice Jackson, who had died the previous October. The mood was guardedly optimistic. Only Justice Black, from Alabama, expected his fellow southerners to resist the proposed integration order for another generation. "It is futile to think," he said, "that in these cases we can settle segregation in the

South." At best, a short, direct decree might get the process under way by ordering that the children who had brought the *Brown* suits be admitted to the schools that had barred them. Justice Frankfurter saw the integration of schools in Maryland, West Virginia, and Kentucky during the past year as a good omen for the Deep South falling into line. Justice Clark commented that he hadn't noticed "too much trouble in Texas," his native state. Even Justice Reed, the last holdout in the original decision, thought that southerners would generally cooperate with the Court's order.

When Chief Justice Earl Warren read the unanimous opinion in *Brown II* to a packed courtroom on May 31, 1955, he sounded as if he wanted to meet halfway the critics who had attacked the 1954 *Brown* decision as overweening. The Court was leaving "primary responsibility" for integrating schools to the "school authorities" in each district. Federal district courts would oversee the process to ensure that school boards were guided by "a practical flexibility," taking into account "different local conditions." The Supreme Court insisted only that the defendants "make a prompt and reasonable start," and offered a list of factors for which courts could provide school boards extra time to comply, including the physical condition of school buildings, the transportation system, and necessary adjustments in district lines. The opinion ended by ordering the admission of black children "to public schools on a racially nondiscriminatory basis with all deliberate speed." Unintended or not, the last four words were taken as a hint by district court judges to allow school officials to stall year after year. Ten years later, only one percent of black children in the South were attending school with whites—not even a single child in Mississippi or Alabama.

As forthright as the 1954 *Brown* decision had been, the 1955 enforcement order sounded as if the Court was willing to accept excuses for the endless procrastination of southern states. Mississippi Governor Hugh L. White offered outright defiance: "We're not going to pay any attention to the Supreme Court decision. We don't think it will have any effect on us down here at all." Governor James F. Byrnes of South Carolina, who had been a Supreme Court Justice in 1940–1941 before taking a New Deal economic appointment, expressed "supreme confidence that we will find ways to lawfully maintain segregation." Arkansas Governor Orval Faubus, who had been moderate on racial issues, now took a hard-line stand against segregated schools to ensure his re-election to a third term.

Faubus's extremism pushed him into a confrontation with President Eisenhower, who had up to this time not expressed any opinion on *Brown*. Eisenhower had simply said that as the chief executive he had to enforce the Constitution as interpreted by the Supreme Court. In the fall of 1957, however, when nine black students appeared at Central High School in Little Rock, in line with an integration plan the school board had filed with the district court, they found their way barred. Faubus had declared the school "off limits" and surrounded the building with National Guardsmen to defend it against a "mob" that failed to materialize. Despite a further court order to proceed with integration, the Guard troops blocked the entrance for three more weeks. When the black students finally entered the school on September 23, the police made them leave—because now there really was a white mob outside. Eisenhower ordered a thousand paratroopers to appear in Little Rock the next day and to be joined by the federalized Guard. The students were escorted to school by soldiers for the rest of the school year, past segregationists who spat on them, kicked them, and even poured soup on one youngster in the cafeteria.

In February 1958 the Little Rock school board asked the court for an extension of the integration order for another two and a half years, in view of the "chaos, bedlam, and turmoil" that the police would not be able to control after federal troops left. The trial court granted the request, only to be overruled by a federal appeals court. The Supreme Court heard the case in a special session before the 1958 school year began. Warren spoke for a unanimous Court, saying that neither violence nor the threat of violence could serve as an excuse for delaying school desegregation and that Governor Faubus was restrained from nullifying "a federal court order." Justice Frankfurter added, in a concurring opinion, "Violent resistance to law cannot be made a reason for its suspension."

Still, in hundreds of other cases, school districts employed obfuscation and red tape to delay the enrollment of black children in white schools, using interminable analysis of each applicant's academic, moral, and physical condition via so-called pupil placement laws, with little reaction from the Supreme Court. The justices seemed content to see a trickle of black students breaking the color barrier as a sign that the Court's order was being heeded.

It took until 1964 for the justices to express their exasperation with the snail's pace of southern school integration. Black plaintiffs in Prince Edward County, Virginia, had begun to seek admission of their children in white schools in 1951. Despite the original 1954 *Brown* ruling, ten years later, in 1964, not a single black child had been enrolled since 1960, when the state had designated state-funded private schools for white children. Justice Black wrote the Court's opinion on the case, *Griffin v. County School Board*, acidly stating that "there has been entirely too much deliberation and not enough speed in enforcing the constitutional rights" affirmed in *Brown*. Seven justices ordered the district court to end state grants of tuition and tax credits to parents of children in private schools, although Justices Clark and Harlan dissented from the majority that ordered the reopening of public schools.

What caused the Court to respond so forcefully in 1964 to the

South's resistance to school integration? Among the factors was a change of direction from the White House, a powerful response from Congress, and more confrontational tactics by civil rights groups. President Eisenhower's attitude of caution in 1955, when he expected southern resistance to integration, had given way to John F. Kennedy's, and in 1963 to Lyndon B. Johnson's, more open commitment to civil rights.

Congress had responded by passing a strong Civil Rights Act in 1964, which, among other things, authorized the Justice Department to bring suit "for the orderly achievement of desegregation in public education." It also gave the Department of Health, Education, and Welfare the power to cut off federal funds from school districts failing to integrate their schools. Southern officials, faced with new economic pressure from Washington, combined with the rulings of district court judges against the exclusion of black children from white schools and of so-called freedom of choice plans to provide private alternatives for white children, generally yielded.

In 1970 the NAACP filed suit to achieve integration in Detroit, a northern city that had experienced "white flight" to the suburbs. The city's school district—fifth largest in the country—covered 140 square miles, with about 290,000 children, 65 percent black and 35 percent white. Federal district court judge Stephen Roth linked city schools with fifty-three predominantly white systems in the suburbs, but Michigan Governor William Milliken lodged a legal challenge to the busing plan. The appeals court approved the plan, to avert a situation that would "nullify *Brown v. Board of Education*" and revert to the "separate but equal" conditions of *Plessy.* In 1974 Chief Justice Burger spoke for a 5-to-4 majority in overturning the busing decree: for the first time in more than two decades, an NAACP suit for a desegregation order had been defeated. Burger's sweeping conclusion held that since the suburban districts had not caused the city's segregation, they need not help to solve the problem. Thurgood Marshall, who had been appointed to the Court in 1967, said sadly, in dissent, that the majority was now turning back the clock, in response to "a perceived public mood that we have gone far enough in enforcing the Constitution's guarantee of equal justice."

Burger's opinion had erected a new hurdle for black plaintiffs hoping to overcome segregation: they had to identify a person or group responsible for the denial of their basic rights before they could claim their full equality as United States citizens. The Court had not set up such a condition when it ruled for the excluded schoolchildren in *Brown v. Board of Education* twenty years earlier, nor in the enforcement orders that it had approved in the interim. Now the burden of proof shifted, from the authorities who had been operating a racially biased system to the victims who sought a remedy for their disadvantaged status. It would grow increasingly hard to find someone to blame as an agent of the discrimination, based on legally valid proof that they—as the schools in the Detroit suburbs, for example—had deliberately sought to keep black children out. Now not just specific plaintiffs but entire communities stood to lose the talents of youngsters who were being miseducated in inadequate inner-city schools.

In 1972 nearly half of the South's black children were finally attending integrated schools. They were benefiting from equal rights, and so were their parents, who had begun to find opportunities to run for and win public office, use public facilities, and attain a decent standard of living. But in 1974 a federal order to bus children in Boston in order to achieve racial balance had led to a major explosion; by 1976 some twenty thousand white students had left the city's public schools for Catholic or private education. This left black children in the majority in public schools—and their parents questioning if it had been worth subjecting them to the harassment they had had to endure. With judges ordering busing to overcome racially segregated residential patterns, school integration was as confrontational as it had been right after *Brown v. Board of Education*. Ironically, the busing stratagem had first been used successfully in the South in 1971, when white resistance had melted away.

Where had the civil rights movement come since that day in Montgomery, Alabama, on December 1, 1954, when Rosa Parks, a forty-two-year-old seamstress, refused to give up her seat on a bus to a standing white passenger? By that time, buses had replaced the trains of Homer Plessy's act of protest in 1892 as the standard means of urban transportation. Parks held her ground against the threats of the bus driver to have her arrested and, like Plessy, she was taken by the police first to the police station and then to the city jail. She later recalled, "I simply decided that I would not get up. I was tired . . . and I was not feeling well. I had felt for a long time that if I was told to get up so that a white person could sit, that I would refuse to do so."

Rosa Parks was no more an isolated actor on the historical stage than Homer Plessy had been. That became clear when Jo Ann Robinson, an English professor at Alabama State College and president of the Women's Political Council, called for a boycott of the Montgomery City Lines on Monday, December 5, the day Rosa Parks was scheduled to go to trial. The women had begun plans to protest the systematic humiliation and insults of black passengers by bus drivers, but their central role was soon overshadowed by Martin Luther King Jr., the new minister at the Dexter Avenue Baptist Church. Thousands of the women's pamphlets asked "every Negro to stay off the buses," because the next arrest would be "you, or your daughter, or mother." On Monday more than 90 percent of the thousands of Montgomery African

Americans who normally took the bus walked, caught rides, or took mules or wagons to their jobs.

Amazingly, the black community followed the call of the twenty-six-year-old Dr. King to resist oppression and be guided by a Christian spirit and the same nonviolent tactics that had been used by Mohandas K. Gandhi to secure India's independence from the British. And Montgomery's fifty thousand black citizens did this in the face of civil suits and police harassment, not for the week or two they had originally expected, but for 381 days before the courts finally decided the issue. City officials threatened to fine black cab drivers who were charging less than set fares and to issue tickets to participants in carpools. On January 26, 1956, King himself was arrested for allegedly driving five miles over the 25-mile-per-hour speed limit. Four days later, his house was dynamited, but fortunately no one was hurt, and he told his supporters to keep loving their enemies. He replied to his critics: "The tension we see in Montgomery today is the necessary tension that comes when the oppressed rise up and start to move forward toward a permanent, positive peace."

On February 21 a hundred boycotters, including King, were threatened with arrest under a 1921 Alabama law making it a crime to hinder a business without "just cause or legal excuse." At his trial, King was fined a thousand dollars, or 386 days at hard labor, but was released on bail until his appeal. He later said, "I knew that I was a convicted criminal, but I was proud of my crime." His opponents "thought they were dealing with a group who could be cajoled or forced to do whatever the white man wanted them to do. They were not aware that they were dealing with Negroes who had been freed from fear."

On April 23, 1956, the Supreme Court upheld a ruling that the segregated buses in Columbia, South Carolina, were illegal. The Montgomery bus system announced that its drivers would no longer enforce racially separate seating either, but W. A. Gayle, the city's mayor, ordered them to continue to enforce segregation, on pain of arrest.

On May 11, 1956, a federal appeals court heard NAACP attorney Robert Carter present the case against the segregated buses in Montgomery, as violating the *Brown* ruling that had overturned the "separate but equal" formula of *Plessy*. City attorneys countered that integrating the buses would provoke racial violence and bloodshed. One of the three judges asked: "Is it fair to command one man to surrender his constitutional rights, in order to prevent another man from committing a crime?" That foreshadowed the 2-to-1 decision on July 4 declaring the Alabama bus segregation law unconstitutional.

King was back in city court on November 13, facing a suit against the carpools as breaching the city's exclusive contract with the bus company when, during a recess, he learned that the Supreme Court had affirmed an order ending segregation on Montgomery's buses. (The city judge had ruled against the carpools, but his decision was overturned by the Supreme Court on December 20.)

The next morning, King was the first passenger on a city bus, seated next to Glenn Smiley, a white minister from Texas.

Later that year, other southern cities, including Tallahassee, also abandoned racially separate seating. "We seek an integration based on mutual respect," King told his supporters, "As we go back to the buses, let us be loving enough to turn an enemy into a friend. We must now move from protest to reconciliation." It seemed that the nonviolent resistance of Homer Plessy had finally been vindicated.

King's steadfastness and eloquence had helped him become the spokesman for civil rights groups throughout the South, but his very prominence made the Southern Christian Leadership

Conference (SCLC), over which he presided, a target for segregationists. For the next three years, white racist groups managed to stymie further advances in integration.

Then, on Monday, February 1, 1960, four black freshmen from North Carolina Agricultural and Technical College sat down at the "whites only" lunch counter in a Woolworth's store in downtown Greensboro, North Carolina, and began a dynamic new chapter in the history of the civil rights movement. The waitress explained to Joseph McNeill, Ezell Blair Jr., Franklin McCain, and David Richmond that the counter was for whites only and that they would have go to the "colored" counter before she could serve them. They refused to move and waited for their coffee and doughnuts until the store closed.

The four students were back at Woolworth's on the next day, this time with twenty-three others. By the end of the week, their number had grown to three hundred. Before long, word spread to Virginia and Florida, and thousands of black protestors—joined by students from nearby white colleges—were conducting sit-ins and pickets at segregated stores throughout the South. At a Woolworth's in Nashville, Tennessee, white hecklers spat on the students and pressed their lit cigarettes to the backs of black girls seated at the white lunch counter, yet police arrested only the students, not their attackers. In Orangeburg, South Carolina, police used fire hoses and tear gas against students who had joined a march in support of a sit-in. Hundreds of them were arrested and jailed, many pushed soaking wet and shivering into a chicken coop that served as a makeshift cell.

In May 1960 the protestors formed the Student Nonviolent Coordinating Committee (SNCC, or "Snick") and gained nationwide support from white youngsters—and from leaders such as John F. Kennedy, then campaigning for the presidency, who quipped: "It is in the American tradition to stand up for one's rights—even if the new way is to sit down." Snick adapted its non-violent tactics from King's SCLC and the more venerable Congress of Racial Equality (CORE), founded in 1942. The NAACP continued to work within the law on such projects as registering black voters, while King's forces were at times ready to compromise in pursuing their goals; but the youthful cadres of Snick and a renascent CORE captured national attention with their spontaneous activism.

In 1961 the Jim Crow system in southern transportation that Homer Plessy had contested in 1892 was still a fact of life. It had lingered on, just as the Supreme Court's "separate but equal" decision in *Plessy* had haunted the struggle for integration in schools, housing, health care, public places, and even cemeteries. James Farmer, executive director of CORE, organized "freedom rides" to desegregate buses and terminals nonviolently and, if repulsed, to provoke the government into action. In May a bus loaded with freedom riders was set afire by a mob in Anniston, Alabama; freedom riders in Birmingham were met by a gang of whites who beat them with lead pipes, baseball bats, and bicycle chains; a third attack took place in Montgomery, the state capital. The police stayed away. Attorney General Robert Kennedy dispatched five hundred federal marshals to Montgomery to guard the demonstrators, who had been joined by the Reverend Martin Luther King.

In Mississippi hundreds of freedom riders were packed into jail for "inflammatory traveling." With President John F. Kennedy goaded into action, the Interstate Commerce Commission pressed for enforcement of the rules against segregated bus terminals. To avoid threatened lawsuits in federal court, most southern states took down the "WHITES ONLY" signs; those who resisted were served with Justice Department injunctions to comply with the law. By the end of 1962, CORE was able to announce the virtual end of segregation in interstate travel—on buses, on trains, and at airports—seventy years after Homer Plessy's interrupted journey in New Orleans.

Two years later, the civil rights movement shifted into high gear to secure the voting rights of African Americans in the Deep South. The Council of Federated Organizations, an umbrella group including SNCC and CORE, announced in January 1964 that it would send northern volunteers to Mississippi for a "Freedom Summer" project to help register black voters. In February the White Knights of the Ku Klux Klan organized to resist this drive and in April burned sixty-one crosses in various locations around the state. On June 21 three civil rights workers— James Chaney, Andrew Goodman, and Michael Schwerner—were murdered in rural Neshoba County. Nineteen men, including the county sheriff and deputy, were identified by the FBI as suspects in the murders, but at a trial in federal court the judge dismissed nearly all the indictments.

National revulsion at the Neshoba County murders helped galvanize Congress to pass the strong Civil Rights Act of July 2, 1964. In November 1965 Thurgood Marshall, whom President Johnson had appointed the first black solicitor general, asked the Supreme Court to invoke a Reconstruction-era law of 1870 to reinstate the indictments of the Klansmen implicated in killing the civil rights workers for depriving their victims of rights "under color of law." On March 28, 1966, a unanimous Court agreed that the Mississippi trial should go forward. The federal jury finally convicted seven of the accused on October 20, 1967, the first jury in that state to convict white men for killing African Americans or civil rights workers.

In 1965 President Johnson pushed for passage of the Voting Rights Act, which barred the "tests and devices" used by state officials to prevent African Americans from voting, and empowered federal observers and registrars to ensure the act's enforcement. For the first time since Reconstruction, black voters were able to constitute a sizeable enough bloc to earn the consideration of white candidates, and even to elect blacks to local and state offices.

There has been impressive, tangible progress as a result of this legislation. In October 2000, Selma, Alabama—scene of the "Bloody Sunday" civil rights march to Montgomery on March 7, 1965—elected James Perkins Jr. its first black mayor; Perkins defeated an avowed segregationist. And in March 2003, Birmingham—a city notorious in the 1960s for a police force under Bull Connor that brutalized civil rights demonstrators with dogs and fire hoses—appointed Annetta W. Nunn, a black woman, chief of police.

But sometimes progress toward true equality for African Americans seems to take two steps forward and one step back. The net gains in the past seventy years are evident in the growing membership of blacks in the middle class, in the various professions, in skilled employment, and in government at all levels—from local school boards to the Cabinet and the Supreme Court. National recognition that the long history of discrimination demanded material forms of compensation led to so-called Affirmative Action programs; and through Title VII of the 1964 Civil Rights Act and subsequent executive orders, employers were directed to offer jobs or contracts to minority members and women to compensate for their past exclusion. In the 1970s and 1980s, the Supreme Court agreed that aptitude tests and educational standards that had led to the rejection of black applicants were illegal. The justices also approved "set asides"—congressionally approved 10 percent shares of federal contracts earmarked for minority business enterprises—against a challenge by white contractors on "due process" grounds.

"Set asides" and affirmative action in the workplace enraged many whites and became an issue so divisive that it threatened to undo what had been achieved by integration. Even greater white hostility, however, was directed at affirmative action programs in universities and professional schools that gave preferential treatment to minority applicants. In a strange twist of legal logic, white (majority) students seized on the equal protection clause of the Fourteenth Amendment to sue for admission slots set aside for minority applicants. What had been legally established in the area of jobs and contracts came to be disputed in higher education.

An ideologically divided Supreme Court was then given the burden of assessing the relative justice of conferring preferred status on black college applicants who presumably would go on to enrich their communities, at the cost of precluding white students with better, but not superlative, test scores, from being accepted by their first-choice school.

The rather muddled answer by the Court came in the case of a thirty-two-year-old white Vietnam War veteran named Allan Paul Bakke, who had been denied admission to the medical school of the University of California at Davis twice, in 1973 and 1974. Bakke had served as a captain in the marines; then, on his GI Bill benefits, had earned an MS degree in mechanical engineering at Stanford while working for NASA. Determined to become a physician, he had applied to eleven medical schools but was not accepted by any of them—including Davis, where his test score was two points too low. Bakke, who had been one of 2,664 applicants for 100 slots, learned that 16 of those slots had been set aside for minority students because of faculty concern over the shortage of African American, Latino, Asian, and Native American physicians. He decided to sue the medical school.

The legal battle around Bakke centered on whether the admissions reserved for minorities constituted a "quota" (a loaded term, especially in the period before World War II when the Ivy League and other leading universities had admitted only a token number of Jews). Was it fair to use the word "quota," the same word that had been used to exclude a minority, for the positive practice of benefiting one? The same question attaches to the novel term "reverse discrimination," seemingly an oxymoron, that became a weapon used by members of the white majority to sue for the loss of their rights and privileges as a result of preferential treatment for nonwhites. It is also apparent that American universities have long provided preference in admissions, without legal challenge, to promising athletes, the children of potential major contributors, and so-called legacies, the offspring of alumni. Yet for a medical school to give a small edge to minority applicants whose communities had a chronic shortage of physicians, was seen by some judges as a fatal flaw in the "merit system," a system that relied primarily on aptitude tests of questionable validity in predicting the abilities of future healers.

The California courts ruled in favor of Bakke, labeling the Davis admissions system a quota, which they deemed illegal in the absence of proof that the school was trying to remedy prior discrimination. Bakke's actual admission, however, had been stayed until the university could obtain a definitive judgment from the Supreme Court. After hearing the case in October 1977, the nine justices of the Court offered six different opinions on June 28, 1978. Four of the justices joined in an opinion by John Paul Stevens, who ordered Bakke admitted because Title VI of the 1964 Civil Rights Act prohibited excluding any individual on racial grounds. Four others rallied around William J. Brennan in affirming that "race-conscious" policies that had been found permissible in employment under Title VII as well as the Constitution were also legitimate in education. The ninth justice, Lewis F. Powell, fashioned a compromise, agreeing in part with the contending sides.

In what became the patched-together majority opinion, 5 to 4, Powell agreed with Stevens that setting aside a specific number of admissions for Negro, Asian, and Chicano applicants had deprived Bakke of the right to compete for those seats; hence, his total exclusion from the competition for all available slots had deprived him of his rights to "equal protection." Powell rejected the university's rationale for distinguishing applicants by race— that it would improve the health services of underserved communities—as insufficient, since it would have such minimal impact. Powell also rejected the premise of the Brennan group, that the university's preference system was justified as a way of compensating minority applicants for injuries that their groups had suffered in the past.

The joint opinion of Justices Brennan, Byron R. White, Marshall, and Harry A. Blackmun had taken a pathfinding turn when it stated "that state governments may adopt race-conscious programs if the purpose of such programs is to remove the disparate racial impact . . . itself the product of past discrimination, whether its own or that of society at large." According to that logic, Bakke was not an innocent victim of current racial preference policies but heir to white society's past discrimination against minorities. Powell distanced himself from "the breadth of this hypothesis," which he called "unprecedented in our constitutional system." Instead, he ordered the admission by the U.C. Davis Medical School of persons like Bakke "who bear no responsibility for whatever harm the beneficiaries of the special admissions program are thought to have suffered."

Yet Powell left a major loophole for affirmative action programs that avoided quotas for groups but awarded a "plus" to individuals "to promote beneficial educational pluralism." He cited as an example the admissions program of Harvard College, which included students from "disadvantaged economic, racial and ethnic groups." To the extent that U.C. Davis could recast its program with the goal of achieving "a diverse student body," Powell said, it could pass the Court's "strict scrutiny" test under the equal protection clause by balancing it with the "compelling interest" test of academic freedom under the First Amendment. Powell's compromise had been ingenious, but it left open for future cases the question: was it just one man's idiosyncratic opinion, or the holding of all four justices around Brennan who had gone along with Powell in endorsing Harvard-type diversity as it remedied "the lingering effects of past discrimination"? For the next two decades, *Bakke* was generally accepted as a precedent set by the Court majority; but then federal appeals courts began to go their own separate ways, challenging the Court to set more clearly defined limits to affirmative action in education.

The issue surfaced in 1992 when Cheryl J. Hopwood, a white woman, applied for admission to the University of Texas Law School—the same institution that had kept walling off Heman Sweatt in the mid-1940s until ordered by the Supreme Court to admit him to its white classes. Hopwood's suit stressed that her test scores had been higher than those of blacks or Mexican Americans who had been admitted under the school's affirmative action program. Two years later, on the eve of the scheduled federal trial, the law school decided to abandon its minority program; after that, the subcommittee administering the program was superseded by a single admissions committee, as the judge had urged, citing Powell's strictures against separate racial admissions in *Bakke*. A federal appeals court ruled in March 1996 that the trial court had been wrong: Powell had been speaking only for himself in *Bakke*, and he had erred in finding diversity to be a "compelling interest," since it frustrated the overriding goal of equal protection.

The number of minority students at U.T. Law subsequently

dwindled, with some resurgence after George W. Bush, as governor, introduced a measure to admit the top 10 percent of high-school graduates to the state university. Similar schemes have been adopted in Florida and California, with parallel results—a drop in the enrollment of minority students at the most prestigious state campuses. A more basic flaw in this roundabout means of recruiting minority applicants is that it presumes the continued existence of high schools with similar ratios of minority to white students. Indeed, a black or Hispanic high school student could switch to the worst school in his or her school district to increase the odds of graduating in the top decile.

At this writing it is also apparent that the fiscal crisis in the state of Texas is leading to tuition increases beyond the ability of poor students to afford—even if they do graduate at the top of their high school classes. In 1973 the Supreme Court ruled 5 to 4 against black parents in Texas who contested the state's school financing system; it was based on property taxes, which left inner-city schools with higher tax rates but less funding per pupil than in wealthy white districts. Where a unanimous Court had held in *Brown* that education "is the very foundation of good citizenship," the majority in *San Antonio's School District v. Rodriguez*, nearly twenty years later, denied that education is even "among the rights afforded protection under our Federal Constitution."

Since the 1970s, the quality gap between wealthy and poor school districts has widened in tandem with the steadily increasing gap between the richest and poorest Americans. A further consequence of this widening class gap is that despite the growing presence of African Americans in the middle and upper classes, a disproportionate number are still poor. When there is "white flight" from urban districts and some inner suburbs, the result is that the schools these white children leave behind are often the most crowded and most ill-equipped in the country.

This is one aspect of what has been called the resegregation of schools, which has recently extended into the suburbs as well.

Gary Orfield, a professor at the Harvard School of Education, has done pioneering research into the trend toward segregation of black and Latino children that he traces from the 1990s—a trend that he contends has been "largely ignored" by "national political leaders." Orfield further argues that resegregation has accelerated in the wake of Supreme Court decisions since 1991 that put time limits on desegregation plans, leading at least nine major school districts to abandon ongoing plans, while others are embroiled in litigation.

While Professor Orfield has many tables confirming the trend to resegregation, he has not correlated it with the continuing spread between white and black children's performance in achievement tests. There is, however, little doubt that the two developments are causally related. No researcher has offered any inherent reason for the lower scores of black and Latino students, leaving two likely explanations: that socioeconomic handicaps of minority families affect the academic performance of their children, and/or that the school environment offers them less encouragement to learn. The American public has shown little inclination to engage this problem, while the federal government has been fixating on increased use of tests as a barometer of success or failure in schools. It has also sporadically advocated the use of school vouchers to offer more choices to parents, without substantially transforming ineffective public schools.

In a sense, the current national debate about affirmative action serves to distract the public from the need to reform elementary, middle, and high schools. By the time minority students are of college age, it may be too late to remedy basic deficiencies in their education during the preceding twelve years. Yet it is the zero-sum game of competing for admission to prestigious colleges and professional schools that preoccupies high school seniors and their parents. What amounts to a system that leaves a negligible number of slots as token rewards for minority students has also come under intense scrutiny by the courts.

In the spring of 2003 two cases from the University of Michigan and its law school were submitted to the Supreme Court: *Jennifer Gratz and Patrick Hamacher v. Lee Bollinger et al.* and *Barbara Grutter v. Lee Bollinger et al.*, respectively. At issue was whether the university was justified in awarding 20 out of a possible 150 points (100 of these points are needed to guarantee admission) to certain minorities, socioeconomically disadvantaged students, or athletes—with only one type of bonus per applicant. Further, the courts had examined the law school's use of an individualized system, with minority status one of several plus factors, and had come up with contrary opinions.

Bernard A. Friedman, the federal district judge who heard the Michigan law school case, ruled that it violated the equal protection clause, but the U.S. Appeals Court overruled him on May 14, 2002. Its chief judge, Boyce F. Martin Jr., for the majority, found that the program fell within the bounds of Justice Powell's *Bakke* decision, but the dissenters saw the program that awarded pluses to minority applicants as a mere camouflage for a quota system. Judge Boggs, in a separate dissent, accused the majority judges of having used biased procedures to have the case heard by a court that would favor the Michigan law school program, before it could be joined by two other newly appointed justices. Justice Karen Nelson Moore took issue with this charge as "baseless" and "inaccurate," in a vitriolic personal exchange rarely seen in court records. This fascinating 154-page opinion came under review by the U.S. Supreme Court, which split into similarly contentious blocs before a majority crystallized in June 2003.

In the oral argument before the Court on April 1, 2003, the

justices seemed to be searching for a middle ground between the plaintiff's lawyer, who argued for so-called race-neutral alternatives to affirmative action, and the defense attorney, who cited the historical record, replete with decisions that made allowance for granting special consideration to minorities. Justice Sandra Day O'Connor, who is often the swing vote between two blocs of her colleagues, interrupted the plaintiff's attorney, Kirk O. Kolbo: was he saying that race "can't be a factor at all," even "one of many factors?" she asked. Kolbo replied that "race itself should not be a factor among others in choosing students because of the Constitution." O'Connor referred to precedents with the contrary conclusion. "The Court," she said, "obviously has upheld the use of race in making selections or choices in certain contexts. . . . You are speaking in absolutes and it isn't quite that."

It was significant that Theodore B. Olson, the solicitor general, expressed what was taken to be President George W. Bush's hostility to the Michigan program. When he was in private practice, Olson had argued against affirmative action at the University of Texas in the *Hopwood* case. Now he was being challenged by Justice Ruth Bader Ginsburg to explain whether the "race preference programs" at the service academies were illegal. Olson retreated, claiming that his office had not "examined that" yet and had omitted mention of the academies in its brief. Further, the negative voice from the executive branch was offset by a "friend of the court" brief by twenty-nine retired military and civilian leaders, including General Norman H. Schwarzkopf; it argued for continued affirmative action in ROTC and the service academies in order to produce the officers essential to preserve the nation's fighting ability. Another surprising amicus brief in support of the Michigan plan was submitted by sixty-five of the biggest corporations, including General Electric and Coca-Cola. The 102 pro and con amicus briefs was a new record.

While the conservative temper of the times seems to be jeop-
ardizing virtually any admissions program that favors minority
applicants, the Michigan case has been solidly based on twin
goals: attaining racial diversity to deepen the learning experience
on campus, and training minority students to become the nation's
leaders. To the extent that it is vulnerable to the charge of con-
cealing quotas, the university program may face the judicial
scalpel for granting discrete bonus points to minority applicants.
Harvard College, whose admissions plan Justice Powell held up as
a model in *Bakke*, never disclosed the relative weight it gave to
racial as opposed to strictly academic factors. By contrast, the
Michigan numbers appear to give a decisive edge to minority
applicants—without which, according to the U.S. Appeals Court
opinion, their admission totals would be cut by more than two-
thirds. As the majority argued, however, while affirmative action
has been crucial for those students, it has scarcely affected the
totals of white students admitted—if affirmative action were abolished, only about one percent more of their marginally qualified
white applicants would find extra slots available.

The Supreme Court's decision of June 23, 2003, hinged on the
vote of Justice O'Connor. Hers was the fifth vote rejecting the
practice of giving extra points to minority applicants to the University of Michigan, on the basis that the university had an unconstitutional "quota." Then she joined another group of four to
make a 5-to-4 majority that ruled as legitimate the University of
Michigan Law School's indeterminate weighting of race as one of
many factors ensuring diversity. She thereby validated the logic
used by Justice Powell in *Bakke* in 1978. She even expanded on
that precedent by commenting on the role of selective universities
in training a leadership corps, which could help to heal the racial
and ethnic tensions of American society. However, she saw affirmative action as limited in time: "We expect that 25 years from

now the use of racial preferences will no longer be necessary to further the interest approved today."

The most bitter dissent came from Justice Clarence Thomas, the Court's lone African American member. Ironically, though he had been a beneficiary of affirmative action as a law school student, he wanted to strike all such programs, as they cast a shadow on the merits of anyone given special consideration on racial or ethnic grounds. He also argued against the professed role of law schools or universities in selecting society's elites.

Still, the narrow majority opinion is the law of the land for some time to come. It will lead state universities and professional schools to revive recruitment of minority applicants in states such as Texas and Florida, where such programs were struck down by federal appeals courts, and in California, where affirmative action was rejected in a referendum. At least to a limited degree, in an era of high tuition costs, the green light from the Supreme Court will reverse the trend toward strict "merit systems" based exclusively on test scores. Despite the seductiveness of test-based merit as a shibboleth, tests are known to be flawed arbiters of merit in any number of ways, not the least of which is that scores can be appreciably augmented by coaching and tutoring programs that are beyond the financial reach of many minority families.

The educational scene has been compared to a shopping-center parking lot, where a few spaces are reserved for the "handicapped." While the availability of these spaces might arouse the ire of able-bodied drivers who can't find parking, eliminating them would cause considerable hardship for the handicapped without any appreciable alleviation of crowding for the general public. The parallel derives its force from the centuries of slavery during which Negroes were forced by threats and punishment to remain illiterate.

A problem with such analogies, however, is that the Court has been asking whether affirmative action programs are designed to last forever. The Court's response in the University of Michigan case was that there is a built-in shutoff mechanism to the consideration of "race and ethnicity"—"until it becomes possible to enroll a 'critical mass' of underrepresented minority students through race-neutral means."

The "Constitution is color-blind, and neither knows nor tolerates classes among citizens," said Justice Harlan in his 1896 *Plessy* dissent. From even a cursory look at Harlan's related opinions, it becomes clear that he was directing his ire at the biased "Jim Crow" laws in the South, not the Reconstruction measures that were designed to aid the newly freed slaves. It is ironic that this metaphor has been used recently by those opponents of affirmative action who argue against policies that marginally diminish the perquisites of the majority. Surely, judges need to take cognizance of existing racial inequities in order to measure the effectiveness of remedial programs; as Justice O'Connor has said, the Court has repeatedly had to use race "in making selections or choices in certain contexts."

Since 1619, when the first slaveship arrived in America, its exhausted passengers were forced to contribute their labor at the cost of their fractured lives. Even after the slaves were freed during the Civil War, they had to endure another ninety years of segregation and unequal citizenship. Has the past fifty years of fitful integration really satisfied the demand for justice? Or does history require yet another measure of restitution for the scales of justice to finally be balanced?

The most ethical policy would be to assure African American children access to the best education, from primary schools to universities, benefiting not only them and their families but all of us who stand to share in the enjoyment of their skills and talents.

# APPENDIX A:

## *Plessy v. Ferguson*, DECISION BY JUSTICE H. B. BROWN

May 18, 1896

This case turns upon the constitutionality of an act of the General Assembly of the State of Louisiana, passed in 1890, providing for separate railway carriages for the white and colored races. (Acts 1890, No. 111, p. 152.)

The first section of the statute enacts "that all railway companies carrying passengers in their coaches in this State, shall provide equal but separate accommodations for the white, and colored races, by providing two or more passenger coaches for each passenger train, or by dividing the passenger coaches by a partition so as to secure separate accommodations. *Provided*, That this section shall not be construed to apply to street railroads. No person or persons shall be admitted to occupy seats in coaches, other than the ones assigned to them, on account of the race they belong to."

By the second section it was enacted "that the officers of such passenger trains shall have power and are hereby required to assign each passenger to the coach or compartment used for the race to which such passenger belongs; any passenger insisting on going into a coach or compartment to which by race he does not belong, shall be liable to a fine of twenty-five dollars, or in lieu thereof to imprisonment for a period of not more than twenty days in the parish prison, and any officer of any railroad insisting on assigning a passenger to a coach or compartment other than the one set aside for the race to which said passenger belongs, shall be liable to a fine of twenty-five dollars, or in lieu thereof to imprisonment for a period of not more than twenty days in the parish prison; and should any passenger refuse to occupy the coach or compartment to which he or she is assigned by the officer of such railway, said officer shall have power to refuse to carry such passenger on his train, and for such refusal neither he nor the railway company shall be liable for damages in any courts of this State."

The third section provides penalties for the refusal or neglect of the officers, directors, conductors, and employes of railway companies to comply with the act, with a proviso that "nothing in this act shall be construed as applying to nurses attending children of the other race." The fourth section is immaterial.

The information filed in the criminal district court charged, in substance, that Plessy, being a passenger between two stations within the State of Louisiana, was assigned by officers of the company to the coach used for the race to which he belonged, but he insisted on going into a coach used by the race to which he did not belong. Neither in the information or plea was his particular race or color averred.

The petition for the writ of prohibition averred that petitioner was seven-eighths Caucasian and one-eighth African blood; that the mixture of colored blood was not discernible in him; and that he was entitled to every right, privilege, and immunity secured to citizens of the United States of the white race; and that, upon such theory, he took possession of a vacant seat in a coach where passengers of the white race were accommodated, and was ordered by the conductor to vacate said coach and take a seat in another, assigned to persons of the colored race, and, having refused to comply with such demand, he was forcibly ejected, with the aid of a police officer, and imprisoned in the parish jail to answer a charge of having violated the above act.

The constitutionality of this act is attacked upon the ground that it conflicts both with the Thirteenth Amendment of the Constitution, abolishing slavery, and the Fourteenth Amendment, which prohibits certain restrictive legislation on the part of the States.

1. That it does not conflict with the Thirteenth Amendment, which abolished slavery and involuntary servitude, except as punishment for crime, is too clear for argument. Slavery implies involuntary servitude—a state of bondage; the ownership of mankind as a chattel, or, at least, the control of the labor and services of one man for the benefit of another, and the absence of a legal right to the disposal of his own person, property, and services. This amendment was said in the *Slaughter-House Cases*, 16 Wall. 36, to have been intended primarily to abolish slavery, as it had been previously known in this country, and that it equally forbade Mexican peonage or the Chinese coolie trade, when they amounted to slavery or involuntary servitude, and that the use of the word "servitude" was intended to prohibit the use of all forms of involuntary slavery, of whatever class or name. It was intimated, however, in that case, that this amendment was regarded by the statesmen of that day as insufficient to protect the colored race from certain laws which had been enacted in the southern States, imposing upon the colored race onerous disabilities and burdens, and curtailing their rights in the pursuit of life, liberty, and property to such an extent that their freedom was of little value; and that the Fourteenth Amendment was devised to meet this exigency.

So, too, in the Civil Rights Cases, 109 U.S. 3, 24, it was said that the act of a mere individual, the owner of an inn, a public conveyance or place of amusement, refusing accommodation to colored people, cannot be justly regarded as imposing any badge of slavery or servitude upon the applicant, but only as involving an ordinary civil injury, properly cognizable by the laws of the State, and presumably subject to redress by those laws until the contrary appears. "It would be running the slavery question into the ground," said Mr. Justice Bradley, "to make it apply to every act of discrimination which a person may see fit to make as to the guests he will entertain, or as to the people he will take into his coach or cab or car, or admit to his concert or theater, or deal with in other matters of intercourse or business."

A statute which implies merely a legal distinction between the white and colored races—a distinction which is founded in the color of the two races, and which must always exist as long as white men are distinguished from the other race by color—has no tendency to destroy the legal equality of the two races, or re-establish a state of involuntary servitude. Indeed, we do not understand that the Thirteenth Amendment is strenuously relied upon by the plaintiff in error in this connection.

2. By the Fourteenth Amendment, all persons born or naturalized in the United States, and subject to the jurisdiction thereof, are made citizens of the United States and of the State wherein they reside; and the States are forbidden from making or enforcing any law which shall abridge the privileges or immunities of citizens of the United States, or shall deprive any person of life, liberty, or property without due process of law, or deny to any person within their jurisdiction the equal protection of the laws.

The proper construction of this amendment was first called to the attention of this court in the *Slaughter-House Cases*, 16 Wall. 36, which involved, however, not a question of race, but one of exclusive privileges. The case did not call for any expression of opinion as to the exact rights it was intended to secure to the colored race, but it was said generally that its main purpose was to establish the citizenship of the Negro, to give definitions of citizenship of the United States and of the States, and to protect from the hostile legislation of the States the privileges and immunities of citizens of the United States, as distinguished from those of citizens of the States.

The object of the amendment was undoubtedly to enforce the absolute equality of the two races before the law, but, in the nature of things, it could not have been intended to abolish distinctions based upon color, or to enforce social, as distinguished from political, equality, or a commingling of the two races upon terms unsatisfactory to either. Laws permitting, and even requiring, their separation, in places where they are liable to be brought into contact, do not necessarily imply the inferiority of either race to the other, and have been generally, if not universally, recognized as within the competency of the state legislatures in the exercise of their police power. The most common instance of this is connected with the establishment of separate schools for white and colored children, which has been held to be a valid exercise of the legislative power even by courts of States where the political rights of the colored race have been longest and most earnestly enforced.

One of the earliest of these cases is that of *Roberts v. City of Boston*, 5 Cush. 198, in which the Supreme Judicial Court of Massachusetts held that the general school committee of Boston had power to make provision for the instruction of colored children in separate schools established exclusively for them, and to prohibit their attendance upon the other schools. "The great principle," said Chief Justice Shaw, p. 206, "advanced by the learned and eloquent advocate for the plaintiff," (Mr. Charles Sumner), "is that, by the constitution and laws of Massachusetts, all persons, without distinction of age or sex, birth or color, origin or condition, are equal before the law. . . . But when this great principle comes to be applied to the actual and various conditions of persons in society, it will not warrant the assertion that men and women are legally clothed with the same civil and political powers, and that children and adults are legally to have the same functions and be subject to the same treatment; but only that the rights of all, as they are settled and regulated by law, are equally entitled to the paternal consideration and protection of the law for their maintenance and security." It was held that the powers of the committee extended to the establishment of separate schools for children of different ages, sexes and colors, and that they might also establish separate schools for poor and neglected children, who have become too old to attend the primary school, and yet have not acquired the rudiments of learning, to enable them to enter the ordinary schools. Similar laws have been enacted by Congress under its general power of legislation over the District of Columbia, as well as by the legislatures of many of the States, and have been generally, if not uniformly, sustained by the courts. *State v. McCann*, 21 Ohio St. 198; *Lehew v. Brummel*, 15 S.W. Rep. 765; *Ward v. Flood*, 48 Cal. 36; *Bertonneau v. School Directors*, 3 Woods 177; *People v. Gallagher*, 93 N.Y. 438; *Cory v. Carter*, 48 Ind. 337; *Dawson v. Lee*, 83 Ky. 49.

Laws forbidding the intermarriage of the two races may be said in a technical sense to interfere with the freedom of contract, and yet have been universally recognized as within the police power of the State. *State v. Gibson*, 36 Ind. 389.

The distinction between laws interfering with the political equality of the Negro and those requiring the separation of the two races in schools, theaters, and railway carriages has been frequently drawn by this Court. Thus, in *Strauder v. West Virginia*, 100 U.S. 303, it was held that a law of West Virginia limiting to white male persons 21 years of age, and citizens of the State, the right to sit upon juries, was a discrimination which implied a legal inferiority in civil society, which lessened the security of the right of the colored race, and was a step toward reducing them to a condition of servility. Indeed, the right of a colored man that, in the selection of jurors to pass upon his life, liberty, and property, there shall be no exclusion of his race, and no discrimination against them because of color, has been asserted in a number of cases. *Virginia v. Rives*, 100 U.S. 313; *Neal v. Delaware*, 103 U.S. 370; *Bush v. Kentucky*, 107 U.S. 110; *Gibson v. Mississippi*, 162 U.S. 565. So, where the laws of a particular locality or the charter of a particular railway corporation has provided that no person shall be excluded from the cars on account of color, we have held that this meant that persons of color should travel in the same car as white ones, and that the enactment was not satisfied by the company's providing cars assigned exclusively to people of color, though they were as good as those which they assigned exclusively to white persons. *Railroad Company v. Brown*, 17 Wall. 445.

Upon the other hand, where a statute of Louisiana required those engaged in the transportation of passengers among the States to give to all persons travelling within that State, upon vessels employed in that business, equal rights and privileges in all parts of the vessel, without distinction on account of race or color, and subjected to an action for damages the owner of such a vessel who excluded colored passengers on account of their color from the cabin set aside by him for the use of whites, it was held to be, so far as it applied to interstate commerce, unconstitutional and void. *Hall v. De Cuir*, 95 U.S. 485. The court in this case, however, expressly disclaimed that it had anything whatever to do with the statute as a regulation of internal commerce, or affecting anything else than commerce among the States.

In the Civil Rights Cases, 109 U.S. 3, it was held that an act of Congress entitling all persons within the jurisdiction of the United States to the full and equal enjoyment of the accommodations, advantages, facilities, and privileges of inns, public conveyances, on land or water, theaters, and other places of public amusement, and made applicable to citizens of every race and color, regardless of any previous condition of servitude, was unconstitutional and void, upon the ground that the Fourteenth Amendment was prohibitory upon the States only, and the legislation authorized to be adopted by Congress for enforcing it was not direct legislation on matters respecting which the States were prohibited from making or enforcing certain laws, or doing certain acts, but was corrective legislation, such as might be necessary for counteracting and redressing the effects of such laws or acts. In delivering the opinion of the court, Mr. Justice Bradley observed that the Fourteenth Amendment "does not invest Congress with power to legislate upon subjects that are within the domain of state legislation, but to provide modes of relief against state legislation or state action of the kind referred to. It does not authorize Congress to create a code of municipal law for the regulation of private rights, but to provide modes of redress against the operation of state laws, and the action of state officers, executive or judicial, when these are subversive of the fundamental rights specified in the amendment. Positive rights and privileges are undoubtedly secured by the Fourteenth Amendment; but they are secured by way of prohibition against state laws and state proceedings affecting those rights and privileges, and by power given to Congress to legislate for the purpose of carrying such prohibition into effect; and such legislation must necesarily be predicated upon such supposed state laws or state proceedings, and be directed to the correction of their operation and effect."

Much nearer, and, indeed, almost directly in point, is the case of the *Louisville, New Orleans &c. Railway v. Mississippi*, 133 U.S. 587, wherein the railway company was indicted for a violation of a statute of Mississippi, enacting that all railroads carrying passengers should provide equal, but separate, accommodations for the white and colored races, by providing two or more passenger cars for each passenger train, or by dividing the passenger cars by a partition, so as to secure separate accommodations. The case was presented in a different aspect from the one under consideration, inasmuch as it was an indictment against the railway company for failing to provide the separate accommodations, but the question considered was the constitutionality of the law. In that case, the Supreme Court of Mississippi, 66 Miss. 662, had held that the statute applied solely to commerce within the State, and, that being the construction of the state statute by its highest court, was accepted as conclusive. "If it be a matter," said the court, p. 591, "respecting commerce wholly within a State, and not interfering with commerce between the States, then, obviously, there is no violation of the commerce clause of the Federal Constitution. . . . No question arises under this section as to the power of the State to separate in different compartments interstate passengers, or affect, in any manner, the privileges and rights of such passengers. All that we can consider is whether the State has the power to require that railroad trains within her limits shall have separate accommodations for the two races. That affecting only commerce within the State is no invasion of the power given to Congress by the commerce clause."

A like course of reasoning applies to the case under consideration, since the Supreme Court of Louisiana, in the case of *State ex rel. Abbott v. Hicks, Judge, et al.*, 44 La. Ann. 770, held that the statute in question did not apply to interstate passengers, but was confined in its application to passengers travelling exclusively within the borders of the State. The case was decided largely upon the authority of *Railway Co. v. State*, 66 Miss. 662, and affirmed by this Court in 133 U.S. 587. In the present case no question of interference with interstate commerce can possibly arise, since the East Louisiana Railway appears to have been purely a local line, with both its termini within the State of Louisiana. Similar statutes for the separation of the two races upon public conveyances were held to be constitutional in *West Chester &c. Railroad v. Miles*, 55 Pa. St. 209; *Day v. Owen*, 5 Mich. 520; *Chicago &c. Railway v. Williams*, 55 Ill. 185; *Chesapeake &c. Railroad v. Wells*, 85 Tenn. 627; *The Sue*, 22 Fed. Rep. 843; *Logwood v. Memphis &c. Railroad*, 23 Fed. Rep. 318; *McGuinn v. Forbes*, 37 Fed. Rep. 639; *People v. King*, 18 N.E. Rep. 245; *Houck v. South Pac. Railway*, 38 Fed. Rep. 226; *Heard v. Georgia Railroad Co.*, 3 Int. Com. Com'n. 111; *S.C.*, 1 Ibid. 428.

While we think the enforced separation of the races, as applied to the internal commerce of the State, neither abridges the privileges or immunities of the colored man, deprives him of his property without due process of law, nor denies him the equal protection of the laws, within the meaning of the Fourteenth Amendment, we are not prepared to say that the conductor, in assigning passengers to the coaches according to their race, does not act at his peril, or that the provision of the second section of the act that denies to the passenger compensation in damages for a refusal to receive him into the coach in which he properly belongs is a valid exercise of the legislative power. Indeed, we understand it to be conceded by the State's attorney that such part of the act as exempts from liability the railway company and its officers is unconstitutional. The power to assign to a particular coach obviously implies the power to determine to which race the passenger belongs, as well as the power to determine who, under the laws of the particular State, is to be deemed a white, and who a colored, person. This question, though indicated in the brief of the plaintiff in error, does not properly arise upon the record in this case, since the only issue made is as to the unconstitutionality of the act, so far as it requires the railway to provide separate accommodations, and the conductor to assign passengers according to their race.

It is claimed by the plaintiff in error that, in any mixed community, the reputation of belonging to the dominant race, in this instance the white race, is "property," in the same sense that a right of action or of inheritance is property. Conceding this to be so, for the purposes of this case, we are unable to see how this statute deprives him of, or in any way affects his right to, such property. If he be a white man, and assigned to a colored coach, he may have his action for damages against the company for being deprived of his so called "property." Upon the other hand, if he be a colored man, and be so assigned, he has been deprived of no property, since he is not lawfully entitled to the reputation of being a white man.

In this connection, it is also suggested by the learned counsel for the plaintiff in error that the same argument that will justify the state legislature in requiring railways to provide separate accommodations for the two races will also authorize them to require separate cars to be provided for people whose hair is of a certain color, or who are aliens, or who belong to certain nationalities, or to enact laws requiring colored people to walk upon one side of the street, and white people upon the other, or requiring white men's houses to be painted white, and colored men's black, or their vehicles or business signs to be of different colors, upon the theory that one side of the street is as good as the other, or that a house or vehicle of one color is as good as one of another color. The reply to all this is that every exercise of the police power must be reasonable, and extend only to such laws as are enacted in good faith for the promotion of the public good, and not for the annoyance or oppression of a particular class. Thus, in *Yick Wo v. Hopkins*, 118 U.S. 356, it was held by this court that a municipal ordinance of the city of San Francisco, to regulate the carrying on of public laundries within the limits of the municipality, violated the provisions of the Constitution of the United States, if it conferred upon the municipal authorities arbitrary power, at their own will, and without regard to discretion, in the legal sense of the term, to give or withhold consent as to persons or places, without regard to the competency of the persons applying or the propriety of the places selected for the carrying on of the business. It was held to be a covert attempt on the part of the municipality to make an arbitrary and unjust discrimination against the Chinese race. While this was the case of a municipal ordinance, a like principle has been held to apply to acts of a state legislature passed in the exercise of the police power. *Railroad Company v. Husen*, 95 U.S. 465; *Louisville & Nashville Railroad v. Kentucky*, 161 U.S. 677, and cases cited on p. 700; *Daggett v. Hudson*, 43 Ohio St. 548; *Capen v. Foster*, 12 Pick. 485; *State ex rel. v. Wood v. Baker*, 38 Wis. 71; *Monroe v. Collins*, 17 Ohio St. 665; *Hulseman v. Rems*, 41 Pa. St. 396; *Osman v. Riley*, 15 Cal. 48.

So far, then, as a conflict with the Fourteenth Amendment is concerned, the case reduces itself to the question whether the statute of Louisiana is a reasonable regulation, and with respect to this there must necessarily be a large discretion on the part of the legislature. In determining the question of reasonableness, it is at liberty to act with reference to the established usages, customs, and traditions of the people, and with a view to the promotion of their comfort, and the preservation of the public peace and good order. Gauged by this standard, we cannot say that a law which authorizes or even requires the separation of the two races in public conveyances is unreasonable, or more obnoxious to the Fourteenth Amendment than the acts of Congress requiring separate schools for colored children in the District of Columbia, the constitutionality of which does not seem to have been questioned, or the corresponding acts of state legislatures.

We consider the underlying fallacy of the plaintiff's argument to consist in the assumption that the enforced separation of the two races stamps the colored race with a badge of inferiority. If this be so, it is not by reason of anything found in the act, but solely because the colored race chooses to put that construction upon it. The argument necessarily assumes that if, as has been more than once the case, and is not unlikely to be so again, the colored race should become the dominant race in the state legislature, and should enact a law in precisely similar terms, it would thereby relegate the white race to an inferior position. We imagine that the white race, at least, would not acquiesce in this assumption. The argument also assumes that social prejudices may be overcome by legislation, and that equal rights cannot be secured to the negro except by an enforced commingling of the two races. We cannot accept this proposition. If the two races are to meet upon terms of social equality, it must be the result of natural affinities, a mutual appreciation of each other's merits, and a voluntary consent of individuals. As was said by the Court of Appeals of New York in *People v. Gallagher*, 93 N.Y. 438, 448, "This end can neither be accomplished nor promoted by laws which conflict with the general sentiment of the community upon whom they are designed to operate. When the government, therefore, has secured to each of its citizens equal rights before the law and equal opportunities for improvement and progress, it has accomplished the end for which it was organized, and performed all of the functions respecting social advantages with which it is endowed." Legislation is powerless to eradicate racial instincts, or to abolish distinctions based upon physical differences, and the attempt to do so can only result in accentuating the difficulties of the present situation. If the civil and political rights of both races be equal, one cannot be inferior to the other civilly or politically. If one race be inferior to the other socially, the Constitution of the United States cannot put them upon the same plane.

It is true that the question of the proportion of colored blood necessary to constitute a colored person, as distinguished from a white person, is one upon which there is a difference of opinion in the different States, some holding that any visible admixture of black blood stamps the person as belonging to the colored race (*State v. Chavers*, 5 Jones [N.C.] 1, p. 11); others, that it depends upon the preponderance of blood (*Gray v. State*, 4 Ohio 354; *Monroe v. Collins*, 17 Ohio St. 665); and still others, that the predominance of white blood must only be in the proportion of three-fourths (*People v. Dean*, 14 Mich. 406; *Jones v. Commonwealth*, 80 Va. 538). But these are questions to be determined under the laws of each State, and are not properly put in issue in this case. Under the allegations of his petition, it may undoubtedly become a question of importance whether, under the laws of Louisiana, the petitioner belongs to the white or colored race.

The judgment of the court below is, therefore,

*Affirmed.*

# APPENDIX B:
## *Plessy v. Ferguson,* DISSENT BY JUSTICE J. M. HARLAN

By the Louisiana statute the validity of which is here involved, all railway companies (other than street-railroad companies) carrying passengers in that State are required to have separate but equal accommodations for white and colored persons, "by providing two or more passenger coaches for each passenger train, or by dividing the passenger coaches by a partition so as to secure separate accommodations." Under this statute, no colored person is permitted to occupy a seat in a coach assigned to white persons; nor any white person to occupy a seat in a coach assigned to colored persons. The managers of the railroad are not allowed to exercise any discretion in the premises, but are required to assign each passenger to some coach or compartment set apart for the exclusive use of his race. If a passenger insists upon going into a coach or compartment not set apart for persons of his race, he is subject to be fined, or to be imprisoned in the parish jail. Penalties are prescribed for the refusal or neglect of the officers, directors, conductors, and employes of railroad companies to comply with the provisions of the act.

Only "nurses attending children of the other race" are excepted from the operation of the statute. No exception is made of colored attendants travelling with adults. A white man is not permitted to have his colored servant with him in the same coach, even if his condition of health requires the constant, personal assistance of such servant. If a colored maid insists upon riding in the same coach with a white woman whom she has been employed to serve, and who may need her personal attention while travelling, she is subject to be fined or imprisoned for such an exhibition of zeal in the discharge of duty.

While there may be in Louisiana persons of different races who are not citizens of the United States, the words in the act, "white and colored races," necessarily include all citizens of the United States of both races residing in that State. So that we have before us a state enactment that compels, under penalties, the separation of the two races in railroad passenger coaches, and makes it a crime for a citizen of either race to enter a coach that has been assigned to citizens of the other race.

Thus the State regulates the use of a public highway by citizens of the United States solely upon the basis of race.

However apparent the injustice of such legislation may be, we have only to consider whether it is consistent with the Constitution of the United States.

That a railroad is a public highway, and that the corporation which owns or operates it is in the exercise of public functions, is not, at this day, to be disputed. Mr. Justice Nelson, speaking for this Court in *New Jersey Steam Navigation Co. v. Merchants' Bank*, 6 How. 344, 382, said that a common carrier was in the exercise of "a sort of public office, and has public duties to perform, from which he should not be permitted to exonerate himself without the assent of the parties concerned." Mr. Justice Strong, delivering the judgment of this court in *Olcott v. The Supervisors*, 16 Wall. 678, 694, said: "That railroads, though constructed by private corporations and owned by them, are public highways, has been the doctrine of nearly all the courts ever since such conveniences for passage and transportation have had any existence. Very early the question arose whether a State's right of eminent domain could be exercised by a private corporation created for the purpose of constructing a railroad. Clearly it could not, unless taking land for such a purpose by such an agency is taking land for public use. The right of eminent domain nowhere justifies taking property for a private use. Yet it is a doctrine universally accepted that

346

a state legislature may authorize a private corporation to take land for the construction of such a road, making compensation to the owner. What else does this doctrine mean if not that building a railroad, though it be built by a private corporation, is an act done for public use?" So, in *Township of Pine Grove v. Talcott*, 19 Wall. 666, 676: "Though the corporation [a railroad company] was private, its work was public, as much so as if it were to be constructed by the State." So, in *Inhabitants of Worcester v. Western Railroad Corporation*, 4 Metc. [Mass.] 564, "The establishment of that great thoroughfare is regarded as a public work, established by public authority, intended for the public use and benefit, the use of which is secured to the whole community, and constitutes, therefore, like a canal, turnpike, or highway, a public easement." "It is true that the real and personal property, necessary to the establishment and management of the railroad, is vested in the corporation; but it is in trust for the public."

In respect of civil rights, common to all citizens, the Constitution of the United States does not, I think, permit any public authority to know the race of those entitled to be protected in the enjoyment of such rights. Every true man has pride of race, and under appropriate circumstances, when the rights of others, his equals before the law, are not to be affected, it is his privilege to express such pride and to take such action based upon it as to him seems proper. But I deny that any legislative body or judicial tribunal may have regard to the race of citizens when the civil rights of those citizens are involved. Indeed, such legislation as that here in question is inconsistent not only with that equality of rights which pertains to citizenship, National and State, but with the personal liberty enjoyed by every one within the United States.

The Thirteenth Amendment does not permit the withholding or the deprivation of any right necessarily inhering in freedom. It not only struck down the institution of slavery as previously existing in the United States, but it prevents the imposition of any burdens or disabilities that constitute badges of slavery or servitude. It decreed universal civil freedom in this country. This Court has so adjudged. But, that amendment having been found inadequate to the protection of the rights of those who had been in slavery, it was followed by the Fourteenth Amendment, which added greatly to the dignity and glory of American citizenship, and to the security of personal liberty, by declaring that "all persons born or naturalized in the United States, and subject to the jurisdiction thereof, are citizens of the United States and of the State wherein they reside," and that "no State shall make or enforce any law which shall abridge the privileges or immunities of citizens of the United States; nor shall any State deprive any person of life, liberty or property without due process of law, nor deny to any person within its jurisdiction the equal protection of the laws." These two amendments, if enforced according to their true intent and meaning, will protect all the civil rights that pertain to freedom and citizenship. Finally, and to the end that no citizen should be denied, on account of his race, the privilege of participating in the political control of his country, it was declared by the Fifteenth Amendment that "the right of citizens of the United States to vote shall not be denied or abridged by the United States or by any State on account of race, color or previous condition of servitude."

These notable additions to the fundamental law were welcomed by the friends of liberty throughout the world. They removed the race line from our governmental systems. They had, as this Court has said, a common purpose, namely, to secure "to a race recently emancipated, a race that through many generations have been held in slavery, all the civil rights that the superior race enjoy." They declared, in legal effect, this Court has further said, "that the law in the States shall be the same for the black as for the white; that all persons, whether colored or white, shall stand equal before the laws of the States; and in regard to the colored race, for whose protection the amendment was primarily designed, that no discrimination shall be made against them by law because of their color." We also said: "The words of the amendment, it is true, are prohibitory, but they contain a necessary implication of a positive immunity, or right, most valuable to the colored race—the right to exemption from unfriendly legislation against them distinctively as colored; exemption from legal discriminations, implying inferiority in civil society, lessening the security of their enjoyment of the rights which others enjoy; and discriminations which are steps toward reducing them to the condition of a subject race." It was, consequently, adjudged that a state law that excluded citizens of the colored race from juries, because of their race, however well qualified in other respects to discharge the duties of jurymen, was repugnant to the Fourteenth Amendment. *Strauder v. West Virginia*, 100 U.S. 303, 306, 307; *Virginia v. Rives*, 100 U.S. 313; *Ex parte Virginia*, 100 U.S. 339; *Neal v. Delaware*, 103 U.S. 370, 386; *Bush v. Kentucky*, 107 U.S. 110, 116. At the present term, referring to the previous adjudications, this Court declared that "underlying all of those decisions is the principle that the Constitution of the United States, in its present form, forbids, so far as civil and political rights are concerned, discrimination by the General Government or the States against any citizen because of his race. All citizens are equal before the law." *Gibson v. Mississippi*, 162 U.S. 565.

The decisions referred to show the scope of the recent amendments of the Constitution. They also show that it is not within the power of a State to prohibit colored citizens, because of their race, from participating as jurors in the administration of justice.

It was said in the argument that the statute of Louisiana does not discriminate against either race, but prescribes a rule applicable alike to white and colored citizens. But this argument does not meet the difficulty. Every one knows that the statute in question had its origin in the purpose, not so much to exclude white persons from railroad cars occupied by blacks, as to exclude colored people from coaches occupied by or assigned to white persons. Railroad corporations of Louisiana did not make discrimination among whites in the matter of accommodation for travellers. The thing to accomplish was, under the guise of giving equal accommodation for whites and blacks, to compel the latter to keep to themselve while travelling in railroad passenger coaches. No one would be so wanting in candor as to assert the contrary. The fundamental objection, therefore, to the statute is that it interferes with the personal freedom of citizens. "Personal liberty," it has been well said, "consists in the power of locomotion, of changing situation, or removing one's person to whatsoever places one's own inclination may direct, without imprisonment or restraint, unlesss by due course of law." 1 Bl. Com. 134. If a white man and a black man choose to occupy the same conveyance on a public highway, it is their right to do so; and no government, proceeding alone on grounds of race, can prevent it without infringing the personal liberty of each.

It is one thing for railroad carriers to furnish, or to be required by law to furnish, equal accommodations for all whom they are under a legal duty to carry. It is quite another thing for government to forbid citizens of the white and black races from travelling in the same public conveyance, and to punish officers of railroad companies for permitting persons of the two races to occupy the same passenger coach. If a State can prescribe, as a rule of civil conduct, that whites and blacks shall not travel as passengers in the same railroad coach, why may it not so regulate the use of the streets of its cities and towns as to compel white citizens to keep on one side of a street, and black citizens to keep on the other? Why may it not, upon like grounds, punish whites and blacks who ride together in street cars or in open vehicles on a public road or street? Why may it not require sheriffs to assign whites to one side of a court room, and blacks to the other? And why may it not also prohibit the commingling of the two races in the galleries of legislative halls or in public assemblages convened for the consideration of the political questions of the day? Further, if this statute of Louisiana is consistent with the personal liberty of citizens, why may not the State require the separation in railroad coaches of native and naturalized citizens of the United States, or of Protestants and Roman Catholics?

The answer given at the argument to these questions was that regulations of the kind they suggest would be unreasonable, and could not, therefore, stand before the law. Is it meant that the determination of questions of legislative power depends on the inquiry whether the statute whose validity is questioned is, in the judgment of the courts, a reasonable one, taking all the circumstances into consideration? A statute may be unreasonable merely because a sound public policy forbade its enactment. But I do not understand that the courts have anything to do with the policy or expediency of legislation. A statute may be valid, and yet, upon grounds of public policy, may well be characterized as unreasonable. Mr. Sedgwick correctly states the rule when he says that, the legislative intention being clearly ascertained, "the courts have no other duty to perform than to execute the legislative will, without any regard to their views as to the wisdom or justice of the particular enactment." Stat. & Const. Constr. 324. There is a dangerous tendency in these latter days to enlarge the functions of the courts, by means of judicial interference with the will of the people as expressed by the legislature. Our institutions have the distinguishing characteristic that the three departments of government are co-ordinate and separate. Each must be kept within the limits defined by the Constitution. And the courts best discharge their duty by executing the will of the law-making power, constitutionally expressed, leaving the results of legislation to be dealt with by the people through their representatives. Statutes must always have a reasonable construction. Sometimes they are to be construed strictly, sometimes liberally, in order to carry out the legislative will. But, however construed, the intent of the legislature is to be respected if the particular statute in question is valid, although the courts, looking at the public interests, may conceive the statute to be both unreasonable and impolitic. If the power exists to enact a statute, that ends the matter so far as the courts are concerned. The adjudged cases in which statutes have been held to be void, because unreasonable, are those in which the means employed by the legislature were not at all germane to the end to which the legislature was competent.

The white race deems itself to be the dominant race in this country. And so it is, in prestige, in achievements, in education, in wealth, and in power. So, I doubt not, it will continue to be for all time, if it remains true to its great heritage and holds fast to the principles of constitutional liberty. But in view of the Constitution, in the eye of the law, there is in this country no superior, dominant, ruling class of citizens. There is no caste here. Our Constitution is color-blind, and neither knows nor tolerates classes among citizens. In respect of civil rights, all citizens are equal before the law. The humblest is the peer of the most powerful. The law regards man as man, and takes no account of his surroundings or of his color when his civil rights as guaranteed by the supreme law of the land are involved. It is therefore to be regretted that this high tribunal, the final expositor of the fundamental law of the land, has reached the conclusion that it is competent for a State to regulate the enjoyment by citizens of their civil rights solely upon the basis of race.

In my opinion, the judgment this day rendered will, in time, prove to be quite as pernicious as the decision made by this tribunal in the *Dred Scott* case.

It was adjudged in that case that the descendants of Africans who were imported into this country and sold as slaves were not included nor intended to be included under the word "citizens" in the Constitution, and could not claim any of the rights and privileges which that instrument provided for and secured to citizens of the United States; that, at the time of the adoption of the Constitution, they were "considered as a subordinate and inferior class of beings, who had been subjugated by the dominant race, and, whether emancipated or not, yet remained subject to their authority, and had no rights or privileges but such as those who held the power and the government might choose to grant them." 19 How. 393, 404. The recent amendments of the Constitution, it was supposed, had eradicated these principles from our institutions. But it seems that we have yet, in some of the States, a dominant race—a superior class of citizens—which assumes to regulate the enjoyment of civil rights, common to all citizens, upon the basis of race. The present decision, it may well be apprehended, will not only stimulate aggressions, more or less brutal and irritating, upon the admitted rights of colored citizens, but will encourage the belief that it is possible, by means of state enactments, to defeat the beneficent purposes which the people of the United States had in view when they adopted the recent amendments of the Constitution, by one of which the blacks of this country were made citizens of the United States and of the States in which they respectively reside, and whose privileges and immunities, as citizens, the States are forbidden to abridge. Sixty millions of whites are in no danger from the presence here of eight millions of blacks. The destinies of the two races, in this country, are indissolubly linked together, and the interests of both require that the common government of all shall not permit the seeds of race hate to be planted under the sanction of law. What can more certainly arouse race hate, what more certainly create and perpetuate a feeling of distrust between these races, than state enactments, which, in fact, proceed on the ground that colored citizens are so inferior and degraded that they cannot be allowed to sit in public coaches occupied by white citizens? That, as all will admit, is the real meaning of such legislation as was enacted in Louisiana.

The sure guarantee of the peace and security of each race is the clear, distinct, unconditional recognition by our governments, National and State, of every right that inheres in civil freedom, and of the equality before the law of all citizens of the United States, without regard to race. State enactments regulating the enjoyment of civil rights upon the basis of race, and cunningly devised to defeat legitimate results of the [Civil] war, under the pretense of recognizing equality of rights, can have no other result than to render permanent peace impossible, and to keep alive a conflict of races, the continuance of which must do harm to all concerned. This question is not met by the suggestion that social equality cannot exist between the white and black races in this country. That argument, if it can be properly regarded as one, is scarcely worthy of consideration; for social equality no more exists between two races when travelling in a passenger coach or a public highway than when members of the same races sit by each other in a street car or in the jury box, or stand or sit with each other in a political assembly, or when they use in common the streets of a city or town, or when they are in the same room for the purpose of having their names placed on the registry of voters, or when they approach the ballot box in order to exercise the high privilege of voting.

There is a race so different from our own that we do not permit those belonging to it to become citizens of the United States. Persons belonging to it are, with few exceptions, absolutely excluded from our country. I allude to the Chinese race. But, by the statute in question, a Chinaman can ride in the same passenger coach with white citizens of the United States, while citizens of the black race in Louisiana, many of whom, perhaps, risked their lives for the preservation of the Union, who are entitled, by law, to participate in the political control of the State and nation, who are not excluded, by law or by reason of their race, from public stations of any kind, and who have all the legal rights that belong to white citizens, are yet declared to be criminals, liable to imprisonment, if they ride in a public coach occupied by citizens of the white race. It is scarcely just to say that a colored citizen should not object to occupying a public coach assigned to his own race. He does not object, nor, perhaps, would he object to separate coaches for his race if his rights under the law were recognized. But he does object, and ought never to cease objecting, to the proposition that citizens of the white and black races can be adjudged criminals because they sit, or claim the right to sit, in the same public coach on a public highway. The arbitrary separation of citizens, on the basis of race, while they are on a public highway, is a badge of servitude wholly inconsistent with the civil freedom and the equality before the law established by the Constitution. It cannot be justified upon any legal grounds.

If evils will result from the commingling of the two races upon public highways established for the benefit of all, they will be infinitely less than those that will surely come from state legislation regulating the enjoyment of civil rights upon the basis of race. We boast of the freedom enjoyed by our people above all other peoples. But it is difficult to reconcile that boast with a state of the law which, practically, puts the brand of servitude and degradation upon a large class of our fellow-citizens, our equals before the law.

The thin disguise of "equal" accommodations for passengers in railroad coaches will not mislead any one, nor atone for the wrong this day done.

The result of the whole matter is that while this Court has frequently adjudged, and at the present term has recognized the doctrine, that a State cannot, consistently with the Constitution of the United States, prevent white and black citizens, having the required qualifications for jury service, from sitting in the same jury box, it is now solemnly held that a State may prohibit white and black citizens from sitting in the same passenger coach on a public highway, or may require that they be separated by a "partition" when in the same passenger coach. May it not now be reasonably expected that astute men of the dominant race, who affect to be disturbed at the possibility that the integrity of the white race may be corrupted, or that its supremacy will be imperiled, by contact on public highways with black people, will endeavor to procure statutes requiring white and black jurors to be separated in the jury box by a "partition," and that, upon retiring from the court room to consult as to their verdict, such partition, if it be a movable one, shall be taken to their consultation room, and set up in such a way as to prevent black jurors from coming too close to their brother jurors of the white race. If the "partition" used in the court room happens to be stationary, provision could be made for screens with openings through which jurors of the two races could confer as to their verdict without coming into personal contact with each other. I cannot see but that, according to the principles this day announced, such state legislation, although conceived in hostility to, and enacted for the purpose of humiliating, citizens of the United States of a particular race, would be held to be consistent with the Constitution.

I do not deem it necessary to review the decisions of state courts to which reference was made in argument. Some, and the most important, of them are wholly inapplicable, because rendered prior to the adoption of the last amendments of the Constitution, when colored people had very few rights which the dominant race felt obliged to respect. Others were made at a time when public opinion, in many localities, was dominated by the institution of slavery; when it would not have been safe to do justice to the black man; and when, so far as the rights of blacks were concerned, race prejudice was, practically, the supreme law of the land. Those decisions cannot be guides in the era introduced by the recent amendments of the supreme law, which established universal civil freedom, gave citizenship to all born or naturalized in the United States and residing here, obliterated the race line from our systems of governments, National and State, and placed our free institutions upon the broad and sure foundation of the equality of all men before the law.

I am of opinion that the statute of Louisiana is inconsistent with the personal liberty of citizens, white and black, in that State, and hostile to both the spirit and letter of the Constitution of the United States. If laws of like character should be enacted in the several States of the Union, the effect would be in the highest degree mischievous. Slavery, as an institution tolerated by law, would, it is true, have disappeared from our country; but there would remain a power in the States, by sinister legislation, to interfere with the full enjoyment of the blessings of freedom; to regulate civil rights, common to all citizens, upon the basis of race; and to place in a condition of legal inferiority a large body of American citizens, now constituting a part of the political community called the "People of the United States," for whom, and by whom through representatives, our government is administered. Such a system is inconsistent with the guarantee given by the Constitution to each State of a republican form of government, and may be stricken down by Congressional action, or by the courts in the discharge of their solemn duty to maintain the supreme law of the land, anything in the constitution or laws of any State to the contrary notwithstanding.

For the reasons stated, I am constrained to withhold my assent from the opinion and judgment of the majority.

[Mr. Justice Brewer did not hear the argument or participate in the decision of this case.]

# BIBLIOGRAPHY

Aldred, Lisa. *Thurgood Marshall*. New York: Chelsea House, 1990.

Allport, Gordon. *The Nature of Prejudice*. Boston: Addison-Wesley, 1954.

Ames, Blanche A. *Adalbert Ames, 1835–1933: General, Senator, Governor*. New York: Argosy-Antiquarian, 1964.

Arbeitman, Lee, and Richard L. Roe. *Great Trials in American History*. St. Paul, Minn.: West, 1985.

Baker, Leonard. *Brandeis and Frankfurter: A Dual Biography*. New York: Harper & Row, 1984.

Baker, Ray Stannard. *Following the Color Line: American Negro Citizenship in the Progressive Era*. New York: Harper & Row, 1964.

Bancroft, Frederic. *Calhoun and the South Carolina Nullificaation Movement*. Gloucester, Mass.: Peter Smith, 1966.

Bardolph, Richard. *The Civil Rights Record: Black Americans and the Law, 1849–1970*. New York: Thomas Y. Crowell, 1970.

Barnes, Catherine A. *Journey from Jim Crow: The Desegregation of Southern Transit*. New York: Columbia University Press, 1983.

Beard, Charles A. and Mary R., *The Rise of American Civilization*. New York: Macmillan, 1927.

Bell, Caryn Cossé. *Revolution, Romanticism and the Afro-Creole Protest Tradition in Louisiana, 1718–1868*. Baton Rouge: Louisiana State University Press, 1997.

Berman, Daniel L. *It Is So Ordered: The Supreme Court Rules on School Desegregation*. New York: W. W. Norton, 1966.

Blassingame, John W. *Black New Orleans: 1860–1880*. Chicago: Chicago University Press, 1973.

Blumberg, Rhoda L. *Civil Rights: The 1960s Struggle*. Boston: Twayne, 1991.

Boritt, Gabor S., ed. *Lincoln's Generals*. New York: Oxford University Press, 1994.

Capers, Gerald M. *John C. Calhoun, Opportunist: A Reappraisal*. Gainesville: University of Florida Press, 1960.

Carnegie, Andrew. *The Gospel of Wealth, and Other Timely Essays*. New York: Century, 1900.

Chalmers, David M. *Hooded Americanism: The First Century of the Ku Klux Klan, 1865–1965*. Garden City, N.Y.: Doubleday, 1965.

Chicago Commission on Race Relations. *The Negro in Chicago*. Chicago: Chicago University Press, 1922.

Cohen, William. *At Freedom's Edge: Black Mobility and the Southern White*

*Quest for Racial Control, 1861–1915.* Baton Rouge: Louisiana State University Press, 1991.

Cook, Blanche Wiesen. *Eleanor Roosevelt.* New York: Viking, 1999.

Craven, Avery. *Reconstruction: The Ending of the Civil War.* New York: Holt, Rinehart and Winston, 1969.

Crété, Liliane. *Daily Life in Louisiana, 1815–1830.* Baton Rouge: Louisiana State University Press, 1981.

Current, Richard Nelson. *Those Terrible Carpetbaggers.* New York: Oxford University Press, 1988.

Desdunes, Rodolphe Lucien. *Our People and Our History.* Baton Rouge: Louisiana State University Press, 1973.

Dibble, Roy F. *Albion W. Tourgée.* Port Washington, N.Y.: Kennikat Press, 1921.

Du Bois, W. E. B. *The Autobiography of W. E. B. Du Bois.* New York: International, 1968.

——. *Black Reconstruction in America.* New York: Atheneum, 1935.

Eastland, Terry. *Ending Affirmative Action: The Case for Colorblind Justice.* New York: Basic Books, 1996.

Fehrenbacher, Don E. *The Dred Scott Case: Its Significance in American Law and Politics.* New York: Oxford University Press, 1978.

Fireside, Harvey. *The "Mississippi Burning" Civil Rights Murder Conspiracy Trial.* Berkeley Heights, N.J.: Enslow, 2002.

——. *New York Times v. Sullivan: Affirming Freedom of the Press.* Springfield, N.J.: Enslow, 1999.

Flack, Horace E. *The Adoption of the Fourteenth Amendment.* Gloucester, Mass.: Peter Smith, 1965.

Foner, Eric. *A Short History of Reconstruction, 1863–1877.* New York: Harper & Row, 1990.

——, and Olivia Mahoney. *America's Reconstruction: People and Politics after the Civil War.* New York: Harper Perennial, 1995.

Franklin, John Hope. *Reconstruction after the Civil War.* Chicago: Chicago University Press, 1994.

Friedman, Leon, and Fred I. Israel, eds. *The Justices of the United States Supreme Court, 1789–1969: Their Lives and Major Opinions.* New York: R.R. Bowker, 1969.

Garner, James Wilford. *Reconstruction in Mississippi.* Gloucester, Mass.: Peter Smith, 1964.

Garrow, David. *Bearing the Cross: Martin Luther King and the Southern Christian Leadership Conference.* New York: William Morrow, 1986.

——, ed. *The Montgomery Bus Boycott and the Women Who Started It: The*

*Memoir of Jo Ann Gibson Robinson.* Knoxville: University of Tennessee Press, 1987.

Gehman, Mary. *The Free People of Color of New Orleans: An Introduction.* New Orleans: Margaret Media, 1994.

Goldman, Roger, and David Gallen. *Thurgood Marshall: Justice for All.* New York: Carroll & Graf, 1992.

Goodman, James. *Stories of Scottsboro.* New York: Pantheon, 1994.

Goodwin, Doris Kearns. *No Ordinary Time: Eleanor and Franklin Roosevelt: The Home Front in World War II.* New York: Simon & Schuster, 1994.

Graf, LeRoy P., and Ralph W. Haskins, eds. *The Papers of Andrew Johnson,* 2 vols. Knoxville: University of Tennessee Press, 1967–1989.

Grodinsky, Julius. *Jay Gould: His Business Career, 1867–1892.* Philadelphia: University of Pennsylvania Press, 1957.

Gross, Theodore L. *Albion W. Tourgée.* New York: Twayne, 1963.

Halberstam, David. *The Fifties.* New York: Villard, 1993.

Hall, Kermit L., ed. *The Oxford Companion to the Supreme Court of the United States.* New York: Oxford University Press, 1992.

Harlan, Malvina Shanklin. *Some Memories of a Long Life, 1854–1911.* New York: Modern Library, 2002.

Harris, William Charles. *The Day of the Carpetbagger: Republican Reconstruction in Mississippi.* Baton Rouge: Louisiana State University Press, 1979.

Haskins, James. *The First Black Governor, Pinkney [sic] Benton Stewart Pinchback.* Trenton, N.J.: Africa World Press, 1973.

Hearn, Chester M. *When the Devil Came to Dixie: Ben Butler in New Orleans.* Baton Rouge: Louisiana State University Press, 1992.

Hirsch, Arnold R., and Joseph Logsdon, eds. *Creole New Orleans: Race and Americanization.* Baton Rouge: Louisiana State University Press, 1992.

Holzman, Robert S. *Stormy Ben Butler.* New York: Macmillan, 1954.

Johnson, Charles Spurgeon. *Patterns of Negro Segregation.* New York: Harper & Bros., 1943.

Jordan, David M. *Roscoe Conkling of New York: Voice in the Senate.* Ithaca, N.Y.: Cornell University Press, 1971.

Josephson, Matthew. *The Robber Barons: The Great American Capitalists, 1861–1901.* New York: Harcourt, Brace & World, 1962.

Kennedy, John F. *Profiles in Courage.* New York: Cardinal edition, 1957.

Killenbeck, Mark R. *The Tenth Amendment and State Sovereignty: Constitutional History and Contemporary Issues.* Lanham, Md.: Rowman & Littlefield, 2002.

King, Grace Elizabeth, and John R. Ficklen. *A History of Louisiana.* New York: University Publishers, 1893.

King, Martin Luther, Jr. *Stride Toward Freedom.* New York: Harper, 1958.

Kluger, Richard. *Simple Justice: The History of Brown v. Board of Education and Black America's Struggle for Equality.* New York: Random House, 1975.

Kousser, J. Morgan, and James M. McPherson, eds. *Region, Race, and Reconstruction: Essays in Honor of C. Vann Woodward.* New York: Oxford University Press, 1982.

Kozol, Jonathan. *Death at an Early Age: The Destruction of the Hearts and Minds of Negro Children in the Boston Public Schools.* Boston: Houghton Mifflin, 1967.

Kurland, Philip, and Gerhard Casper. *Landmark Briefs and Arguments of the Supreme Court of the United States: Constitutional Law.* Arlington, Va.: University Publications of America, 1958.

Lewis, Anthony. *Make No Law: The Sullivan Case and the First Amendment.* New York: Random House, 1991.

Lewis, David L. *W. E. B. Du Bois: The Fight for Equality and the American Century, 1919–1963.* New York: Henry Holt, 2000.

Lincoln, Abraham. *Collected Works of Abraham Lincoln.* New Brunswick, N.J.: Rutgers University Press, 1953–1955.

Lively, Donald E. *The Constitution and Race.* New York: Praeger, 1992.

Lofgren, Charles A. *The Plessy Case: A Legal-Historical Interpretation.* New York: Oxford University Press, 1987.

Logan, Rayford W. *The Betrayal of the Negro: From Rutherford B. Hayes to Woodrow Wilson.* New York: Collier, 1954.

Madison, James, Alexander Hamilton, and John Jay. *The Federalist Papers.* New York: New American Library, 1961.

McDonald, Forrest. *States' Rights and the Union: Imperium in Imperio, 1776–1876.* Lawrence: University Press of Kansas, 2000.

Marmor, Theodore R. *The Career of John C. Calhoun: Politician, Social Critic, Political Philosopher.* New York: Garland, 1988.

Mason, Alpheus T., and William M. Beaney. *American Constitutional Law: Introductory Essays and Selected Cases.* Englewood Cliffs, N.J.: Prentice-Hall, 1964.

Miller, Loren. *The Petitioners: The Story of the Supreme Court of the United States and the Negro.* New York: Pantheon, 1966.

Morison, Samuel Eliot. *The Oxford History of the American People.* New York: Oxford University Press, 1965.

Myrdal, Gunnar. *An American Dilemma: The Negro Problem and Modern Democracy.* New York: Harper & Brothers, 1944.

NAACP Legal Defense and Educational Fund. *Toward Equal Justice.* New York: NAACP, n.d.

O'Brien, David M. *Constitutional Law and Politics: Civil Rights and Liberties.* New York: W. W. Norton, 1991.

Olson, Otto H. *A Carpetbagger: Albion W. Tourgée and Reconstruction in North Carolina.* Baltimore: Johns Hopkins University [PhD], 1959.

——. *Carpetbagger's Crusade: The Life of Albion Winegar Tourgée.* Baltimore: Johns Hopkins University Press, 1965.

——. *The Thin Disguise: Plessy v. Ferguson, A Documentary Presentation (1864–1896).* New York: Humanities Press, 1967.

Orfield, Gary, and John T. Yu. The *Resegregation in American Schools.* Cambridge, Mass.: Harvard University, 1999.

Ovington, Mary White. *How the National Association for the Advancement of Colored People Began.* New York: NAACP, 1914.

Painter, Nell Irvin. *Standing at Armageddon: The United States, 1887–1919.* New York: W. W. Norton, 1987.

Perman, Michael. *The Road to Redemption: Southern Politics, 1869–1879.* Chapel Hill: University of North Carolina Press, 1984.

Polakoff, Keith Ian. *The Politics of Inertia: The Election of 1876 and the End of Reconstruction.* Baton Rouge: Louisiana State Unviersity Press, 1973.

Polenberg, Richard. *One Nation Divisible: Class, Race, and Ethnicity in the United States Since 1938.* New York: Viking, 1980.

Pollack, Jack Harrison. *Earl Warren, the Judge Who Changed America.* Englewood Cliffs, N.J.: Prentice Hall, 1979.

Przybyszewski, Linda. *The Republic According to John Marshall Harlan.* Chapel Hill: University of North Carolina Press, 1999.

Rabinowitz, Howard N. *Race Relations in the Urban South, 1865–1890.* New York: Oxford University Press, 1978.

*Recipes and Reminiscences of New Orleans*, vol. II, *Our Cultural Heritage.* New Orleans: Ursuline Academy, 1981.

*Reporting Civil Rights I.* New York: Library of America, 2003.

Rogers, Kim Lacy. *Righteous Lives: Narratives of the New Orleans Civil Rights Movement.* New York: New York University Press, 1993.

Sarratt, Reed. *The Ordeal of Segregation: The First Decade.* New York: Harper & Row, 1966.

Scheiner, Seth M., ed. *Reconstruction: A Tragic Era?* New York: Holt, Rinehart & Winston, 1968.

Schwartz, Bernard, ed. *The Fourteenth Amendment: Centennial Volume.* New York: New York University Press, 1970.

——. *A History of the Supreme Court.* New York: Oxford University Press, 1993.

——. *Super Chief: Earl Warren and His Supreme Court, a Judicial Biography.* New York: New York University Press, 1983.

Sindler, Allan P. *Bakke, De Funis, and Minority Admissions: The Quest for Equal Opportunity*. New York: Longman, 1978.

Sitkoff, Harvey. *The Struggle for Black Equality, 1954–1992*. New York: Hill & Wang, 1993.

Stampp, Kenneth M. *The Era of Reconstruction, 1865–1877*. New York: Knopf, 1965.

———, and Leon F. Litwack, eds. *Reconstruction: An Anthology of Revisionist Writings*. Baton Rouge: Louisiana State University Press, 1969.

Stephenson, Gilbert T. *Race Distinctions in American Law*. New York: Appleton, 1910.

Taeuber, Karl E. and Alma F. *Negroes in Cities: Residential Segregation and Neighborhood Change*. Chicago: Aldine, 1965.

Taylor, Joe Gray. *Louisiana Reconstructed, 1863–1877*. Baton Rouge: Louisiana State University Press, 1974.

Thomas, Brook, ed. *Plessy v. Ferguson: A Brief History with Documents*. Boston: Bedford/St. Martin's, 1997.

Thompson, Daniel C. *The Negro Leadership Class*. Englewood Cliffs, N.J.: Prentice-Hall, 1963.

Tinker, Edward Larocque. *Creole City: Its Past and Its People*. New York: Longmans, Green, 1953.

Thornbrough, Emma Lou. *Black Reconstructionists*. Englewood Cliffs, N.J.: Prentice Hall, 1972.

Tourgée, Albion Winegar. *A Fool's Errand*. Cambridge, Mass.: Harvard University Press, 1961.

Trefousse, Hans Louis. *Ben Butler: The South Called Him Beast!* New York: Twayne, 1957.

Ture, Kwame (Stokely Carmichael), and Charles V. Hamilton. *Black Power: The Politics of Liberation in America*. New York: Vintage, 1992.

Tushnet, Mark. *The NAACP's Legal Strategy Against Segregated Education, 1925–1950*. Chapel Hill: University of North Carolina Press, 1987.

United States Commission on Civil Rights. *Twenty Years after Brown*. Washington: U.S. Government Printing Office, 1975.

Veit, Helen E., et al., eds. *Creating the Bill of Rights*. Baltimore: Johns Hopkins University Press, 1991.

Warren, Earl. *The Memoirs of Earl Warren*. Garden City, N.Y.: Doubleday, 1977.

Warlich, Robert. *"Beast" Butler: The Incredible Career of Major General Benjamin Franklin Butler*. Washington: Quaker Press, 1962.

Warmoth, Henry Clay. *War, Politics, and Reconstruction*. New York: Macmillan, 1930.

Washington, Booker T. *Up from Slavery*. New York: Lancer, 1968.

Weaver, John Downing. *Warren: The Man, the Court, the Era*. Boston: Little, Brown, 1967.

West, Richard S. *Lincoln's Scapegoat General: A Life of Benjamin F. Butler, 1818–1893*. Boston: Houghton Mifflin, 1965.

Wilkinson, J. Harvie III. *From Brown to Bakke: The Supreme Court and School Integration, 1954–1978*. New York: Oxford University Press, 1979.

Wiltse, Charles M. *John C. Calhoun: 1840–1850 Sectionalist*. Indianapolis: Bobbs-Merrill, 1957.

Wish, Harvey, ed. *Reconstruction in the South, 1865–1877*. New York: Farrar, Straus and Giroux, 1965.

Woodward, C. Vann. *Reunion and Reaction: The Compromise of 1877 and the End of Reconstruction*. Boston: Little, Brown, 1966.

——. *The Strange Career of Jim Crow*. New York: Oxford University Press, 1974.

Wilson, Theodore Brantner. *The Black Codes of the South*. University: University of Alabama Press, 1965.

Yarbrough, Tinsley E. *Judicial Enigma: The First Justice Harlan*. New York: Oxford University Press, 1995.

# NOTES

## Chapter 1: An Interrupted Journey

1. On June 7, 1892 . . . commit a crime: Keith W. Medley, "The Sad Story of How 'Separate But Equal' Was Born," *Smithsonian*, February 1994, pp. 106–107.

2. Dowling told him . . . minstrel show: Morison, p. 792.

2–3. "remaining in a compartment . . . the State": *Plessy v. Ferguson*, 163 U.S. 537 (1892), Albion W. Tourgée and James C. Walker, "Brief for Plaintiff in Error," pp. 8–9.

3. The Plessys lived in . . . New Orleans: Medley, *op. cit.*

3. Adams claimed . . . for whites: Cited in Olsen, *Thin Disguise*, pp. 70–71.

4. Although slavery . . . a segregated "colored car": Lofgren, p. 41.

4–5. "distinction and discrimination . . . the Federal Constitution": *Plessy v. Ferguson*, Tourgée and Walker, p. 9.

5. He claimed . . . to be near each other: Cited in Olsen, *Thin Disguise*, p. 11.

6. "respectably and cleanly . . . any noxious [i.e., infectious] disease": *Plessy v. Ferguson*, Tourgée and Walker, p. 9.

6. Judge Ferguson . . . "learning and ability": Cited in Olsen, *Thin Disguise*, p. 14.

7. "that what he says . . . this law": *Ibid.*, p. 71.

7. A caustic commentary . . . "better for them": *Ibid.*, p. 14.

7. So much for . . . Supreme Court annals: *Washington Post*, 11 October 1949, editorial, p. 14, also rates the *Plessy* decision the "worst" after *Dred Scott*, cited in Logan, p. 121.

8. Mainly in New Orleans . . . in 1803: Gehman, p. 20.

9. The French administrators . . . New Orleans: Jerah Johnson, "Colonial New Orleans: A Fragment of the Eighteenth-Century Ethos," in Hirsch and Logsdon, p. 53.

9. More than six hundred . . . the conflict: Gehman, p. 59.

10. The term "mulatto" . . . through the 1850s: *Ibid.*, p. 60.

10. The brightest . . . education: Blassingame, p. 195.

11. Then they bulled their way . . . to block the river: Morison, p. 641.

11. General Butler . . . subject to confiscation: *Ibid.*, p. 653.

11. "a woman of the town. . . . ": Franklin, p. 3.

12. "compulsory free labor system": Blassingame, pp. 29–30.

12. "equal but separate" railway cars: Joseph Logsdon and Caryn Cossé Bell, "The Americanization of Black New Orleans 1850–1900," in Hirsch and Logsdon, pp. 256–257.

12. "We'll make a case . . . to travel through the State unmolested": *Plessy v. Ferguson*, "Act No. 111," in Supreme Court Briefs.

12–13. Money and support . . . bitter years of slavery: "An Appeal," Tulane University Archives (New Orleans: September 5, 1891), unpaged.

13. . . . rich and poor African Americans . . . grimy Jim Crow cars . . . : Polakoff, pp. 298–299.

13. If these members . . . Confederate states: *Ibid.*, p. 313.

14. Thousands of Tilden ballots . . . a major defeat: Woodward, *Reunion*, pp. 18–19.

14. Whoever dared . . . violence in state after state: *Ibid.*, p. 8.

15. "It was a murder . . . without the shadow of necessity": Wish, pp. 52–53.
15. It divided the South . . . the rights of freedmen: Current, p. 66.
15. Seymour may have . . . win the contest: Morison, pp. 721–722.
15–16. Despite repeated setbacks . . . President Rutherford B. Hayes: La Wanda and John H. Cox, "Civil Rights: The Issue of Reconstruction," in Scheiner, pp. 37–47.
16. At least since . . . *Gone with the Wind*: Logan, pp. 350–351.
17. Soon after . . . threw the Negro pupils out: Louis R. Harlan, "Desegregation of New Orleans Public Schools During Reconstruction," *American Historical Review*, LXVII, pp. 663–675.
17–18. In 1868 Warmoth . . . as his lieutenant governor: Current, pp. 75–78.
18. Next in line . . . attained that office in the United States: *Ibid.*, pp. 276–281.
18. He was succeeded . . . C. C. Antoine, who served from 1872 to 1876: Logsdon and Bell, p. 251.
18. Other black officials . . . 1872–1876: John Hope Franklin, "A Re-evaluation of Negro Participation," in Scheiner, p. 55.
19. If the majority . . . fit in to the new political order: Wish, p. xxiv.
19. W. E. B. Du Bois . . . against corrupt state officials: W. E. B. Du Bois, "Reconstruction and Its Benefits," *American Historical Review*, XV, pp. 781–799.
19. In April . . . Republicans Grant and Schuyler Colfax: Current, p. 78. *Cf.* Thornbrough, p. 39, giving April totals of 61,152 for Warmouth, 43,739 against.
20. Gone were the Radical Republicans . . . the Pullman Strike of 1894: Morison, p. 740.
20. True, the Court's last word . . . public amusement: Civil Rights Cases, 109 U.S. 3.
21. "badges of slavery": *Ibid.*
22. Although Harlan . . . a leading supporter of Negro rights: Yarbrough, pp. 28–33.
22. Indeed, in an authoritative history . . . a contributor: Desdunes, p. 142. However, biographers of Justice Harlan discount the claim of his financial support to the plaintiff as incredible, given his strict code of ethics.
22–23. Albion W. Tourgée . . . to rule in Plessy's favor: Albion W. Tourgée to Louis A. Martinet, 31 October 1893, Tourgée Papers, cited in Olsen, *Thin Disguise*, p. 78.
23. This senior counsel . . . was freed in an exchange: John Hope Franklin, "Introduction," in Albion W. Tourgée, *A Fool's Errand*, pp. viii–ix.
23. Tourgée . . . elected a judge of the superior court: Current, pp. 52–65.
24. He accepted . . . without fee: Lofgren, p. 30.
24. Their first volunteer . . . Rodolphe Desdunes: Thomas, p. 5.
26. In brief . . . "without due process of law": Howard J. Graham, "The 'Conspiracy Theory' of the Fourteenth Amendment" (originally in *Yale Law Journal*, XLVIII, 1938), reprinted in Stampp and Litwack, p. 108.
26. *The Gospel of Wealth*: Matthew Josephson, *The Robber Barons: The Great American Capitalists, 1861–1901* (New York: Harcourt Brace Jovanovich, 1962), p. v.
27. Rodolphe Desdunes . . . of voting age: Desdunes, p. 144.

## Chapter 2: Reconstruction Promises Never Kept
29. "With malice toward none . . . all nations": Abraham Lincoln, "Second Inaugural Address," in Lincoln, VIII, p. 333.

30. "Founded in . . . of justice": Abraham Lincoln, "Peoria Speech, 1851," in *ibid.*, II, p. 271.

30. "A house divided . . . half *free*": Abraham Lincoln, "Douglas Debates, 1858," in *ibid.*, II, p. 463.

30–31. "who think slavery . . . end to it": Abraham Lincoln, in *ibid.*, II, p. 276.

31. "If each state . . . have decided": Stephen A. Douglas, "Quincy Speech, 1858," in *ibid.*, III, pp. 266, 273.

31. "I will say . . . white people": Abraham Lincoln, "Douglas Debates, 1858," in *ibid.*, III, p. 145. Some historians (e.g., Wilson, p. 141) seem to have mistakenly identified the site as Charleston, S.C., indicating a "southern audience" that Lincoln was placating. Indeed, Lincoln cited his words from the Illinois speech a year later, September 16, 1858, in Columbus, Ohio (*ibid.*, p. 400).

32. "My paramount object . . . destroy slavery": Abraham Lincoln, "Letter to Horace Greeley, 1862," in *ibid.*, V., p. 388.

32. "The moment came . . . in bondage": Foner, *Short History*, pp. 1–2.

32. A meeting . . . the cotton trade: Abraham Lincoln, "To the Workingmen of Manchester," in Lincoln, VI, pp. 63–65.

32. "Shall be, then . . . forever free": Abraham Lincoln, "Emancipation Proclamation," in *ibid.*, pp. 28–31.

33. "The North went to war . . . to secure this result": Du Bois, *Black Reconstruction*, p. 716.

33. "Without the military . . . have been won": *Ibid.*

33. In proportion . . . "they were fighting": *Ibid.*, p. 717.

34. "believe the Negro . . . and suffrage": *Ibid.*, p. 731.

34. "all the forces . . . of barbarous freedmen": *Ibid.*, p. 719.

34. "From the Republican policy . . . order of intelligence": *Ibid.*, p. 718.

34. After the war . . . the old slave system: Bardolph, p. 35.

35. On May 25, 1865 . . . he then pardoned: Graf and Haskins, VIII, pp. 128–130.

35. He opposed the congressional . . . and abolished slavery: Craven, p. 71.

36. He was also against . . . the war: *Ibid.*, pp. 143–146.

36–37. In March 1867 . . . executive officials: Morison, p. 720.

37. The Senate trial . . . their political careers: John F. Kennedy included the story of one of these senators, Edmund G. Ross of Kansas, in his 1956 *Profiles in Courage*.

37. It took the U.S. Supreme Court . . . his appointees: *Myers v. United States*, 272 U.S. 52.

37. General Benjamin Butler . . . that of whites. Morison, p. 674.

37–38. A monument . . . "the patriot soldier": *Ibid.*, p. 675.

38. Until his death . . . was never enacted: Craven, p. 136.

38. Under Lincoln the Freedmen's bureau . . . primary schools: Morison, p. 711.

39. One of its first graduates . . . public accommodations: Washington, p. 220.

39. The original promise . . . other supplies: Bardolph, p. 42.

39. When Louisiana free men . . . "a Negro constituency": Du Bois, *Black Reconstruction*, p.156; Taylor, p. 27.

39. The committee . . . in Washington: Bell, pp. 251–252.

40. Lincoln's confidential message . . . "in our ranks": Du Bois, *op. cit.*, p. 157.

40. When Lincoln was asked . . . legal contracts: Franklin, pp. 14–15.

40. Though the bill passed . . . leadership role: Craven, pp. 71–75.

41. After establishing . . . for Negroes: Morison, pp. 714–715.

41. An able associate . . . U.S. circuit court: *Ibid.*, p. 715.

42. Yet at least one respected historian . . . lash out at slavery: *Ibid.*, p. 714.

42. Morison further finds . . . ill-equipped for citizenship: *Ibid.*, p. 715.

43. To separate Negro children . . . later in life: Kluger, pp. 75–76.

43. "must depend upon . . . conditions": *Roberts v. City of Boston*, 5 Cushing 198 (Mass. 1850).

43. Without the support . . . Black Codes: Wilson, p. 146.

44. At the height . . . teeth in it: Bardolph, p. 35.

44–45. Unlike the civil administrators . . . against Negroes: Stampp, pp. 184–185.

46. The antislavery cause . . . in 1833: Kluger, p. 36.

46. On July 13, 1863 . . . four days: Morison, p. 666.

46. In the Confederacy . . . for every twenty slaves: *Ibid.*, p. 667.

47. W. E. B. Du Bois . . . rich and poor: Du Bois, *op. cit.*, p. 460.

47. Forty-two Negroes . . . in the state senate: *Ibid.*, 471.

47–48. The 1868 national election . . . in Louisiana: *Ibid.*, p. 482.

48. The racist campaign . . . of the three: *Ibid.*, p. 474.

48. In the case . . . been illegally ousted: *Ibid.*, 482.

48–49. The Ku Klux Klan . . . from the battlefield: Chalmers, p. 2.

49. By 1869 Forrest . . . habeas corpus: Fireside, *"Mississippi Burning,"* p. 49; see also Miller, p. 97.

49. Grant did . . . violence on freedpeople: Foner and Mahoney, p. 123.

50. Typical of this genre . . . mulatto soldiers: Frederick L. Hoffman, "Race Amalgamation," cited in Thomas, p. 84.

50. Other vital statistics . . . "unaffected by education": *Ibid.*, p. 94.

50. Hoffman quotes . . . "civilization": Cited in *ibid.*, p. 79.

51–52. "If there be on the part of whites . . . pay for them": Henry M. Field, "Capacity of the Negro—His Position in the North," cited in Thomas, p. 102.

52. "We cannot fight against instinct . . . laws": Cited in *ibid.*, p. 119.

52. "the negro [sic] race . . . single great leader": Cited in *ibid.*, p. 103.

52. "where are the men . . . of mediocrity": Cited in *ibid.*, p. 112.

53. "a black skin . . . passion to reason": Lewis, p. 353.

53. "ambitious northern whites . . . Reconstruction governments": Scheiner, p. 47.

53. The result . . . incited racial conflict: *Ibid.*, p. 48.

53. Actually, it was W. G. Brown . . . 1873: Du Bois, *op. cit.*, p. 477.

53. Du Bois, according to his autobiography . . . War: Du Bois, *Autobiography*, pp. 61–62.

53–54. Du Bois says . . . his family's poverty: *Ibid.*, p. 73.

54. Though he was befriended . . . "voluntary segregation": *Ibid.*, p. 133.

54. After a year's . . . association with Atlanta University: *Ibid.*, p. 205. Atlanta, like Fisk, was an institution founded privately for Negroes, in 1865, while Howard University was organized with federal help in 1867.

54. "learn to dignify . . . agitation": *Ibid.*, p. 245.

54–55. Instead of following . . . black community: *Ibid.*, pp. 248–249.

55. The 1906 meeting led to . . . black officer: Ovington, *How the National Association for the Advancement of Colored People Began* (New York: NAACP, 1914), p. 1.

55. "new slavery" of blacks . . . their civil rights: Du Bois, *Black Reconstruction*, p. 153.

## Chapter 3: Carpetbaggers, Scalawags, and Redeemers

58. Some northerners . . . at the time: Stampp, pp. 178–180.
58. Far from . . . "really a small minority": Kenneth M. Stampp, "Radical Rule: The Tragic Decade Thesis Disputed," in Scheiner, pp. 69–79.
58. Some of them . . . as blacks: Foner and Mahoney, pp. 23–29.
59. As for . . . postwar South: Stampp, pp. 184–185.
59. Ames was a native . . . Bull Run: Ames, pp. 1, 64–68.
59. He had . . . Medal of Honor: *Ibid.*, p.71; Current, pp. 112–113.
59. He had risen . . . Europe in 1866: Ames, pp. 223, 229, 234.
59. he presided . . . off the land: Ames, p. 255.
59. On June 15 . . . "Johnson governments": Current, pp. 114–115; Ames, p. 269.
60. so Ames had . . . Humphreys out of the mansion: Ames, pp. 271–273.
60. In November . . . Republican: Current, p. 120.
60. He also . . . impecunious whites: *Ibid.*, p. 173.
60. Democrats . . . Ku Klux Klan: Ames, pp. 272–284.
60–61. Even though . . . new constitution: Current, p. 176.
61. In 1870 . . . to the Union: Morison, p. 724; Ames, p. 286.
61. It took Charles . . . 40 to 12: Ames, pp. 297–312.
61. Ames now felt . . . family home: Ames, pp. 314–323.
61. On March 6 . . . freedmen: Miller, p. 98.
61. Ames spoke forcefully . . . by voting: Ames, pp. 331–334.
61–62. The remaining radicals . . . the state: Current, pp. 190–191.
62. For example . . . "servitude": Ames, p. 345.
62. With predominately . . . "Independent Republican": Ames, pp. 380–382.
62. In the political . . . thousand votes: Current, p. 309. Note that his victory margin is also given as thirty thousand (Ames, p. 385).
62. The two years . . . to eradicate illiteracy: Current, pp. 311–312.
62–63. In 1875 . . . half of the deal: Morison, p. 724.
63. The Democratic . . . Negro voters: Ames, pp. 392–393.
63. Lamar was elected to the U.S. Senate in 1877. In 1885, President Cleveland appointed him Secretary of the Interior, and, in 1888, an associate justice of the Supreme Court. John W. Winkle, "Lucius Quintus Cincinnatus Lamar," in Hall, pp. 494–495.
63. "The whole public . . . part of the government": Morison, p. 724; Ames, pp. 430–433.
63. Without any support . . . state senate: Ames, p. 469.
63. For Ames himself . . . inventive technology: Current, pp. 412–413; Ames, pp. 516–519.
64. Ironically, Ames . . . although unsuccessfully: Kennedy, pp. 136–137; Ames, pp. 549–553.
64. In 1870 the legislature . . . in 1862: Morison, p. 718.
64–65. Samuel Eliot Morison . . . Tennessee: *Ibid.*
65. The 1876 "compromise" . . . decided the issue: *Ibid.*, p. 724.
66. Warmoth managed . . . underestimates: Current, pp. 3–5.
66. Warmoth also managed . . . war's end: *Ibid.*, pp. 8–10.
66–67. After President Johnson . . . Republican party: *Ibid.*, p. 14.
67. This group selected . . . to the Union: Du Bois, *Black Reconstruction*, p. 463.

67. Despite his nondescript . . . after the war: Taylor, p. 79.
67. On the second ballot . . . lieutenant governor: Du Bois, *op. cit.*, p. 469.
67. As the new . . . the Ku Klux Klan: Current, p. 122.
67–68. White supremacists . . . order: Blassingame, p. 189.
68. The legislature . . . Union troops: Current, p. 122.
68. Warmoth saw . . . in Washington: *Ibid.*, p. 124.
68. Blair's public letter . . . racist violence: *Ibid.*, p. 125.
68. Warmoth then wrote . . . carpetbagger: Taylor, p. 171.
69. "barred from . . . dictation": Cited in Current, p. 127.
69. The Louisiana legislature . . . project: Taylor, pp. 177–178.
69. He also vetoed . . . outbreaks: Logsdon and Bell, "The Americanization of Black New Orleans 1850–1900," in Hirsch and Logsdon, p. 249.
69. When the War . . . 243 white officers: Current, p. 129.
69. The election . . . all defeated locally: Taylor, p. 172.
69. Warmoth's cautious advice . . . Creole community: Gehman, p. 89.
70. He even published . . . legislature: Taylor, pp. 196–198.
70. In 1871 . . . market value: Current, pp. 242–244.
70. Warmoth also took credit . . . time: Taylor, pp. 192–194, 250.
70–71. Warmoth's political power . . . minimal violence: Taylor, p. 238.
71. After Dunn's sudden death . . . impeach Warmoth: Du Bois, *op. cit.*, pp. 478–479; Logsdon and Bell, p. 250; Taylor, pp. 211–212.
72. The grounds were . . . bribe: Current, p. 280; Taylor, p. 247.
72. At two separate ceremonies . . . proper governor: Joseph G. Tregle, Jr., "Creoles and Americans," in Hirsch and Logsdon, p. 172.
73. He heard . . . in New Orleans: Blassingame, p. 192.
73. Warmoth wrote . . . of corruption: Cited in Current, p. 295.
73. After a string . . . on the sidelines: Current, pp. 416–417; Taylor, pp. 251, 253–255.
73. For his party . . . New Orleans: Current, p. 418.
73–74. To his dismay . . . had voted: Taylor, p. 508.
74. Warmoth lived . . . racial views: Current, p. 420.
75. In 1865 . . . thirty-nine lashes: Bardolph, pp. 42–44.
75. The states . . . cast their ballots: Stampp, pp. 178–179.
76. Throughout the South . . . in 1795: Du Bois, *op. cit.*, p. 451.
76. John Hope Franklin . . . "it would happen here": Franklin, p. 3.
77. Gordon Allport . . . core of the concept: Allport.
77. And it obfuscated . . . John C. Calhoun: Morison, pp. 432, 435.
78. Like a naïve pilgrim . . . in the South: Olsen, *A Carpetbagger*; see also Olsen, *Carpetbagger's Crusade*.
78–79. He had withdrawn . . . the waist down: Olsen, *A Carpetbagger*, pp. 32–33.
79. He had acquired . . . in an exchange: Foner and Mahoney, p. 116.
79. During this campaign . . . December 6, 1863: Olsen, *Carpetbagger's Crusade*, p. 22.
79–80. Back home . . . someone like himself: *Ibid.*, pp. 26–27.
80. Tourgée would be . . . war injuries: Olsen, *A Carpetbagger*, pp. 52–53.
80. After scouting out . . . a business: *Ibid.*, p. 54.
80. The first was . . . to his neighbors: Olsen, *A Carpetbagger*, p. 80.
80–81. North Carolina . . . much of Holden's work: Olsen, *Carpetbagger's Crusade*, p. 41.

81. Negro leaders had met . . . to vote: Olsen, *A Carpetbagger*, p. 86.

81. Carried away . . . leave the state: *Ibid.*, pp. 115, 121.

81. On his return home . . . "end": Current, p. 63.

81. Tourgée received a range . . . family: Gross, p. 26.

81. He had hopes . . . empty-handed: Olsen, *Carpetbagger's Crusade*, p. 74.

82. General Edward R. S. Canby . . . year before: *Ibid.*, p. 116.

82. Yet Tourgée became . . . freedmen: *Ibid.*, p. 93.

82. His biggest triumph . . . of two hundred dollars: *Ibid.*, p. 118.

83. By all accounts . . . reasonable jurist: Gross, p. 30.

83. A more balanced account . . . "not enter": John Hope Franklin, "Albion Tourgée, Social Critic," intro. to Tourgée, *Fool's Errand*, p. xiv.

83. The Klan . . . summer of 1870: Foner and Mahoney, p. 116.

83. He weathered attempts . . . links to the Klan: Franklin, p. xv.

83–84. He was exposed . . . liaison: Olsen, *Carpetbagger's Crusade*, p. 216.

84. In the wake . . . for that time: Franklin, "Albion Tourgée," p. xxi.

84–85. To today's readers . . . aid for education: *Tourgée*, Chapter XV.

85. If the reader . . . Sunday school: *Tourgée*, Chapter X.

85. He was introduced . . . that project: Franklin, "Albion Tourgée," p. xxii.

86. It was from that hideaway . . . sixty-seven: Dibble, pp. 124–131.

86. In his "Reply to 'A Fool's Errand' " . . . "South": Franklin, "Albion Tourgée," p. xxiv.

86. The fault for . . . North Carolinian: Olsen, *Carpetbagger's Crusade*, p. 141.

86–87. Tourgée had once . . . Reconstruction: *Ibid.*, pp. 270, 346.

## Chapter 4: The "Free People of Color" in New Orleans

90. Butler had only reluctantly . . . armed Negroes: Logsdon and Bell, "The Americanization of Black New Orleans, 1850–1900," in Hirsch and Logsdon, pp. 219–220.

90. He had, however . . . American citizens: *Ibid.*, pp. 222–223.

90–91. By December 1862 . . . white elite: *Ibid.*, p. 223.

91. The original three . . . in combat: Desdunes, p. xiii.

91. A year later . . . proved their mettle: Morison, p. 674.

91. Hundreds of free blacks . . . regiments: Logsdon and Bell, p. 221.

91. Not long afterward . . . his commission: Foner and Mahoney, p. 101; Haskins, pp. 23–24, 46. After his father's death in 1848, Pinchback—the sole support of his family—had worked on gambling boats that plied the Mississippi. In 1862, General Butler authorized him to recruit volunteers for the Union, and at 26 he was made a company commander in the "Corps d'Afrique."

91–92. Thomas O. Moore . . . service chores: Blassingame, p. 34.

92. The black Creoles . . . since the 1830s: Logsdon and Bell, p. 223.

92. Faced with this split . . . George Shepley: *Ibid.*, p. 225.

93. The two emissaries . . . Fifteenth Amendment: *Ibid.*, pp. 225–226.

93. General Banks . . . the publication: *Ibid.*, p. 229.

93. With the backing . . . new name: Desdunes, p. 133.

93. If the leaders . . . grounds: Logsdon and Bell, pp. 201–261.

94. Quite a contrasting . . . white authorities: Blassingame, p. 15.

94–95. They were welcome . . . for blacks: *Ibid.*, pp. 13–17.

95. Since the organized abolition . . . bondsmen: Logsdon and Bell, p. 207.

95. The escalating racial . . . Caribbean: Blassingame, p. 208.

96. Such contradictory . . . dominant whites: Logsdon and Bell, p. 203.

96. Indeed, as a young man . . . Spanish culture: *Ibid.*

96. The white Democrats . . . citizens: *Ibid.*, pp. 202–205.

97. In his history . . . inflated figure: Du Bois, *Black Reconstruction*, p. 154.

97. The Ricaud family . . . this business: Gehman, p. 73.

97. From a group . . . white population: Du Bois, *op. cit.*, p. 154.

97–98. Arthur Estèves . . . in 1847: *Ibid.*, p. 456.

98. It was no accident . . . valises: Desdunes, p. 144.

98. Robert Norbert Rillieux . . . career: Gehman, p. 56.

99. Their two sons . . . in Bordeaux: Du Bois, *op. cit.*, p. 154; Warburg appears also as Warbourg (in French).

99. Twentieth-century accounts . . . plantations: Blassingame, pp. 2–11.

99. These unions . . . rules: *Ibid.*, pp. 17–20.

100. In the city's annals . . . in 1845: Blassingame, p. 10.

100. Aristide Mary . . . philanthropist: *Ibid.*, p. 11.

100. Until it was drawn . . . worshippers: *Ibid.*, p. 13.

100. The original ten . . . public schools: *Ibid.*, pp. 107–109.

101. Sisters of the Holy Family . . . in 1837: Gehman, pp. 74–76.

101. By 1860 . . . from the outset: Logsdon and Bell, pp. 211–214.

102. By 1865 . . . self-seeking politicians: *Ibid.*, pp. 238–240.

103. The National Equal Rights . . . suffrage: *Ibid.*, p. 231.

103. This landmark . . . including Louisiana: Bell, p. 255.

103. The black Creoles . . . its organ: Logsdon and Bell, p. 229.

103. The Freedmen's Aid . . . farmers: Blassingame, pp. 56–57.

103. By August . . . property: *Ibid.*, pp. 57–58.

104. In January 1865 . . . June 10, 1865: Bell, p. 256.

104. This group . . . founded in July: Du Bois, *op. cit.*, p. 462.

104. The FUS . . . of Louisiana: Current, p. 13.

104. However, the black . . . Congress: *Ibid.*, p. 14.

105. In April 1868 . . . volunteers: *Ibid.*, p. 76.

105. Warmoth selected . . . the ticket: Logsdon and Bell, pp. 248–249.

105. Nearly 48 percent . . . leaders: *Ibid.*, p. 241.

105. Upon Louisiana's readmission . . . businesses: Bell, p. 272.

105. Warmoth's advice . . . Creole leaders: Foner and Mahoney, p. 101.

105–106. Warmoth . . . impeachment trial: Du Bois, *op. cit.*, p. 469; King and Fickler, p. 238.

106. Pinchback agreed . . . would attend: Logsdon and Bell, p. 252.

106. They tried . . . the U.S. Senate: *Ibid.*, p. 251.

106. With Congress hamstrung . . . Kellogg: Current, pp. 279–281.

107. Legal segregation . . . A. J. Dumont: Logsdon and Bell, p. 202.

107. Blacks who openly resisted . . . groups: Du Bois, *op. cit.*, p. 474.

107. Fifty black and white . . . 1879: Logsdon and Bell, pp. 201–202.

107–108. Dr. Louis-Charles Roudanez . . . opportunism of Pinchback: *Ibid.*, pp. 202–203.

108. He began by denouncing . . . advancement: *Ibid.*, p. 252.

108. Desdunes had campaigned . . . twenty years: *Ibid.*, p. 255.

108. In 1887 Desdunes . . . Blacks: *Ibid.*, p. 256.

108. Louis Martinet . . . occasional articles: O'Neill, intro. to Desdunes, p. xvii.
108. Martinet, like Desdunes . . . network: Thompson, p. 38.
109. The editors . . . segregated railroad travel: Logsdon and Bell, p. 257.
109. The committee comprised . . . Antoine: Desdunes, p. 141.
110. . . . on February 24, 1892 . . . white skin: Thomas, p. 5.
110. Rodolphe Desdunes . . . the legislature: Desdunes, p.143.
110. However, the committee . . . without a fee: *Ibid.*, p. 142.
110-111. Only in hindsight . . . the Regent of France: *Recipes and Reminiscences*, p. 1.
111. The white pioneers . . . French jails: *Ibid.*, p. 3.
111. The Acadians . . . bayous to urban life: *Ibid.*, pp. 113–114.
111. The next group . . . in the 1790s: *Ibid.*, p. 4.
111. Other notables . . . in Haiti: *Ibid.*, pp. 4–5.
111. The offspring . . . (in the New World): Crété, p. 69.
112. Until 1730 . . . fifteenth century: Gehman, pp. 8–10.
112. At least those were . . . maltreated: Crété, p. 96.
112. Once freed . . . a white spouse: Tinker, p. 258.
112. When Louisiana was . . . in 1739: Gehman, p. 22.
112-113. Their collective identity . . . the 1790s: *Ibid.*, pp. 31–35.
113. As has been . . . a husband's estate: Tinker, pp. 259–260.
113. The free people . . . of the slaves: Rogers, p. 2.
113. It grew as . . . a Puritanical elite: Gehman, pp. 49–50.

## Chapter 5: *Plessy v. Louisiana*: Searching for Precedents
115. Nichols had held . . . following January: Taylor, pp. 496–497.
116. The Thirteenth Amendment . . . rights: Fehrenbacher, pp. 580–581.
116. Chief Justice Roger B. Taney . . . "respect": *Scott v. Sanford*, 19 Howard 393.
117. That was the Missouri . . . Purchase: Morison, pp. 593–594.
117. His reading of . . . territories: *Scott v. Sanford*.
117-118. One expert analyst . . . 1787: Fehrenbacher, pp. 399–400.
118. Further, Fehrenbacher concludes . . . "accuracy": *Ibid.*, p. 384.
118. The drafters . . . Civil War: *Ibid.*, p. 580.
118. They would also extend . . . Missouri: Kluger, pp. 42–43.
119. A year after . . . civil rights: *Ibid.*, pp. 46–47.
119. If the Thirteenth . . . Negroes: Flack, pp. 127–133.
119. The amendment . . . old plantation jobs: Craven, pp. 117–122.
120. How could . . . "perpetuate race prejudice": *Ex parte Homer A. Plessy*, Brief of Relator for Writs of Prohibition and Certiorari.
120. As for discrimination . . . for whites: *Ibid.*, p. 2.
120. This rationale . . . "steal bread": Anatole France, *Le Lys Rouge* (1894), Chapter 7.
121. Lofgren explicates . . . "writ of certiorari": Lofgren, Chapter 3.
121. These sections . . . Fourteenth Amendment: *Ex parte Plessy*, pp. 1–2.
121-122. Tourgée and Walker . . . "by reputation": *Ibid.*, pp. 11–14.
122. The unjust-discrimination . . . their charge: *Ibid.*, pp. 11, 21.
122. Louisiana law . . . on the subject: *Ibid.*, p. 9.
122-123. In what seems . . . "does not enjoy": *Ibid.*, p. 11.
123. It was obvious . . . "more frequent": *Ibid.*, pp. 4–5.
123. Ferguson had conflated . . . "said regulations": *Ibid.*, p. 4.

123. For example . . . "of the State": *Ibid.*, p. 10.
124. If this was . . . segregated coach: *Ibid.*, p. 9.
124. The same skepticism . . . Jim Crow car: *Ibid.*, pp. 20–21.
124. The second and . . . right to travel: *Ibid.*, pp. 17–18.
125. Such "imprisonment . . . due process of law": *Ibid.*, p. 16.
125. District Attorney Adams . . . recognized authority: Lofgren, pp. 49–50.
125–126. He simply conceded . . . still stand: *Ibid.*, p. 56.
126. The Supreme Court . . . seats by race: *Ibid.*, p. 57.
126. The third part . . . Fourteenth Amendment: *Ex parte Plessy*, Brief for Relator, p. 21.
127. Justice Bushrod Washington . . . inapplicable: *Corfield v. Coryell*, 6 Fed. Cases 546, No. 3230.
127–128. One of the amendment's . . . "good purpose": C. Herman Pritchett, "Privileges and Immunities," in Hall, p. 680.
128. The butchers . . . Amendment: *Slaughter House Cases*, 16 Wall. 36.
128. On behalf . . . "to the States": *Ibid.*
128–129. According to Miller's . . . "Constitution": *Ibid.*
129. Congress could not have . . . "control of Congress": *Ibid.*
129. Howe . . . "could not be law": Miller, p. 107.
129–130. It would be . . . "of all governments": *Ibid.*, p. 108.
130. Another dissenter . . . "rights of citizens": *Ibid.*, p. 108–109.
130–131. Field's theory . . . protected right: *Ex parte Virginia*, 100 U.S. 339.
131. As Judge Loren Miller . . . as well: Miller, p. 134.
131. This 1875 decision . . . *Cruikshank v. United States*: 92 U.S. 542.
132. Three of the killers . . . First Amendment: Fireside, *"Mississippi Burning,"* p. 49.
132. It had not literally . . . "due process of law": *Cruikshank*.
132–133. "the right of the people . . . member of society": *Ibid.*
133. For Plessy's attorneys . . . judicial remedy: *Ex parte Plessy*, Brief for Relator, p. 10.
134. In the case . . . constitutionally invalid: *Ibid.*, p. 5.
134. In *Hall v. DeCuir* . . . "his voyage": *Hall v. DeCuir*, 95 U.S. 485.
134–135. Justice Waite . . . "separate but equal": Robert J. Cottrol, *"Hall v. DeCuir,"* in Hall, p. 359.
135. If an abrupt shift . . . decided in 1890: 133 U.S. 587.
135. . . . although the majority . . . Plessy's case: *Ex parte Plessy*, Brief for Relator, p. 7.
135–136. Brewer's ruling . . . "two races": 133 U.S. 587.
136. Though Harlan . . . "the laws": 109 U.S. 3.
136. The first document . . . "colored race": Lofgren, p. 55.
136–137. Yet the court file . . . "white race": *Ex parte Plessy*, Affidavit "Exhibit A," p. 12.
137. Since Cain's statement . . . "United States": *Ibid.*, "Answer of Respondents," p. 12.
137. As for Tourgée . . . "almost impossible": *Ibid.*, Brief for Relator, p. 22.
137–138. He cited as precedent . . . white travelers: *Logwood and Wife v. Memphis & C.R.R. Co.*
138. Hammond had said . . . "too exacting": *Logwood*, Brief for Relator, p. 4.
138. During the economic . . . segregation: *Munn v. Illinois*, 94 U.S. 113.
139. Fenner said . . . "the subject of slavery": *Ex parte Plessy*, 11 So. Reporter, 948.
140. The first of Fenner's . . . "changed by law": 5 Cushing 198.
140. Justice Daniel Agnew . . . "to intermix": 55 Pennsylvania, St. 209.
140. As for the 1890 . . . "peace and comfort": *Ex parte Plessy*, 11 So. Reporter, 948.

## Chapter 6: The Fourteenth Amendment "Conspiracy"

143. It seems anachronistic . . . Congress: The Confederacy had retrieved the theory of John C. Calhoun, who resigned the vice presidency in 1832 to champion the rights of states to "nullify" federal laws.

143–144. Like the "Gilded Age" . . . innovation: The Gilded Age is generally considered to be the period from 1865 to 1890.

144. They were called . . . market: Josephson, p. vi.

144. Jay Gould . . . Daniel Drew: Grodinsky, p. 30.

144. Gould reflected . . . "kill the other half": Painter, p. 33.

145. For Carnegie . . . humanity: Carnegie.

145–146. It was this clique . . . Amendment: Painter, p. xx.

146. The opening sentence . . . "or denied": 39th Cong., lst Sess., *Congressional Globe*, p. 2543.

146. Senator Jacob M. Howard . . . "fundamental guarantees": Miller, p. 95, citing Kelley's brief in *Brown v. Board*.

146. At the time . . . "aliens": Jordan, p. 66.

147. The *New York Times* . . . patronage. Judith K. Schafer, "Conkling, Roscoe," in Hall, p. 178.

147–148. Even a "most casual . . . over him": *Slaughter House Cases*, 16 Wall. 36.

148. Chief Justice Morrison R. Waite . . . was permissible: *Munn v. Illinois*, 94 U.S. 113.

148. In his *Munn* dissent . . . "receive": *Ibid.*

149. Cooley wanted these barriers . . . or trusts: Mason and Beaney, p. 323.

149–150. He revealed . . . "State and local taxes": Stampp, p. 108.

150. The framers . . . "California to do": *San Mateo County v. Southern Pacific RR*, 116 U.S. 138, transcript of record, cited in Jordan, pp. 417–418.

150. By May 1886 . . . Central Pacific Railroads: *Santa Clara County v. Southern Pacific Railroad*, 118 U.S. 394.

150. Waite said . . . "that it does": *Ibid.*

150–151. By 1896 . . . action against Negroes: Lofgren, p. 70.

151–152. In 1938 Howard Jay Graham . . . "own relation thereto": Howard J. Graham, "The 'Conspiracy' Theory of the Fourteenth Amendment," 47 *Yale Law Journal* 371, reprinted in Stampp and Litwack, p. 107.

152. A look back . . . "Powers of States": Roscoe Conkling, "Speech Delivered in the Senate of the U.S.," Feb. 22, 1870, Washington, D.C.: F. & J. Rives & Ge. A. Binley, 1870.

152. Conkling skips . . . thousand Negroes: *Ibid.*

153. This statute . . . to Congress again: McDonald, p. 213.

153. The first scholarly . . . in 1908: Flack, Johns Hopkins University Press, 1908, reprinted 1965.

154. *Barron v. Baltimore:* 7 Pet. 243.

154. Flack does find . . . and theaters: Flack, p. 41.

154. Among several railway cases . . . "ride": *Ibid.*, p. 46.

155. When the mysterious . . . "property": Stampp, p. 109.

155. Kendrick's version . . . American history: Charles and Mary Beard, II, pp. 112–114.

155. James Madison had intended . . . "government": *Barron v. Baltimore*, 7 Pet. 243.

156. In any case . . . "of the States": Schwartz, *Fourteenth*, p. 2.

156. In the *Santa Clara* . . . "Freedmen": *Ibid.*, p. 102.
156. Chief Justice Earl Warren . . . "civil rights": *Ibid.*, p. 216.
156. Warren singled out . . . "balance": *Ibid.*
158. James Madison . . . "is reserved": Forrest McDonald, "Tenth Amendment," in Hall, p. 861.
158. Madison's response . . . "no harm in making such a declaration": Killenbeck, p. 2.
158. In *The Federalist Papers* . . . yet undefined ways: Madison, Hamilton, and Jay, *Federalist* No. 84, pp. 513–514.
159. In October 1788 . . . to the Constitution: Veit, p. xiii.
159. These laws . . . "to defame" it: O'Brien, p. 392.
159. That same year . . . further prosecutions: A. Lewis, pp. 60–61.
159–160. . . . further prosecutions . . . no longer valid: *New York Times v. Sullivan* (376 U.S. 278). They were still in the statute books, however, until a brilliant brief by Herbert Wechsler in 1960 reminded the Court that it was time to lay the antiquated laws to rest. Wechsler was arguing against libel judgments by Alabama courts against the New York *Times* and civil rights groups because state law allowed awards for persons whose reputation was injured by statements that contained any inaccuracies, no matter how minor. If the damage awards had been sustained, they would have crippled the nascent movement launched by Dr. Martin Luther King in Montgomery, as well as muzzling reporters who covered southern racist incidents. See Fireside, *New York Times*, p. 94.
160. In 1819 . . . classic opinion: *McCulloch v. Maryland*, 4 Wheat. 316.
160. As Marshall parsed . . . "forgoing Powers": Article I, Sect. 8, in *ibid.*
161. He was instrumental . . . nullification: Capers, pp. 115–118.
161. After he returned . . . system: Bancroft, pp. 116–117; Killenbeck, pp. 236–338; Marmor, p. 179.
163. However, Taney's belief . . . *Prigg v. Pennsylvania*: 16 Pet. 539.
164. A slave owner . . . unconstitutional: *Ibid.*
165. Only one independent . . . "of color": *Ibid.*
166. More than nine hundred . . . masters: Miller, p. 52.

## Chapter 7: En Route to the Supreme Court
167. "The sight . . . the system": Harlan, p. 20.
168. The indignant . . . "father's lips": *Ibid.*, p. 21.
168. Malvina's memoir . . . "equality of blacks": Przybyszewski, p. 14.
168. Indeed, the anecdote . . . "of slavery": *Ibid.*, p. 19.
168. The father . . . his household: *Ibid.*, p. 26.
169. These feelings . . . Harlan image: Linda Przybyszewski, "Afterword" to Harlan, p. 228.
169. In October 1893 . . . "stand upon": Oct. 31, 1893 letter from Tourgée to Martinet, in "The Tourgée Papers," Chautauqua, N.Y.: Chautauqua County Historical Society.
170. Justice Harlan . . . *Dred Scott* decision: Harlan, p. 109.
171. This was a view . . . section: 379 U.S. 241.
171. Harlan's dissent . . . of Louisville: Przybyszewski, p. 95.
171. "The opinion . . . Constitution": Undated letter among Harlan papers, Univ. of Louisville, cited in Yarbrough, p. 152.
171. Strong had been . . . "to give them": *Strauder v. West Virginia*, 100 U.S. 303.

171–172. However . . . the Fourteenth Amendment: *Virginia v. Rives*, 100 U.S. 313.

172. Another of Harlan's . . . "the Country": Letter from Swayne to Harlan, Nov. 20, 1883, Harlan papers, Univ. of Louisville, cited in Yarbrough, p. 152.

172. Even Roscoe Conkling . . . "of position": Letter from Conkling to Harlan, Dec. 27, 1883, Harlan Papers, Univ. of Louisville, cited in Yarbrough, p. 152.

172. Frederick Douglass . . . "the multitude": *American Reformer*, Dec. 8, 1883, cited in *ibid.*

173. The record does show . . . slavery: Louis Filler, "John M. Harlan," in Friedman and Israel, p. 1282.

174. He had also grown . . . slavery: Yarbrough, p. 72.

174. The Ku Klux Klan . . . crippled: *Ibid.*, p. 67.

174. Harlan's law firm . . . Harrodsburg: Harlan papers, Library of Congress, cited in *ibid.*, p. 67.

176. First, he had to . . . "stealing the presidency": Yarbrough, p. 109.

177. Watson described . . . speeches: Morison, p. 791.

177. A parallel horror . . . in the West: *Ibid.*, p. 793.

178. During his tenure . . . Sixteenth Amendment: *Pollock v. Farmers' Loan & Trust Co.*, 157 U.S. 429.

178. . . . and finding the Sherman Antitrust . . . "commerce": *U.S. v. E. C. Knight*, 156 U.S. 2.

178. Fuller also announced . . . discrimination: John Orth, "Melville W. Fuller," in Hall, p. 32.

179. White's questionable contribution . . . Court: *Standard Oil v. U.S.*, 211 U.S. 1; Richard Y. Funston, "Edward .D. White," in Hall, p. 928.

179–180. After serving . . . *Ex parte Virginia*, 100 U.S. 339.

180. States had the right . . . "the States": Miller, p. 127.

180. Determined to surpass . . . little work: Loren P. Beth, "Stephen J. Field," in Hall, p. 291.

180–181. Peckham, who had . . . passage of the law: *Lochner v. New York*, 198 U.S. 45.

181. In 1895, he wrote . . . workers' strike: 158 U.S. 564.

181. Court injunctions . . . integrated classes: *Berea College v. Kentucky*, 211 U.S. 45.

181–182. . . . he also found . . . (see Chapter 9): 203 U.S. 1.

182. Gray showed . . . state actions: John Semonche, "Horace Gray," in Hall, p. 345.

182. Using common-law . . . United States: *United States v. Wong Kim Ark*, 169 U.S. 649.

183. What must have . . . "Anglo-Saxon race": Cited in Francis Helminski, "Henry Billings Brown," in Hall, p. 93.

183. His biographer . . . "unexceptional for their time": *Ibid.*

189. Morse cited . . . Chinese owners *Barbier v. Connolly*, 113 U.S. 27.

189. Morse claimed . . . on trains: A. P. Morse, "Brief for Defendant in Error," *Plessy v. Ferguson.*

190. In 1880 . . . "civil society": *Strauder v. West Virginia*, 100 U.S. 303.

190. Morse left the controlling . . . "as to colored persons": *Ibid.*

## Chapter 8: The Decision Comes Down

193. At least two . . . Reconstruction: Lofgren, p. 151, says Tourgée took the train from New York to Washington on April 10. The Washington *Post*, "Capitol Chat," Apr. 14, 1896, has him heading to the Court, though Olsen, in *Carpetbagger's Crusade*, says he was too busy to go.

194–199. We do not know . . . that jusice had been done: *"Plessy v. Ferguson. Argument of A. W. Tourgée,"* ms. #5472, Tourgée Papers, Chautauqua County Historical Society, Westfield, New York.

198. In Miller's parsing . . . their state: 16 Wallace 36.

199. However, only one . . . segregated cars: *Louisville, New Orleans and Texas Railway v. Mississippi,* 133 U.S. 587; Lofgren, p. 173.

200. For example . . . registration lists: *Strauder v. West Virginia,* 100 U.S. 303; *Virginia v. Rives,* 100 U.S. 313.

200–201. Justice David J. Brewer had . . . segregate schools: *Berea College v. Kentucky* decision, 211 U.S. 45.

201. and be allowed . . . Arkansas: *Hodges v. United States,* 203 U.S. 1.

201. Brown was known for . . . "public welfare": *Holden v. Hardy,* 169 U.S. 366, upholding Utah's eight-hour-workday limit for miners.

201–203. On May 18, 1896 . . . "a state of involuntary servitude": *Plessy v. Ferguson,* 163 U.S. 537–593.

203. Brown then buttresses . . . two key decisions: *Slaughter House Cases,* 16 Wall. 36; Civil Rights Cases, 109 U.S. 3, 24.

204. As Bernard Schwartz . . . "discrimination": Schwartz, *History,* p. 188.

205–206. Brown next inquires . . . "particular class": 163 U.S. 544–549.

207–208. Brown disagrees . . . federal amendment: *Ibid.,* 549–551.

208. He may . . . justice like Brown's: Yale professor William Graham Sumner was a very influential member of this school.

208. *Hall v. DeCuir:* 94 U.S. 485.

208. *New Orleans & Texas Railway Co. v. Mississippi:* 133 U.S. 587.

209. *People v. Gallagher:* 93 New York 438.

209. Charles Lofgren . . . could not work: Lofgren, p. 179.

210–211. Lofgren also notes . . . "war of the races": *Clark v. Board of Directors,* cited in Lofgren, p. 181.

211. Moving even further . . . Indiana court decision: 36 Indiana 389.

211–212. Since the preponderance . . . Louisiana railway law: *Plessy v. Ferguson,* 163 U.S. 550.

211. *Yick Wo v. Hopkins:* 118 U.S. 356.

213. Justice Brown, who . . . "the same plane": *Ibid.,* 551–552.

214–215. Richard Kluger . . . "colored passengers": Kluger, p. 79.

215. Indeed, in seven . . . or less: *Ibid.,* p. 80.

215–216. Harlan's opinion . . . same side of a courtroom: 163 U.S. 553–561.

217–218. Then Harlan exhibits . . . "of the United States": *Ibid.,* 559–564.

## Chapter 9: Segregation without Judicial Restraints

221. Taney . . . state law: *Dred Scott v. Sanford,* 19 How. 393.

222–223. The *Times* briefly reported . . . "two races": "Louisiana's Separate Car Law," the New York *Times,* May 19, 1896, part II, p. 3.

223. A dozen contemporary . . . Otto H. Olsen: Olsen, *Thin Disguise,* pp. 123–130.

223. The decision was hailed . . . "Southern railway": "Equality, But Not Socialism," *Daily Picayune,* May 19, 1896, cited in *ibid.*

223–224. This racist sentiment . . . "Southern States": "Hardly Expected," *Dispatch,* May 21, 1896, in *ibid.,* pp. 126–127.

225. By the end . . . and hotels: Stephenson, pp. 216–218.

225. And the plight . . . accommodations: Woodward, *Strange Career*, p. 18.

225. The *Republican* . . . "white men?": "Like the Measles," Springfield, Mass., *Republican*, May 20, 1896, cited in Olsen, *Thin Disguise*, p. 127.

225. The New York *Daily Tribune:* "The Unfortunate Law of the Land," *Tribune*, May 19, 1896, in *ibid.*, p. 130.

225. The newspapers in Rochester . . . Orange Park: "State Sovereignty," Rochester *Union Advertiser*, May 19, 1896, in *ibid.*, p. 125; "A Strange Decision," Rochester *Democrat and Chronicle*, May 20, 1896, in *ibid.*, pp. 123–124.

226. The *Weekly Blade* . . . "most noble": "A Damnable Outrage," Parsons, Kansas *Weekly Blade*, May 30, 1896, in *ibid.*, p. 129.

226. Most pro-business . . . United States: Woodward, *Strange Career*, p. 54.

226–227. Some leading intellectuals . . . from Indiana: *Ibid.*, p. 55.

227. The *A.M.E. Church Review:* "Plausible Sophistry," *A.M.E. Church Review*, XIII (1896), pp. 156–162, in *ibid.*, pp. 125–126.

227–228. The most muted criticism . . . "of the soul": Booker T. Washington, "Who Is Permanently Hurt?"; *Boston Our Day*, June 1896, cited in Thomas, p. 135.

228. A more pointed . . . "The Courts and the Negro": Reprinted in Thomas, pp. 149–160.

229. The defense committee . . . charities: Lofgren, p. 42.

230. Charles S. Johnson . . . club cars: Johnson, p. 45.

230. Ray Stannard Baker . . . "Jim Crow Car": R. Baker, p. 31.

230. In 1944 . . . "forms of segregation": Myrdal, p. 635.

231. In Houston . . . passengers: Johnson, pp. 46–51.

231. When plane travel . . . segregated: Barnes, p. 14.

231. What had been . . . intermarriage: Johnson, pp. 163–164.

231. In one scholar's words . . . "of the white race": Blassingame, p. 113.

231–232. Even in 1896 . . . twenty-one years old: Stephenson, p. 327.

232. By 1904 . . . by 1900: Woodward, *Strange Career*, 1974, p. 85.

232. Even in New Orleans . . . allegiances: Gehman, p. 108.

233. After an initial . . . private club: This practice continued until 1927, when the Supreme Court ruled against white primaries in Texas [*Nixon v. Herndon*, 273 U.S. 536], then, in 1932, allowed a modified version of such primaries as "private" actions [*Grovey v. Townsend*, 295 U.S. 45], but finally reversed that decision in 1944 [*Smith v. Allright*, 321 U.S. 649].

233. The wave . . . "and warning": Logan, pp. 297–298.

233. An article . . . the NAACP: Kluger, pp. 96–97.

235. In its second incarnation . . . Washington, D.C.: Chalmers, p. 4.

235–236. A Klan-related conspiracy . . . 1870 Act: Fireside, *"Mississippi Burning,"* p. 49.

236. Benjamin R. Tillman . . . race-baiting: Logan, p. 349.

236. In addition . . . code of silence: Ernie Suggs, "Moor's Ford Lynching," Atlanta *Journal-Constitution*, Mar. 11, 2001, p. C1.

236. In the 1930s . . . "I walked out": Johnson, p. 53.

236. In Dalton, Georgia . . . died: *Ibid.*, p. 51.

236–237. These cases . . . in the South: Bardolph, p. 42.

237. They began to . . . 1930: Taeuber, p. 3.

237. The demographic . . . 251 percent: Johnson, p. 320.

238. In 1917 . . . Washington, D.C.: *Ibid.*, p. 313.

238. In 1943 . . . victims: Thomas Sancton, "The Race Riots," *The New Republic*, July 5, 1943, reprinted in *Reporting Civil Rights*, p. 37.

239. The sale agreement . . . "is demanded": *Buchanan v. Warley*, 165 Ky. 559, cited in Miller, p. 249.

240. Justice William R. Day's . . . "account of color": 245 U.S. 60.

240. Challenges . . . in 1917: *Koehler v. Rowland*, 275 Mo. 573.

240. and in Michigan . . . "private concern": *Parmalee v. Moris*, 218 Mich. 625, cited in Miller, p. 252.

240. Justice Edward T. Sanford . . . law: *Corrigan v. Buckley*, 271 U.S. 323.

241. During the next four years . . . Race Relations: Chicago Commission on Race Relations, pp. 122–123.

241. From the time the first . . . punishment: Blumberg, pp. 4–5.

241. As has been noted . . . public ones: Lively, p. 92.

242. By 1904 . . . intended by God: Cited in Miller, p. 200.

243. When the case . . . states' rights: *Berea College v. Kentucky*, 211 U.S. 45.

243. Kentucky's attorneys . . . "that race": Cited in Kluger, p. 87.

243. Justice John Marshall Harlan . . . "the law": Cited in Miller, p. 203.

243–244. Further, Harlan . . . "innocent purpose: *Ibid.*, p. 204.

244. He also saw God . . . or safety: Przybyszewski, pp. 107–108.

244. Oliver Wendell Holmes . . . "each other": Cited in John Orth, "John Marshall Harlan," in Hall, p. 363.

245. His Boston Brahmin . . . "enough": *Buck v. Bell*, 274 U.S. 200.

245. "There is still . . . of the Bench": Brown, "Dissenting Opinions of Mr. Justice Harlan," *American Law Review*, 46: 335–38, cited in Thomas, p. 165.

## Chapter 10: The Walls Begin to Crumble

248. After an August 1906 riot . . . discharged: Logan, pp. 347–350.

248. Wilson extended . . . policy: *Ibid.*, pp. 365–366.

249. Representative James B. Madden . . . Caucasian: Cited in *ibid.*, p. 365.

249. In 1914 and in 1916 . . . freed them: Przybyszewski, p. 88.

249. Grimké had led . . . "is unthinkable": Logan, p. 365.

250. Senator Vardaman . . . "equal terms": *Congressional Record*, 63rd Congress, 2nd sess., pp. 2929, 3073, 3118, cited in Logan, p. 369.

250. The work of Linda Przybyszewski . . . blacks and whites: Przybyszewski, Chapter 2.

251. "Of course . . . at public expense": *Berea College v. Kentucky*, 211 U.S. 45.

251 Przybyszewski attributes . . . "miscegenation": Przybyszewski, pp. 100–101.

251. Indeed, in 1882 . . . same-race couple: *Pace v. Alabama*, 106 U.S. 583.

252. *Cummings v. Richmond County Board of Education:* 175 U.S. 528.

252. A Georgia county . . . for Negroes: Cited in Przybyszewski, p. 100.

252. *Guinn v. United States:* 238 U.S. 347.

253. The two judges . . . "the United States": Miller, p. 219.

254. "In no event . . . Texas": Cited in *ibid.*, p. 222.

254. However, enigmatically . . . by law: *Nixon v. Herndon*, 273 U.S. 536.

254. The Texas legislature . . . "qualified to vote": Cited in Miller, p. 223.

254–255. Accordingly, members of the party . . . disenfranchisement: *Nixon v. Condon*, 286 U.S. 73.

255. *Moore v. Dempsey:* 261 U.S. 86.

255–256. It originated in . . . five whites dead: Miller, pp. 232–233.

256. The governor also . . . electric chair: *Ibid.*

257. "If in fact . . . due process of law": *Moore v. Dempsey.*

257. Justices McReynolds and George . . . "lynch law": *Frank v. Mangum,* 237 U.S. 309.

257. American Legion post . . . leave the area: Miller, p. 237.

258. "Regulations which . . . unreasonable": *Chiles v. Chesapeake Railroad Co.,* 218 U.S. 71.

258–259. He was succeeded . . . "real property": Cited in Miller, p. 258.

259. *Powell v. Alabama:* 287 U.S. 45; *Norris v. Alabama:* 294 U.S. 587; *Patterson v. Alabama:* 294 U.S. 600.

260. "I knew if a white . . . not done": Cited in Goodman, *Stories of Scottsboro,* p. 5.

260. Twelve days . . . raped them: *Ibid.,* p. 13.

261. Only the case of Roy Wright . . . penalty: Miller, p. 287.

261. The American Civil Liberties Union . . . "a legal lynching": Goodman, p. 42.

262. *Powell v. Alabama:* 287 U.S. 45.

262. "Whether requested or not . . . or the like": *Ibid.*

262. Butler's opinion . . . "the several states": *Ibid.*

263. The Labor Defense coup . . . hung jury: Goodman, p. 101.

263. Leibowitz . . . citizens of Alabama: Cited in *ibid.,* p. 104.

264. Bates admitted . . . sentenced to death: Cited in Miller, p. 270.

265. This time . . . had convicted him: *Norris v. Alabama,* 294 U.S. 587.

267. Samuel Leibowitz . . . New York Supreme Court: Goodman, pp. 396–397.

269. Postal clerks . . . "race or color": *Mail Handlers Union v. Corsi,* 326 U.S. 88.

269. The Supreme Court ruled . . . state action: *United States v. Classic,* 313 U.S. 299.

269. *Grovey v. Townsend:* 295 U.S. 45.

270. He said that . . . "Fifteenth amendment": *Smith v. Allwright,* 321 U.S. 649.

270–271. While Eleanor Roosevelt . . . black leaders: Cook, Vol. 2, Chapter 10.

271. On the eve . . . "defense employment": Cited in *Reporting Civil Rights,* Part 1, *American Journalism, 1941–1963,* pp. 1–4.

271. Three days before . . . in the army: Goodwin, p. 252.

271. Again, in the midst . . . fellow soldiers: Roi Ottley, "Seething with Resentment," *The New Republic,* Nov. 10, 1941; cited in *Reporting Civil Rights,* p. 5.

271–272. Thirty-one . . . racist police officers: Thomas Sancton, "The Race Riots," *The New Republic,* July 5, 1943; cited in *Reporting Civil Rights* p. 37.

272. The wartime . . . threat of violence: For attacks on Negro passengers in Tennessee and Mississippi, see reports by Bayard Rustin and L. O. Swingler in *ibid.,* pp. 15, 19.

# Chapter 11: *Plessy* Finally Meets Its Match

274. "equal rights . . . real property": Cited in Miller, p. 258.

274. The NAACP used . . . Felix Frankfurter: Mark Tushnet, "Charles V. Hamilton," in Hall, p. 413.

274–275. The state courts . . . law school: *Missouri ex rel. Gaines v. Canada,* 305 U.S. 337.

275. "in conformity with . . . the Fourteenth Amendment: *Sipuel v. Board of Regents,* 332 U.S. 631.

275. She then asked . . . Fourteenth Amendment: *Fisher v. Hurst*, 333 U.S. 147.

276. After a federal court . . . at regular mealtimes: *McLaurin v. Oklahoma State Regents for Higher Education*, 339 U.S. 637.

277. *Sweatt v. Painter*: 339 U.S. 629.

277. A second version . . . not acceptable to Mr. Sweatt: Miller, pp. 338–340.

277. In the next legal round . . . donations: NAACP Legal Defense and Educational Fund, p. 7.

277. When Marshall arrived . . . "Jim Crow in education": Aldred, p. 68.

277–278. The May 1947 trial . . . out of it: Kluger, pp. 262–263.

278. Still, as was expected . . . law school: Cited in Miller, p. 339.

279. Richard Kluger's . . . assigned to himself: Kluger, pp. 280–281.

280. Here Vinson added . . . "traditions and prestige": *Sweatt v. Painter*, 339 U.S. 629.

281. There was no need . . . "racial segregation": *Ibid.*

281–282. Marshall was born . . . a dentist: Aldred, p. 28.

282. "I scrunched": *Ibid.*, p. 31.

283. During his twenty-five years . . . criminal justice: Tushnet, p. 45.

284. She had discovered . . . United States history: Berman, *It Is So Ordered*, p. 9.

284. The notice had not mentioned . . . elsewhere: "Interview with Mrs. Brown," Kansas City *Star*, May 17, 1964, cited in Weaver, p. 211.

284. As Oliver Brown . . . for black children: U.S. Supreme Court, Transcript of Oral Arguments, No. 8, *Brown v. Board of Education*, 1952, pp. 89–90.

285. Fleming said . . . "come up together": Cited in Kluger, p. 411.

286. "that these children . . . voluntarily": U.S. Supreme Court, Transcript of Oral Arguments, *op. cit.*, p. 138.

286. "have the opportunity . . . is to live": *Ibid.*, p. 126.

286. "Segregation of white . . . integrated school system": *Brown v. Board*, 98 F. Supp. 797.

286. "no child . . . the other race": U.S. Supreme Court, Transcript of Oral Arguments, No. 101, *Briggs v. Elliot*, p. 7.

287. Blacks made up . . . illiterate: *Ibid.*, pp. 52–55.

287. Indeed, black children . . . harvesting seasons: *Ibid.*, pp. 59–60.

287. White children . . . per black child: *Ibid.*, pp. 40–41.

287. Pearson recounted . . . harvester: Kluger, p. 18.

288. "The white folks . . . petition": *Ibid.*, p. 23.

288. When the gas station . . . farmlands: *Ibid.*, p. 24.

289. This proved . . . "confusion in his self-image": U.S. Supreme Court, Transcript of Oral Arguments, *op. cit.*, pp. 84–89.

289. The Clarendon County . . . "their own race": *Ibid.*, p. 113.

289. "the public schools" . . . be integrated: *Ibid.*, p. 118.

289. "In perfect candor . . . not be serious": Kurland and Casper, Vol. 49, p. 285.

290. Despite the evident . . . bond issue: *Ibid.*, p. 275.

290. "This is a matter . . . not the courts": *Ibid.*, p. 189.

290. "Segregation in education . . . *per se inequality*": *Ibid.*, p. 208.

290. The NAACP case . . . constitution: *Davis v. County School Board*, 103 F. Supp. 337.

291. A year later . . . below state standards: *Belton v. Gebhart* and *Bulah v. Gebhart*, cited in Kluger, p. 435.

292. In the fall of 1950 . . . "whites only": U.S. Supreme Court, Transcript of Oral Arguments, No. 413, *Bolling v. Sharpe*, pp. 4–5.

292. When Bishop next . . . of Congress: Arbeitman and Roe, p. 85.

292–293. Nabrit, instead . . . skin color: U.S. Supreme Court, Transcript of Oral Arguments, *op. cit.*, pp. 37–41.

293. "What schooling . . . their rights now": *Ibid.*

293. Bastian ruled against . . . Congress: *Bolling v. Sharpe*, 347 U.S. 497.

294. Is there evidence . . . black children?: Kurland and Casper, Vol. 49, p. 285.

294. "things we cannot" . . . schools: *Ibid.*, p. 290.

294. Paul Wilson . . . possible outcome: *Ibid.*, p. 301.

294. Only Justice Felix . . . "man's inhumanity to man?": *Ibid.*, p. 293.

295. Thurgood Marshall . . . "badge of inferiority": *Ibid.*, p. 310.

295. Could the justices . . . segregation "is bad": *Ibid.*, p. 316.

295. Marshall offered . . . "talk that way": *Ibid.*, p. 318.

295. At this conference . . . formula outright: Halberstam, p. 416.

295. Whatever Warren . . . inferior schools: *Ibid.*, p. 420.

296. But even without . . . "ball game": Goldman and Gallen, pp. 93–94.

296. The NAACP lawyers . . . damage them: Kurland and Casper, Vol. 49A, p. 1316.

296. Davis had served . . . for president: Aldred, p. 16.

296. "so often announced . . . disturbance": Kurland and Casper, Vol. 49A, p. 489.

296. "Changed conditions . . . the Constitution": *Ibid.*, p. 333.

297. "a glorified . . . Carolina": *Ibid.*, p. 491.

297. In rebuttal . . . "the minority people": *Ibid.*, p. 339.

297. For the justices . . . into account: *Ibid.*, p. 340.

297. Indeed, after . . . legal contest: NAACP Legal and Educational Defense Fund, pp. 17–18.

297. For Davis . . . to follow: Kurland and Casper, Vol. 49A, p. 491.

297. As for Dr. Clark's . . . white dolls: *Ibid.*, p. 336.

297. Milton Korman . . . "atmosphere": *Ibid.*, p. 429.

297. Instead of . . . culture: *Ibid.*, p. 340.

297. "Those same kids . . . in school": *Ibid.*

298. After the first . . . for integrating schools: L. Baker, p. 479; see also The Frankfurter Papers, Harvard University, cited in Schwartz, *History*, p. 72.

286-287. "This is the first . . . God": Halberstam, p. 416.

298. When the new . . . would arouse: Warren, p. 276.

298. Warren was . . . take over: *Ibid.*, p. 277.

298. When Warren . . . positions: Pollock, *Earl Warren*, p. 174.

298. Perhaps Warren's . . . "the Warren Court": Warren, p. 4.

299. It is not clear . . . black classmates: *Ibid.*

299. For his three . . . "kids felt": Schwartz, *History*, p. 97.

299. First, for the NAACP . . . included: Kurland and Casper, Vol. 49A, pp. 449–458.

299. Justice Frankfurter . . . schools: *Ibid.*, pp. 459–462.

299. Thurgood Marshall . . . failed to act: *Ibid.*, pp. 466–467.

299–300. "an inherent determination . . . stands for": *Ibid.*, p. 523.

300. "It is the position . . . Amendment": *Ibid.*, pp. 534–535.

300. However . . . local judges: *Ibid.*, pp. 538–539.

300. A majority . . . consensus: Pollack, p. 174.

300. Warren told him . . . "for the country": Schwartz, *History*, p. 94.

301. Warren visited him . . . "the announcement": Warren, p. 3.

301. "We conclude . . . are inherently unequal": 347 U.S. 483. See also Robert S. Donovan, "Supreme Court, 9–0, Bans Segregation in Public Schools," New York *Herald-Tribune*, May 18, 1954, reprinted in *Reporting Civil Rights*, Part One, pp. 204–210.

301–302. Warren admitted . . . segregated public schools: *Bolling v. Sharpe*, 347 U.S. 497.

## Chapter 12: Fifty Years of Integration: Half Measures and Halting Progress

304. "In the long run . . . be reaffirmed": Robert H. Jackson Papers, Library of Congress, reprinted in O'Brien, p. 1311.

306. "High Court Bans School Segregation": The New York *Times*, May 18, 1954, p. 1.

306. "the most important . . . a citizen": Frank B. Kent, Jr., "School Segregation Banned in Nation," The Washington *Post*, May 18, 1954, p. 1.

306. "a mere scrap of paper": Roberts, "South's Leaders Are Shocked at School Integration Ruling," *ibid*.

306. "will not abide . . . in education": *Ibid*.

306. schools should be opened . . . a year later: 349 U.S. 294.

307. "send their children . . . not conform": Kurland and Casper, pp. 1167–1168.

307. "popular hostility . . . as feasible": *Brown v. Board of Education*, "Brief for the United States," No. 1, pp. 19, 768.

307. "With all deliberate speed": *Virginia v. West Virginia*, 200 U.S. 1.

307–308. "It is futile . . . the South": Schwartz, *Super*, p. 118.

308. Justice Frankfurter . . . into line: O'Brien, Vol. 2, p. 1318.

308. Justice Clark . . . his native state: Schwartz, *Super*, p. 119.

308. "primary responsibility" . . . in each district: 349 U.S. 294.

308. "to public schools . . . deliberate speed": *Ibid*.

309. "We're not . . . here at all": Sarratt, p. 1.

309. "Supreme confidence . . . segregation: *Ibid*., p. 5.

309. Faubus had declared . . . materialize: Sitkoff, p. 29.

309. Eisenhower ordered . . . cafeteria: Wilkinson, p. 91.

310. "Violent resistance . . . suspension": *Cooper v. Aaron*, 358 U.S. 1.

310. "pupil placement laws": *Shuttlesworth v. Alabama*, 358 U.S. 10.

310. "there has been . . . constitutional rights": *Griffin v. County School Board*, 377 U.S. 218.

311. President Eisenhower's . . . civil rights: Polenberg, p. 190.

311. Congress . . . "public education": P.L. 88-352, Title IV, #407, 1964, (a)(2).

311. Southern officials . . . generally yielded: *Bradley v. Richmond School Board*, 382 U.S. 103; *Green v. County School Board*, 391 U.S. 430; and *U.S. v. Jefferson School Board*, 372 Fed. 836.

312. Burger's sweeping conclusion . . . solve the problem: *Milliken v. Bradley*, 418 U.S. 717.

312. In 1972 . . . standard of living: U.S. Commission on Civil Rights, p. 167.

312–313. This left black children . . . endure: Wilkinson, pp. 213–214.

313. Ironically . . . white resistance had melted away: *Swann v. Charlotte-Mecklenburg Board of Education*, 402 U.S. 1.

313. "I simply decided . . . to do so": Garrow, *Bearing*, p. 12.

313. The women . . . Dexter Avenue Baptist Church: Garrow, *Montgomery*, p. 20.

313. "every Negro . . . or mother": *Ibid.*, p. 46.

314. "The tension . . . positive peace": King, p. 32.

314. "I knew . . . freed from fear": *Ibid.*, p. 122.

315. "Is it fair . . . committing a crime?": *Ibid.*, p. 124.

315. "As we go back . . . reconciliation": *Ibid.*, pp. 137–138.

316. The waitress . . . the store closed: Sitkoff, p. 62.

316–317. "It is . . . to sit down": *Ibid.*, p. 36.

317. Snick: Eventually, by the late 1960s, Snick, led by Stokely Carmichael, also showed its impatience by asserting the right of self-defense against Klan violence, and adopting a slogan for "black power," defined as "a call for black people to define their own goals, to lead their own organizations and to support those organizations." Turé [Carmichael] and Hamilton, *Black Power*, p. 44.

317. James Farmer . . . government into action: Weisbrot, p. 55.

317. "inflammatory traveling": *Ibid.*, p. 61.

318. On June 21 . . . all the indictments: Fireside, *"Mississippi Burning,"* p. 49.

318. On March 28, 1966 . . . go forward: *United States v. Price et al.*, 383 U.S. 787.

319. In October 2000 . . . avowed segregationist: Gettleman, "To Mayor, It's Selma's Statute of Limitations," Los Angeles *Times*, Oct. 22, 2000, p. 2.

319. And in March 2003 . . . chief of police: Halbfinger, "A Black Woman Sits in Bull Connor's Seat," The New York *Times*, May 3, 2002, p. A12.

319. In the 1970s . . . were illegal: *Griggs v. Duke Power Co.*, 401 U.S. 424; *Ward's Cove Packing Co. v. Atonio*, 490 U.S. 642.

319. The justices . . . "due process" grounds: *Fullilove v. Klutznick*, 448 U.S. 448.

320. Determined to become a physician . . . too low: Sindler, pp. 63–78.

320. Bakke, who had been . . . physicians: *Regents of the University of California v. Bakke*, 438 US. 265.

321. After hearing the case . . . contending sides: *Ibid.*

322. The joint opinion . . . against minorities: Sindler, pp. 303–304.

323. Two years later . . . in *Bakke*: Eastland, pp. 69–70.

324. At this writing . . . high-school classes: The University of Texas announced in fall 2003 that tuition will increase by one third in fall 2004.

324. In 1973 . . . wealthy white districts: *San Antonio Independent School District v. Rodriguez*, 411 U.S. 1.

325. Gary Orfield . . . "national political leaders": Orfield and Yu, p. 3.

325. Orfield further . . . in litigation: Decisions cited in *ibid.*, p. 4, include *Dowell*, 1991; *Freeman v. Pitts*, 1992; and *Jenkins*, 1995.

325. No researcher . . . encouragement to learn: See the pioneering study by Jonathan Kozol.

326. Further, the courts . . . contrary opinions: Greenhouse, "Justices Look for Nuance in Race-Preference Case," The New York *Times*, April 2, 2003, p. A1.

326. Justice Karen Nelson Moore . . . court records: *Grutter v. Bollinger*, U.S. Court of Appeals for the Sixth Circuit, Nos. 01–1447/1516, as cited in http://www.umich.edu~urel/admissions/legal/grutter/gru-ap-op.html (5/13/02).

327. "can't be a factor . . . isn't quite that": "Excerpts from Arguments Before the Supreme Court on Affirmative Action," The New York *Times*, April 2, 2003, p. A14.

327. Further, the negative voice . . . The 102: Dworkin, "The Court and the University," *The New York Review*, May 15, 2003, p. 9.

328. As the majority argued . . . slots available: *Grutter v. Bollinger*, as cited above.

328. She thereby validated . . . American society: Nicholas Lemann, "A Decision that Universities Can Relate To," The New York *Times*, June 29, 2003, p. WK14.

328–329. "We expect that . . . interest approved today": Steven A. Holmes and Greg Winter, "Fixing the Race Gap in 25 Years or Less," The New York *Times*, June 29, 2003, p. WK1.

330. The Court's response . . . "race-neutral means": *Grutter v. Bollinger*, p. 21.

# INDEX